DEADLY SINS

nakaba suzuki presents

25

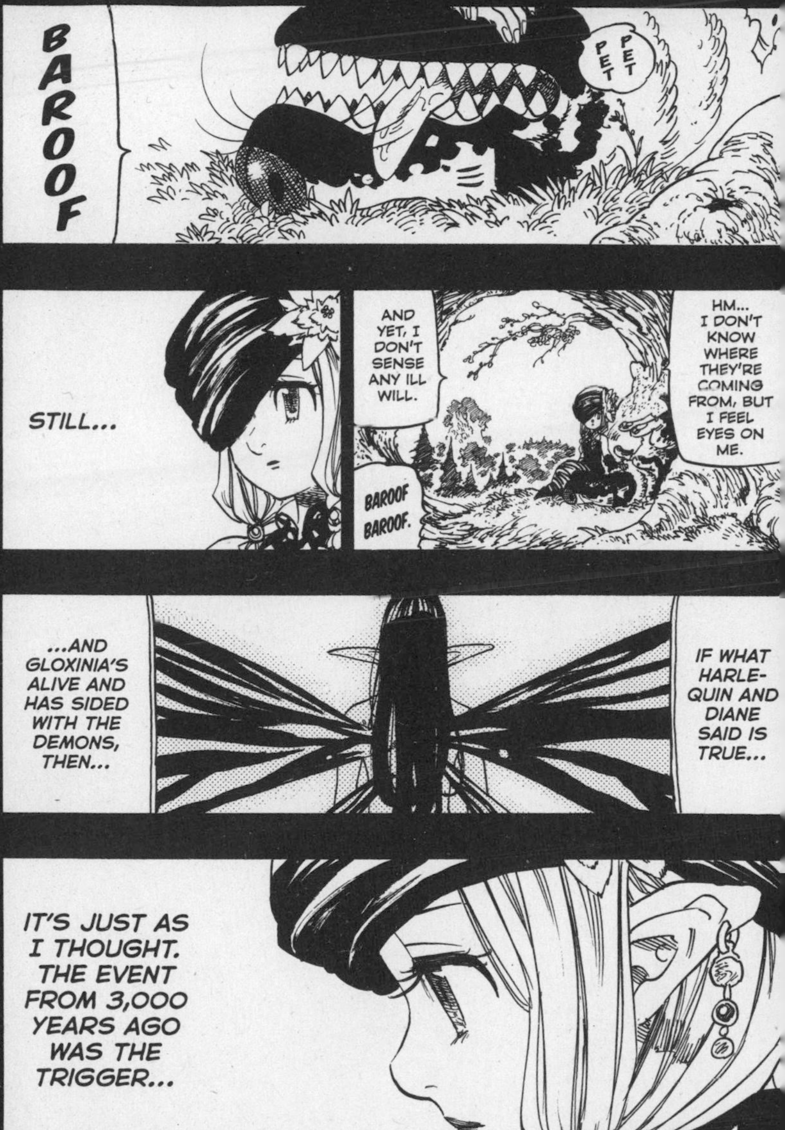
PET PET
BAROOF
HM... I DON'T KNOW WHERE THEY'RE COMING FROM, BUT I FEEL EYES ON ME.
BAROOF BAROOF.
AND YET, I DON'T SENSE ANY ILL WILL.
STILL...
IF WHAT HARLE-QUIN AND DIANE SAID IS TRUE...
...AND GLOXINIA'S ALIVE AND HAS SIDED WITH THE DEMONS, THEN...
IT'S JUST AS I THOUGHT. THE EVENT FROM 3,000 YEARS AGO WAS THE TRIGGER...

CONTENTS

BOAR HAT

The Seven Deadly Sins

Chapter 198 - The Giant & the Fairy

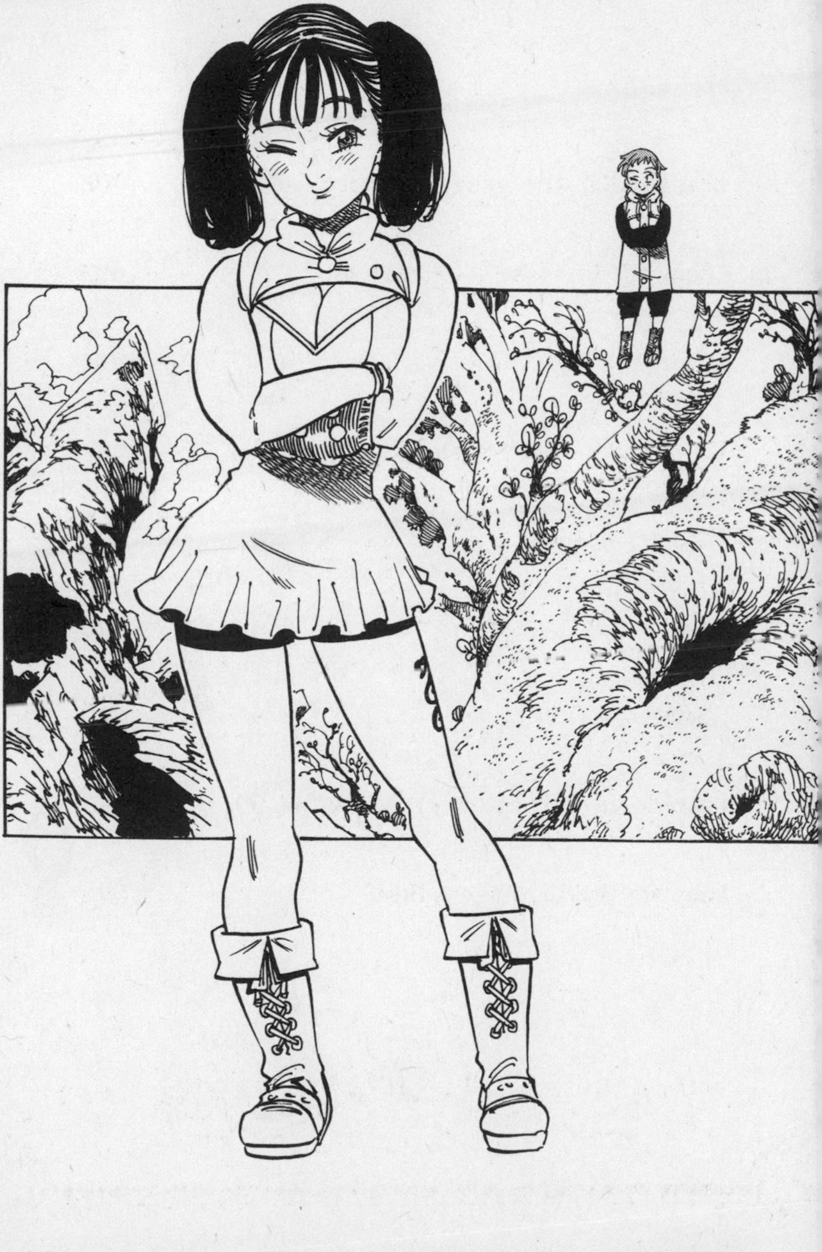

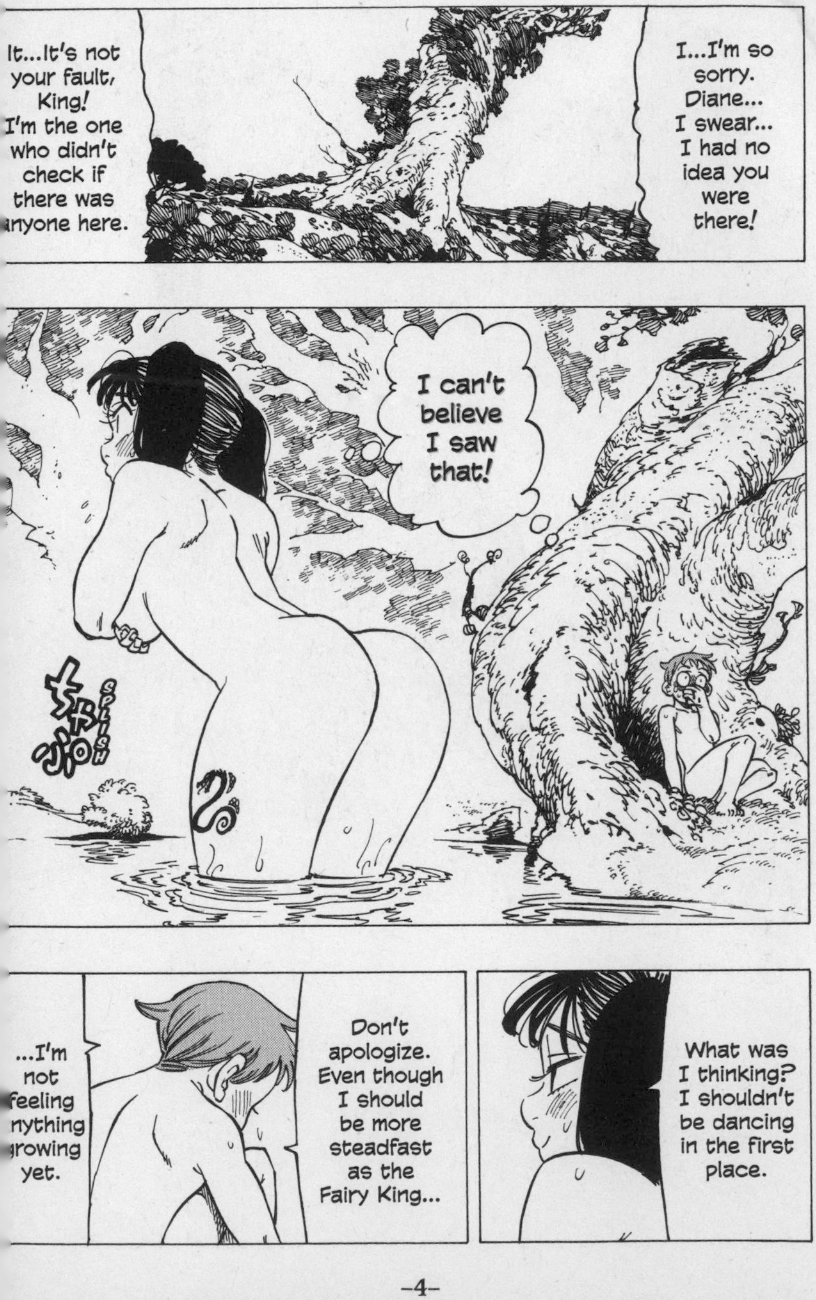
I...I'm so sorry. Diane... I swear... I had no idea you were there!
It...It's not your fault, King! I'm the one who didn't check if there was anyone here.
I can't believe I saw that!
SPLISH
What was I thinking? I shouldn't be dancing in the first place.
Don't apologize. Even though I should be more steadfast as the Fairy King...
...I'm not feeling anything growing yet.

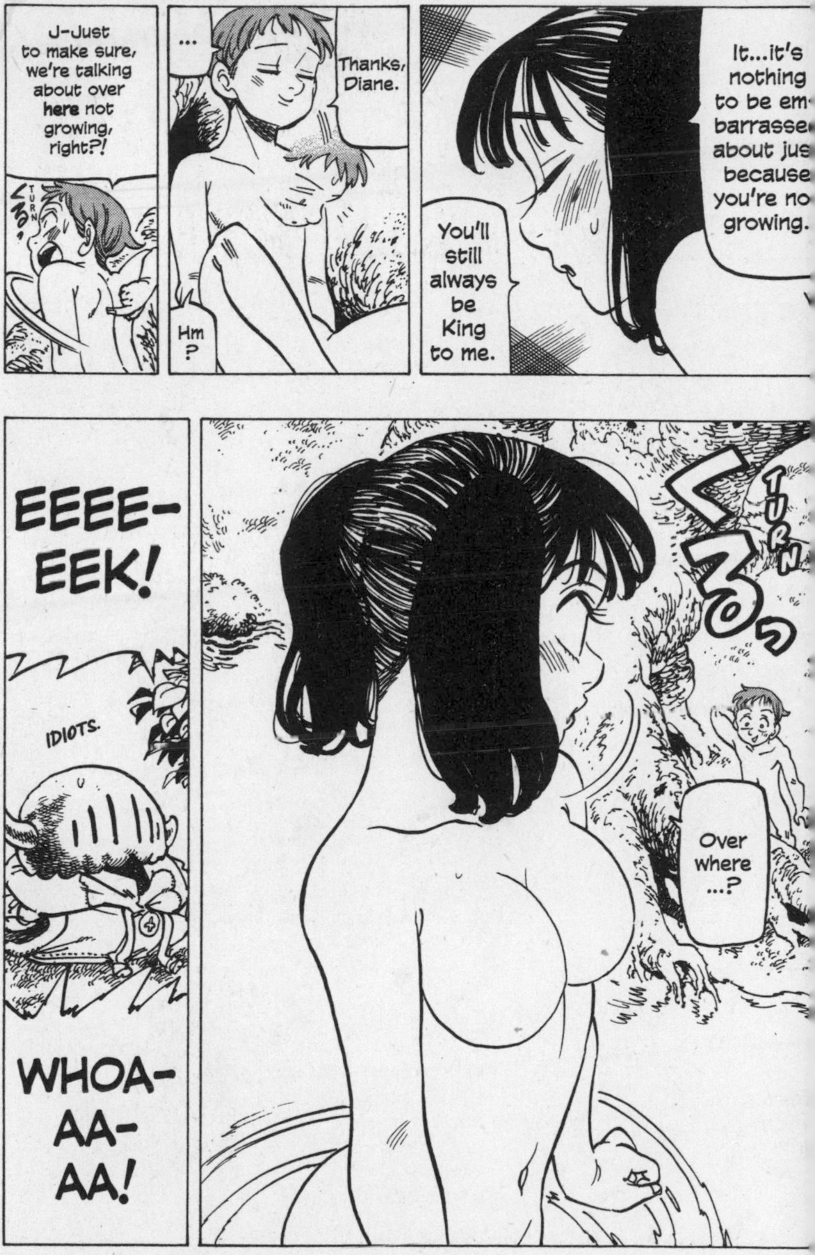
It...it's nothing to be em-barrasse[d] about jus[t] because you're no[t] growing.
You'll still always be King to me.
...
Thanks, Diane.
Hm?
J-Just to make sure, we're talking about over here not growing, right?!
TURN
TURN
Over where ...?
EEEE-EEK!
IDIOTS.
WHOA-AA-AA!

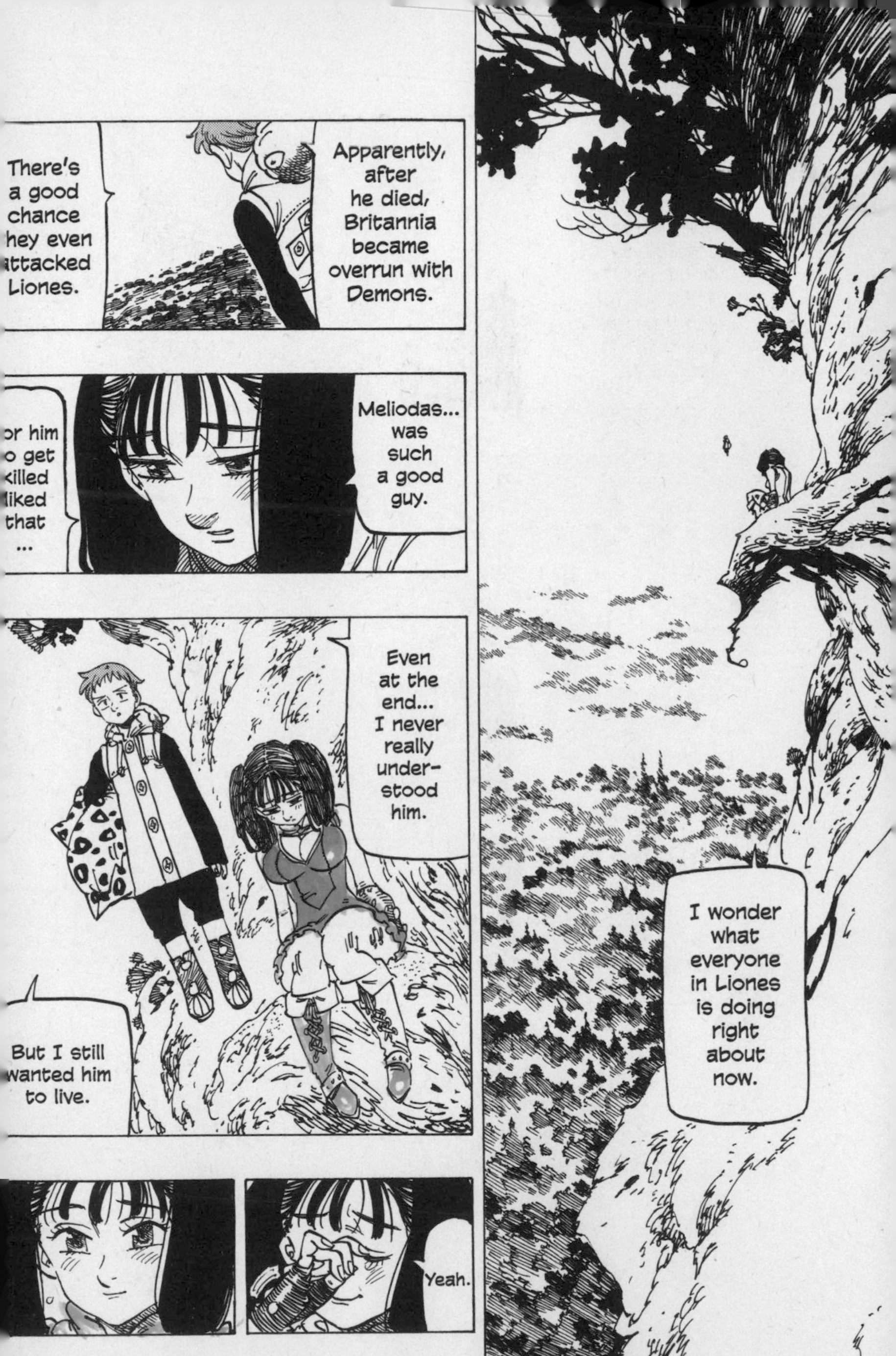
I wonder what everyone in Liones is doing right about now.
Apparently, after he died, Britannia became overrun with Demons.
There's a good chance hey even ttacked Liones.
Meliodas... was such a good guy.
or him o get killed liked that ...
Even at the end... I never really under-stood him.
But I still wanted him to live.
Yeah.

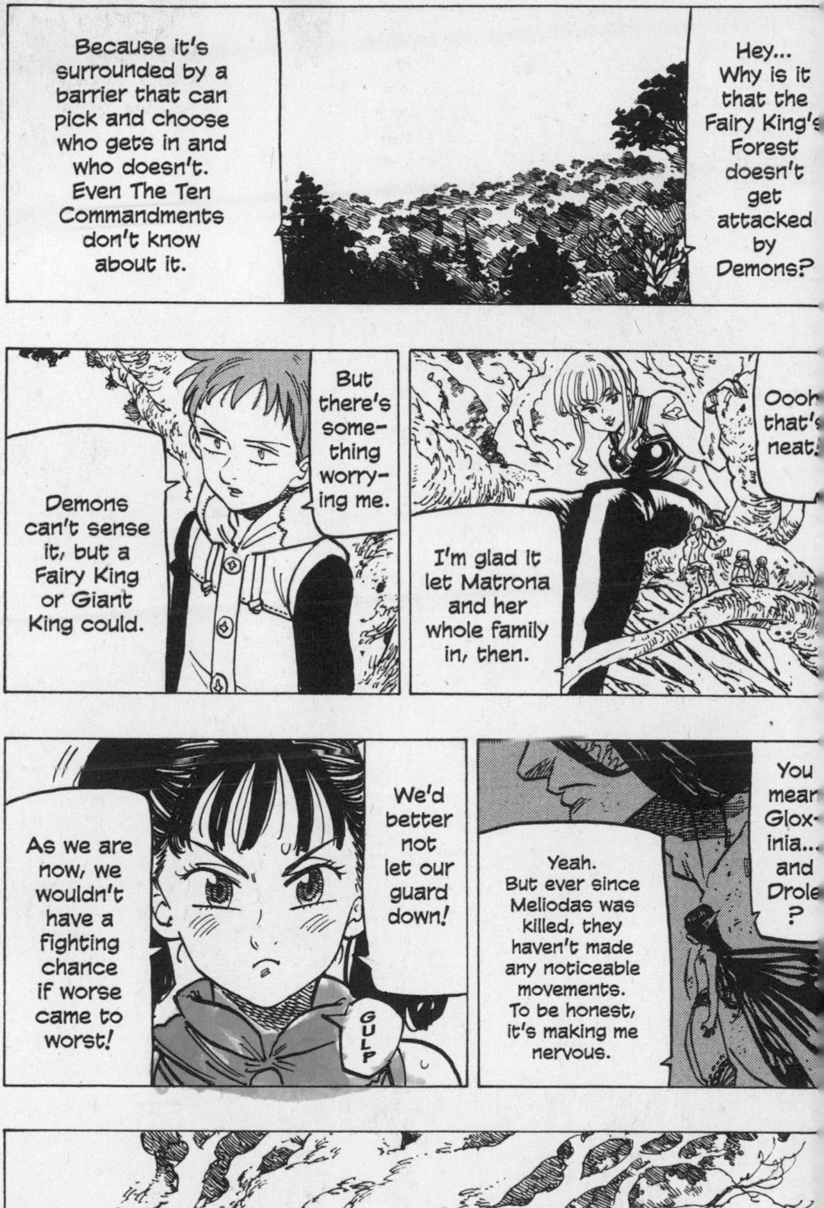
Hey... Why is it that the Fairy King's Forest doesn't get attacked by Demons?
Because it's surrounded by a barrier that can pick and choose who gets in and who doesn't. Even The Ten Commandments don't know about it.
Oooh that's neat!
I'm glad it let Matrona and her whole family in, then.
But there's some-thing worry-ing me.
Demons can't sense it, but a Fairy King or Giant King could.
You mean Glox-inia... and Drole?
Yeah. But ever since Meliodas was killed, they haven't made any noticeable movements. To be honest, it's making me nervous.
We'd better not let our guard down!
GULP
As we are now, we wouldn't have a fighting chance if worse came to worst!

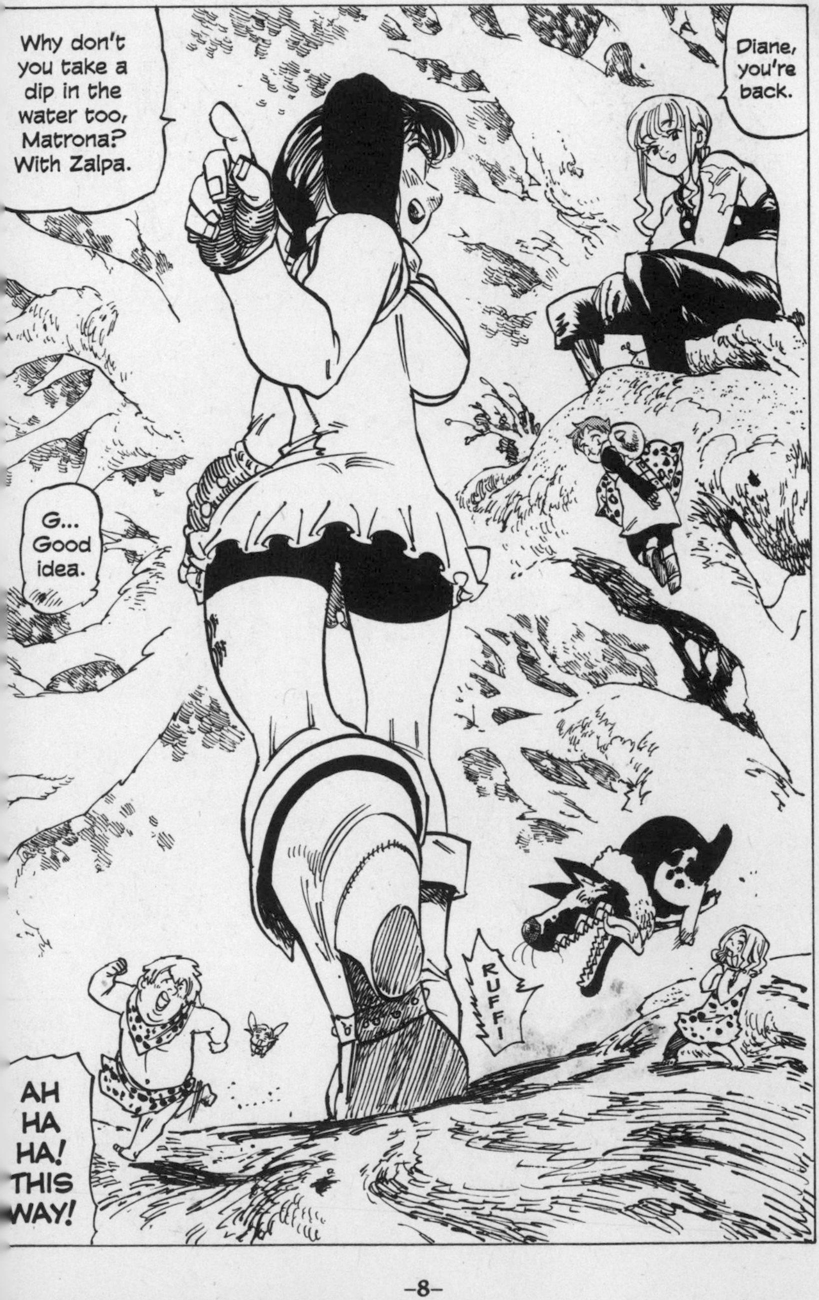
Diane, you're back.
Why don't you take a dip in the water too, Matrona? With Zalpa.
G... Good idea.
RUFF!
AH HA HA! THIS WAY!

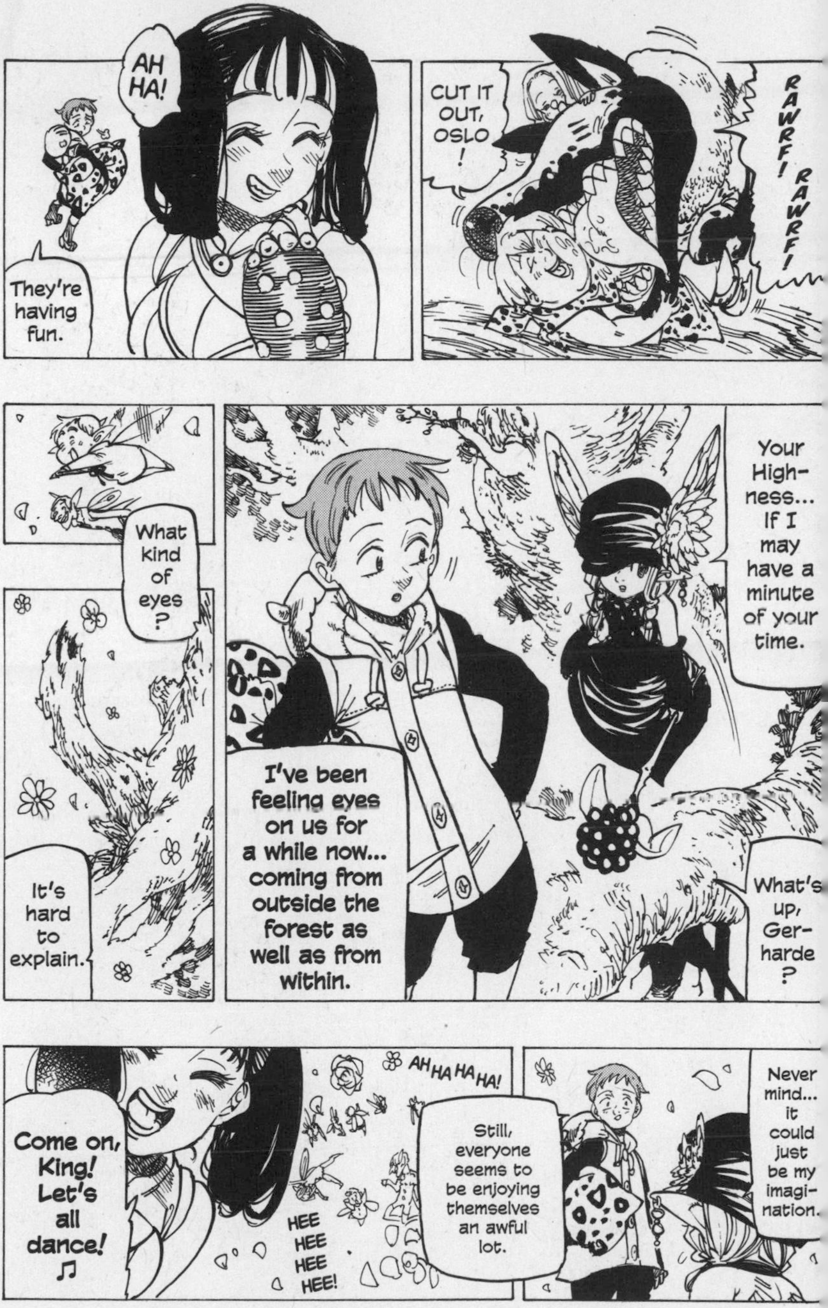
RAWRF! RAWRF!
CUT IT OUT, OSLO!
AH HA!
They're having fun.
Your High-ness... If I may have a minute of your time.
What's up, Ger-harde?
I've been feeling eyes on us for a while now... coming from outside the forest as well as from within.
What kind of eyes?
It's hard to explain.
Never mind... it could just be my imagi-nation.
Still, everyone seems to be enjoying themselves an awful lot.
AH HA HA HA!
HEE HEE HEE HEE!
Come on, King! Let's all dance! ♫

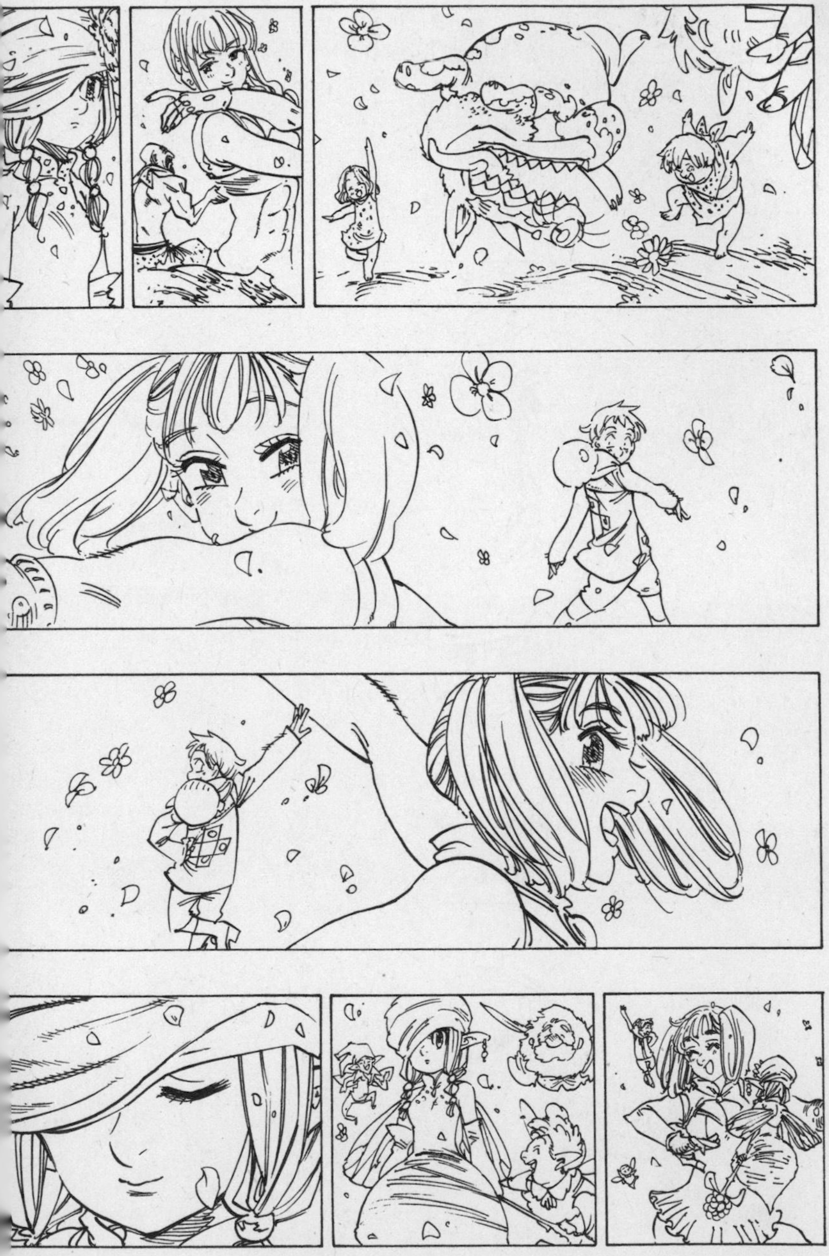

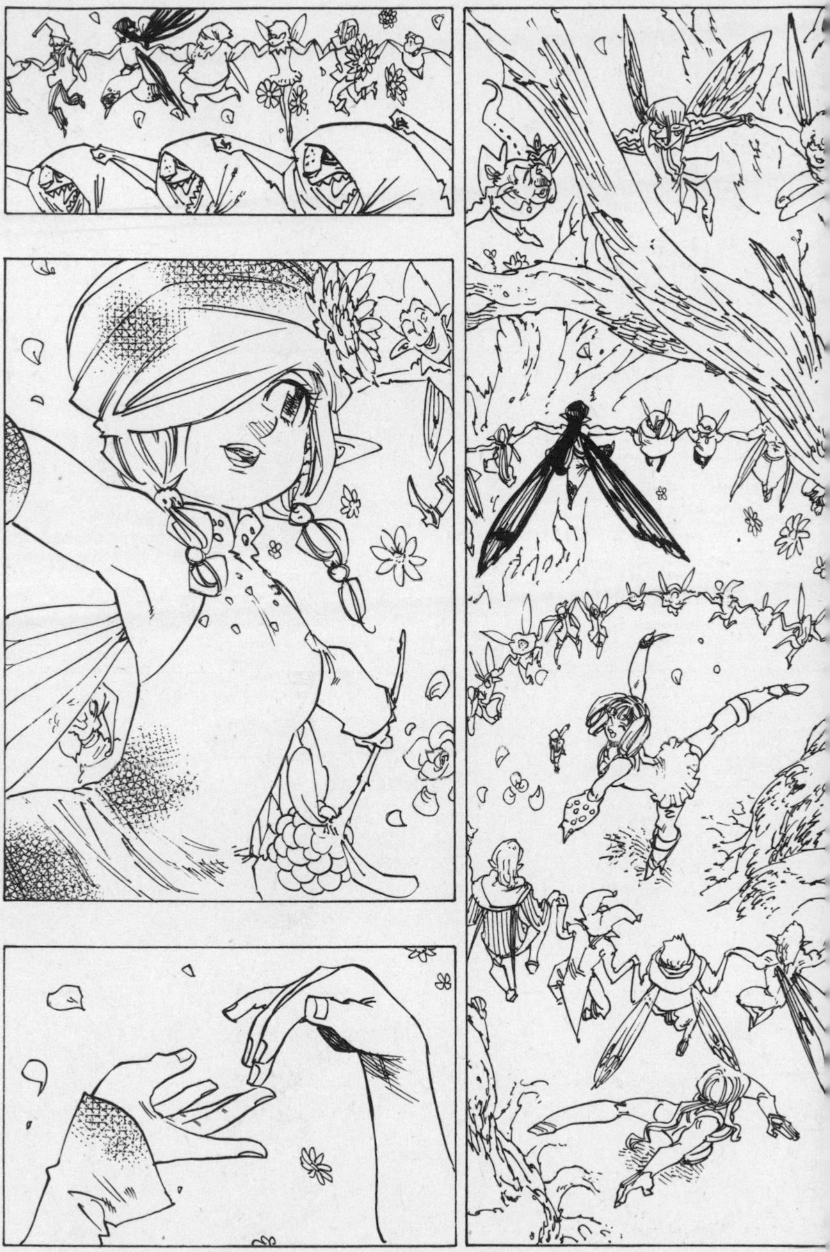

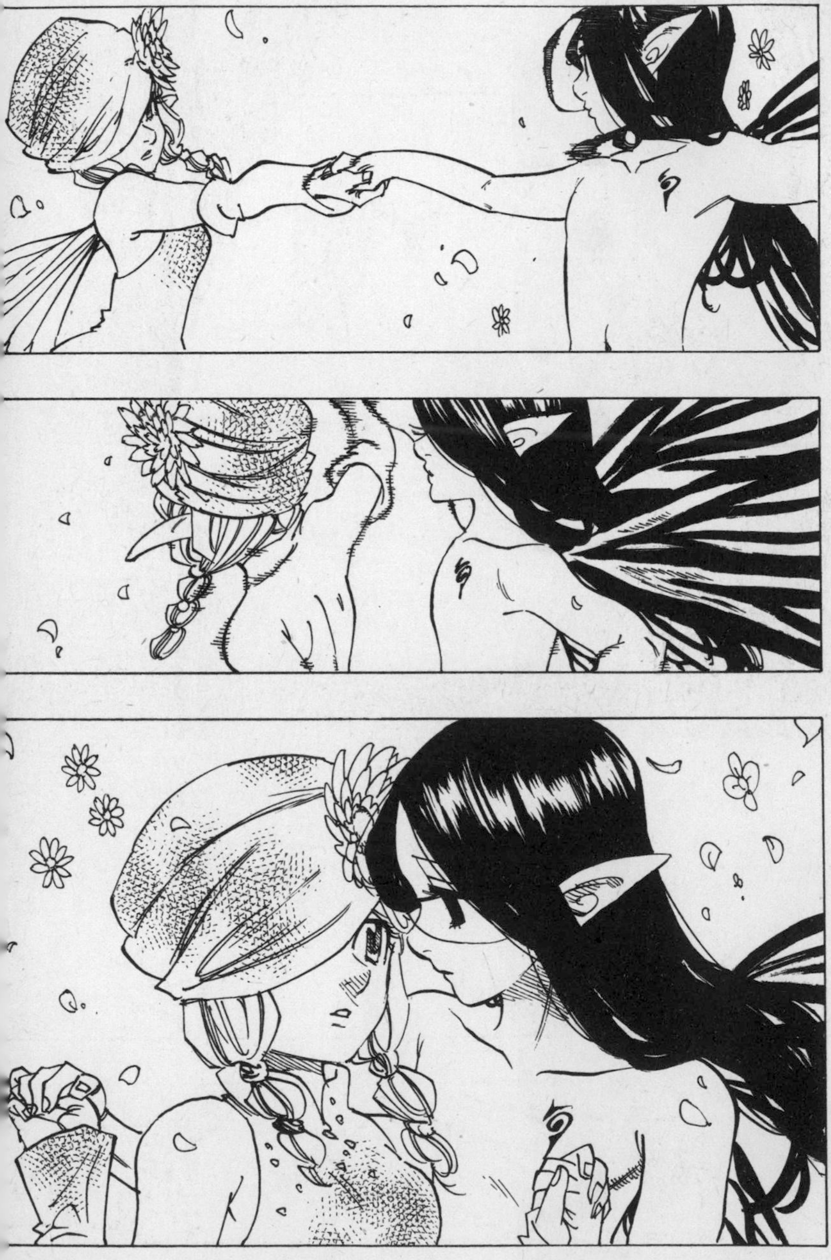

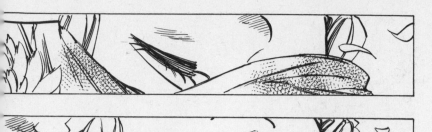

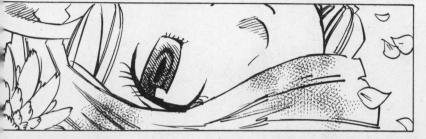

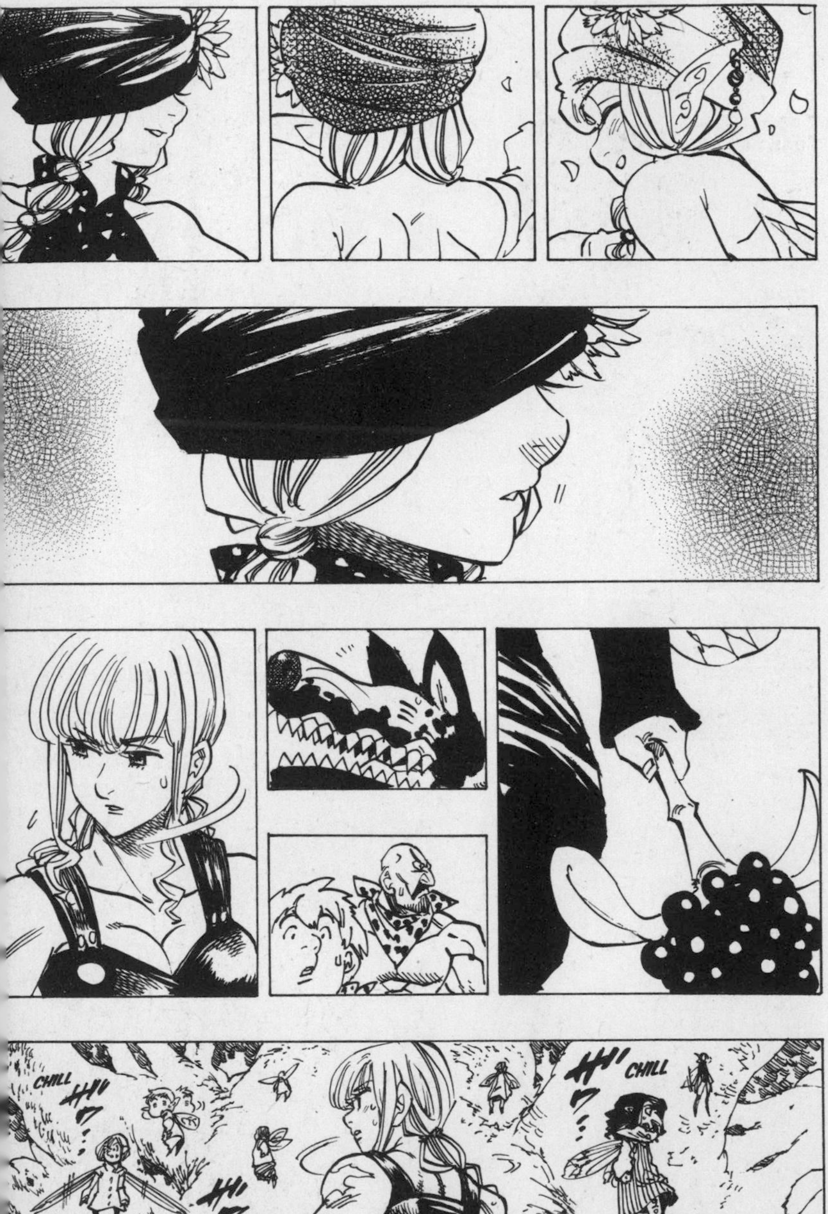
CHILL
CHILL
CHILL

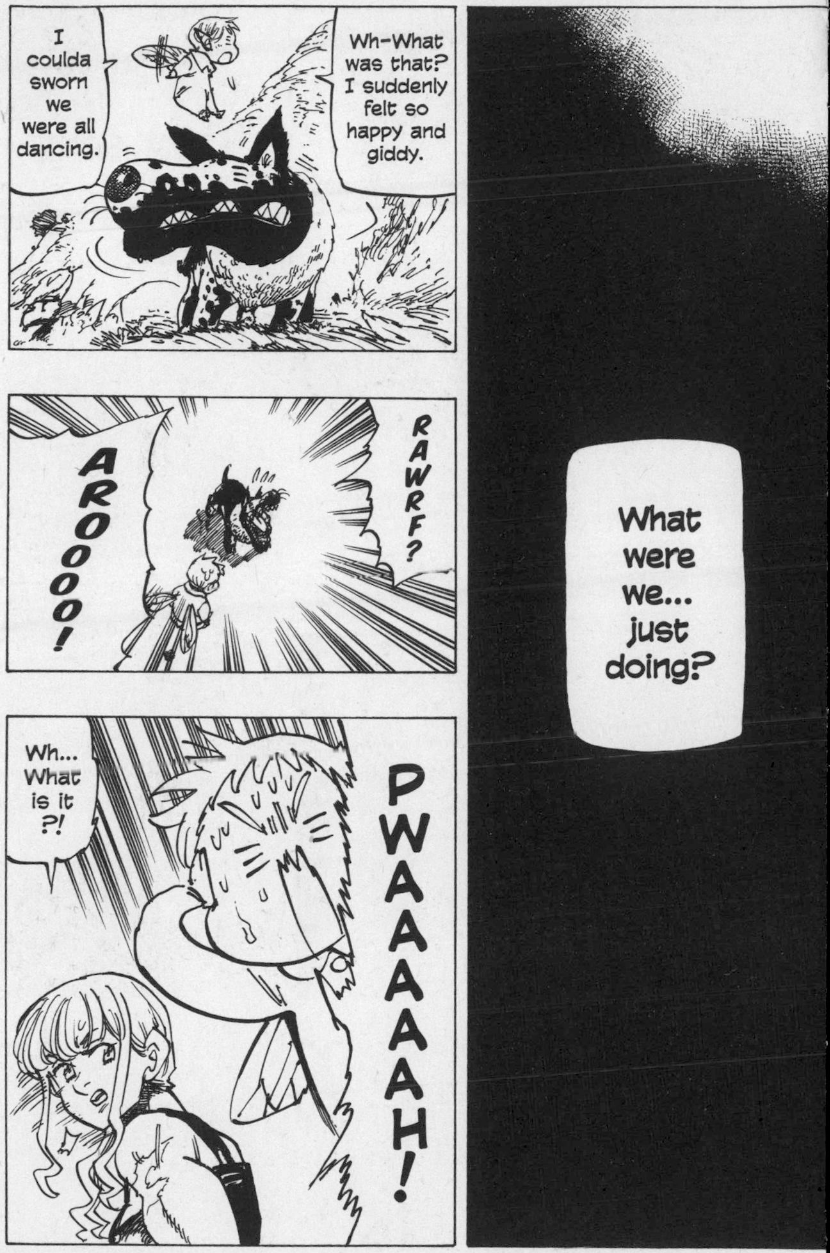
What were we... just doing?
Wh-What was that? I suddenly felt so happy and giddy.
I coulda sworn we were all dancing.
RAWRF?
AROOOOO!
PWAAAAAAH!
Wh... What is it ?!

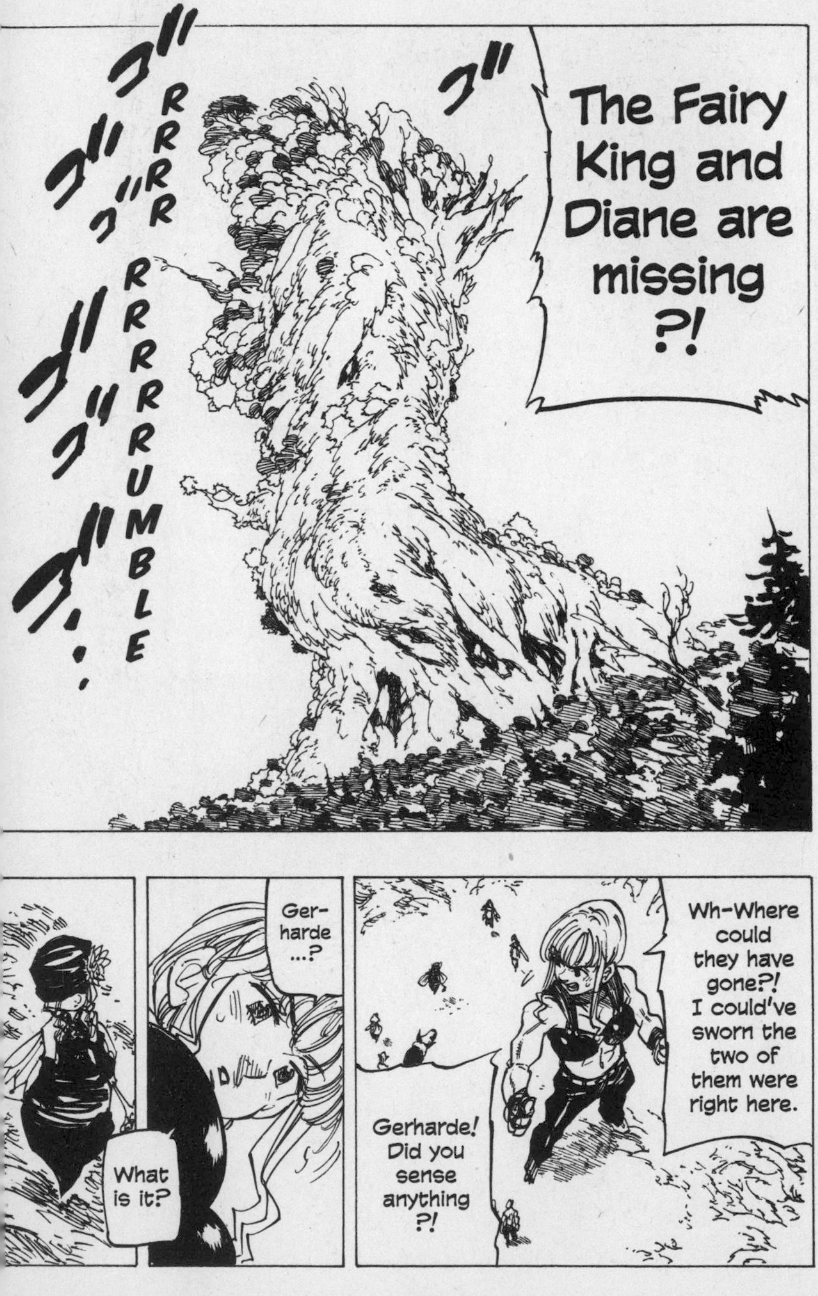
The Fairy King and Diane are missing ?!
RRRRRRRRRRUMBLE
Wh-Where could they have gone?! I could've sworn the two of them were right here.
Gerharde! Did you sense anything ?!
Ger-harde ...?
What is it?

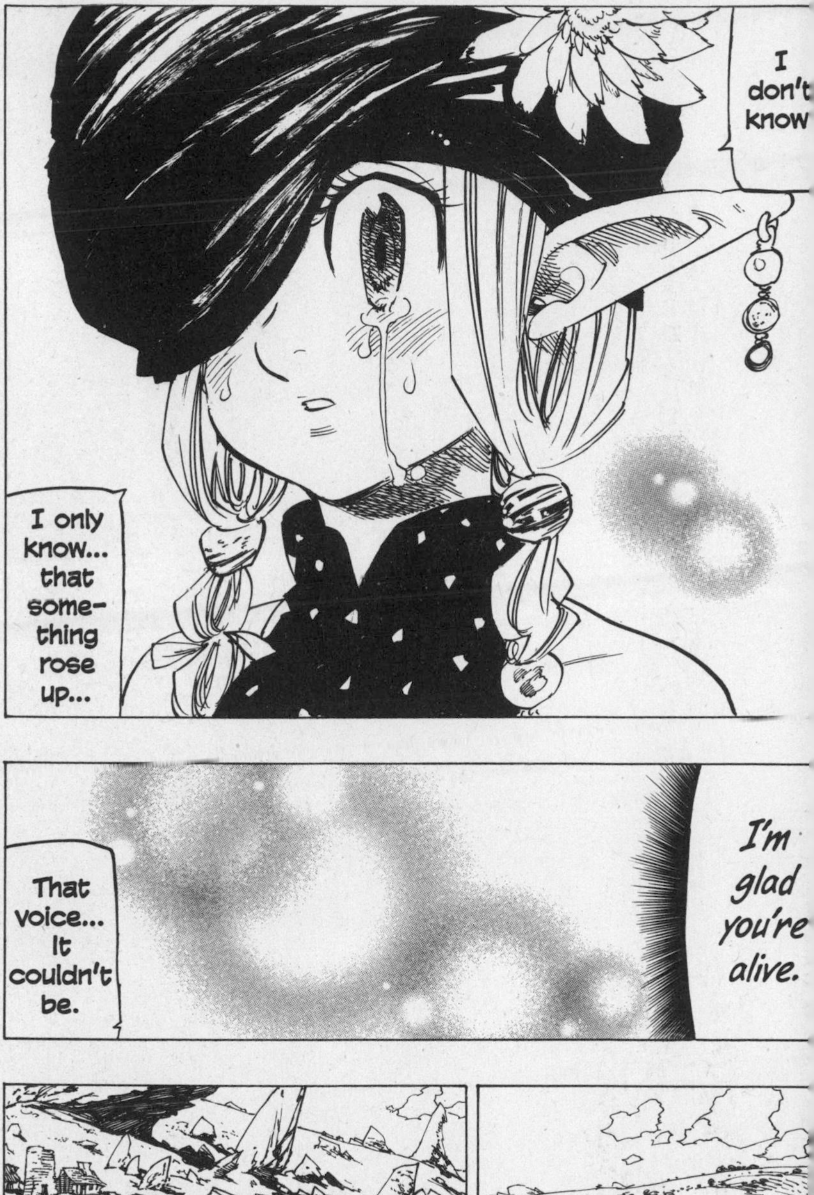
I don't know
I only know... that some-thing rose up...
I'm glad you're alive.
That voice... It couldn't be.

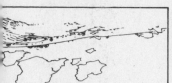

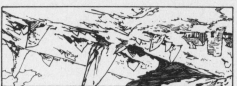

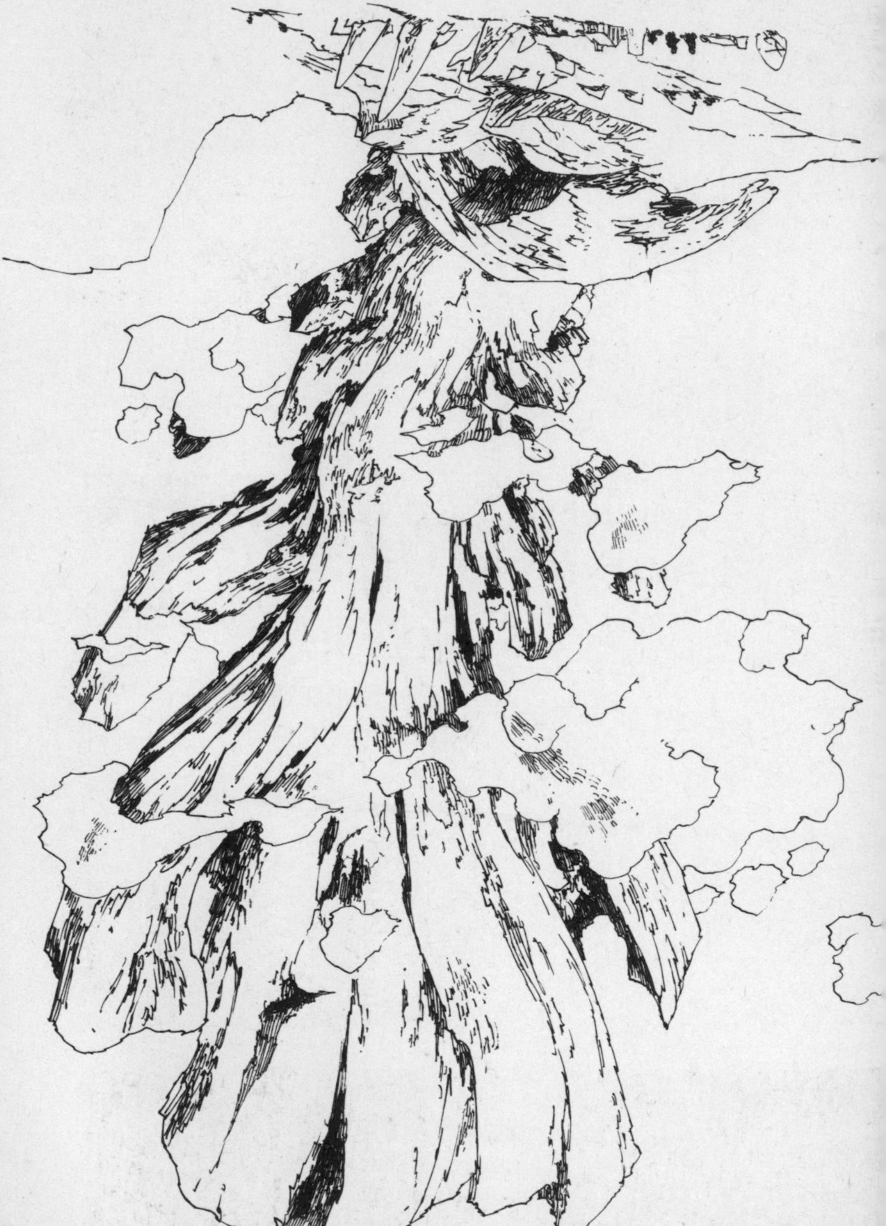

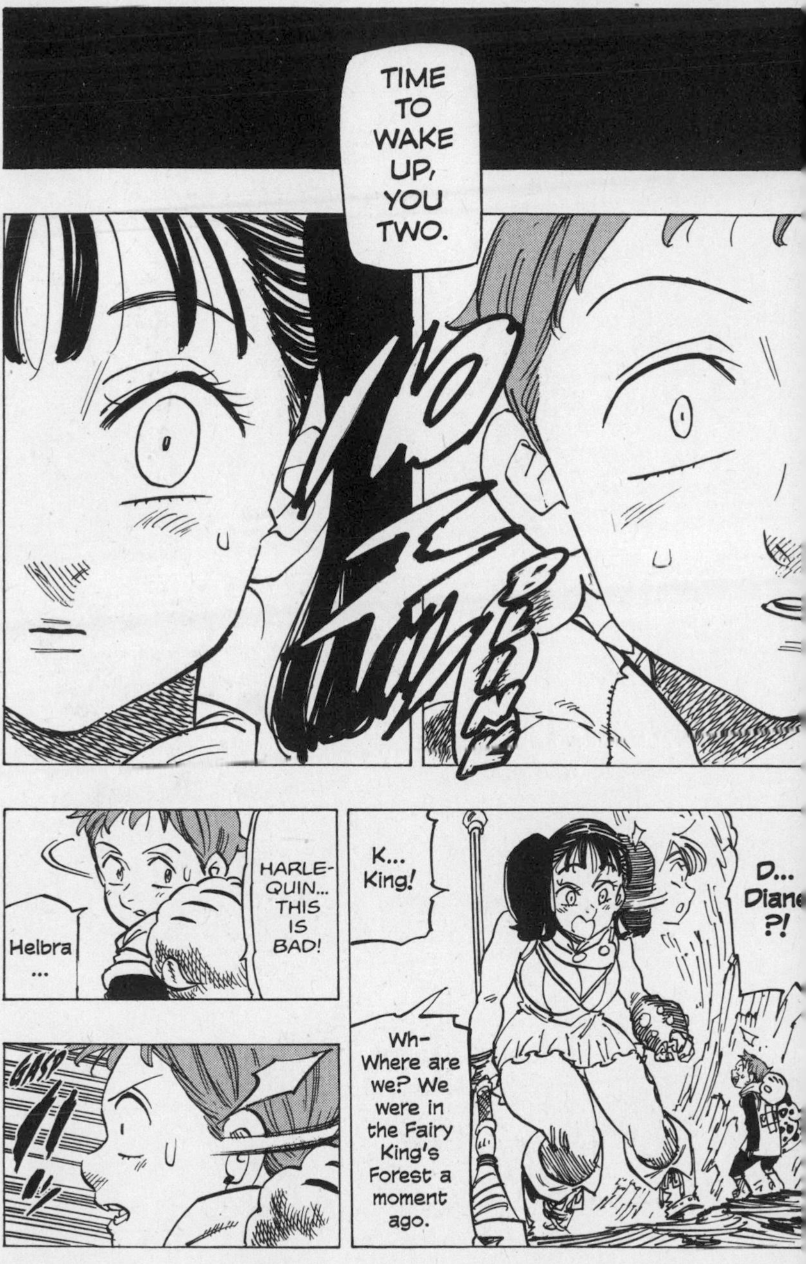
TIME TO WAKE UP, YOU TWO.
D... Diane?!
K... King!
Wh- Where are we? We were in the Fairy King's Forest a moment ago.
HARLEQUIN... THIS IS BAD!
Helbra...
GASP

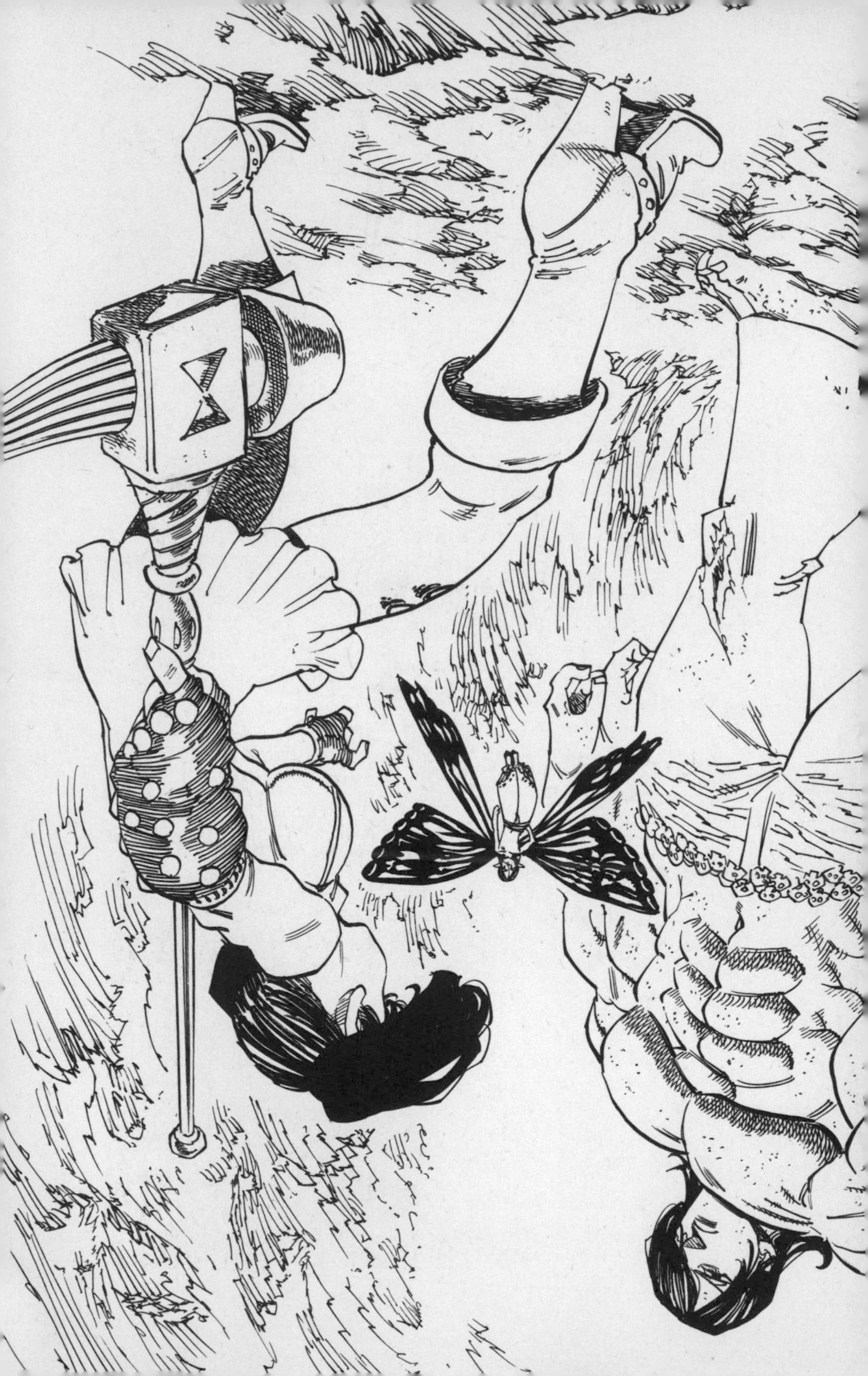

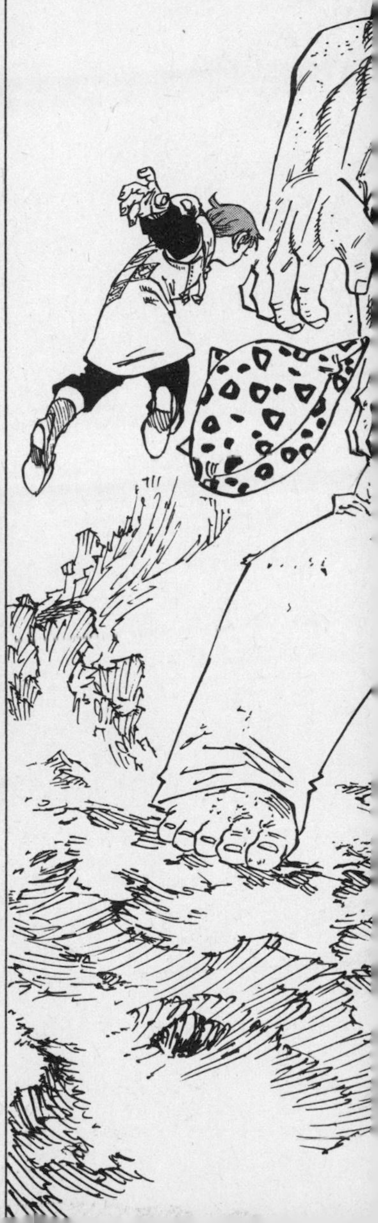

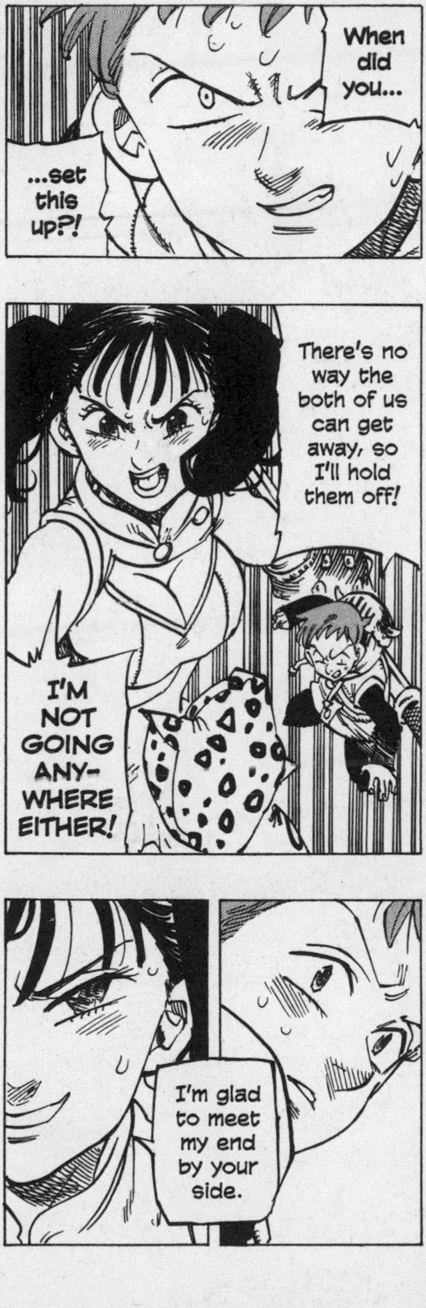
When did you...
...set this up?!
There's no way the both of us can get away, so I'll hold them off!
I'M NOT GOING ANY-WHERE EITHER!
I'm glad to meet my end by your side.

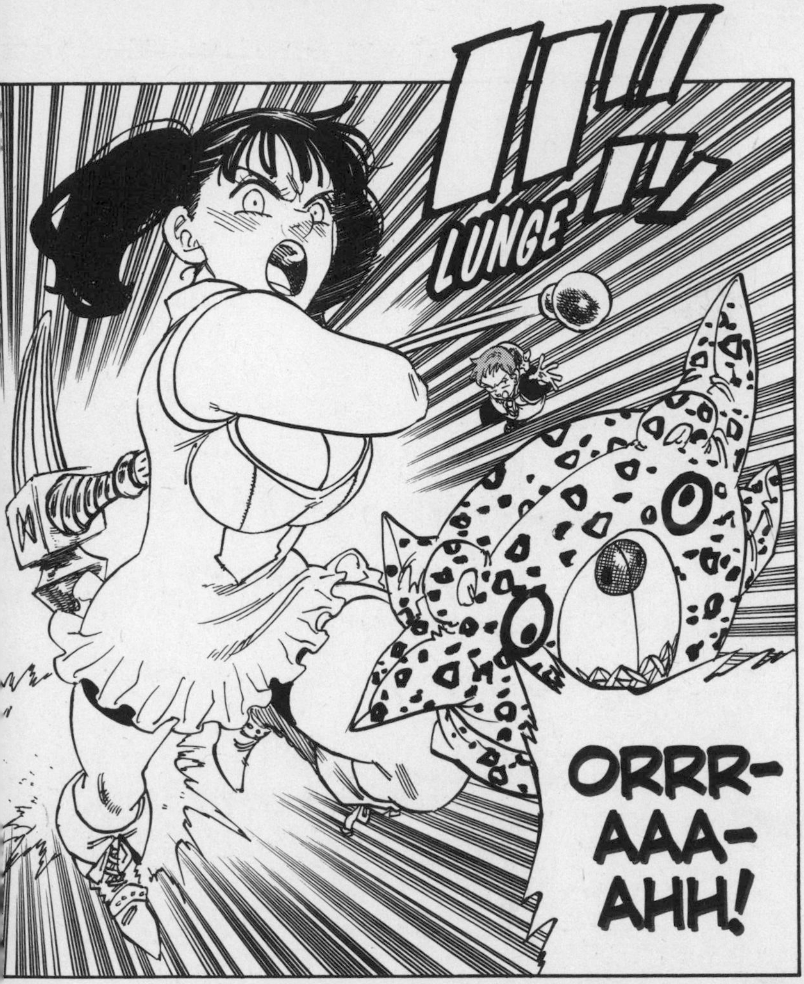
LUNGE
ORRR-AAA-AHH!

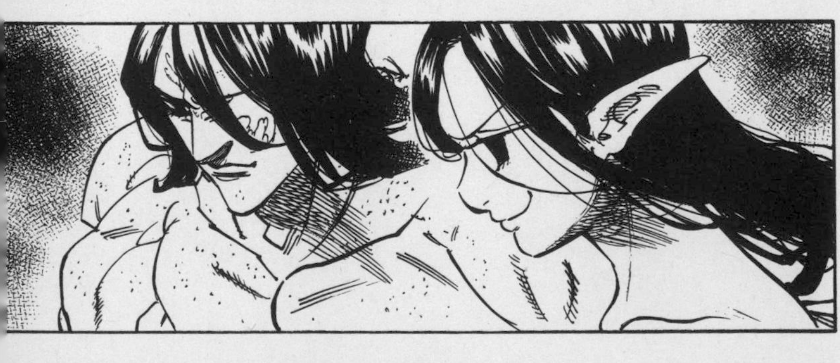

Chapter 199 - Those Without Light

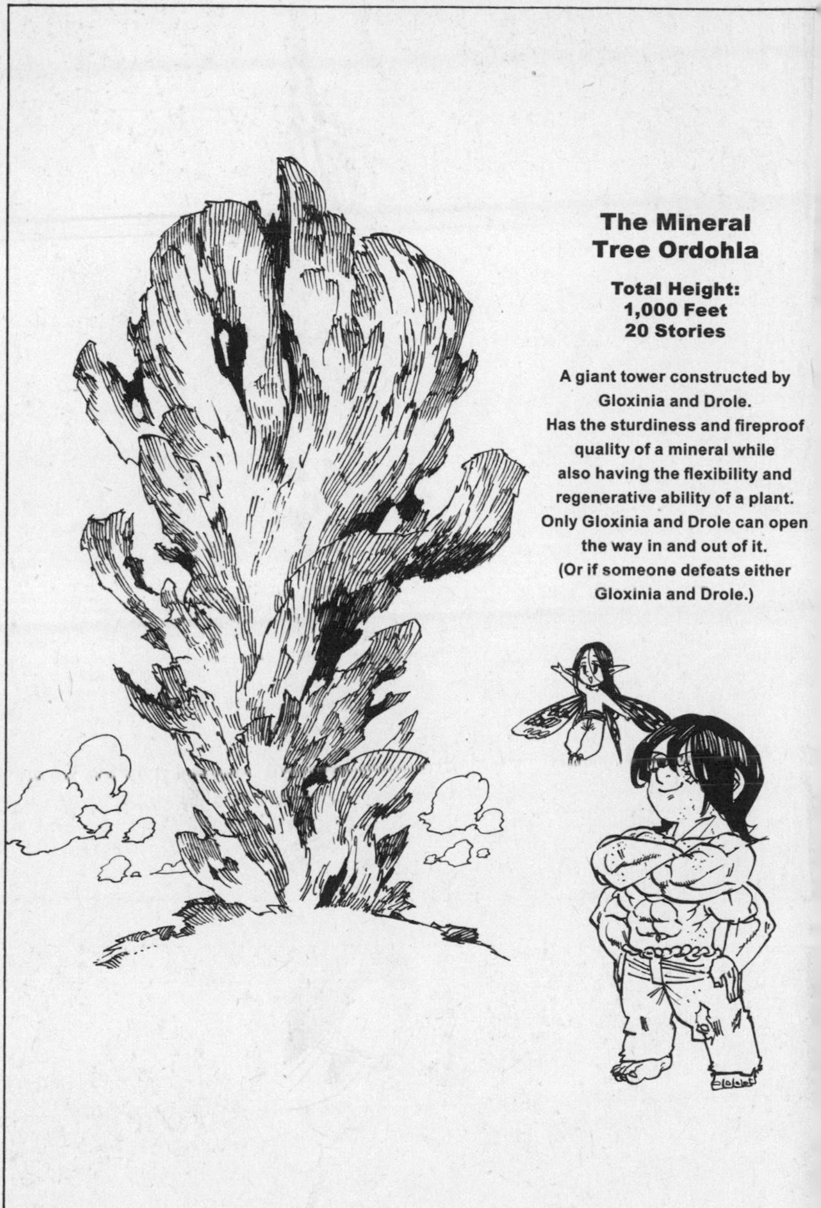
The Mineral
Tree Ordohla
Total Height:
1,000 Feet
20 Stories
A giant tower constructed by
Gloxinia and Drole.
Has the sturdiness and fireproof
quality of a mineral while
also having the flexibility and
regenerative ability of a plant.
Only Gloxinia and Drole can open
the way in and out of it.
(Or if someone defeats either
Gloxinia and Drole.)

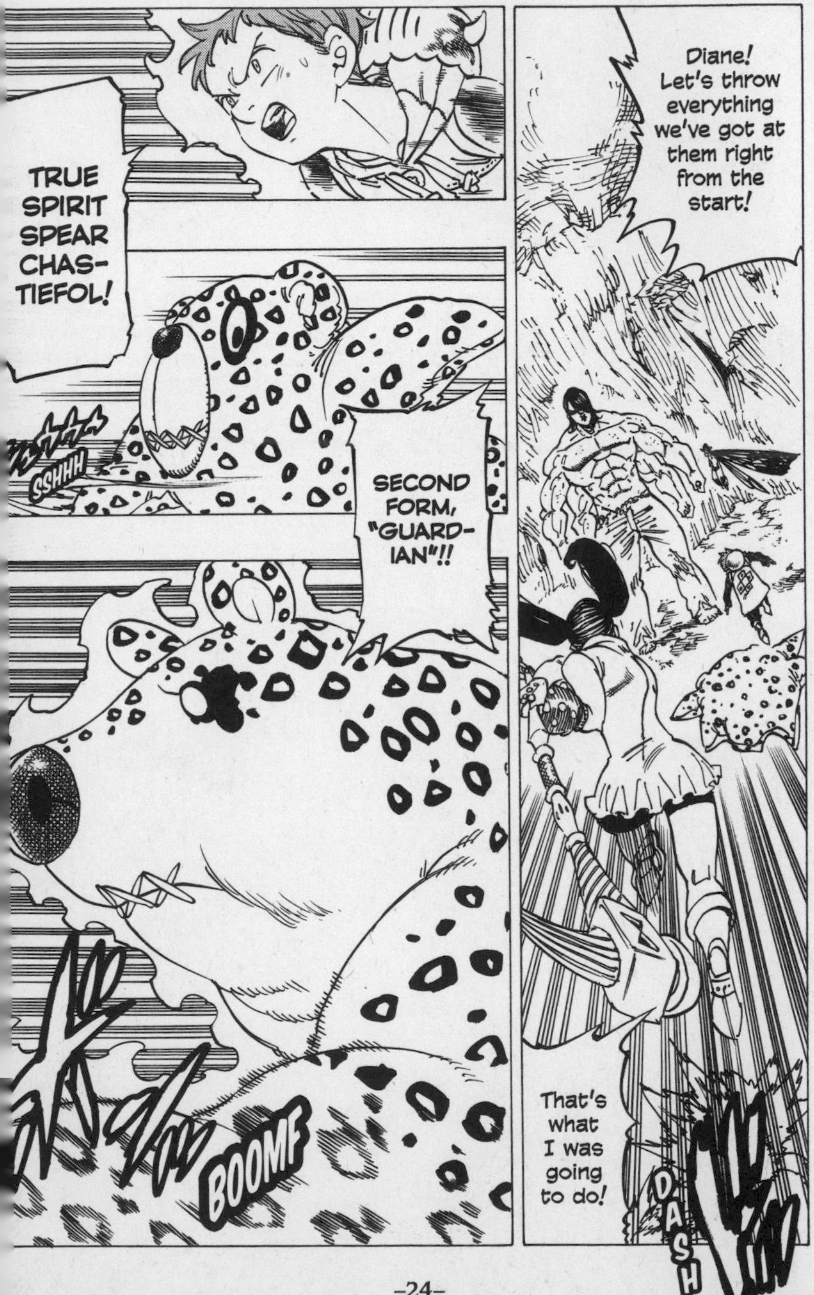
Diane! Let's throw everything we've got at them right from the start!
That's what I was going to do!
DASH
TRUE SPIRIT SPEAR CHAS-TIEFOL!
SSHHH
SECOND FORM, "GUARD-IAN"!!
BOOMF

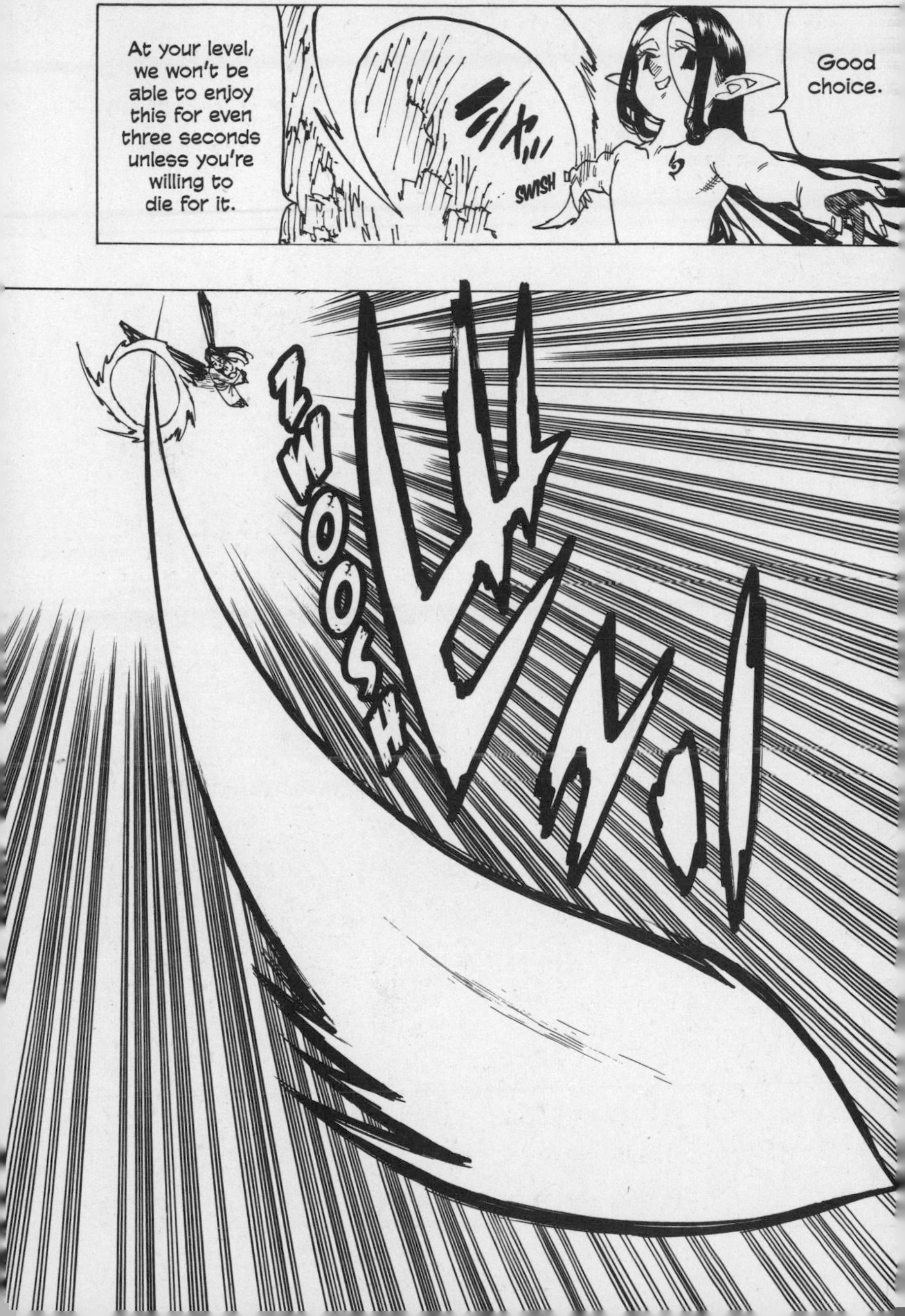
Good choice.
SWISH
At your level, we won't be able to enjoy this for even three seconds unless you're willing to die for it.
ZWOOSH

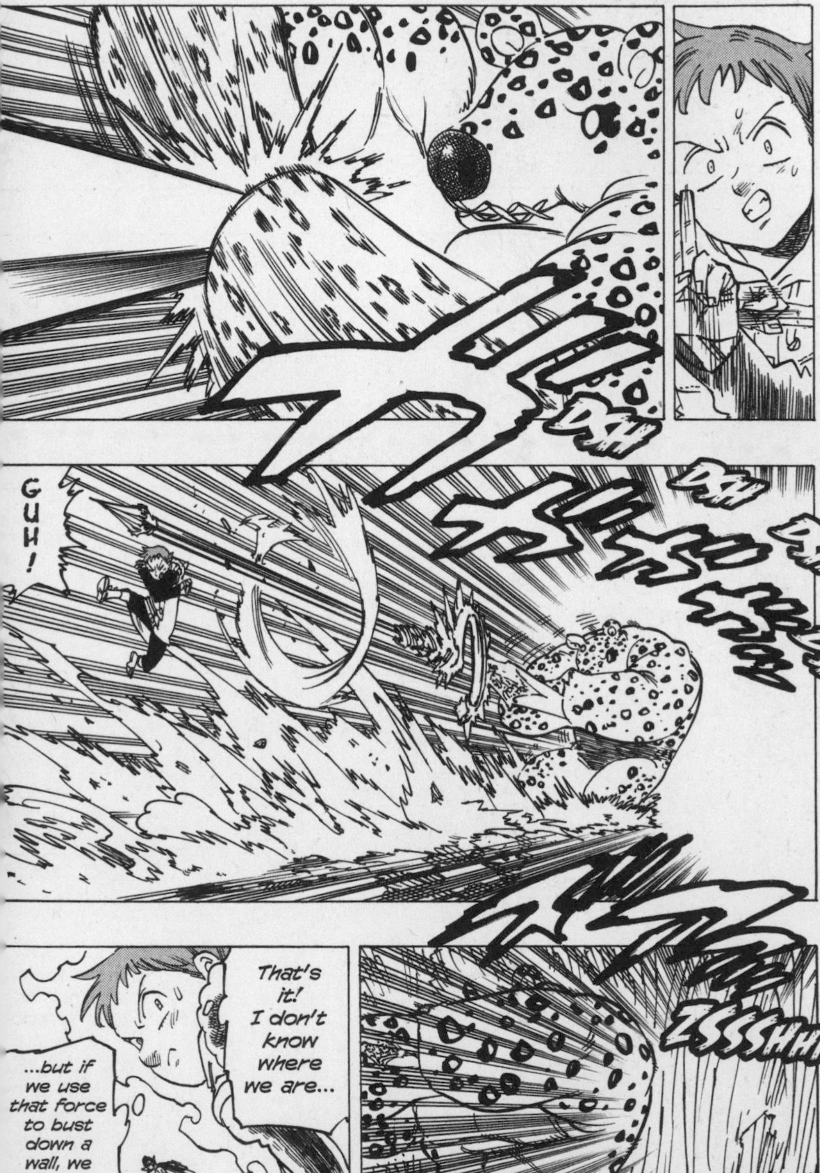
DH DH DH DH
GUH!
ZSSSHHH
That's it! I don't know where we are...
...but if we use that force to bust down a wall, we can open an escape route!

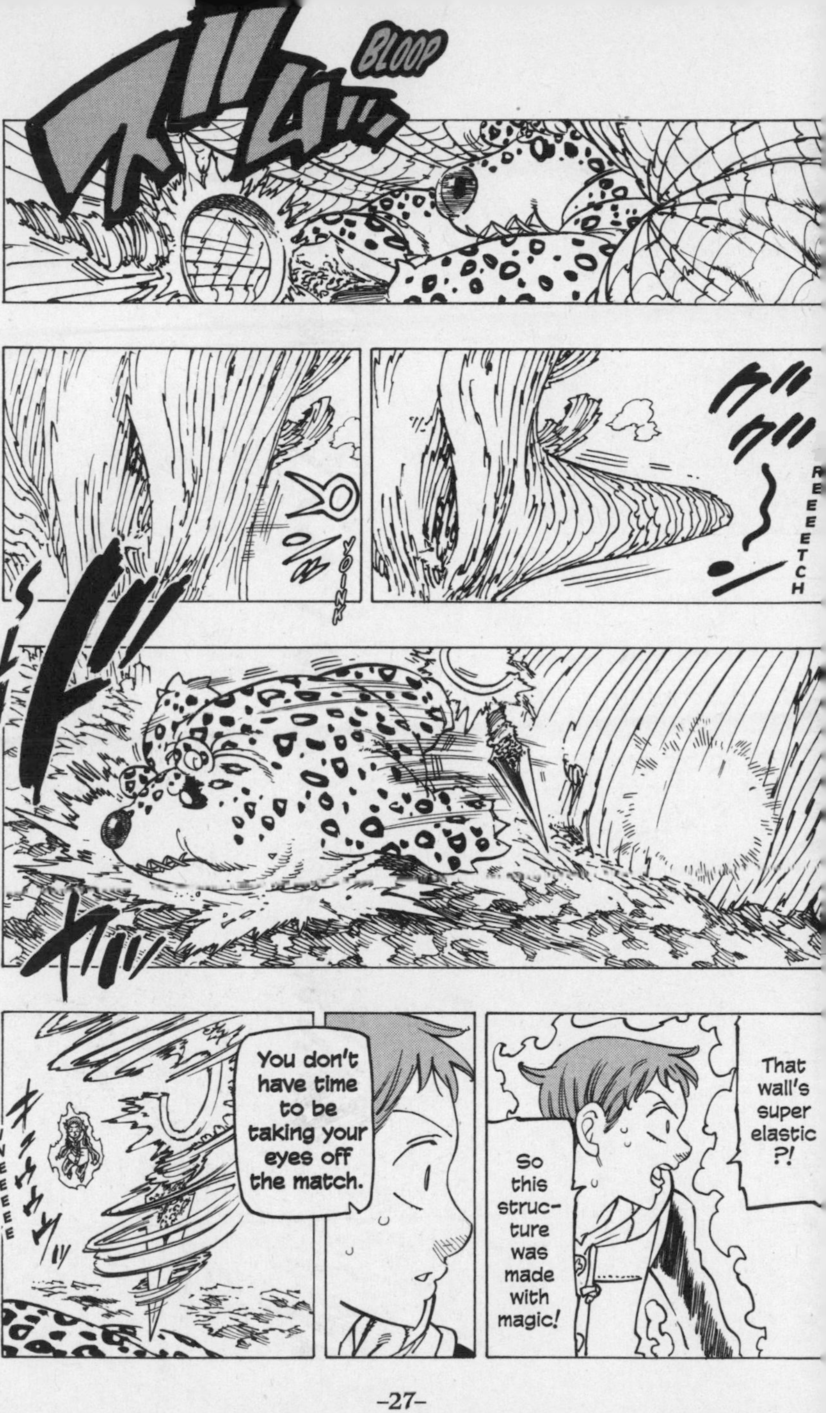
BLOOP
REEEETCH
YOINK
SLAM
That wall's super elastic ?!
So this struc- ture was made with magic!
You don't have time to be taking your eyes off the match.
VWEEEEE

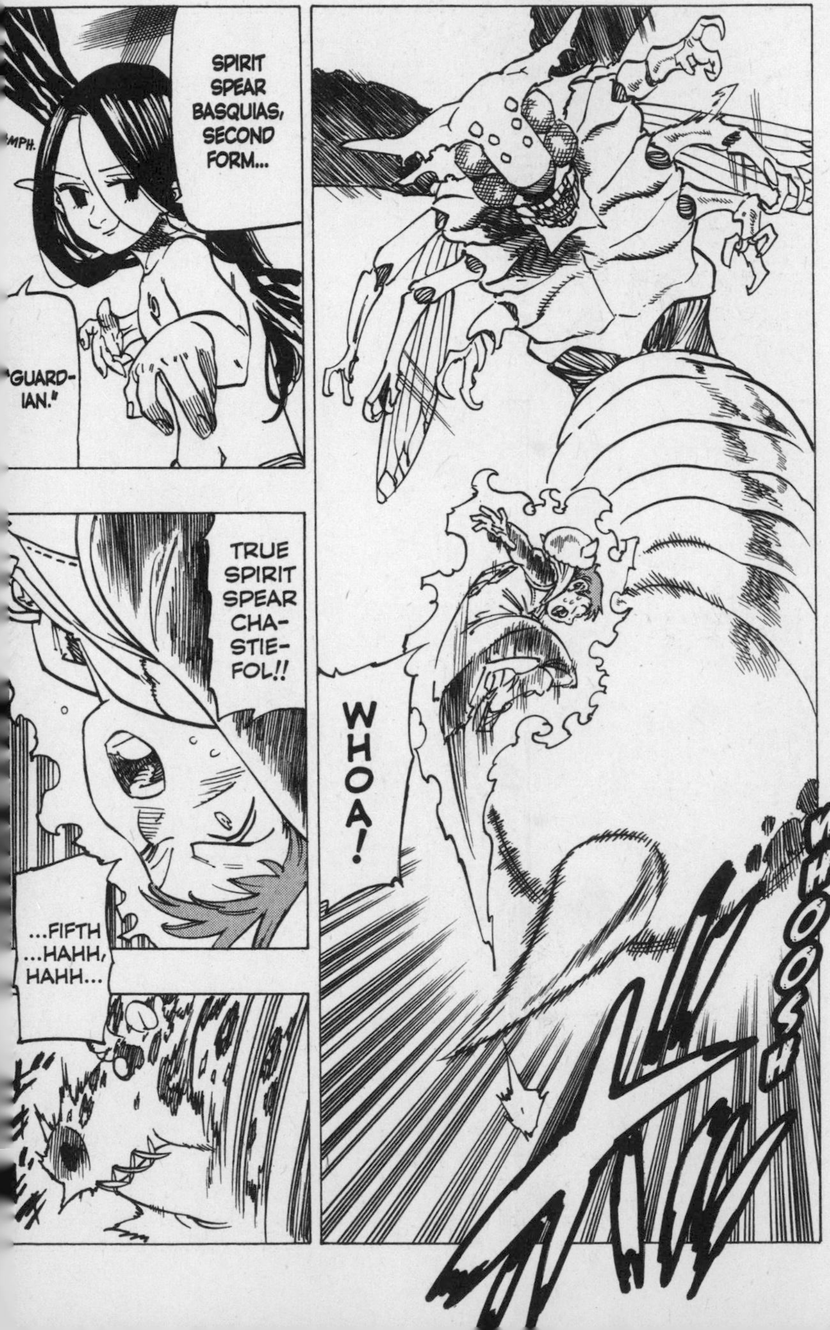
WHOA!
WHOOOSH
MPH.
SPIRIT SPEAR BASQUIAS, SECOND FORM...
"GUARDIAN."
TRUE SPIRIT SPEAR CHASTIEFOL!!
...FIFTH ...HAHH, HAHH...

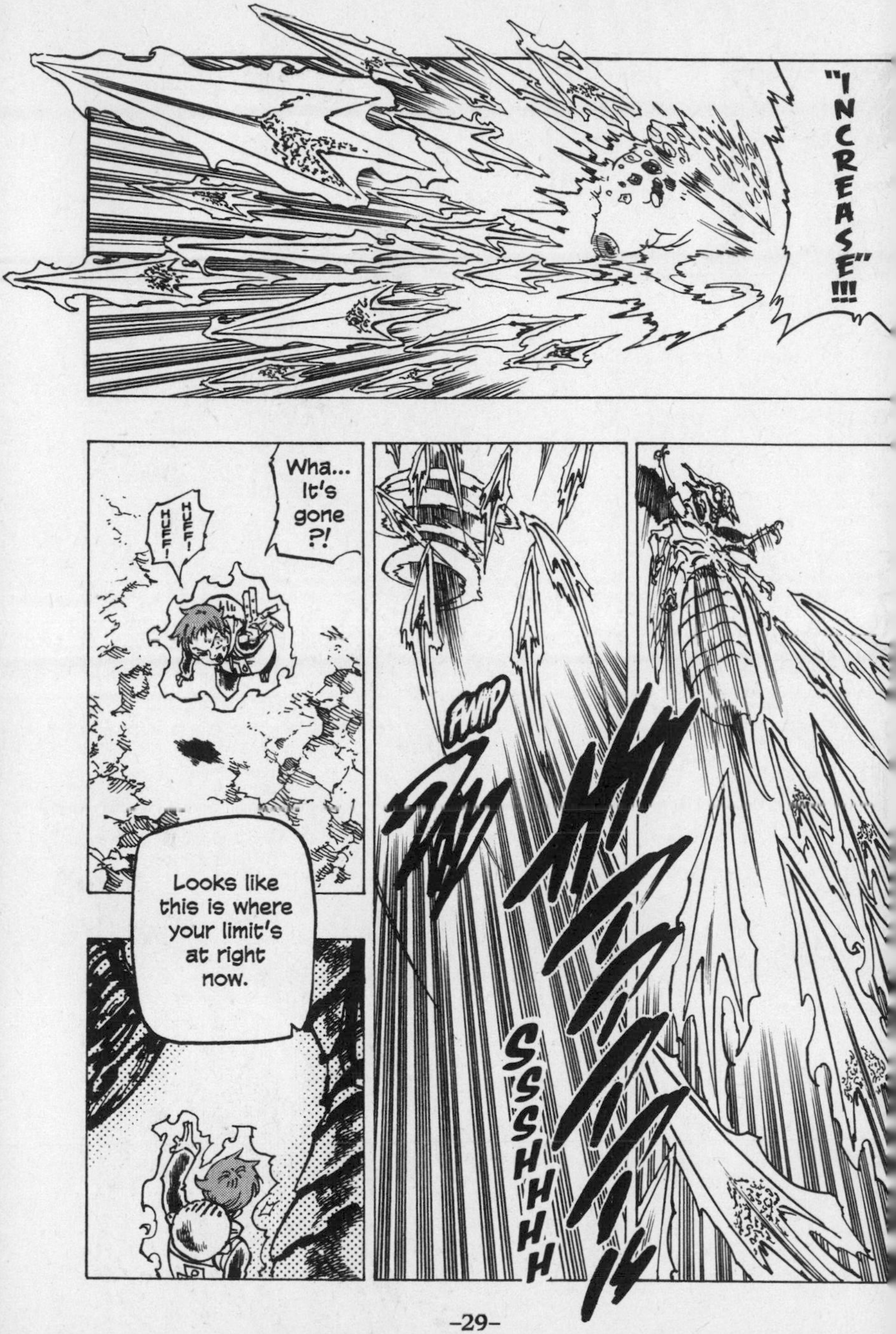
"INCREASE"!!!
FWIP
SSSHHHH
Wha... It's gone?!
HUFF! HUFF!
Looks like this is where your limit's at right now.

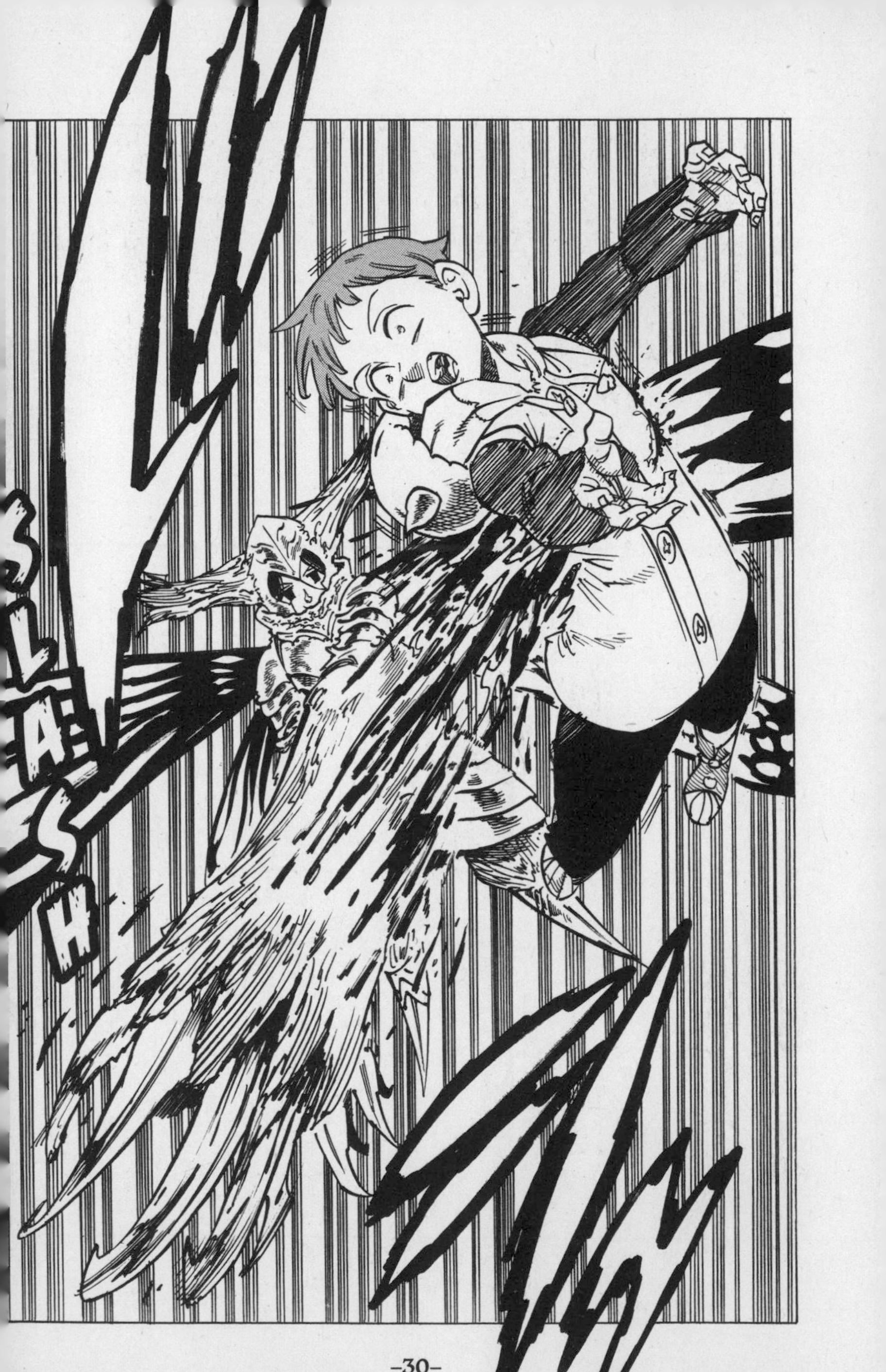
SLASH

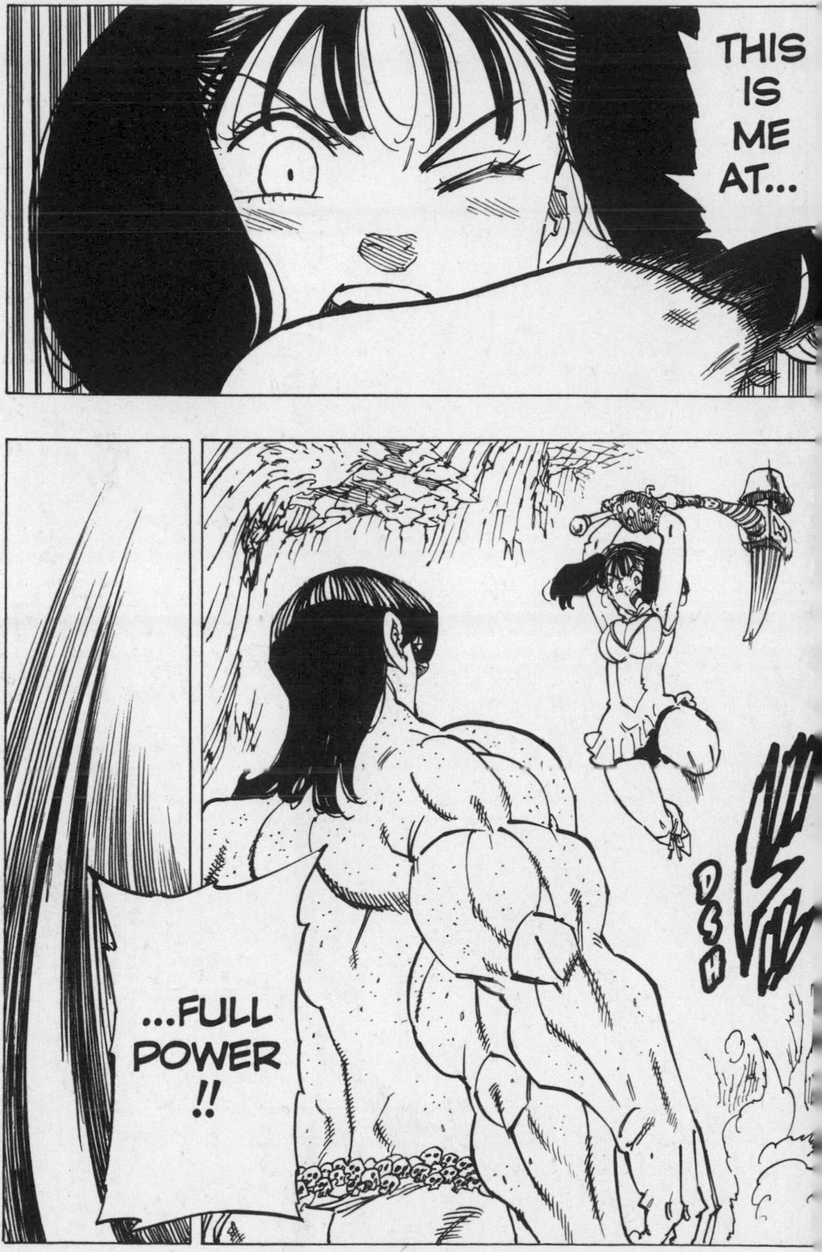
THIS IS ME AT...
DSH
...FULL POWER !!

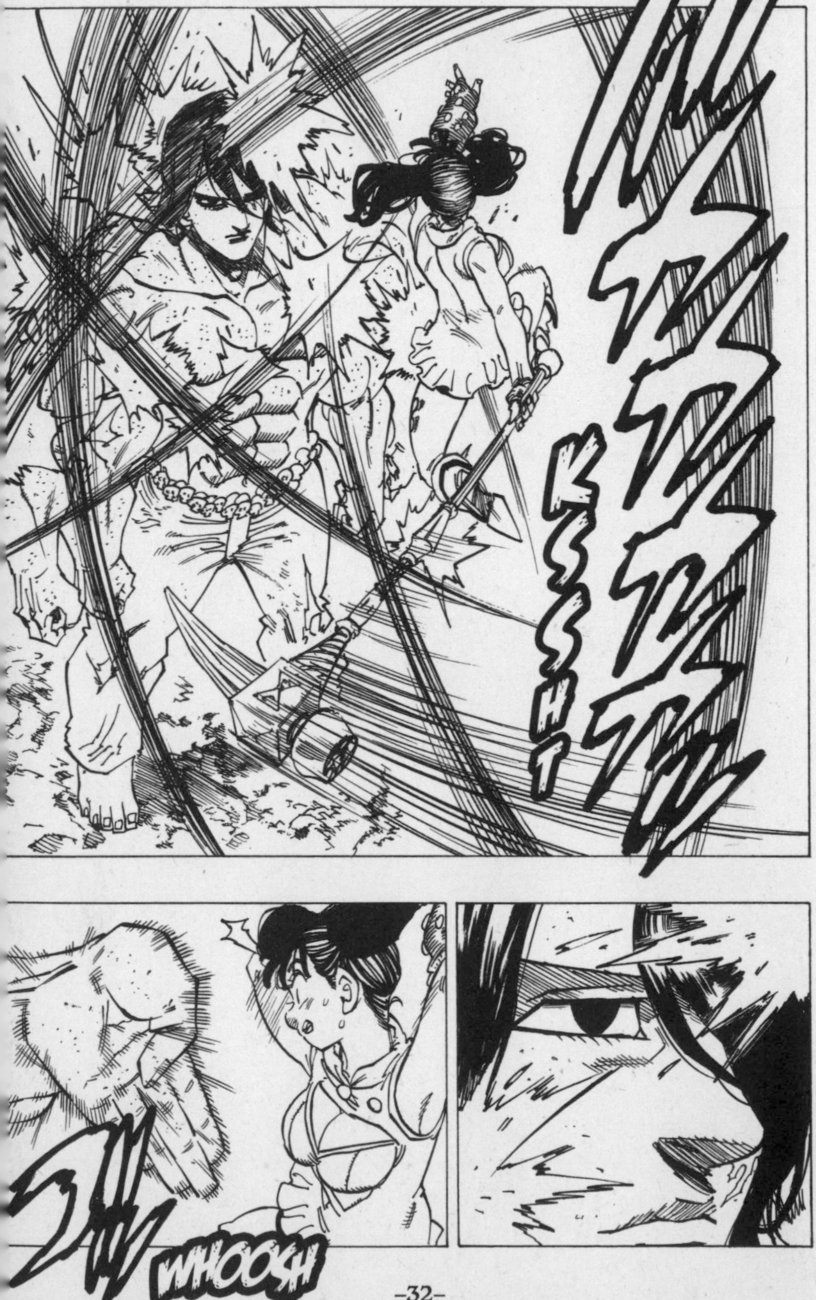
KLISSHT
WHOOSH

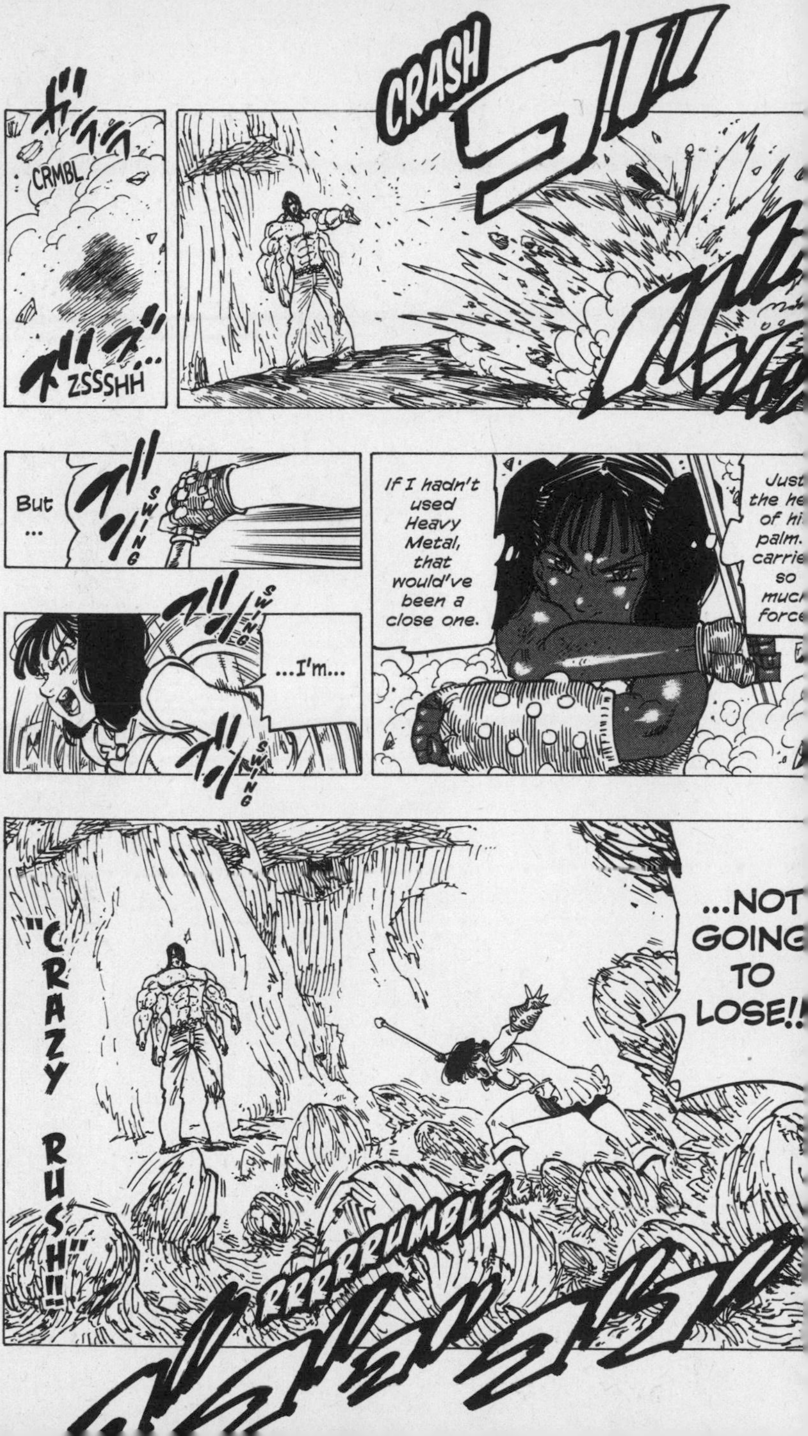
CRASH
CRMBL
ZSSSHH
Just
the he
of hi
palm.
carrie
so
much
force
If I hadn't used Heavy Metal, that would've been a close one.
But ...
SWING
SWING
...I'm...
SWING
...NOT GOING TO LOSE!!
"CRAZY RUSH!!!"
RRRRRUMBLE

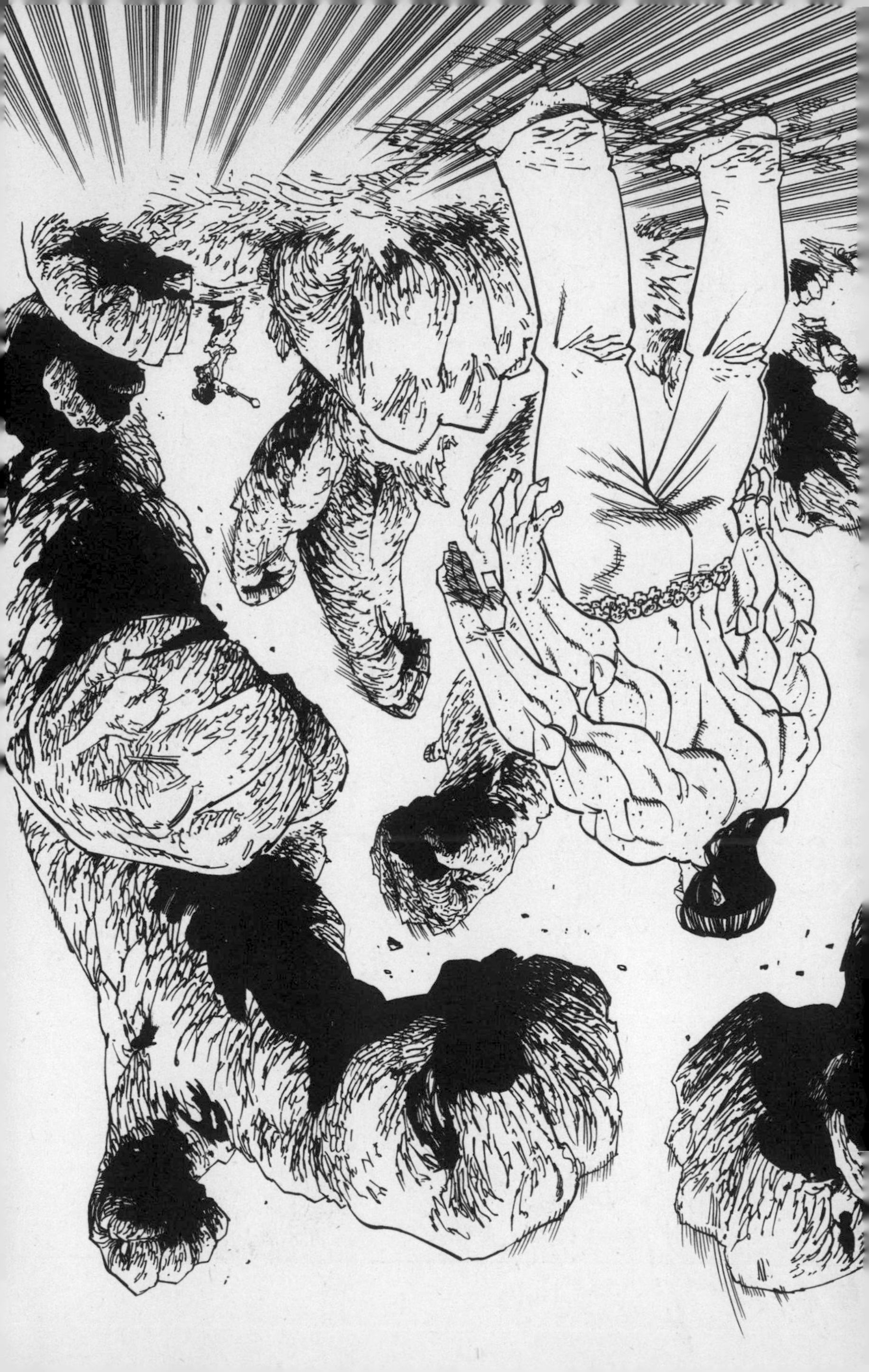

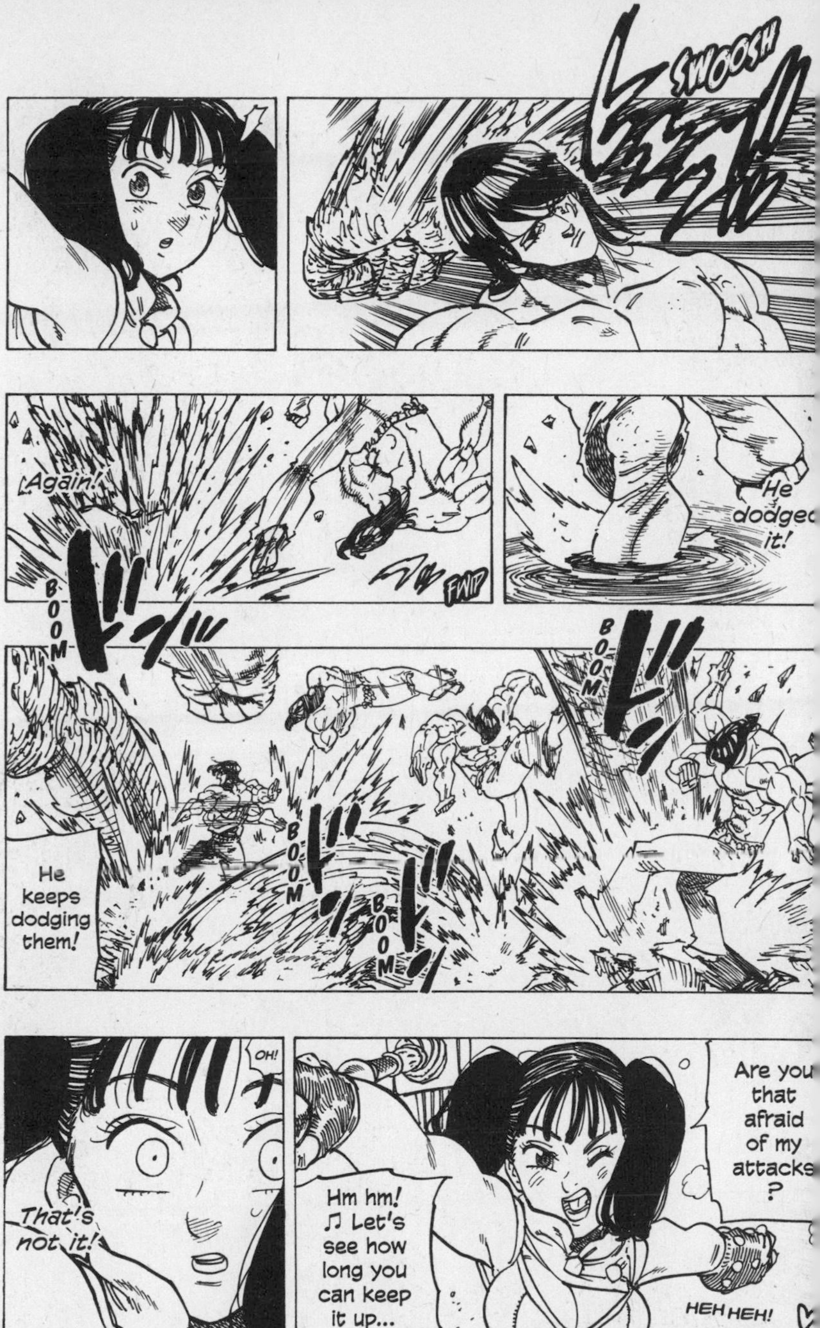
SWOOSH
He dodged it!
Again!
FWIP
BOOM
BOOM
He keeps dodging them!
BOOM
BOOM
BOOM
Are you that afraid of my attacks?
Hm hm! ♫ Let's see how long you can keep it up...
HEH HEH!
OH!
That's not it!

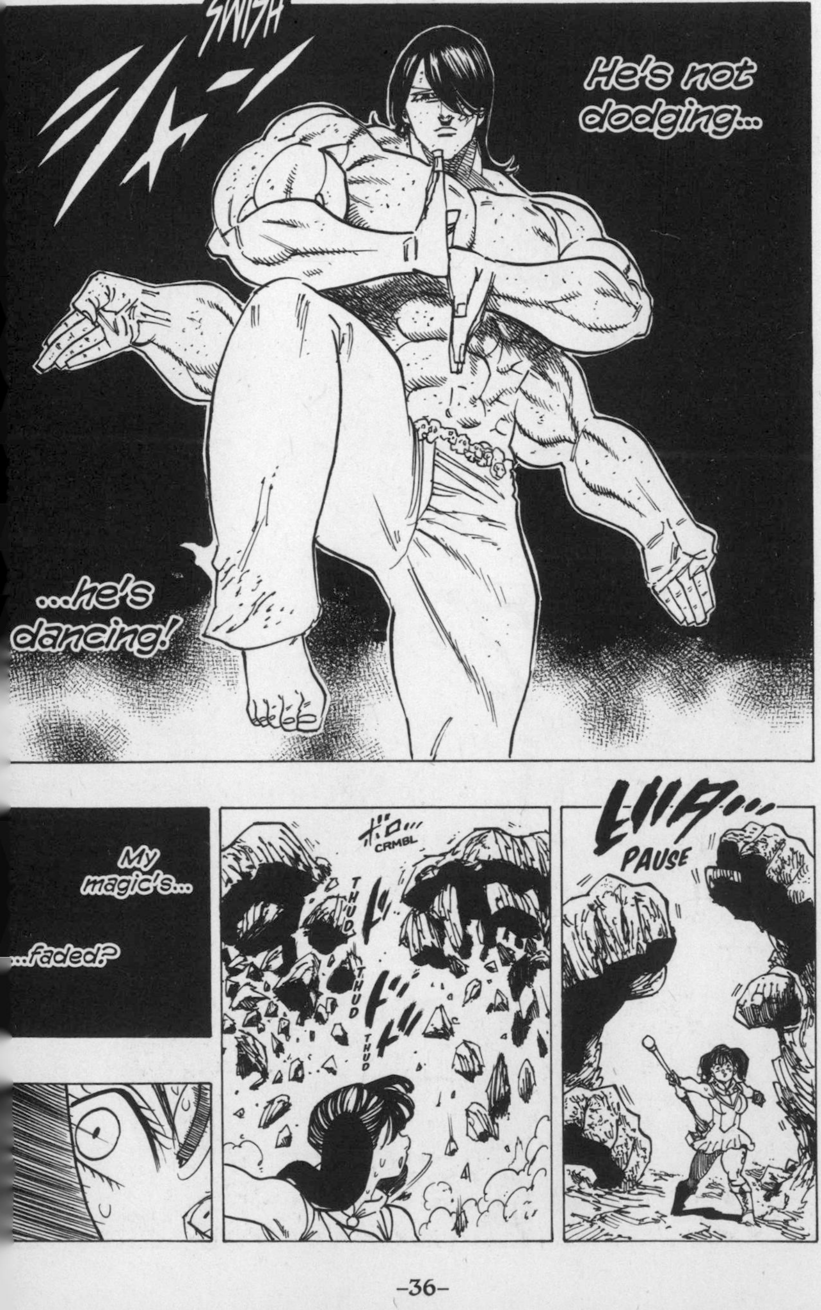
SWISH
He's not dodging...
...he's dancing!
PAUSE
CRMBL
THUD
THUD
My magic's...
...faded?

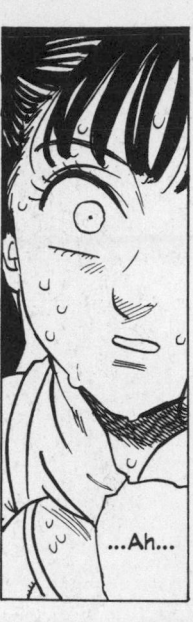

...Ah...

Little girl...
It seems
you don't
understand
a thing.

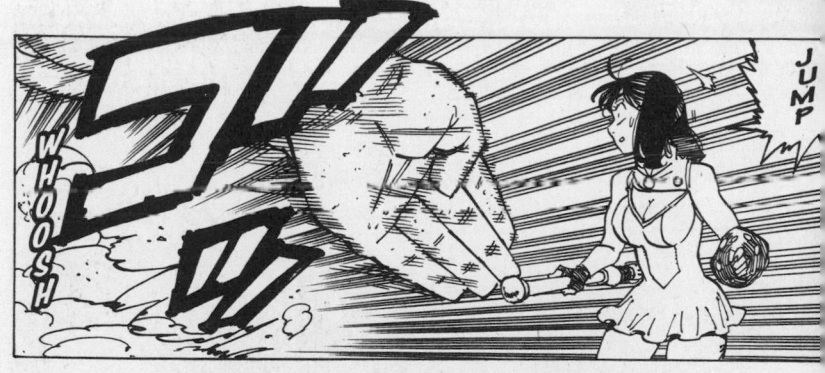

WHOOSH

JUMP

TING

"HEAVY METAL"

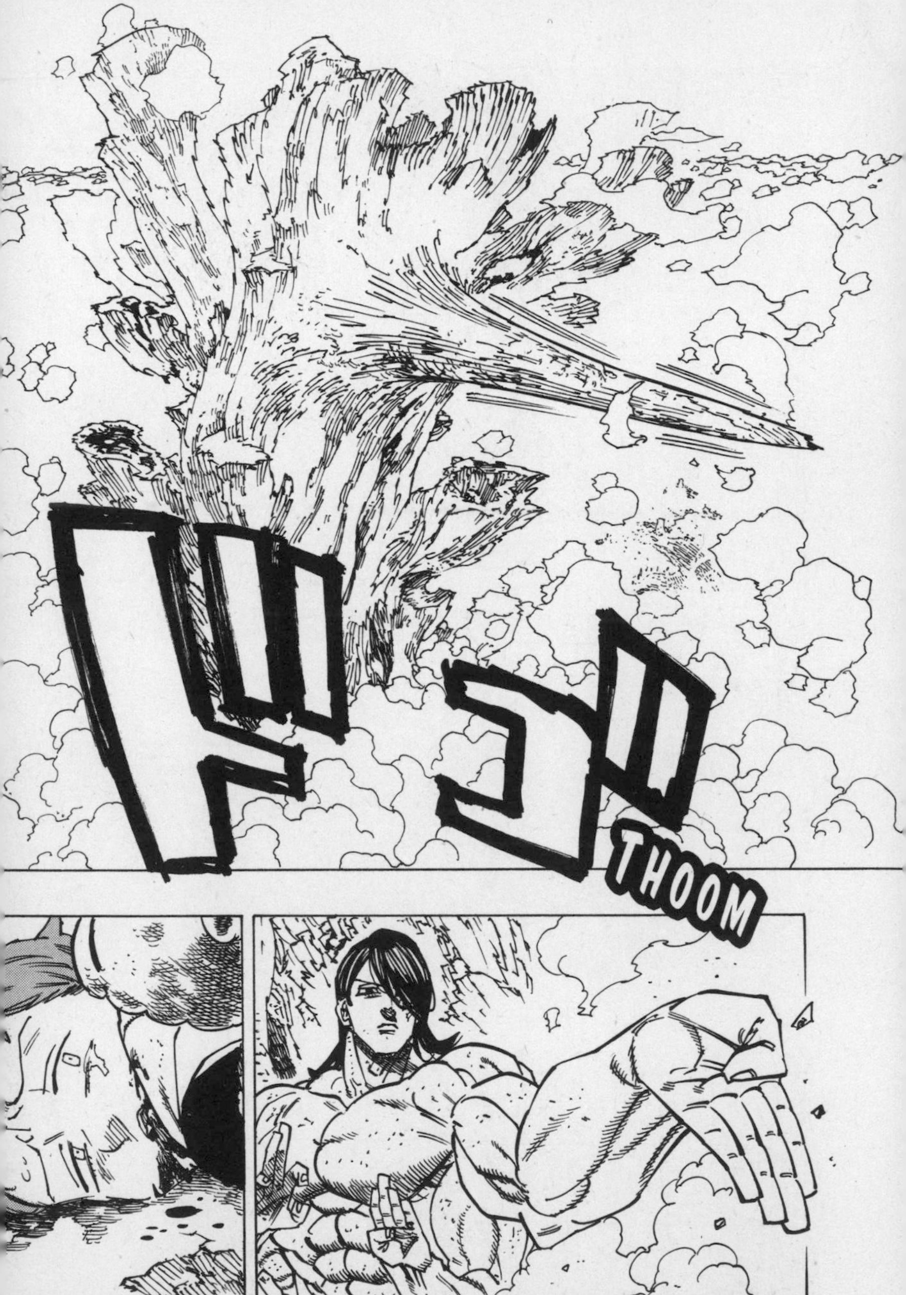
THOOM

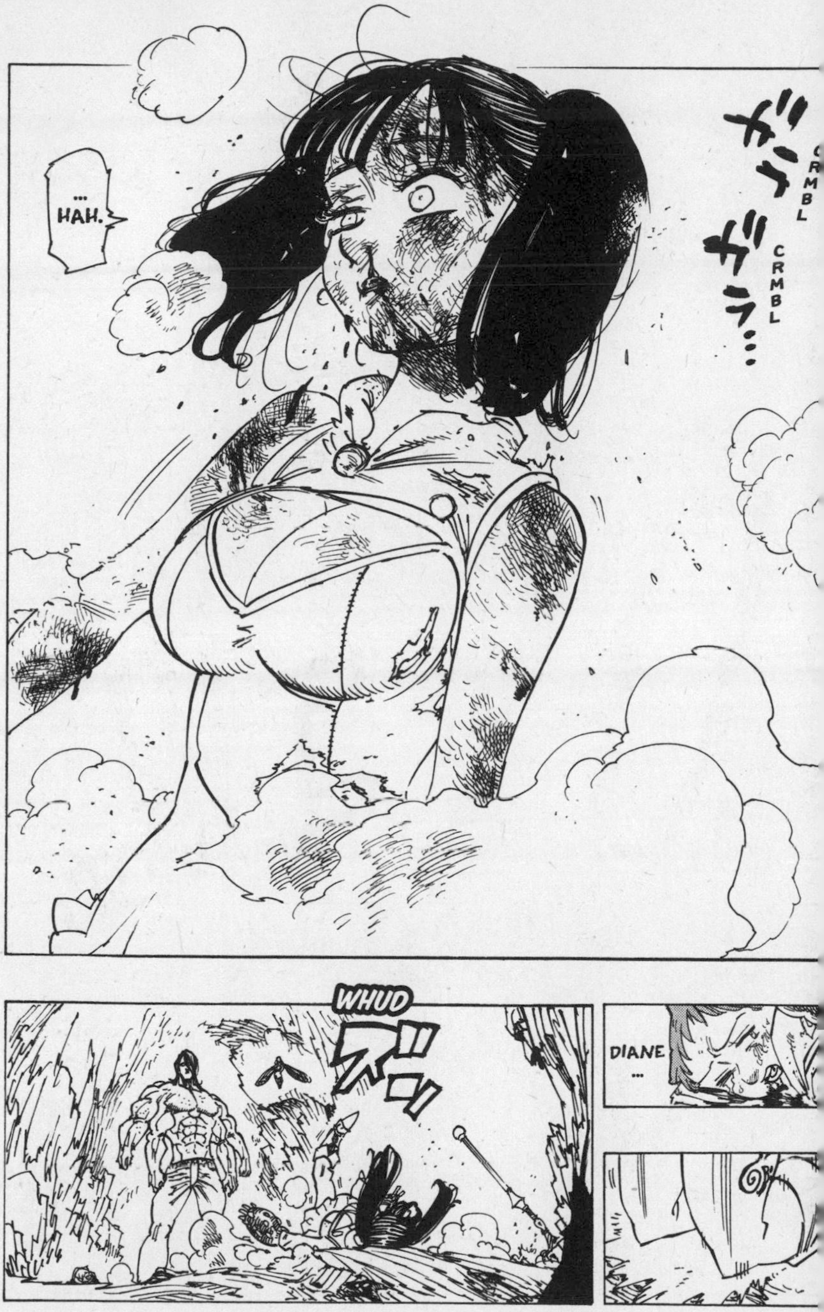
CRMBL
CRMBL
... HAH.
DIANE ...
WHUD

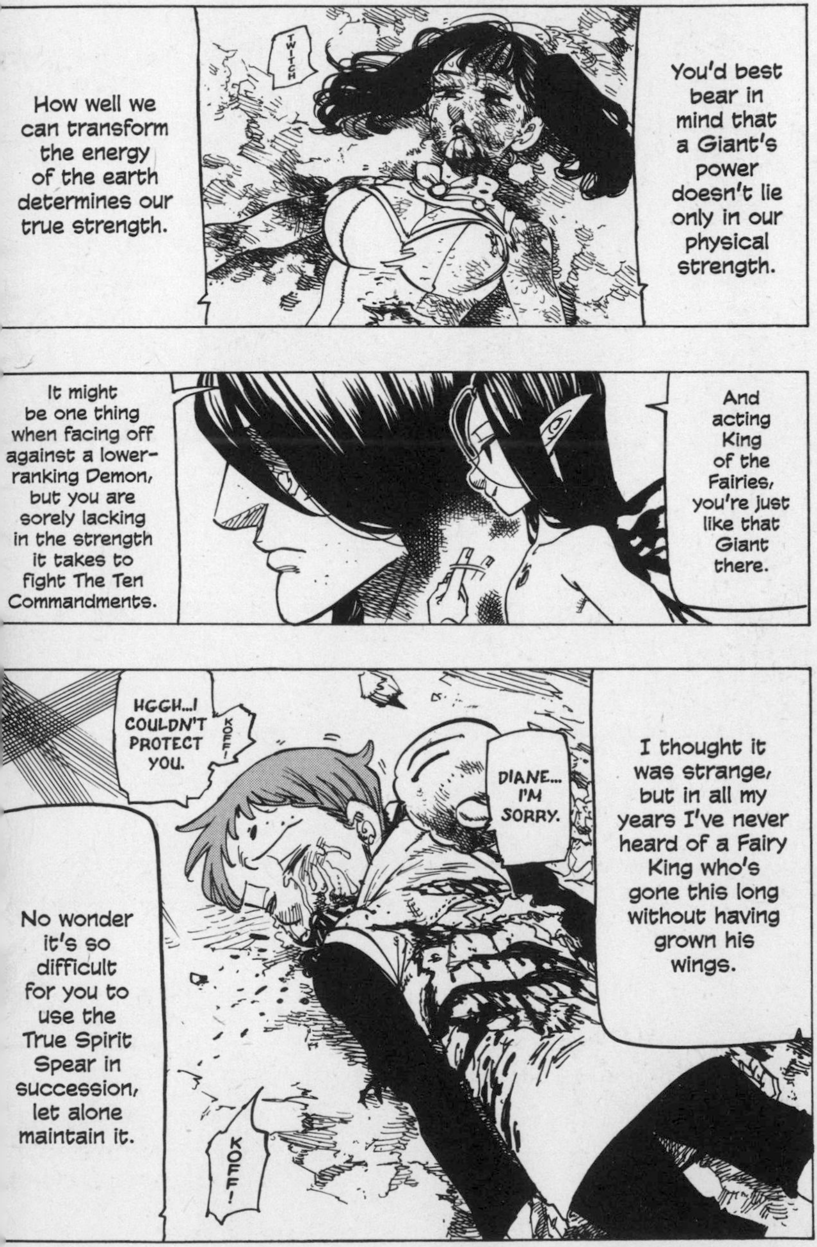
You'd best bear in mind that a Giant's power doesn't lie only in our physical strength.
TWITCH
How well we can transform the energy of the earth determines our true strength.
And acting King of the Fairies, you're just like that Giant there.
It might be one thing when facing off against a lower-ranking Demon, but you are sorely lacking in the strength it takes to fight The Ten Commandments.
I thought it was strange, but in all my years I've never heard of a Fairy King who's gone this long without having grown his wings.
DIANE... I'M SORRY.
KOFF!
HGGH...I COULDN'T PROTECT YOU.
No wonder it's so difficult for you to use the True Spirit Spear in succession, let alone maintain it.
KOFF!

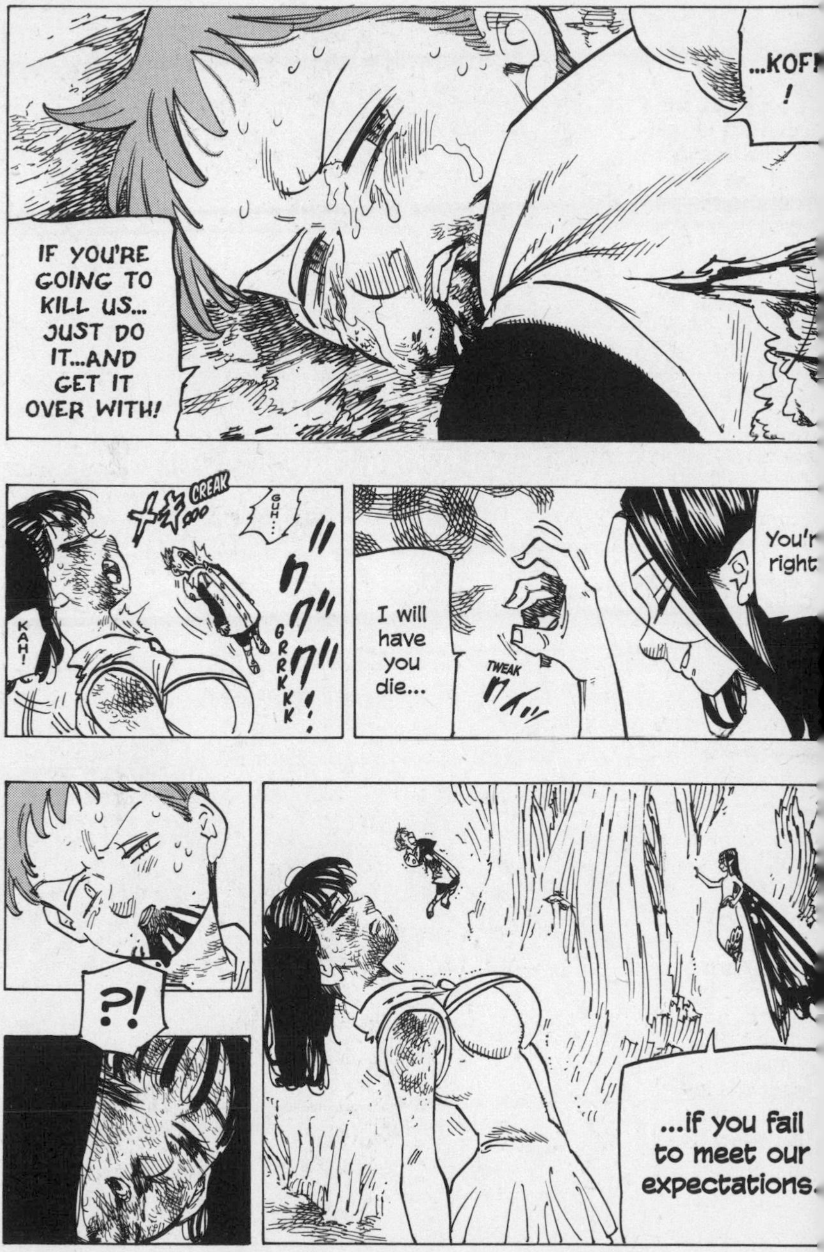
...KOFF
!
IF YOU'RE GOING TO KILL US... JUST DO IT...AND GET IT OVER WITH!
You'r right
I will have you die...
TWEAK
GUH...
CREAK
GRRKKK!!
KAH!
...if you fail to meet our expectations.
?!

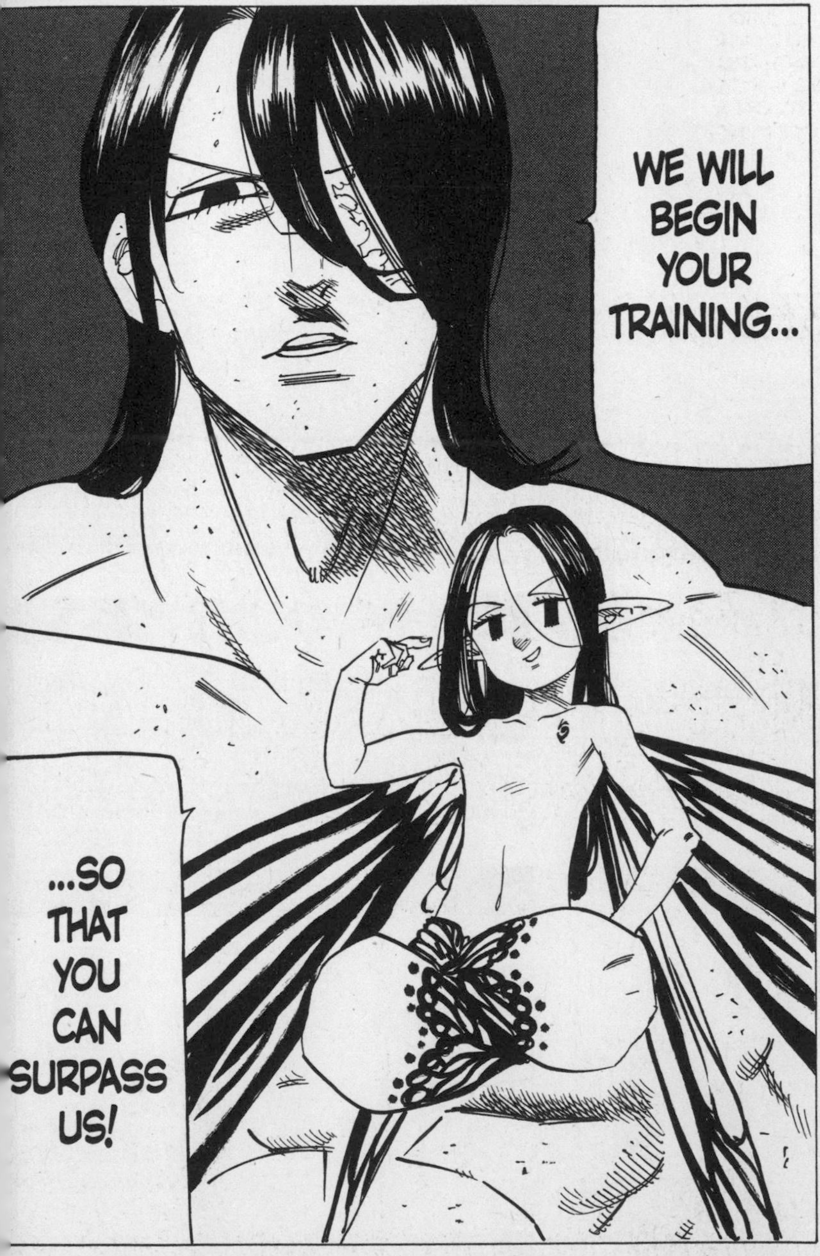
WE WILL BEGIN YOUR TRAINING...
...SO THAT YOU CAN SURPASS US!

Bonus Story - Ruler of the Altar (4)

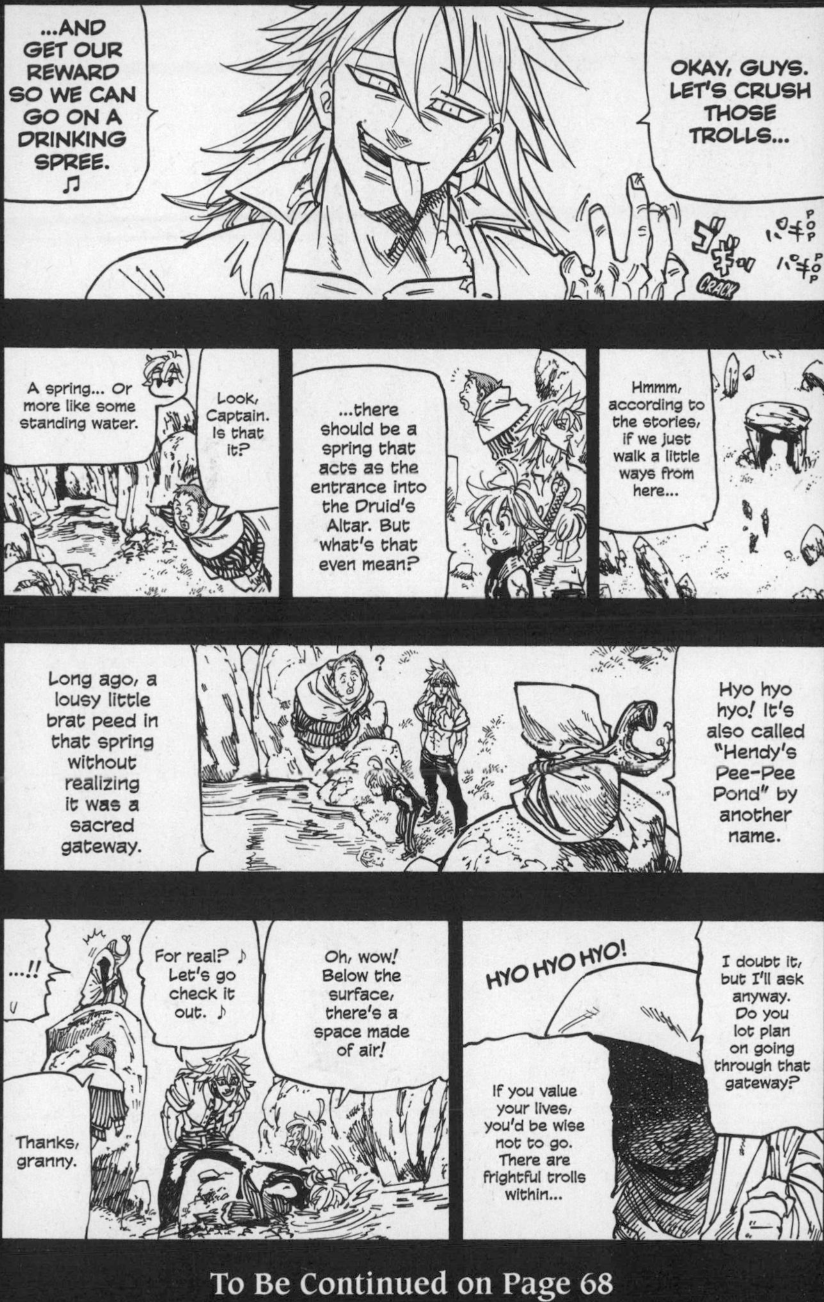

OKAY, GUYS. LET'S CRUSH THOSE TROLLS...
POP POP
CRACK
...AND GET OUR REWARD SO WE CAN GO ON A DRINKING SPREE. ♫
Hmmm, according to the stories, if we just walk a little ways from here...
...there should be a spring that acts as the entrance into the Druid's Altar. But what's that even mean?
Look, Captain. Is that it?
A spring... Or more like some standing water.
Hyo hyo hyo! It's also called "Hendy's Pee-Pee Pond" by another name.
?
Long ago, a lousy little brat peed in that spring without realizing it was a sacred gateway.
I doubt it, but I'll ask anyway. Do you lot plan on going through that gateway?
HYO HYO HYO!
If you value your lives, you'd be wise not to go. There are frightful trolls within...
Oh, wow! Below the surface, there's a space made of air!
For real? ♪ Let's go check it out. ♪
...!!
Thanks, granny.

To Be Continued on Page 68

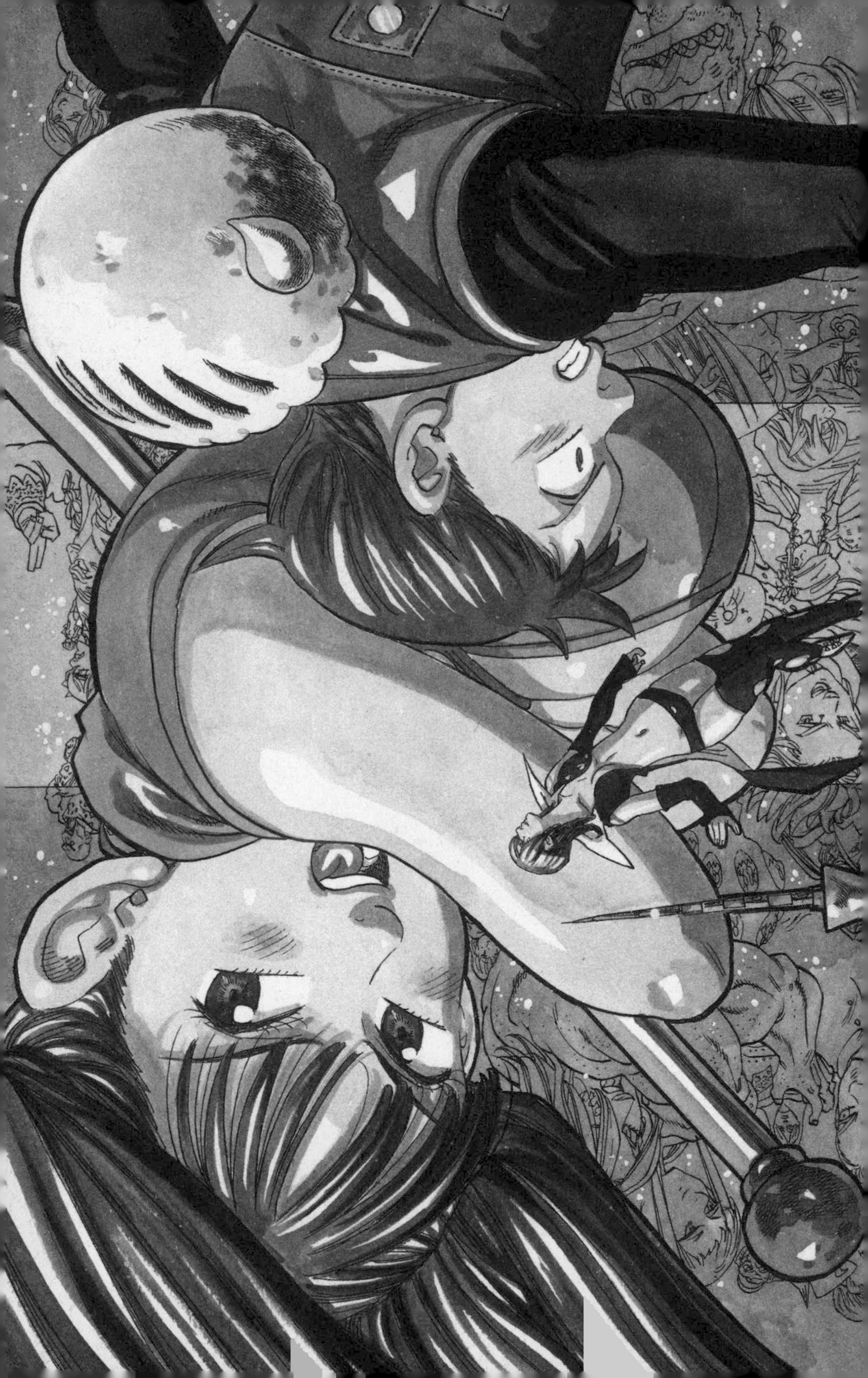

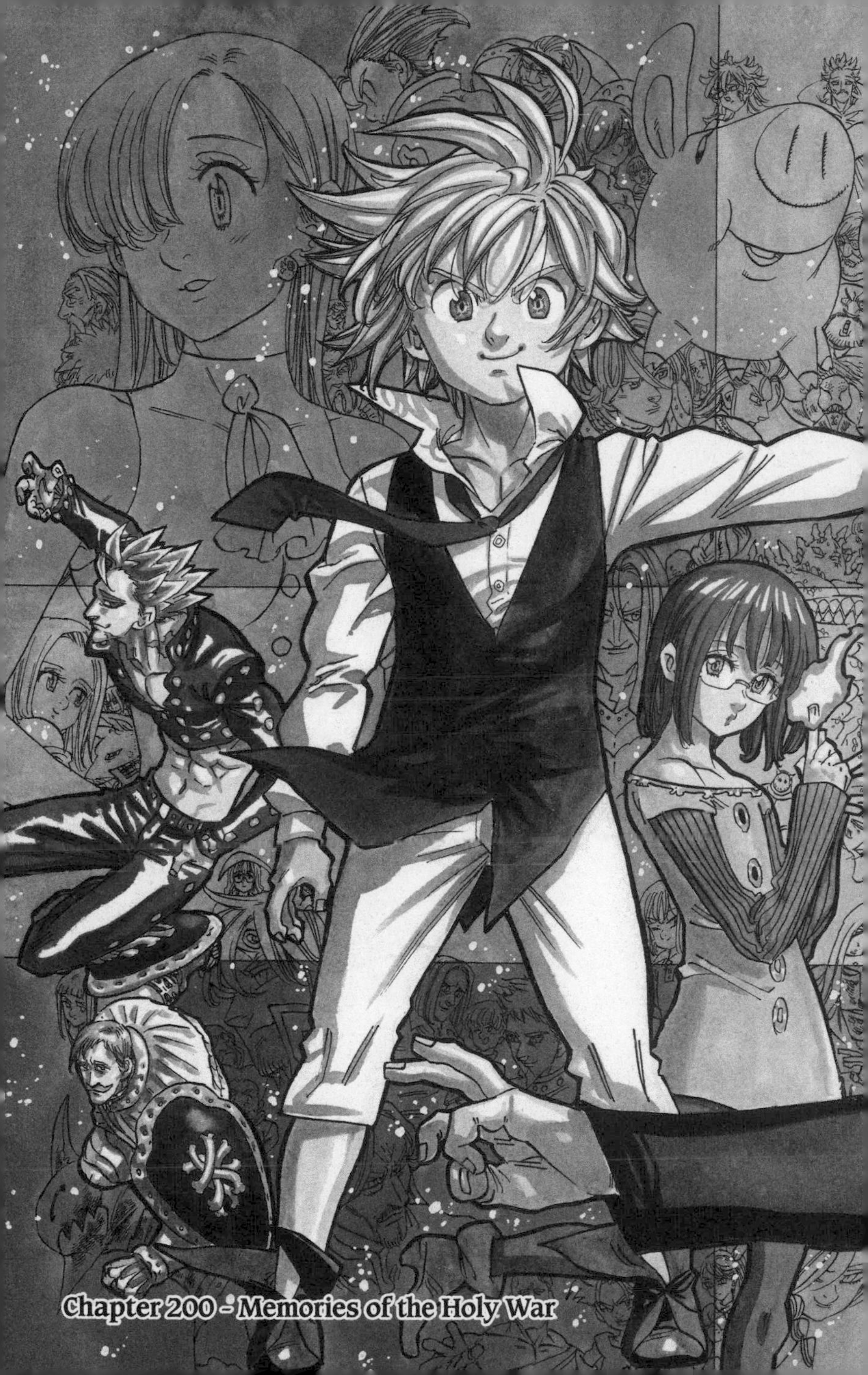
Chapter 200 - Memories of the Holy War

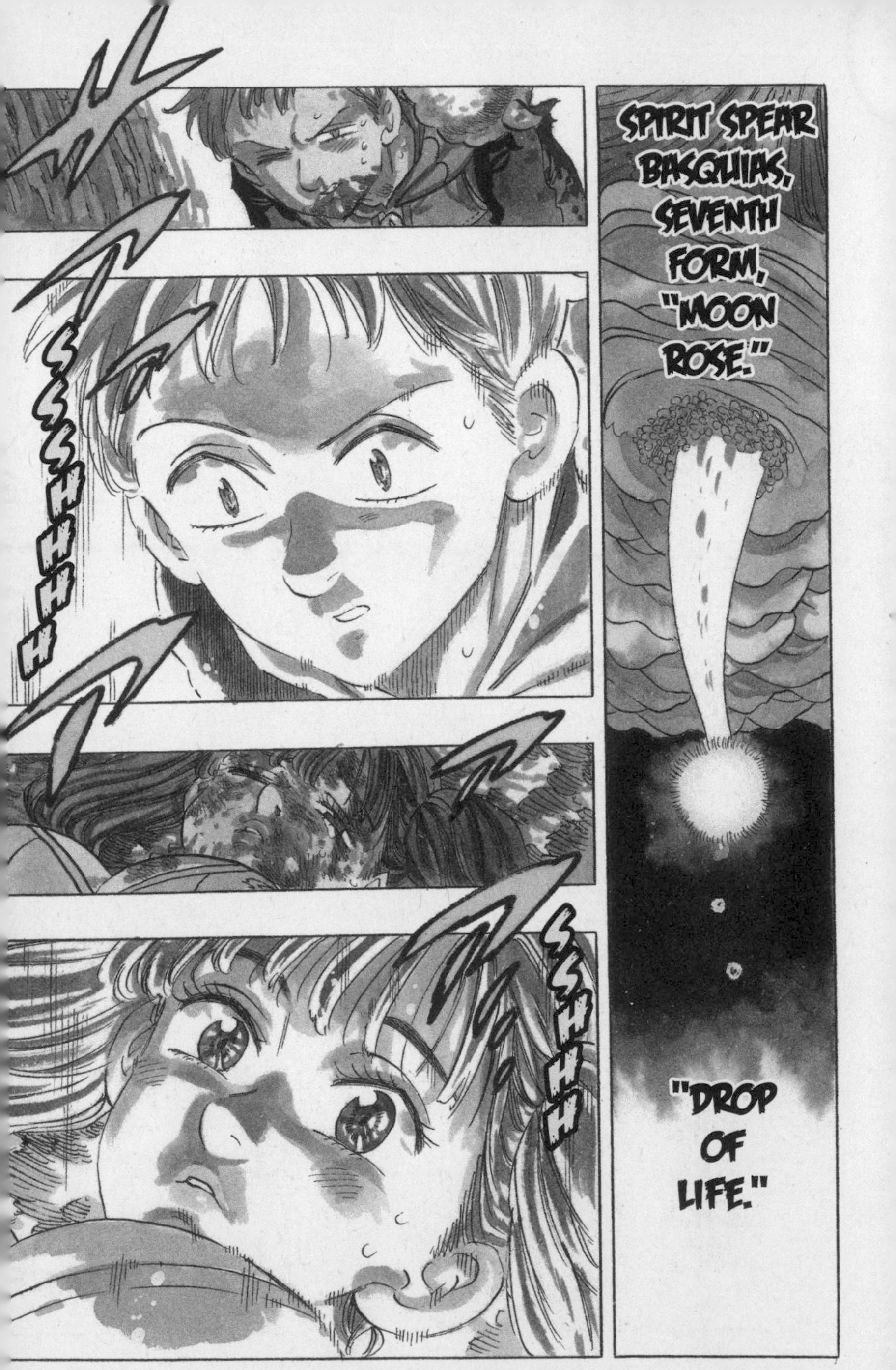
SPIRIT SPEAR BASQUIAS, SEVENTH FORM, "MOON ROSE."
"DROP OF LIFE."
SSHHHH
SSSHHHHHH

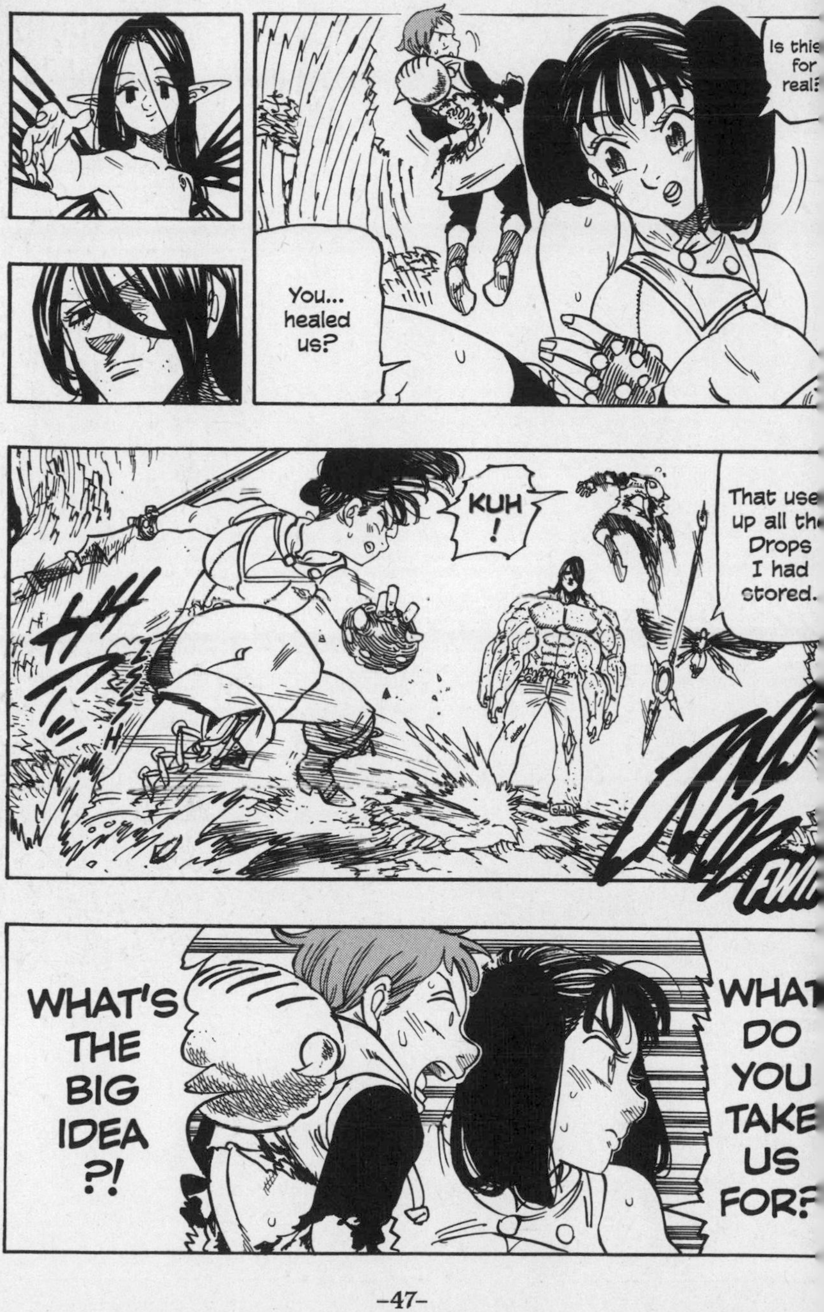
Is this for real?
You... healed us?
That use up all the Drops I had stored.
KUH !
FWI
WHAT DO YOU TAKE US FOR?
WHAT'S THE BIG IDEA ?!

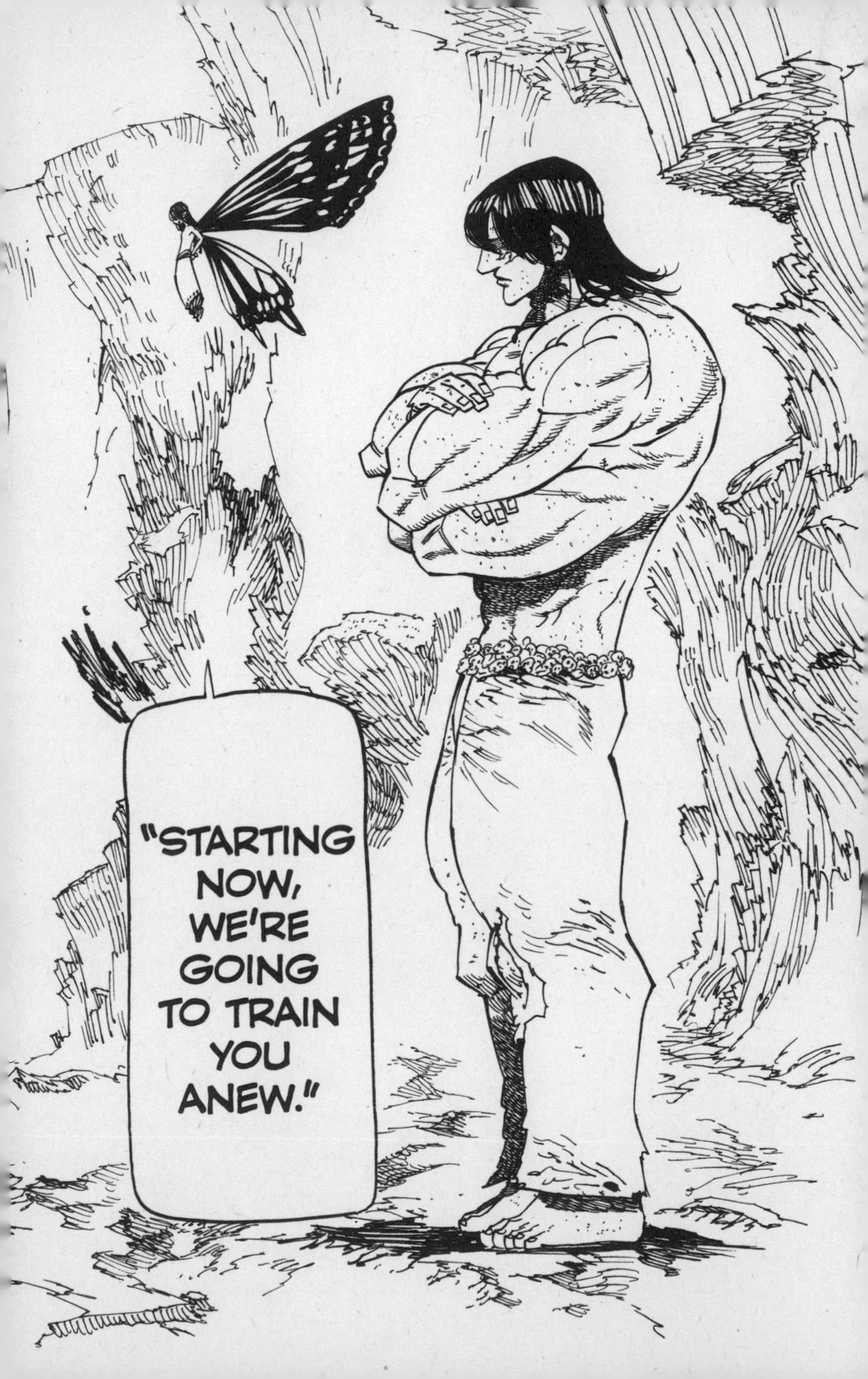
"STARTING NOW, WE'RE GOING TO TRAIN YOU ANEW."

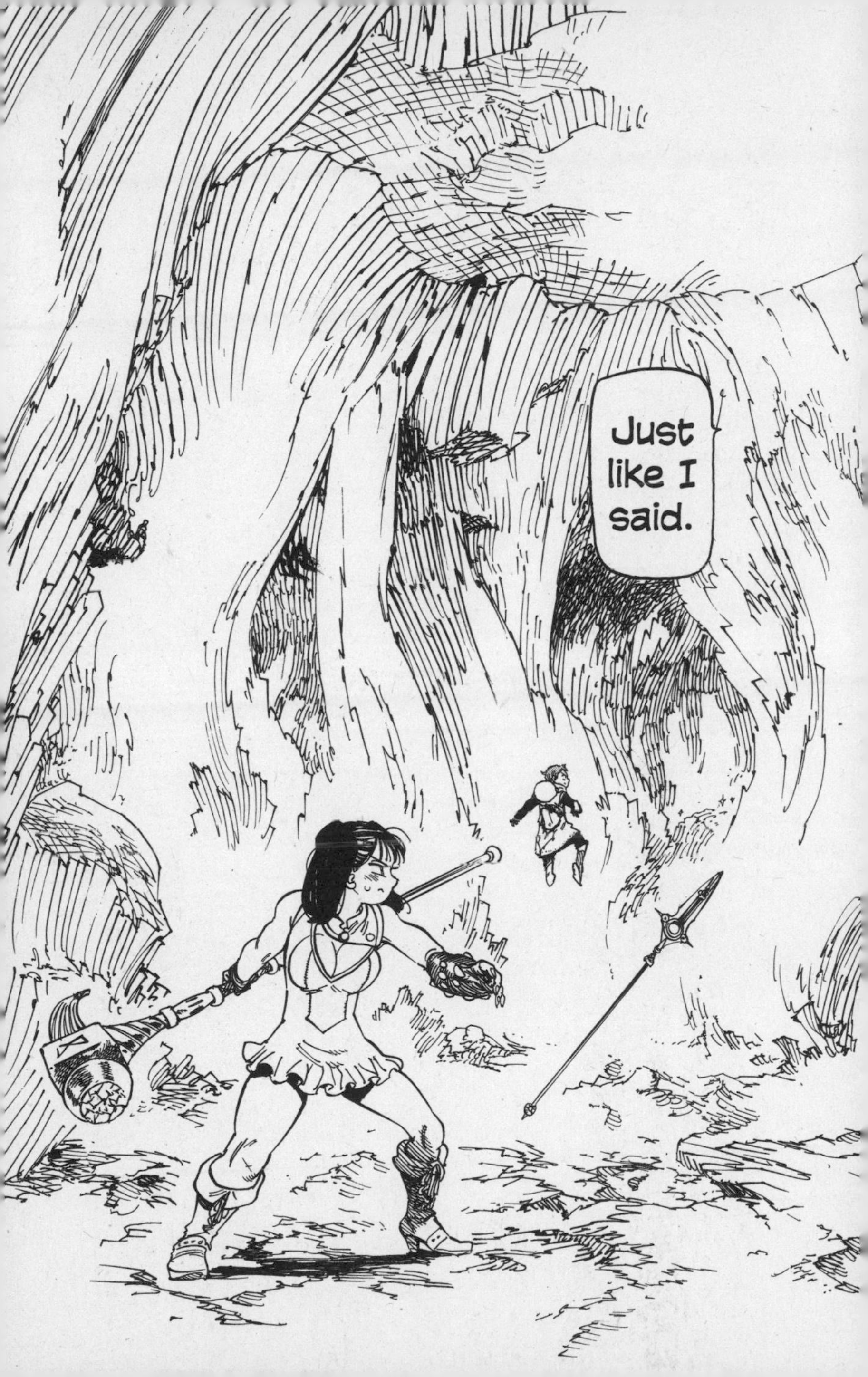
Just like I said.

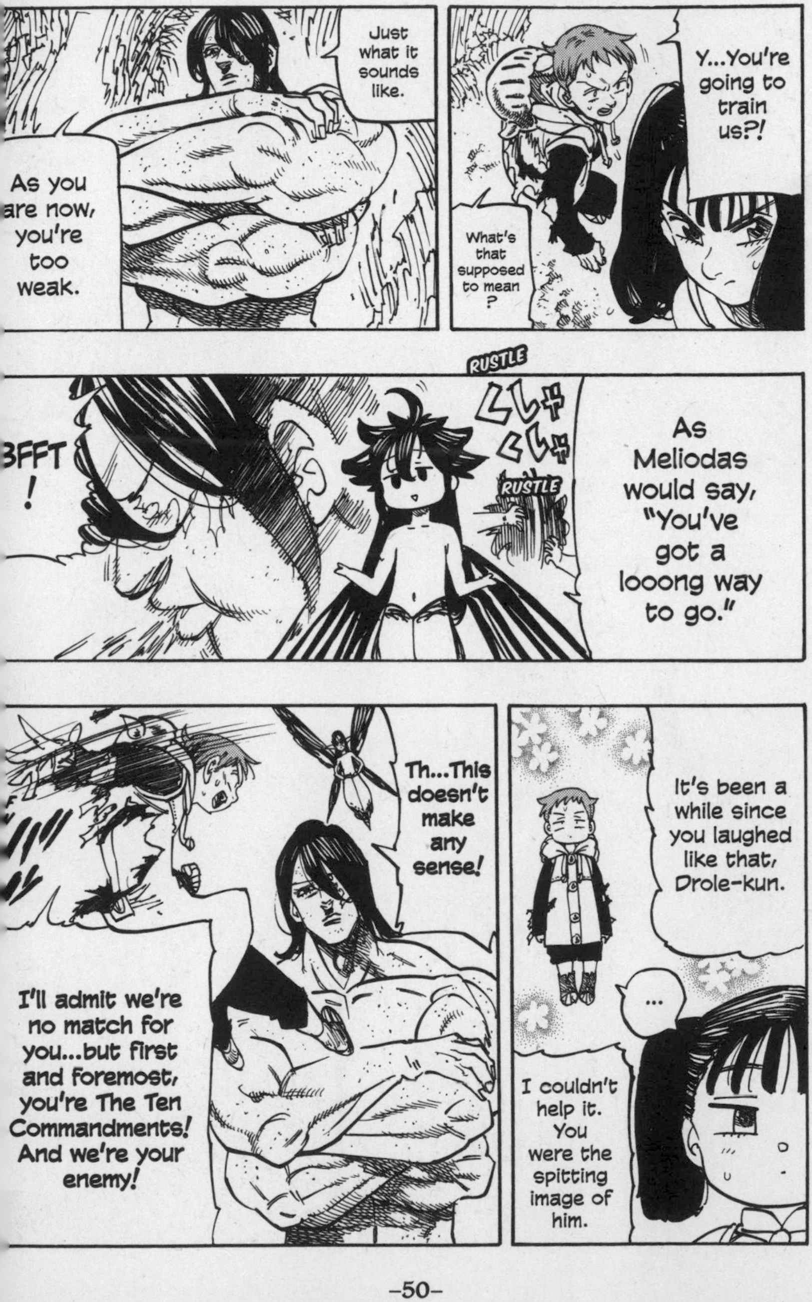
Y...You're going to train us?!
What's that supposed to mean?
Just what it sounds like.
As you are now, you're too weak.
RUSTLE
RUSTLE
As Meliodas would say, "You've got a looong way to go."
BFFT!
It's been a while since you laughed like that, Drole-kun.
...
I couldn't help it. You were the spitting image of him.
Th...This doesn't make any sense!
I'll admit we're no match for you...but first and foremost, you're The Ten Commandments! And we're your enemy!

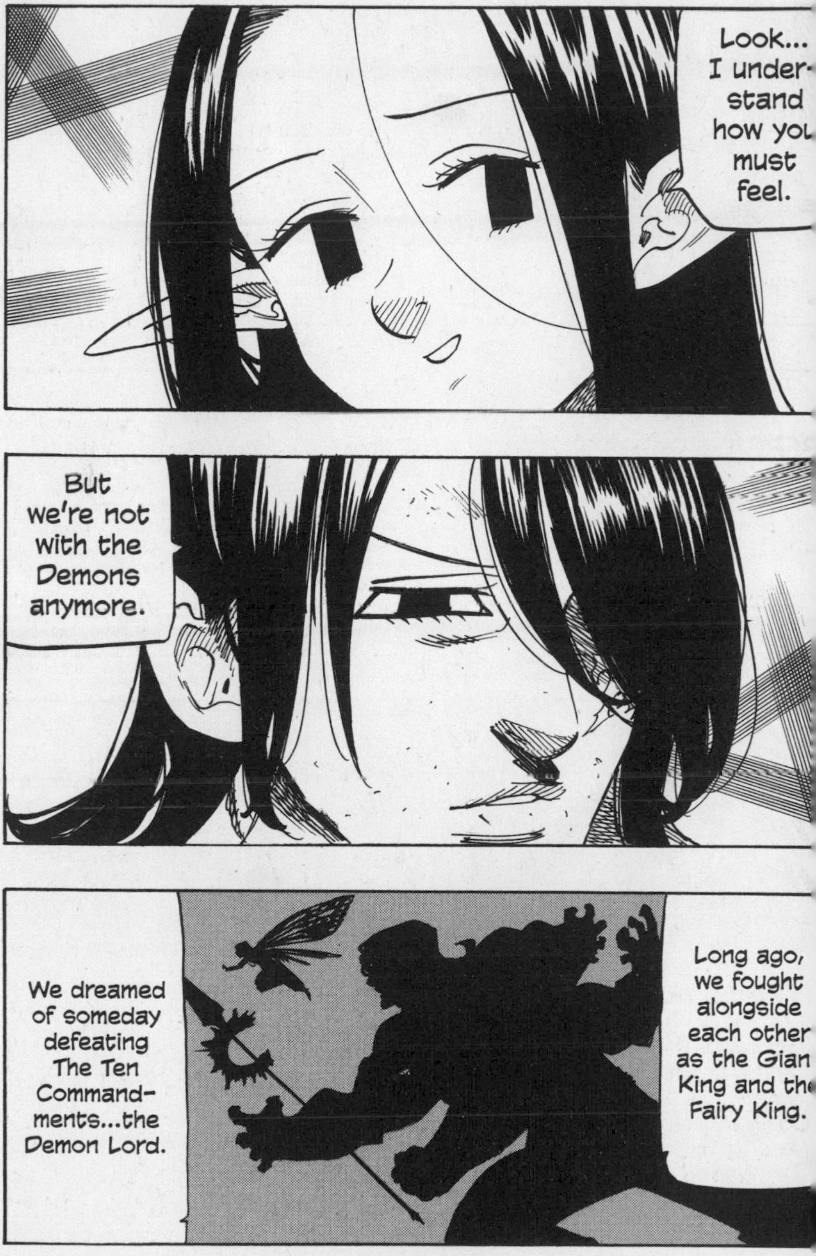
Look... I under-stand how you must feel.
But we're not with the Demons anymore.
Long ago, we fought alongside each other as the Gian King and th Fairy King.
We dreamed of someday defeating The Ten Command-ments...the Demon Lord.

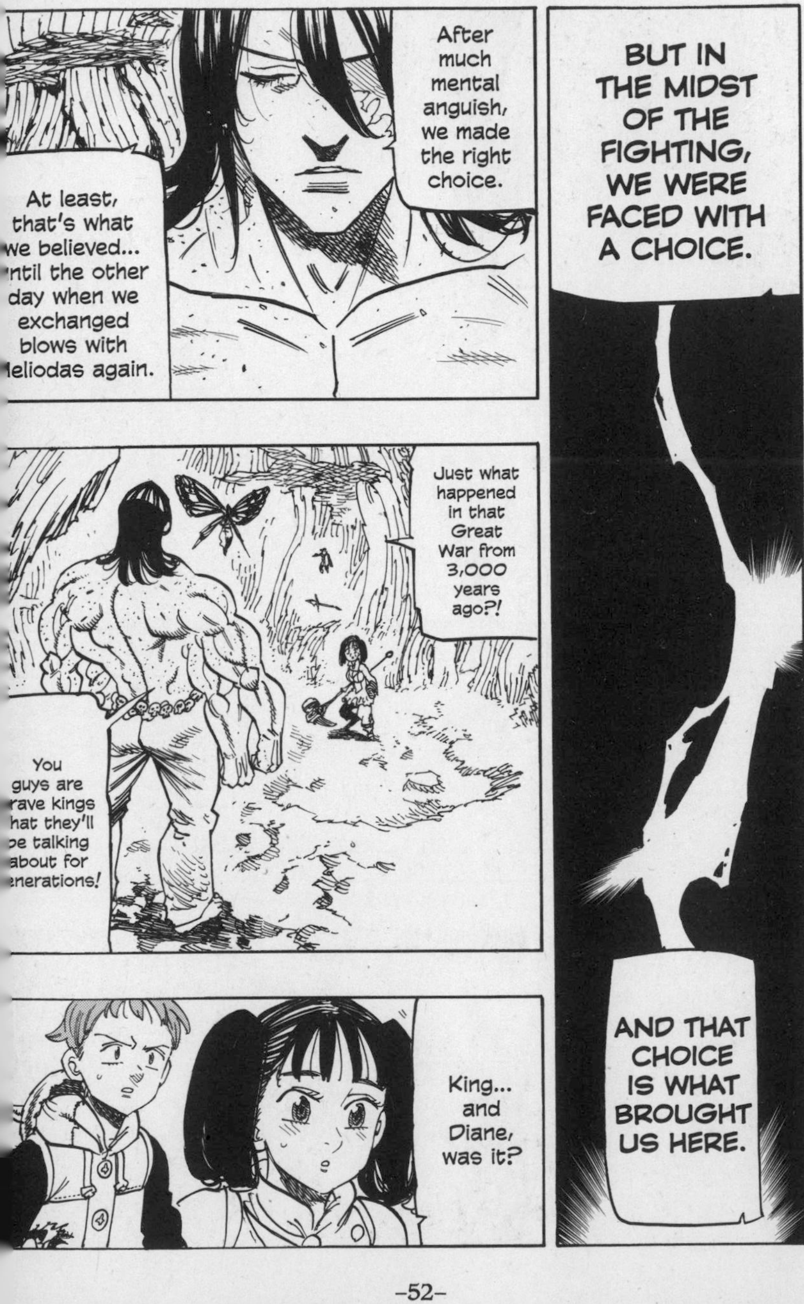
BUT IN THE MIDST OF THE FIGHTING, WE WERE FACED WITH A CHOICE.
AND THAT CHOICE IS WHAT BROUGHT US HERE.
After much mental anguish, we made the right choice.
At least, that's what we believed... until the other day when we exchanged blows with Meliodas again.
Just what happened in that Great War from 3,000 years ago?!
You guys are brave kings that they'll be talking about for generations!
King... and Diane, was it?

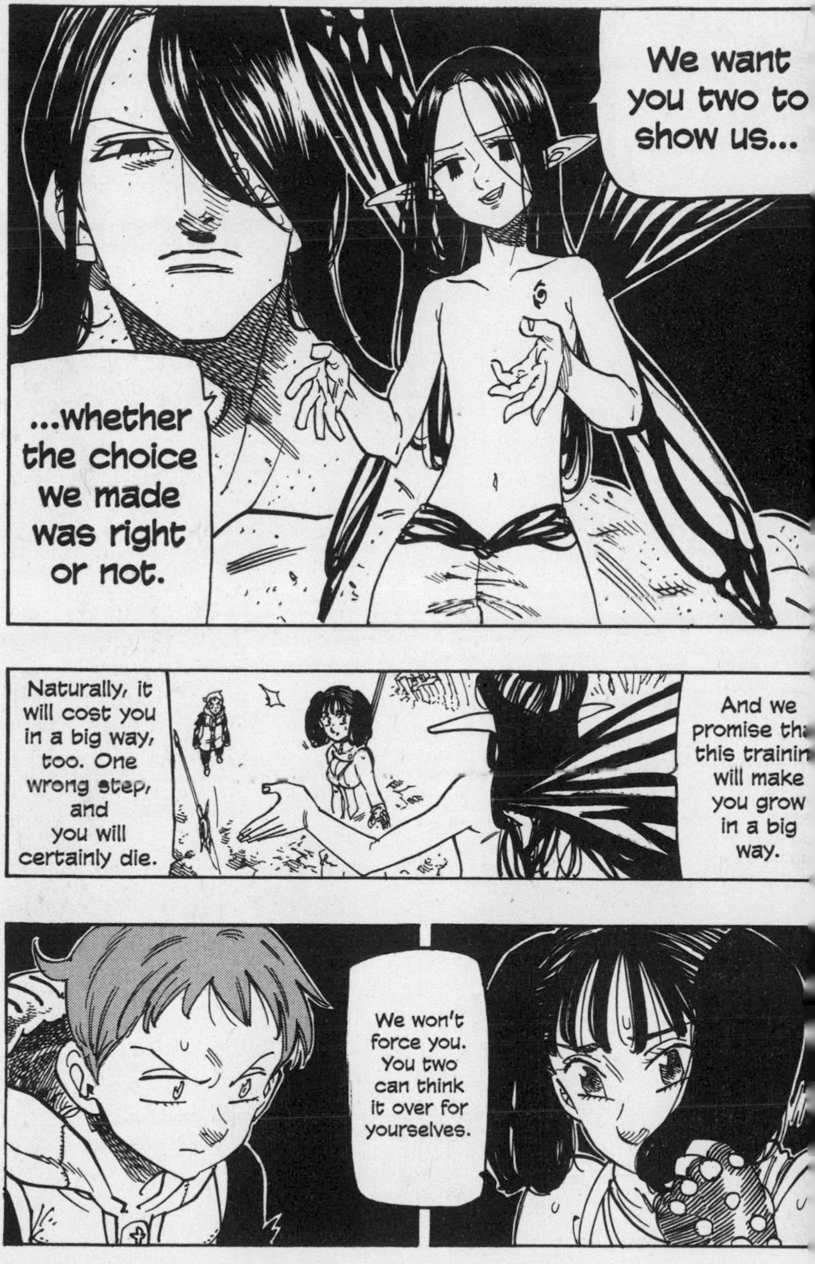
We want you two to show us...
...whether the choice we made was right or not.
And we promise tha this trainin will make you grow in a big way.
Naturally, it will cost you in a big way, too. One wrong step, and you will certainly die.
We won't force you. You two can think it over for yourselves.

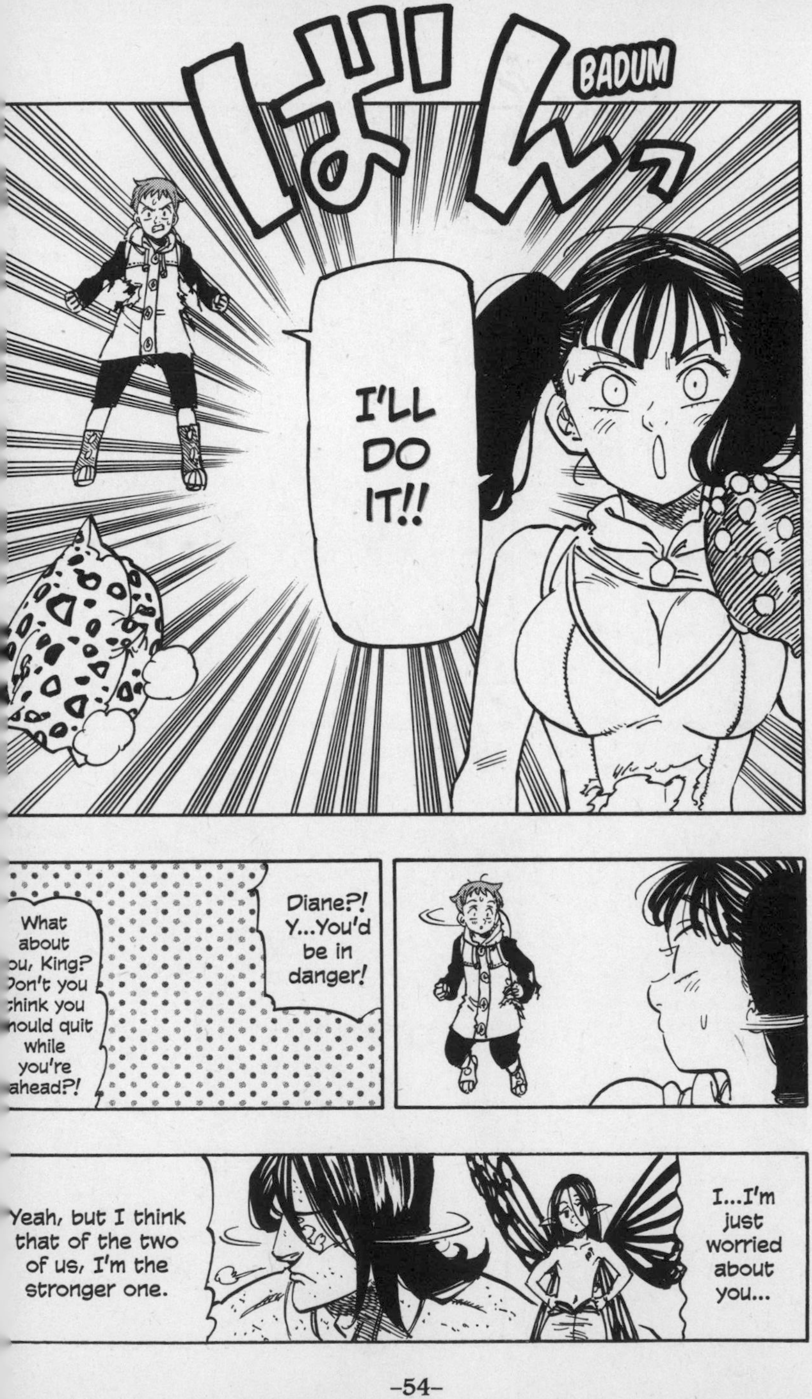
ばん
BADUM
I'LL DO IT!!
Diane?! Y...You'd be in danger!
What about ou, King? on't you hink you hould quit while you're head?!
I...I'm just worried about you...
Yeah, but I think that of the two of us, I'm the stronger one.

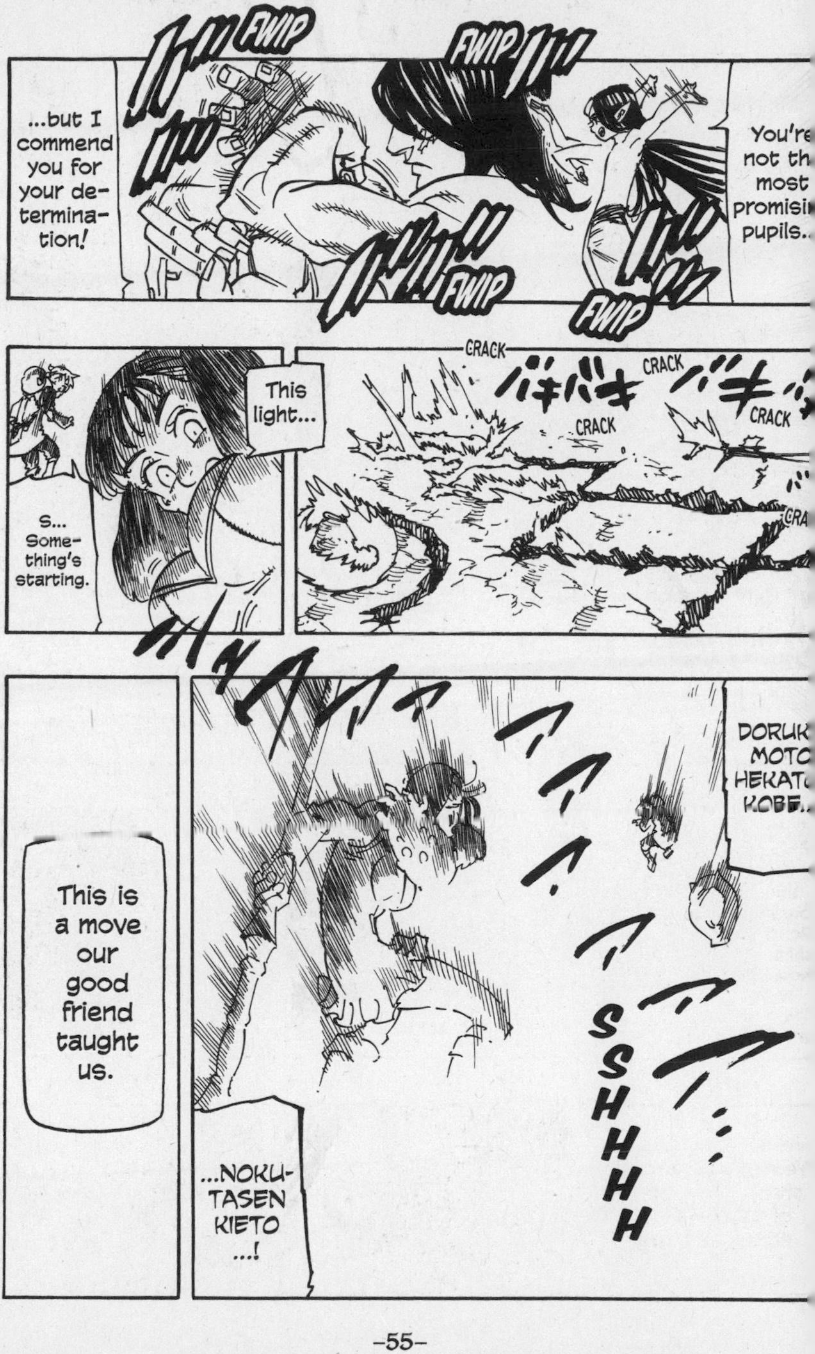
You're
not th
most
promisi
pupils..
...but I commend you for your de-termina-tion!
FWIP
FWIP
FWIP
FWIP
CRACK
CRACK
CRACK
CRACK
This light...
S... Some-thing's starting.
DORUK
MOTO
HEKAT
KOBE...
SSHHHH
...NOKU-TASEN KIETO ...!
This is a move our good friend taught us.

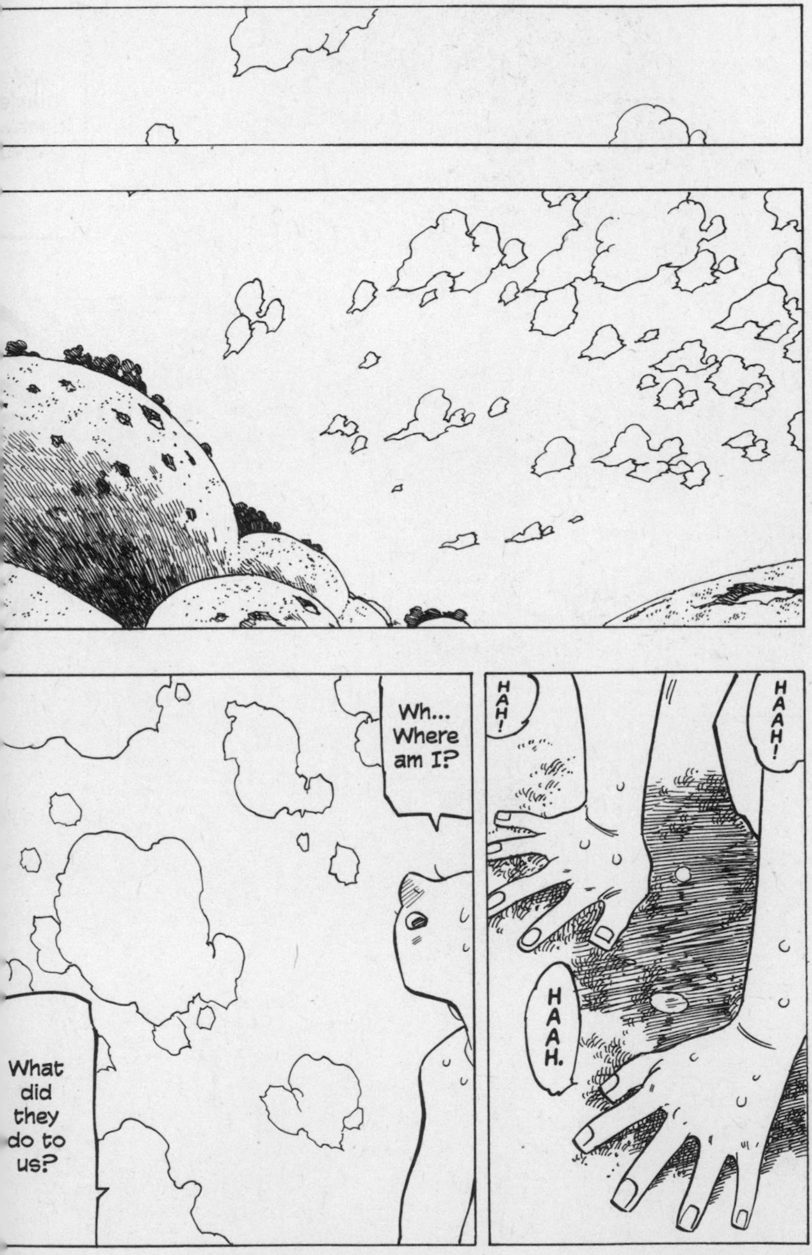
HAAAH!
HAH!
HAAAH.
Wh... Where am I?
What did they do to us?

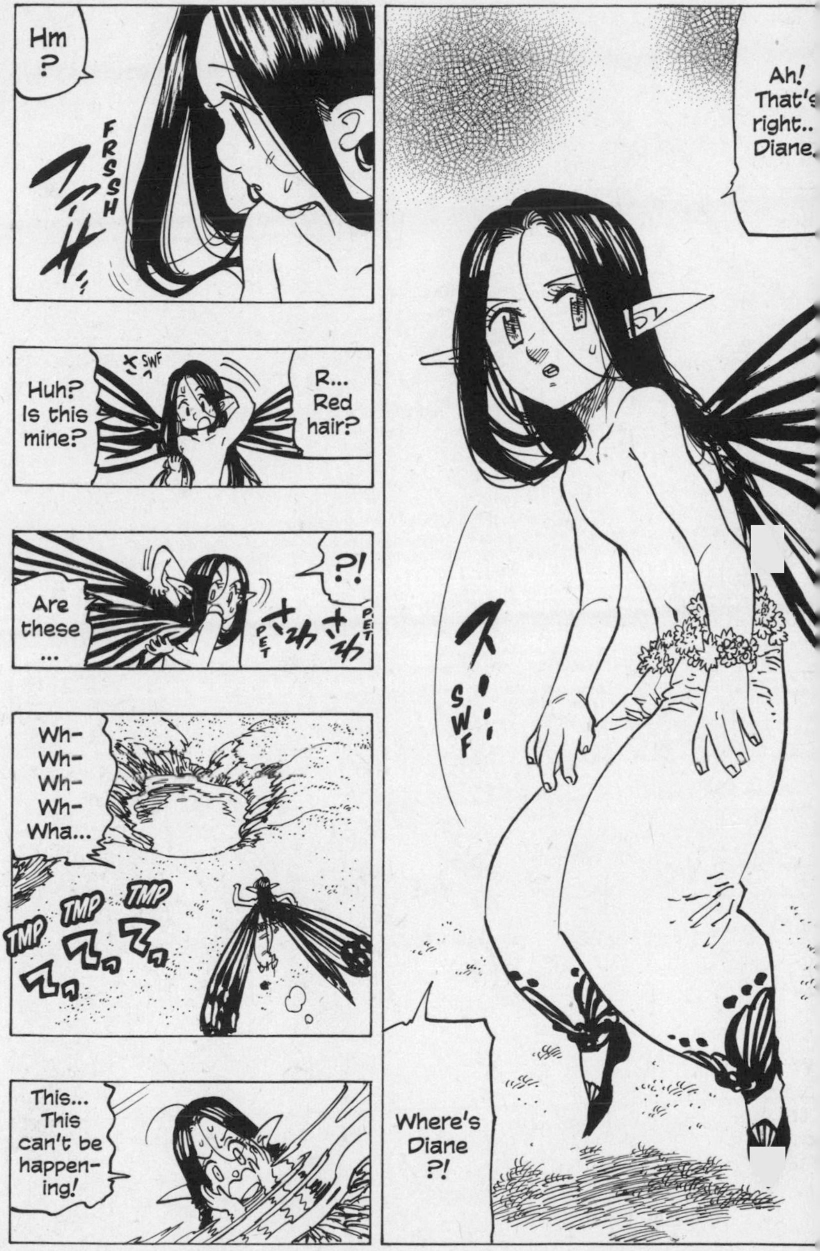
Ah! That's right.. Diane.
SWF
Where's Diane ?!
Hm ?
FRSSH
R... Red hair?
SWF
Huh? Is this mine?
?!
PET PET
Are these ...
Wh- Wh- Wh- Wh- Wha...
TMP TMP TMP
This... This can't be happen-ing!

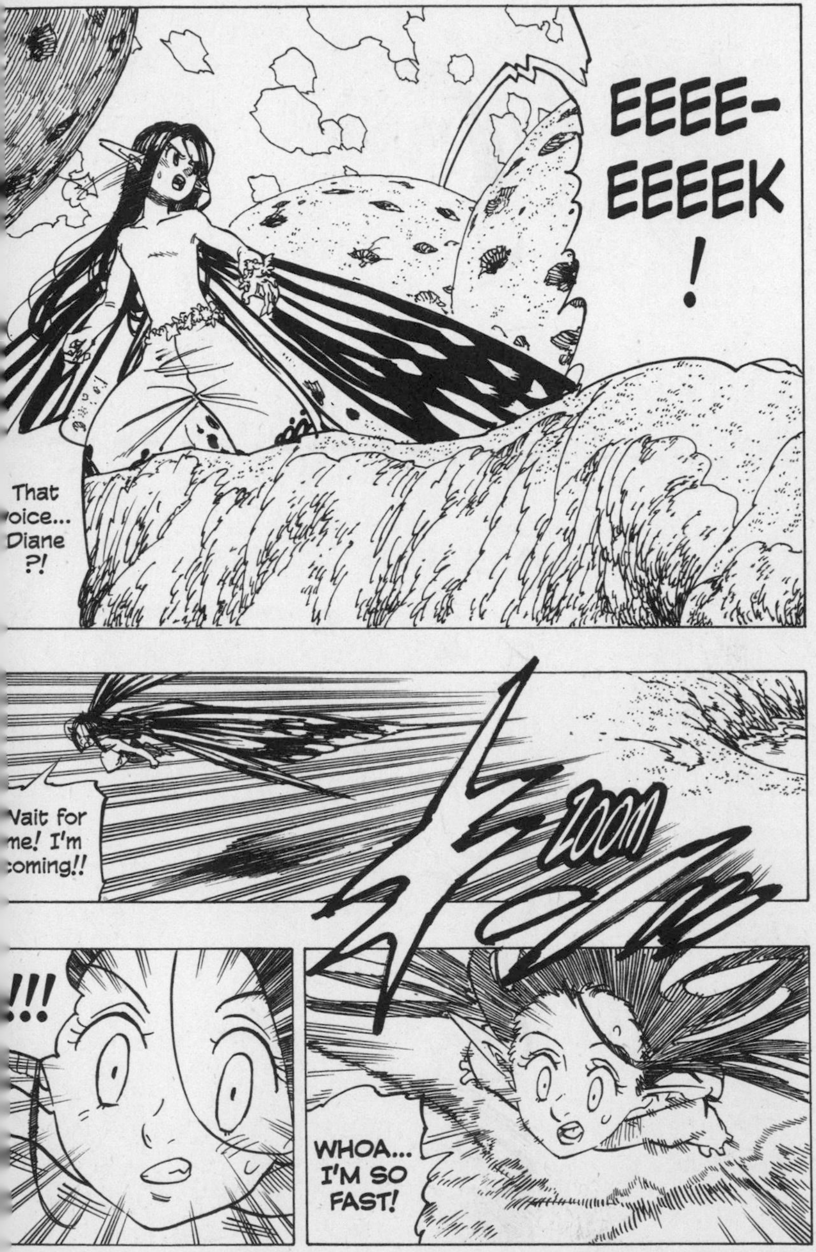
EEEE-EEEEK!
That oice... Diane ?!
ZOOM
Vait for me! I'm coming!!
WHOA... I'M SO FAST!
!!!

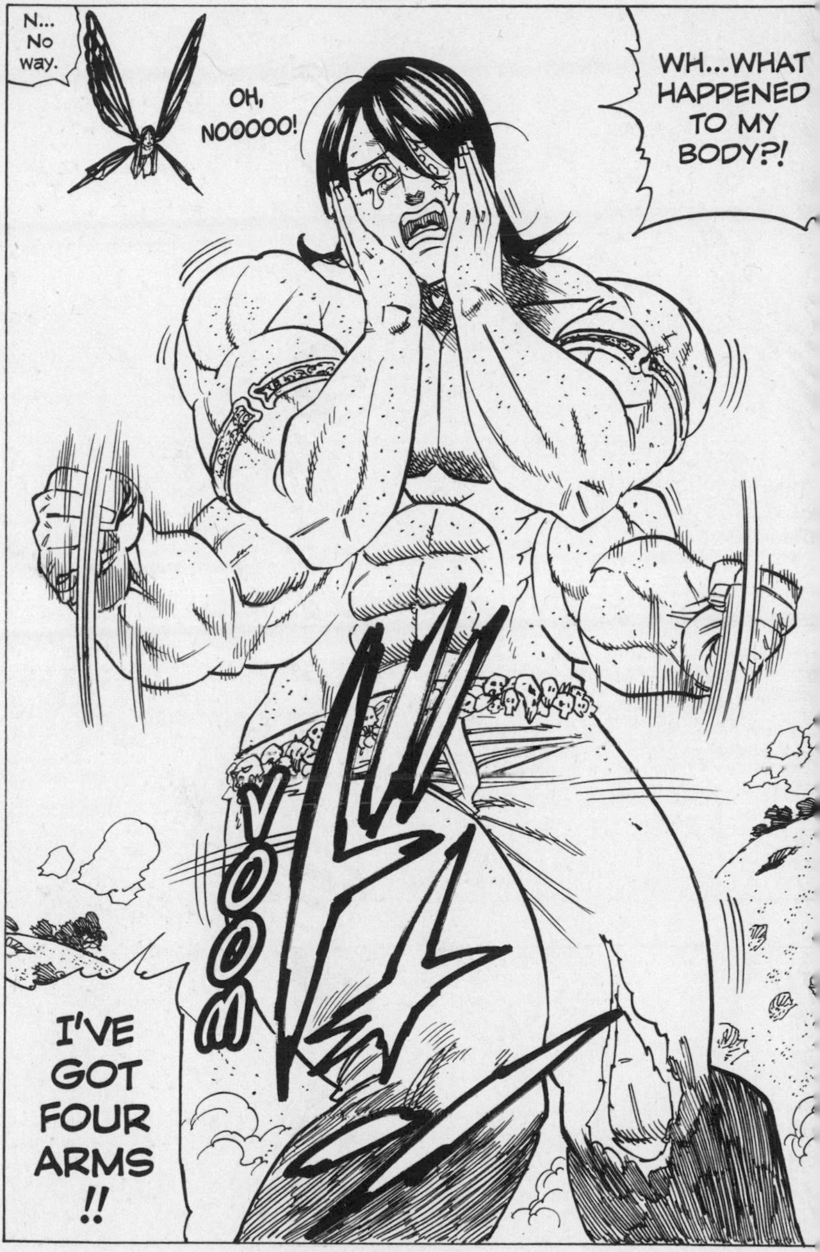
WH...WHAT HAPPENED TO MY BODY?!
OH, NOOOOO!
N... No way.
VOOOOM
I'VE GOT FOUR ARMS !!

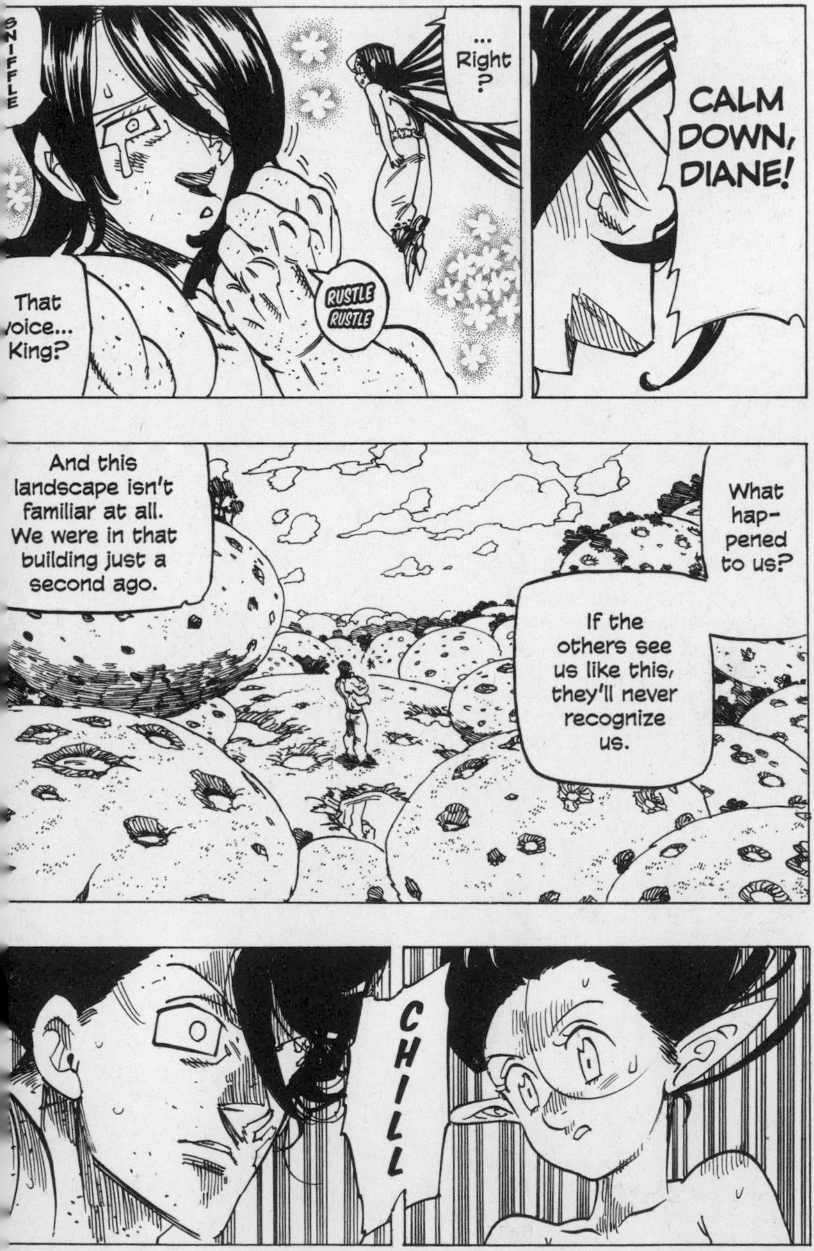
CALM DOWN, DIANE!
...Right?
RUSTLE RUSTLE
SNIFFLE
That voice... King?
What hap-pened to us?
If the others see us like this, they'll never recognize us.
And this landscape isn't familiar at all. We were in that building just a second ago.
CHILL

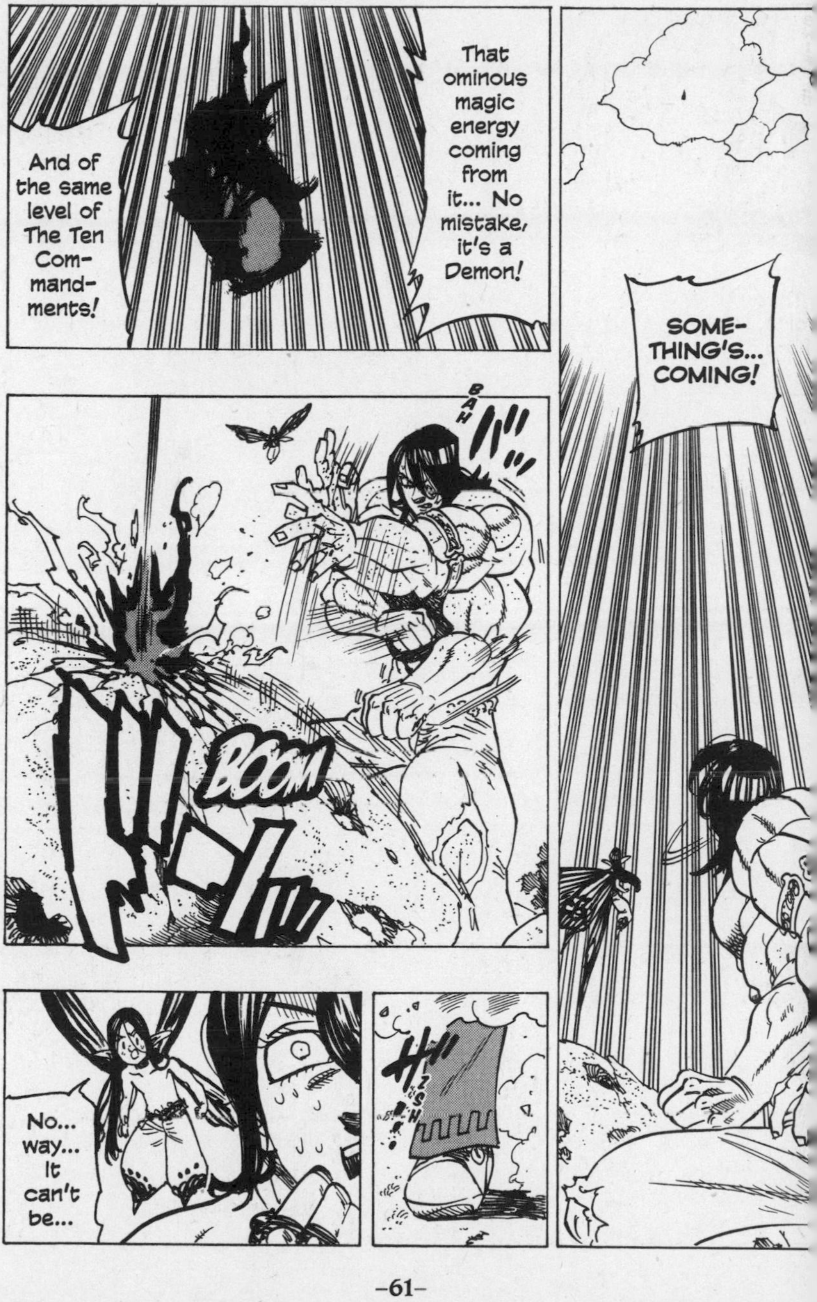
SOME-THING'S... COMING!
That ominous magic energy coming from it... No mistake, it's a Demon!
And of the same level of The Ten Com-mand-ments!
BAH
BOOM
ZSH
No... way... It can't be...

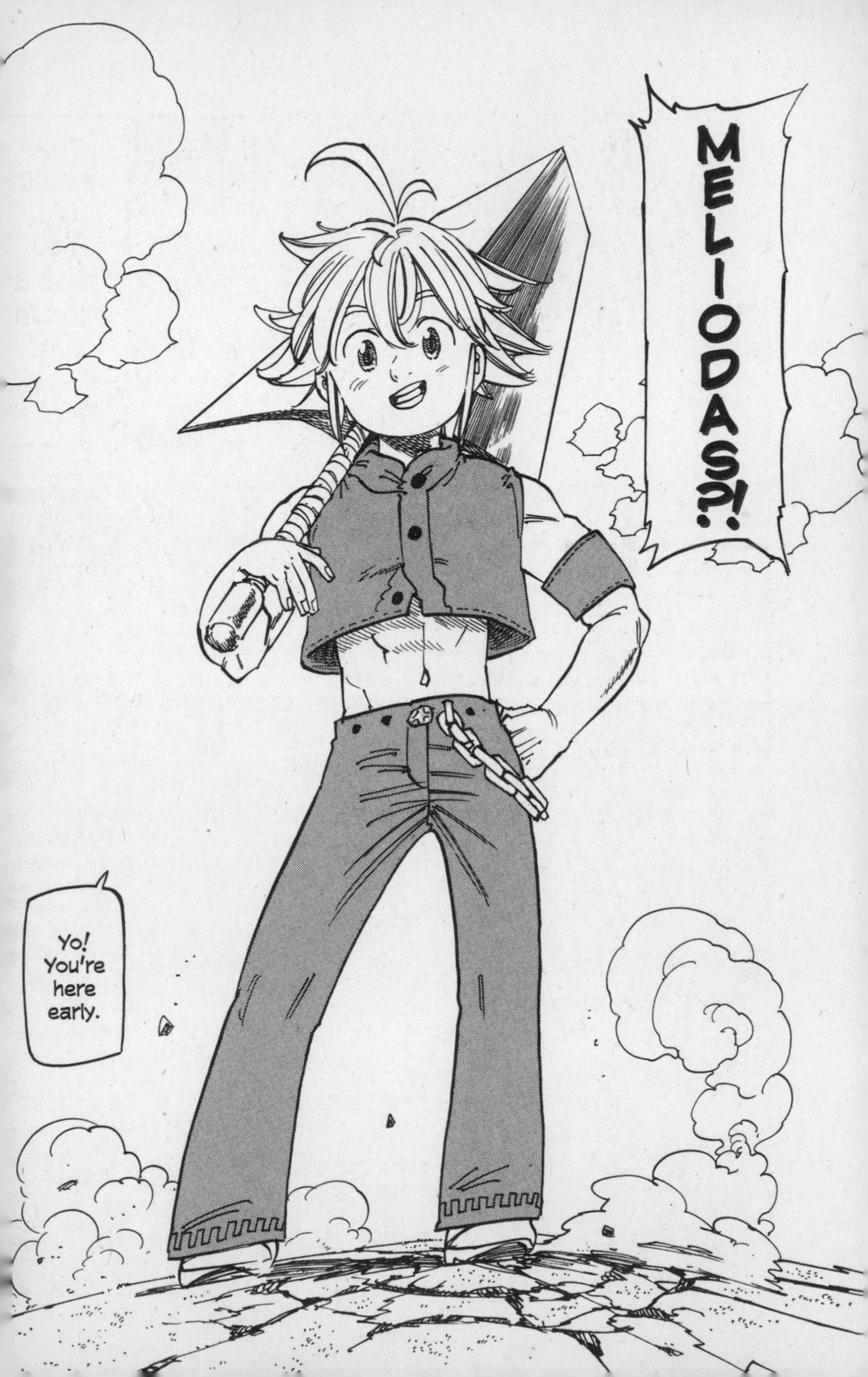
MELIODAS?!
Yo! You're here early.

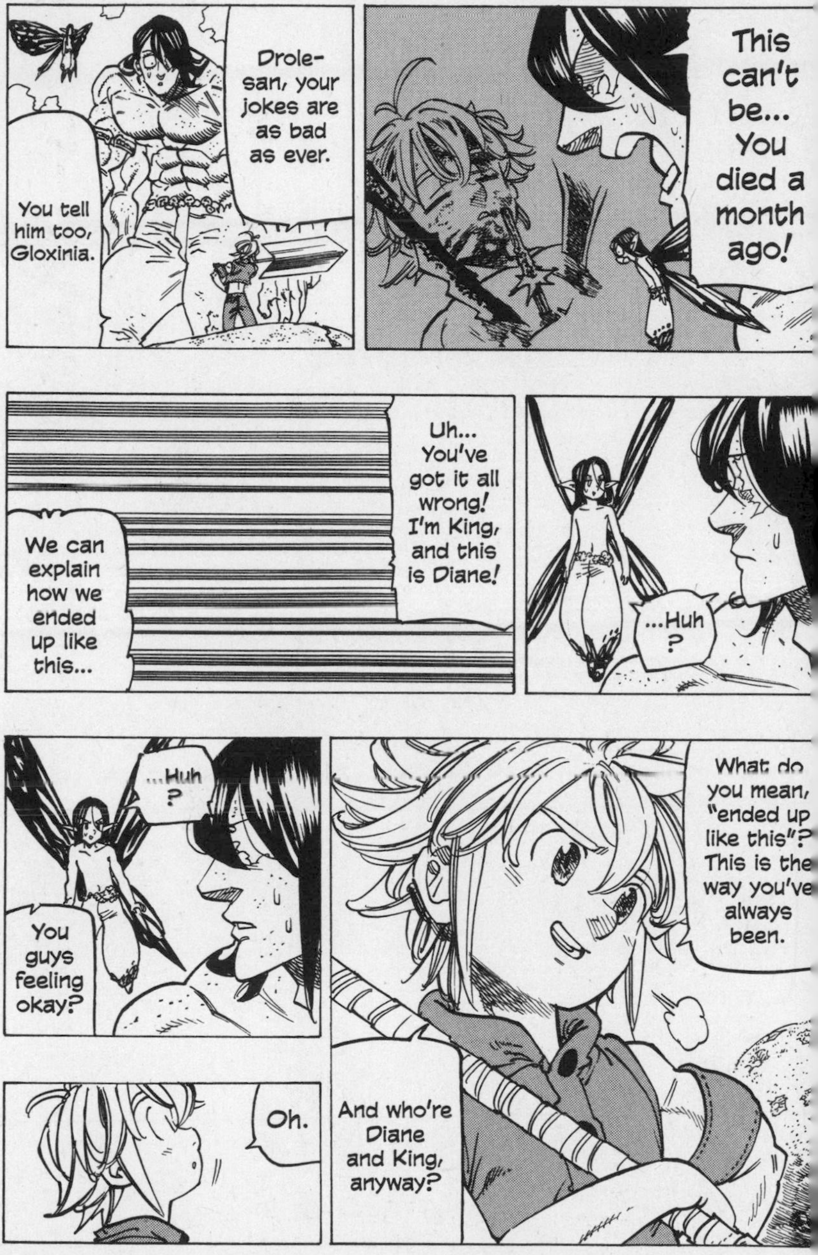
This can't be... You died a month ago!
Drole-san, your jokes are as bad as ever.
You tell him too, Gloxinia.
...Huh?
Uh... You've got it all wrong! I'm King, and this is Diane!
We can explain how we ended up like this...
What do you mean, "ended up like this"? This is the way you've always been.
And who're Diane and King, anyway?
...Huh?
You guys feeling okay?
Oh.

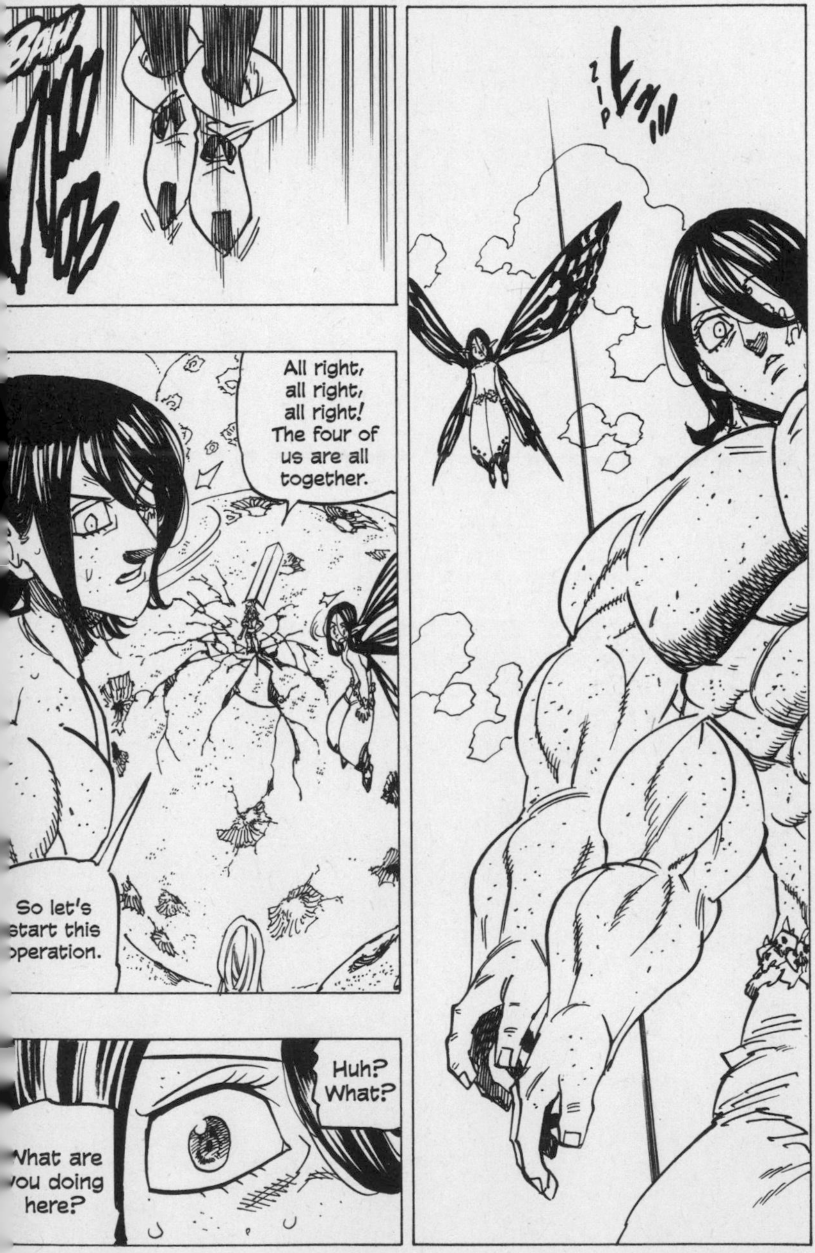
ZIP
BAH
All right, all right, all right! The four of us are all together.
So let's start this operation.
Huh? What?
What are you doing here?

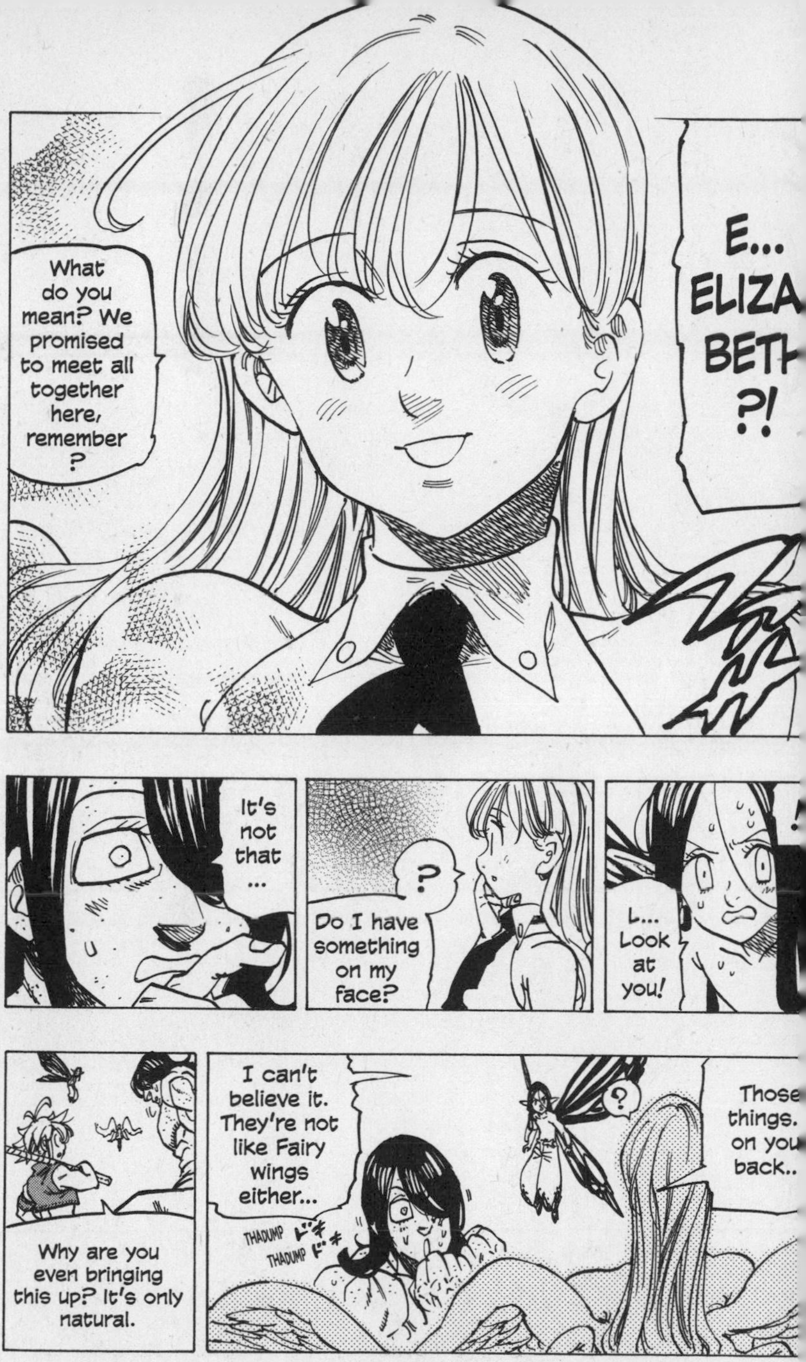
E... ELIZA BETH ?!
What do you mean? We promised to meet all together here, remember ?
L... Look at you!
?
Do I have something on my face?
It's not that ...
Those things. on you back..
?
I can't believe it. They're not like Fairy wings either...
THADUMP
THADUMP
Why are you even bringing this up? It's only natural.

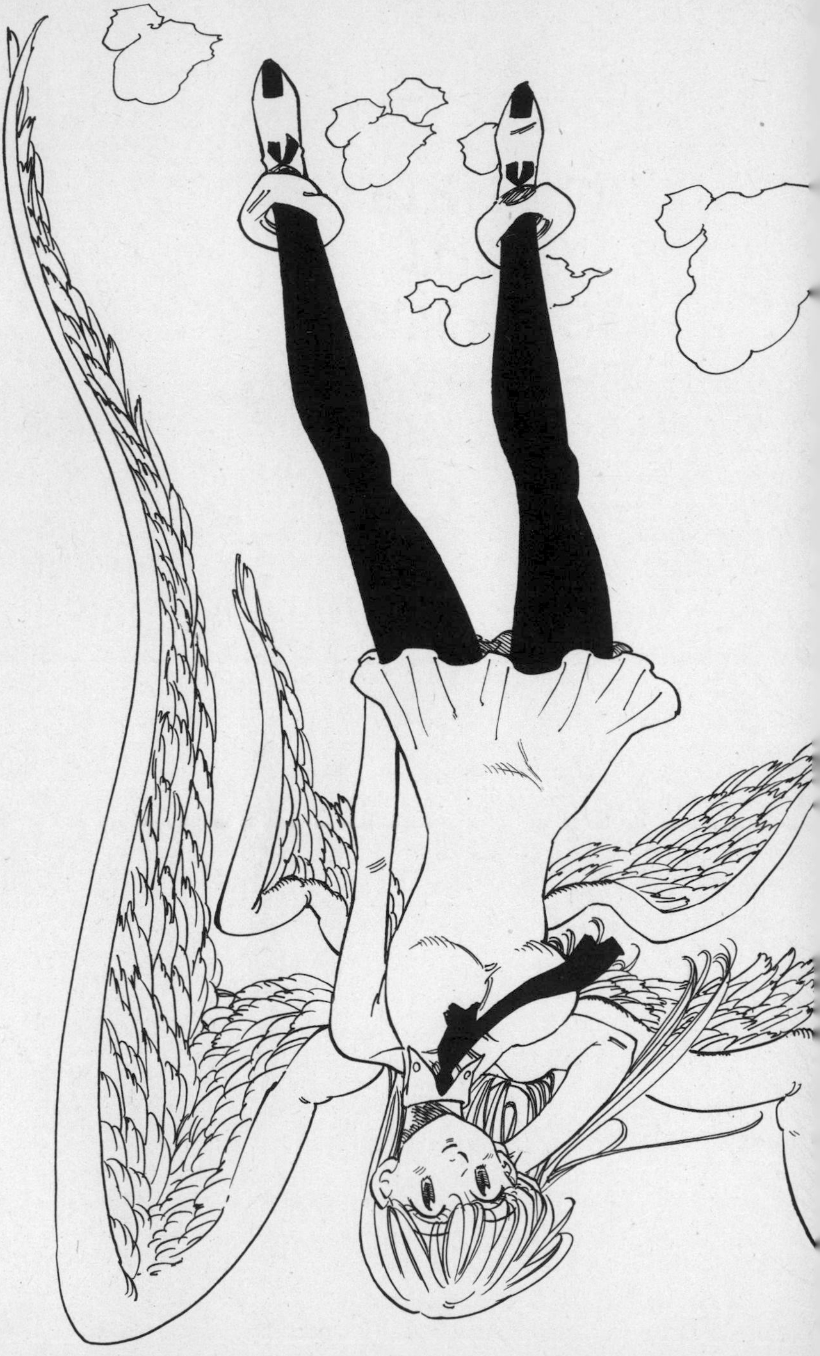

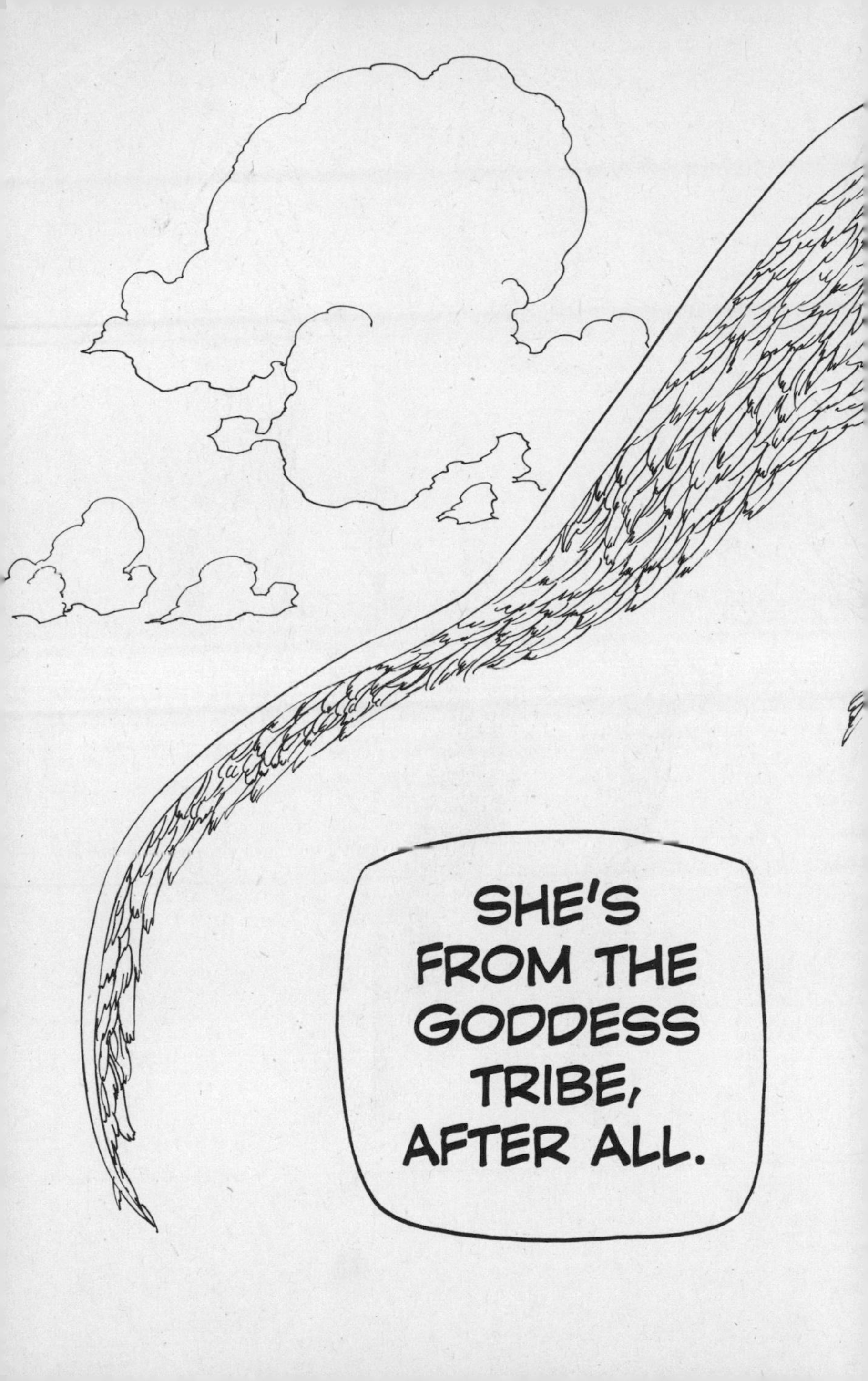
SHE'S FROM THE GODDESS TRIBE, AFTER ALL.

Bonus Story - Ruler of the Altar (5)

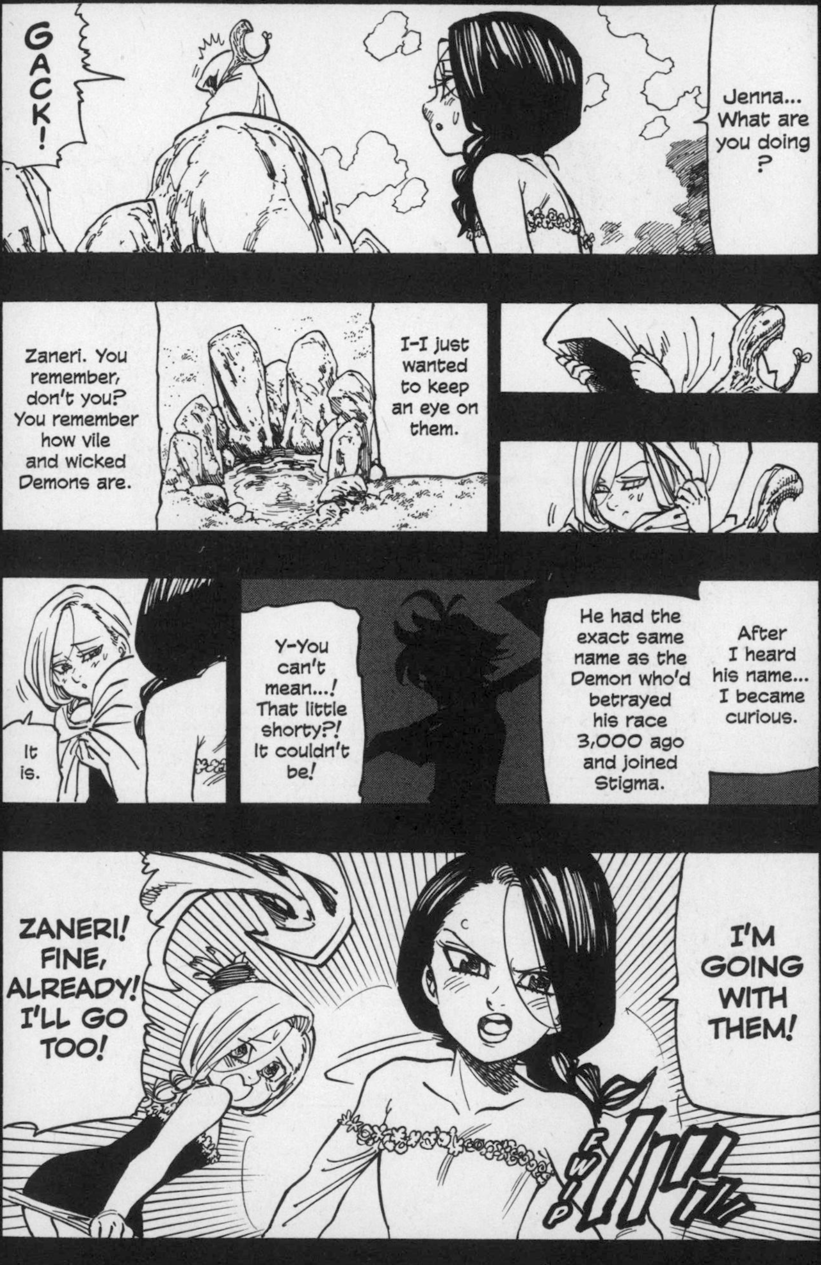
Jenna... What are you doing ?
GACK!
I-I just wanted to keep an eye on them.
Zaneri. You remember, don't you? You remember how vile and wicked Demons are.
After I heard his name... I became curious.
He had the exact same name as the Demon who'd betrayed his race 3,000 ago and joined Stigma.
Y-You can't mean...! That little shorty?! It couldn't be!
It is.
I'M GOING WITH THEM!
ZANERI! FINE, ALREADY! I'LL GO TOO!
FWIP

To Be Continued

Chapter 201 - Those Who Fight in Arms

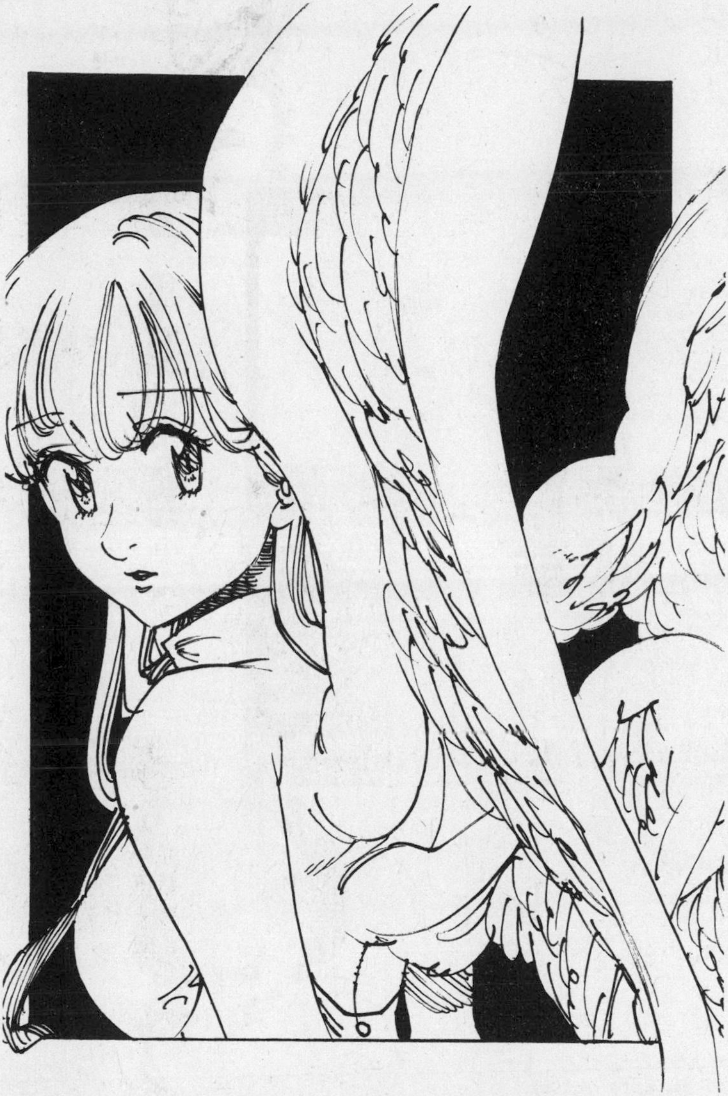

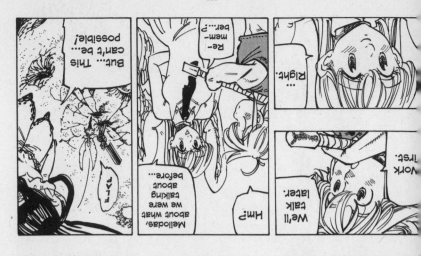

ELIZA-BETH... Y... YOU'RE A GODDESS ?!
FLAP
FLAP
But... This can't be... possible!
Meliodas, about what we were talking about before...
Hm?
Re-mem-ber...?
We'll talk later.
Work first.
... Right.

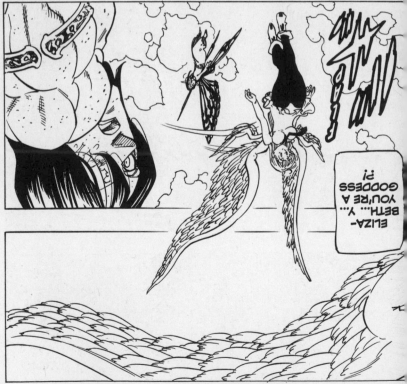

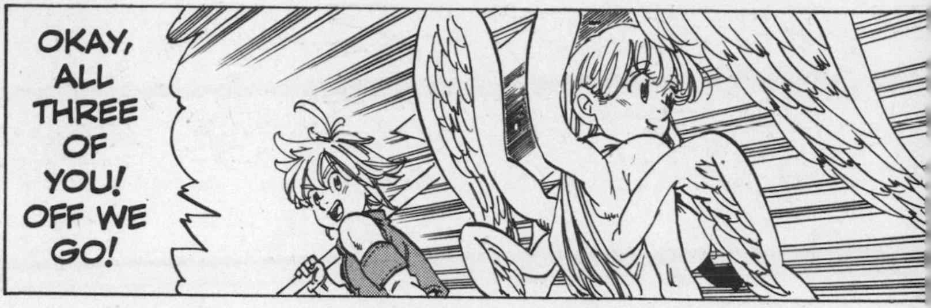
OKAY, ALL THREE OF YOU! OFF WE GO!

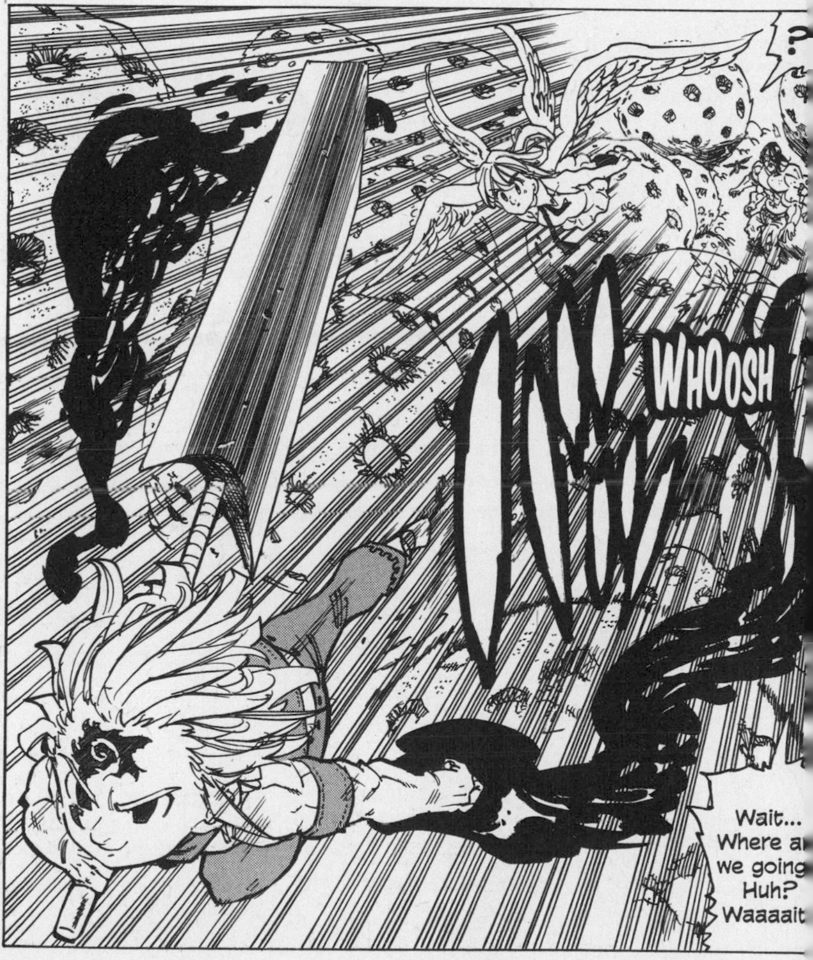
?
WHOOSH
Wait... Where a
we going
Huh? Waaaait

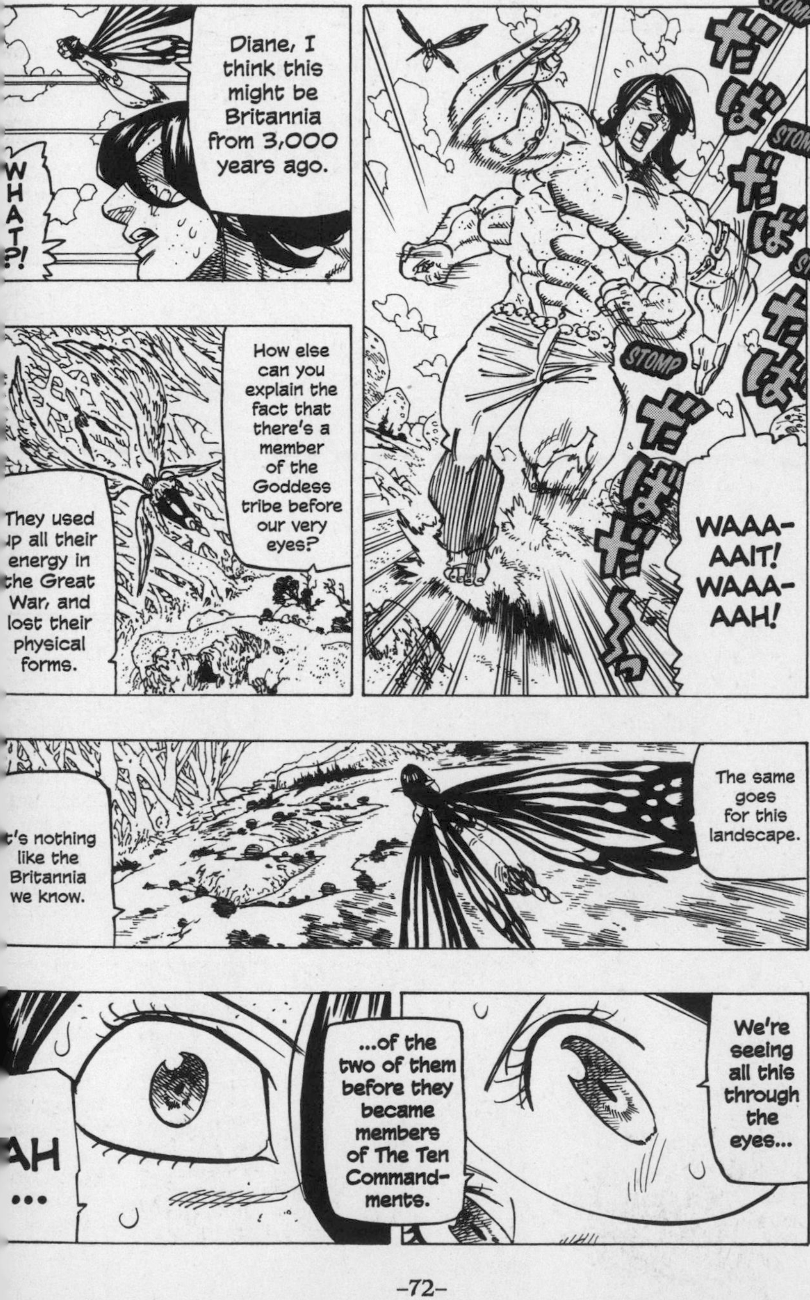
STOMP
STOMP
STOMP
STOMP
WAAA-AAIT! WAAA-AAH!
Diane, I think this might be Britannia from 3,000 years ago.
WHAT?!
How else can you explain the fact that there's a member of the Goddess tribe before our very eyes?
They used up all their energy in the Great War, and lost their physical forms.
The same goes for this landscape.
t's nothing like the Britannia we know.
We're seeing all this through the eyes...
...of the two of them before they became members of The Ten Commandments.
AH
...

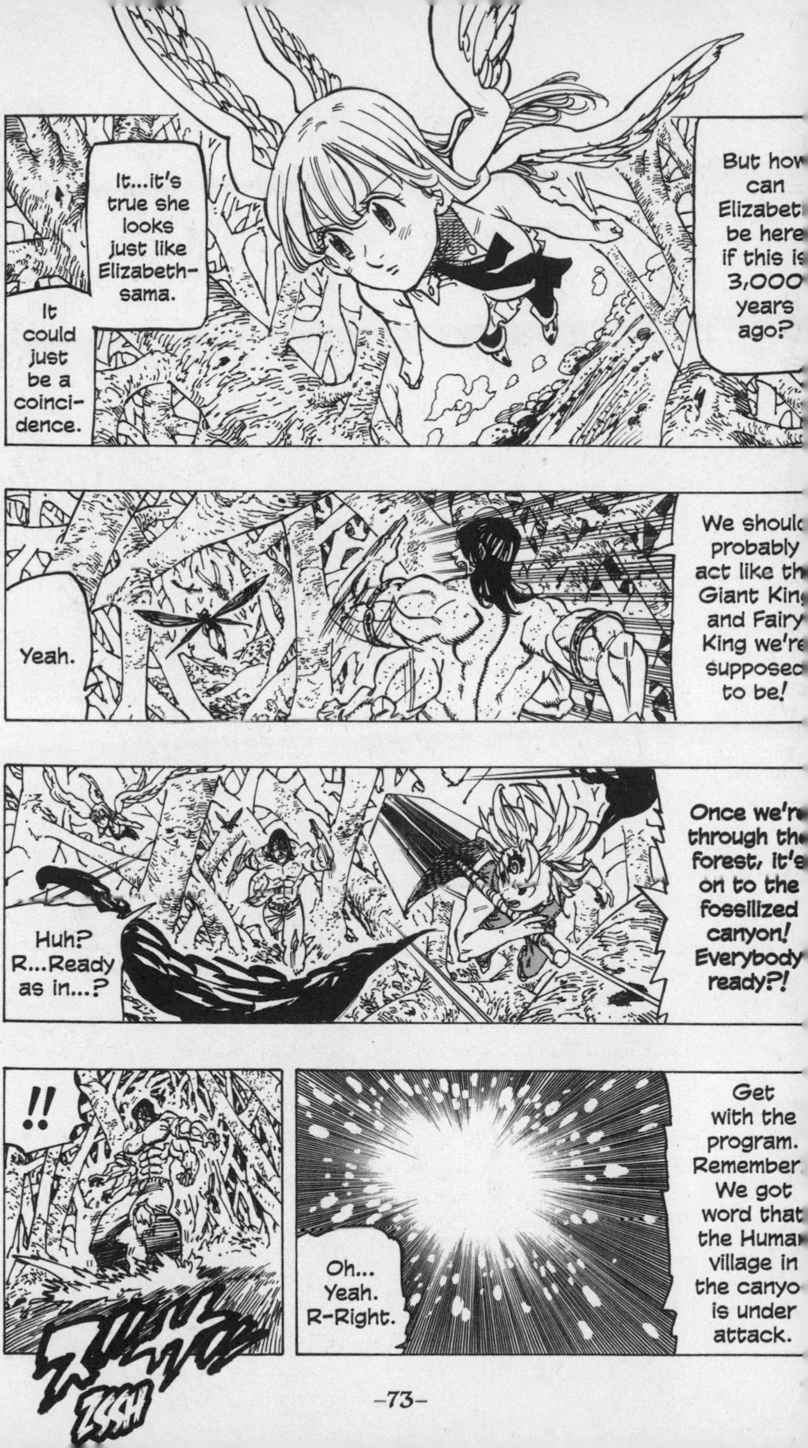
But how can Elizabet be here if this is 3,000 years ago?
It...it's true she looks just like Elizabeth-sama.
It could just be a coincidence.
We should probably act like the Giant King and Fairy King we're supposed to be!
Yeah.
Once we're through the forest, it's on to the fossilized canyon! Everybody ready?!
Huh? R...Ready as in...?
Get with the program. Remember. We got word that the Huma village in the canyo is under attack.
Oh... Yeah. R-Right.
!!
ZSSH

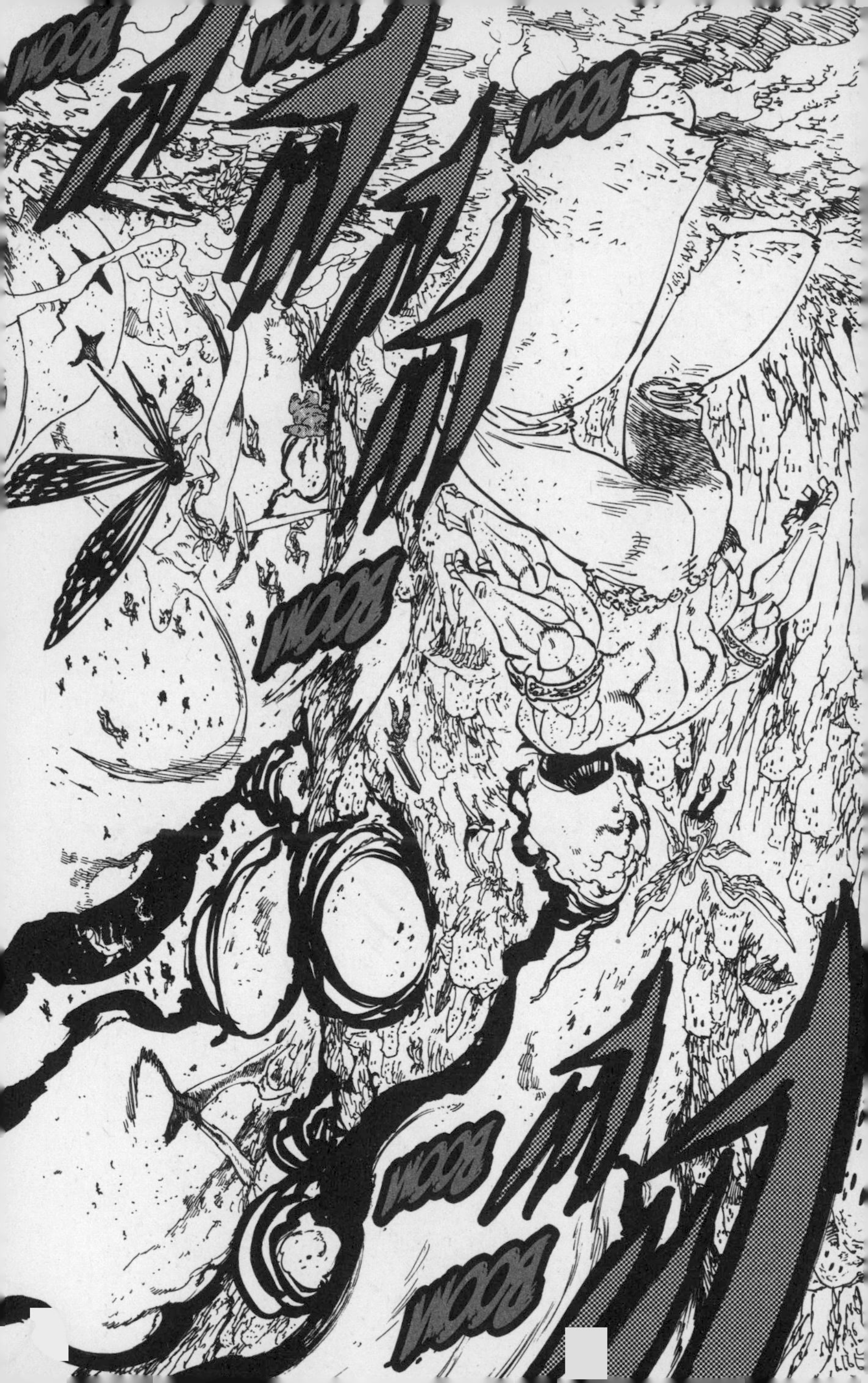
WOOSH
WOOSH
WOOSH
WOOSH
WOOSH
WOOSH

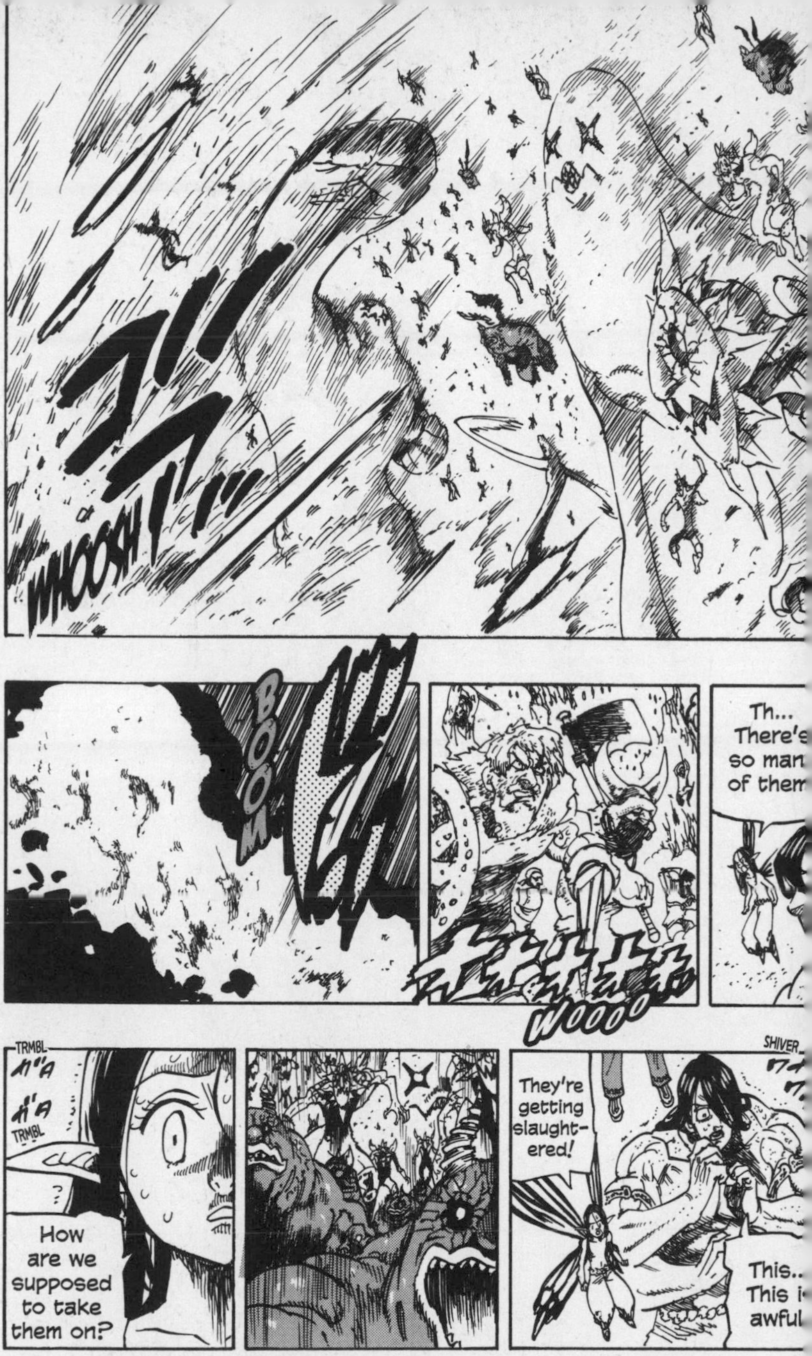
WHOOSH
Th... There's so man of them
WOOOO
BOOM
SHIVER
This... This i awful
They're getting slaught-ered!
TRMBL
TRMBL
How are we supposed to take them on?

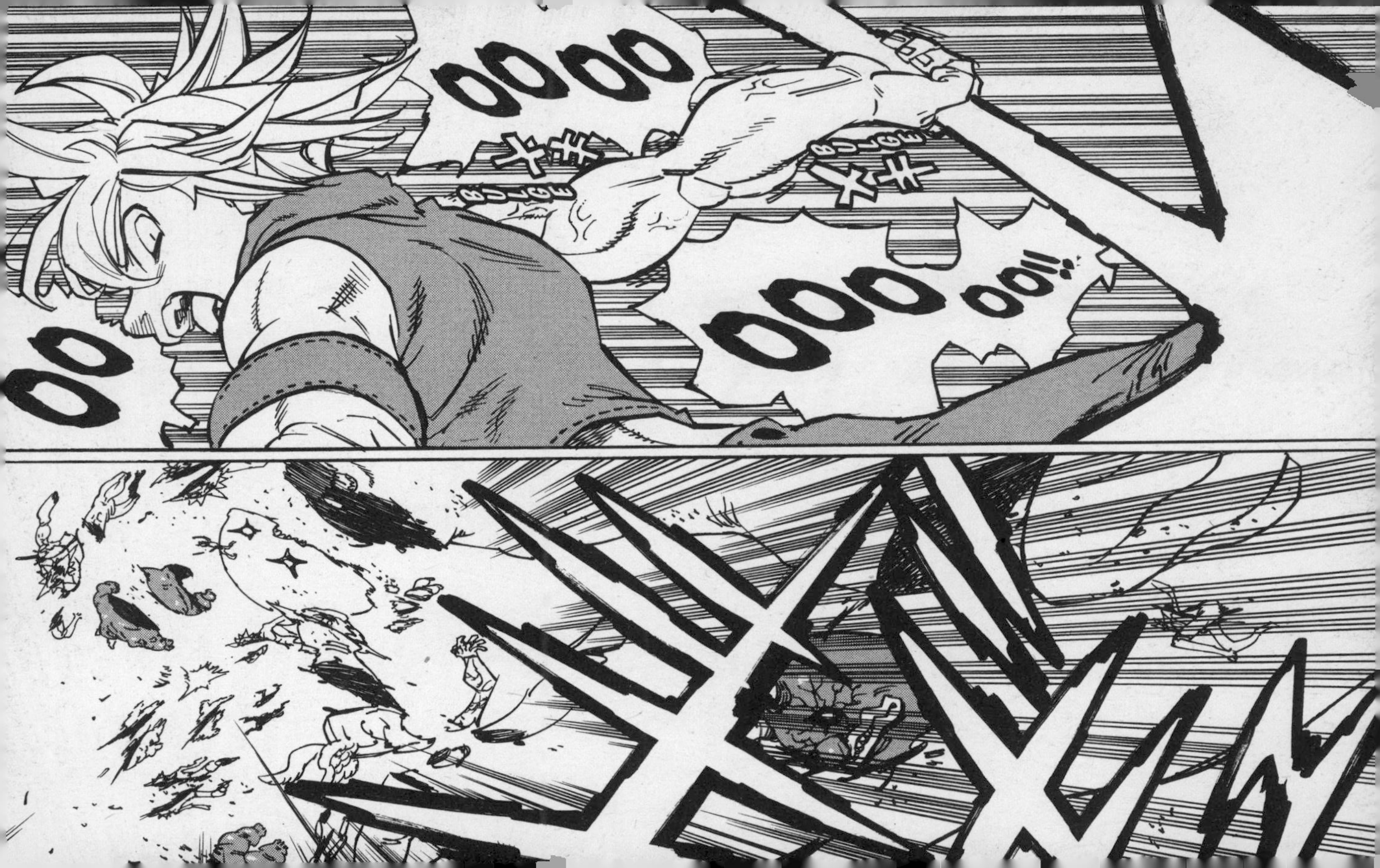
OO
OOOO
OOO
OO!!
キメ
BULGE
キメ
BULGE

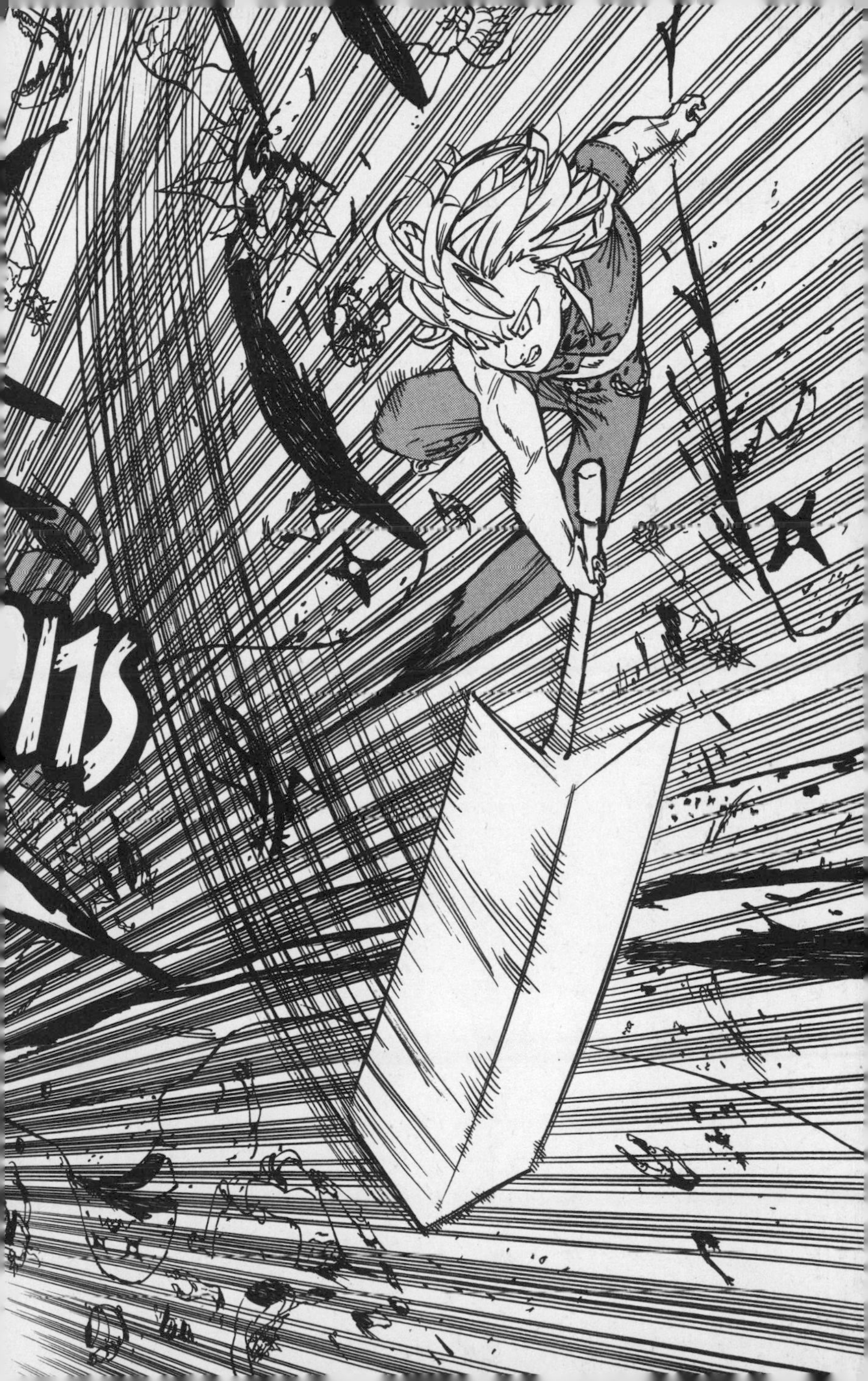

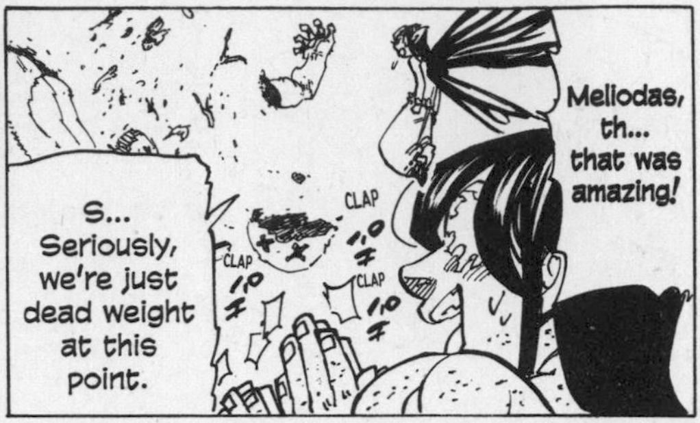
Meliodas, th... that was amazing!
CLAP
CLAP
CLAP
S... Seriously, we're just dead weight at this point.

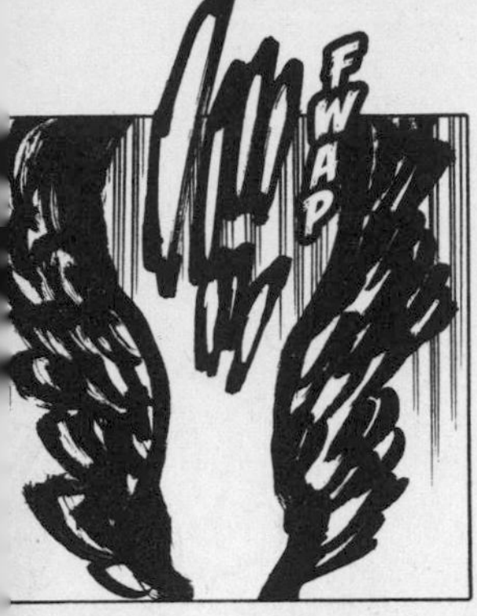
FWAP

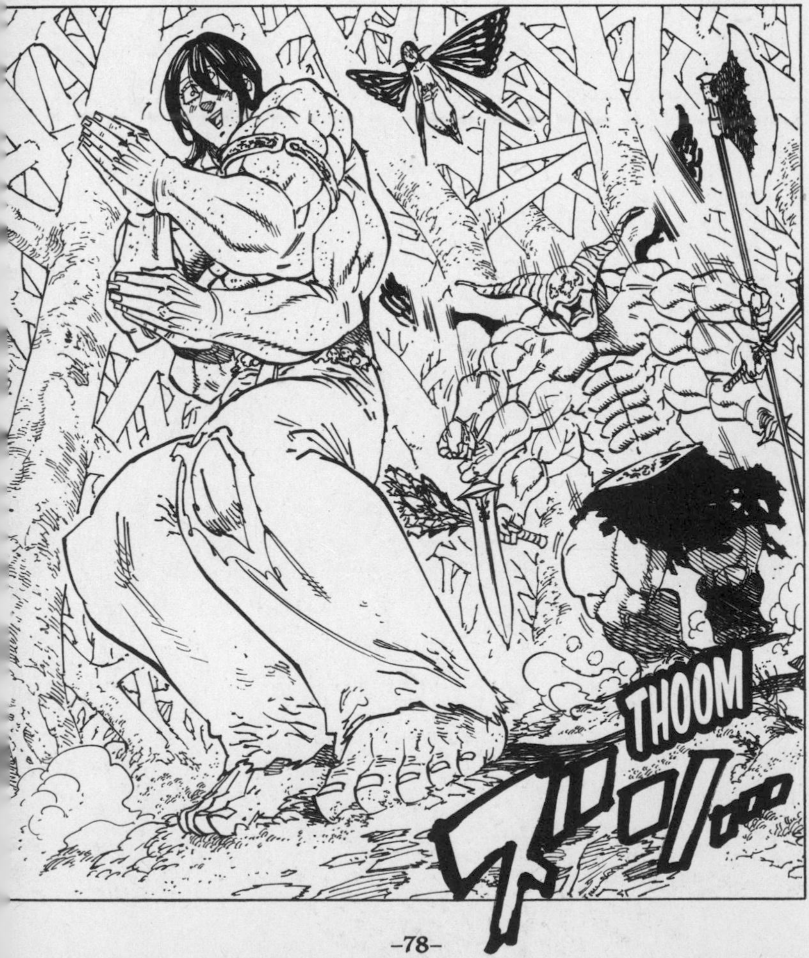
THOOM

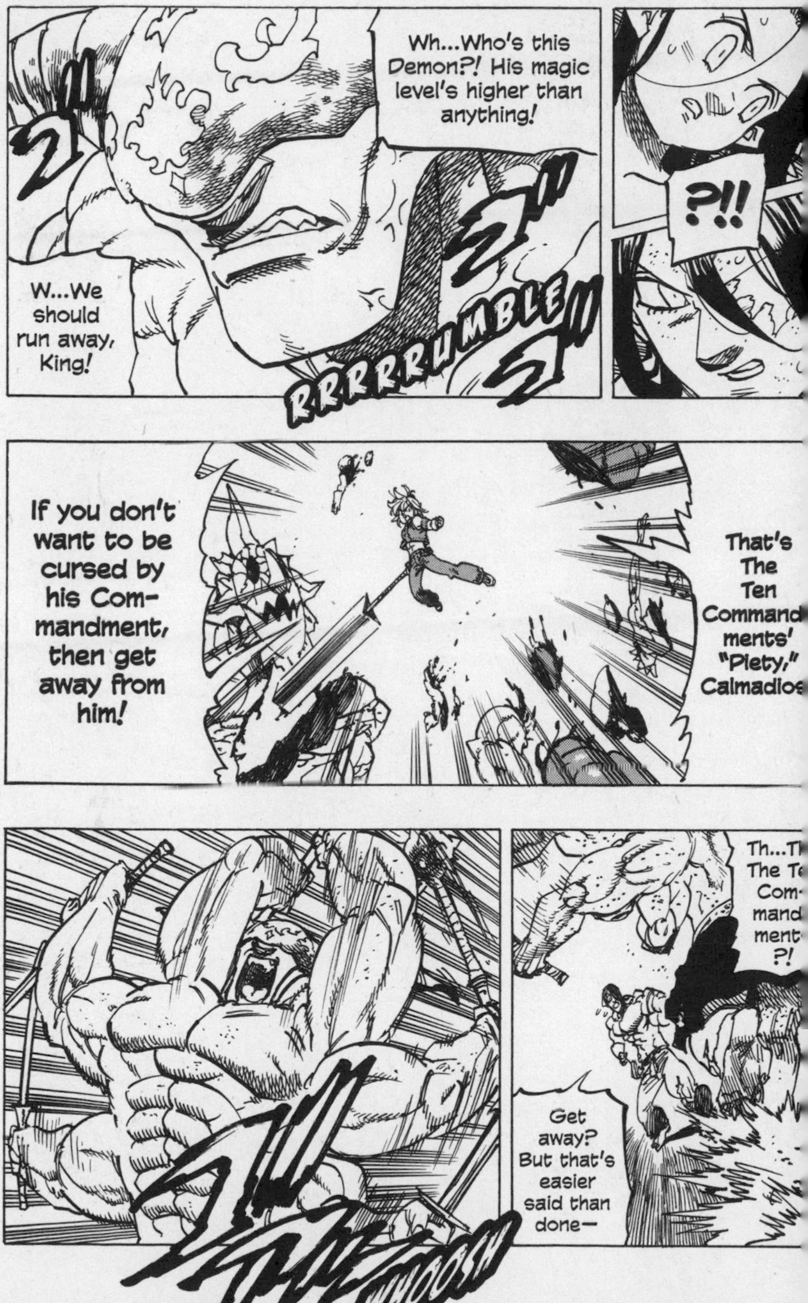
?!!
Wh...Who's this Demon?! His magic level's higher than anything!
RRRRRUMBLE
W...We should run away, King!
That's The Ten Command ments' "Piety," Calmadios
If you don't want to be cursed by his Com- mandment, then get away from him!
Th...Th The Te Com- mand ment ?!
Get away? But that's easier said than done—
WHOOSH

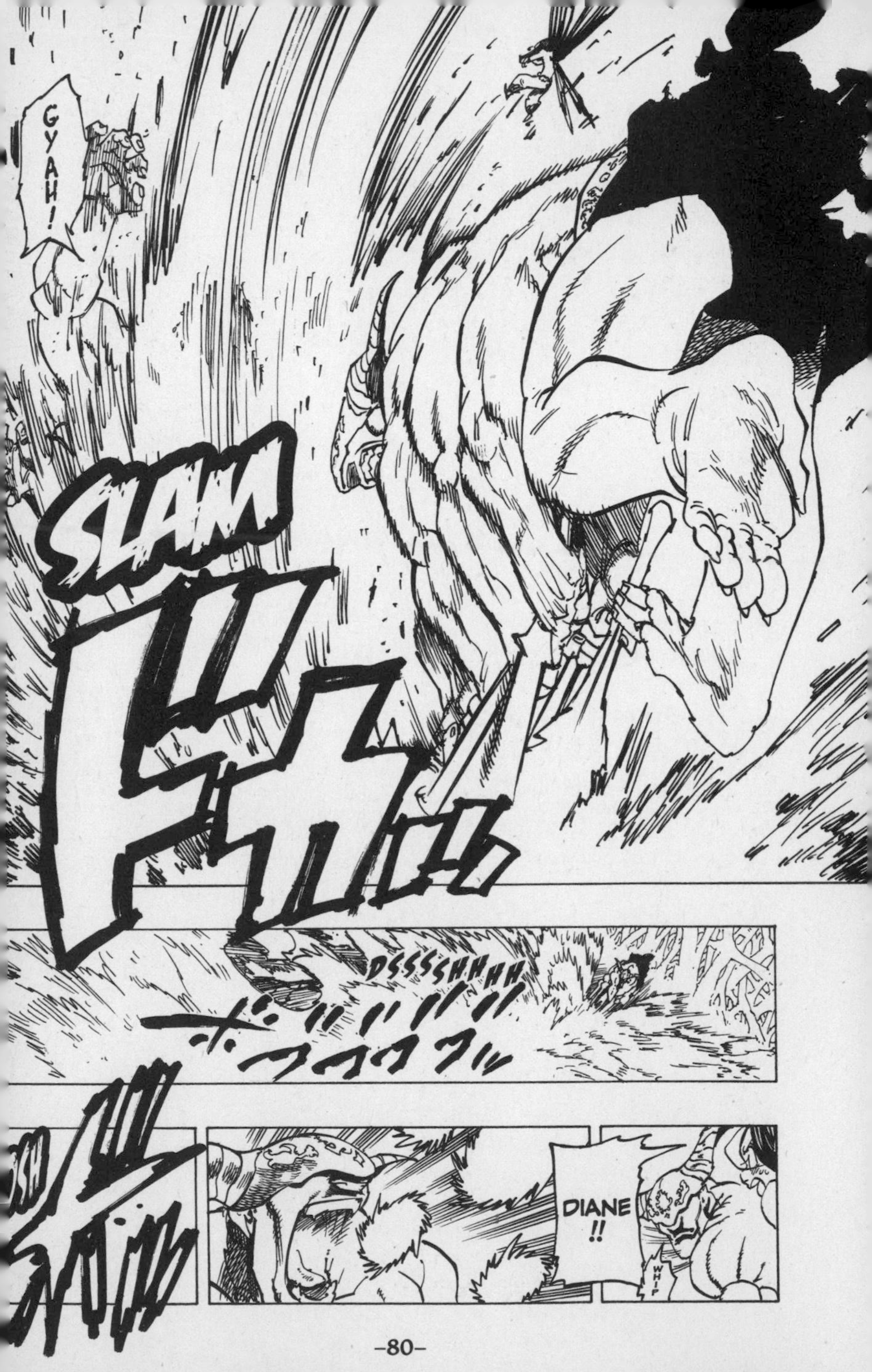
GYAH!
SLAM
DSSSSHHHH
DIANE !!
WHIP

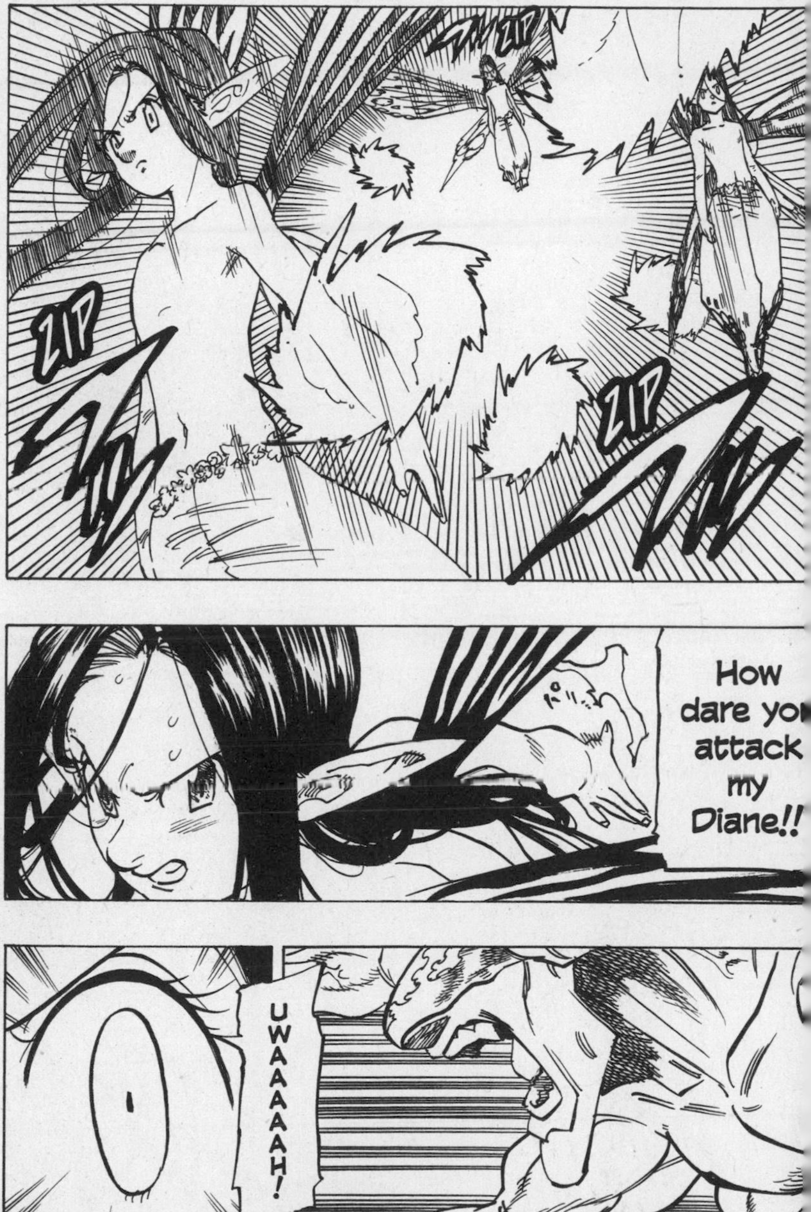
ZIP
ZIP
ZIP
How dare yo attack my Diane!!
UWAAAAAAH!

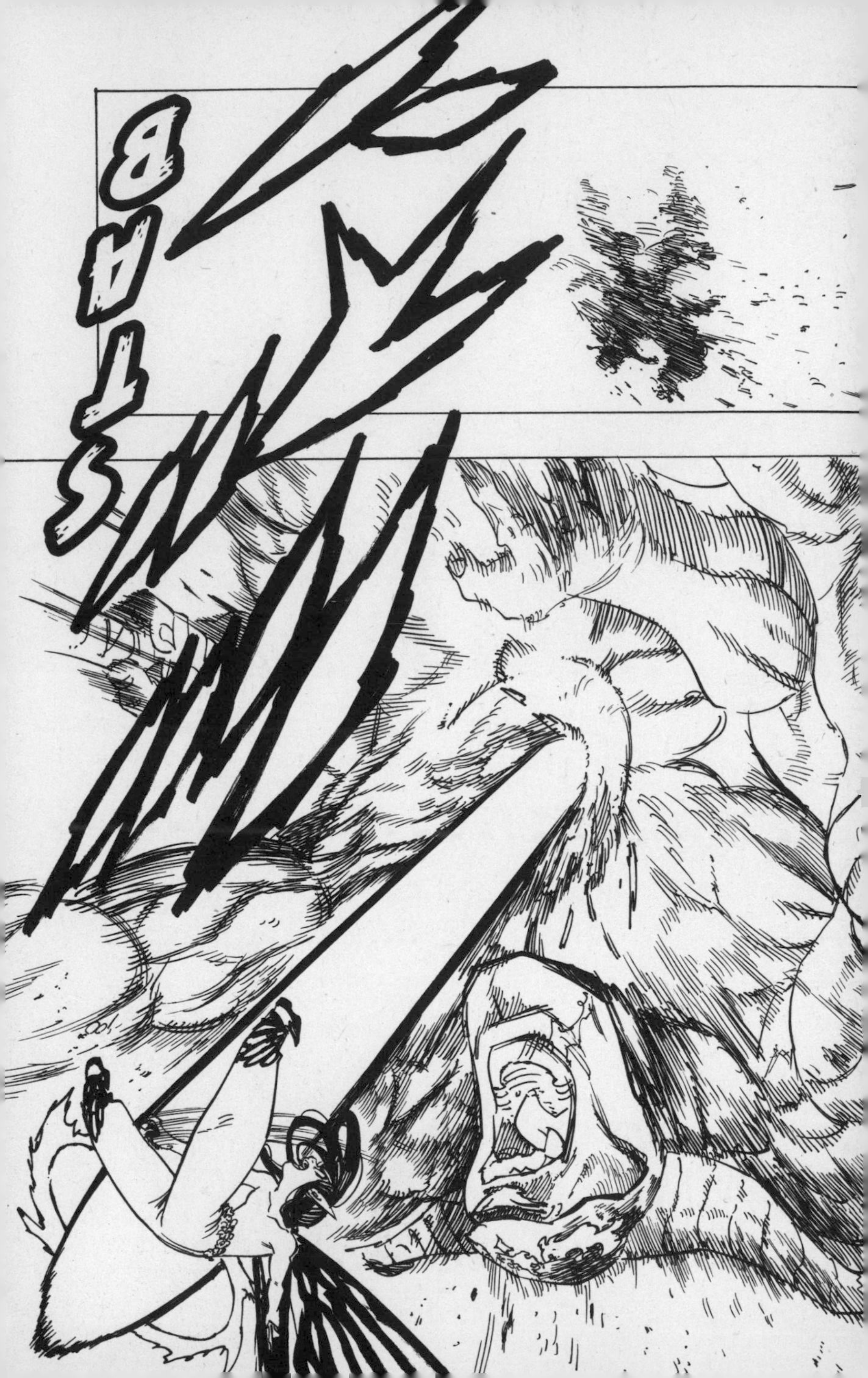
STAB

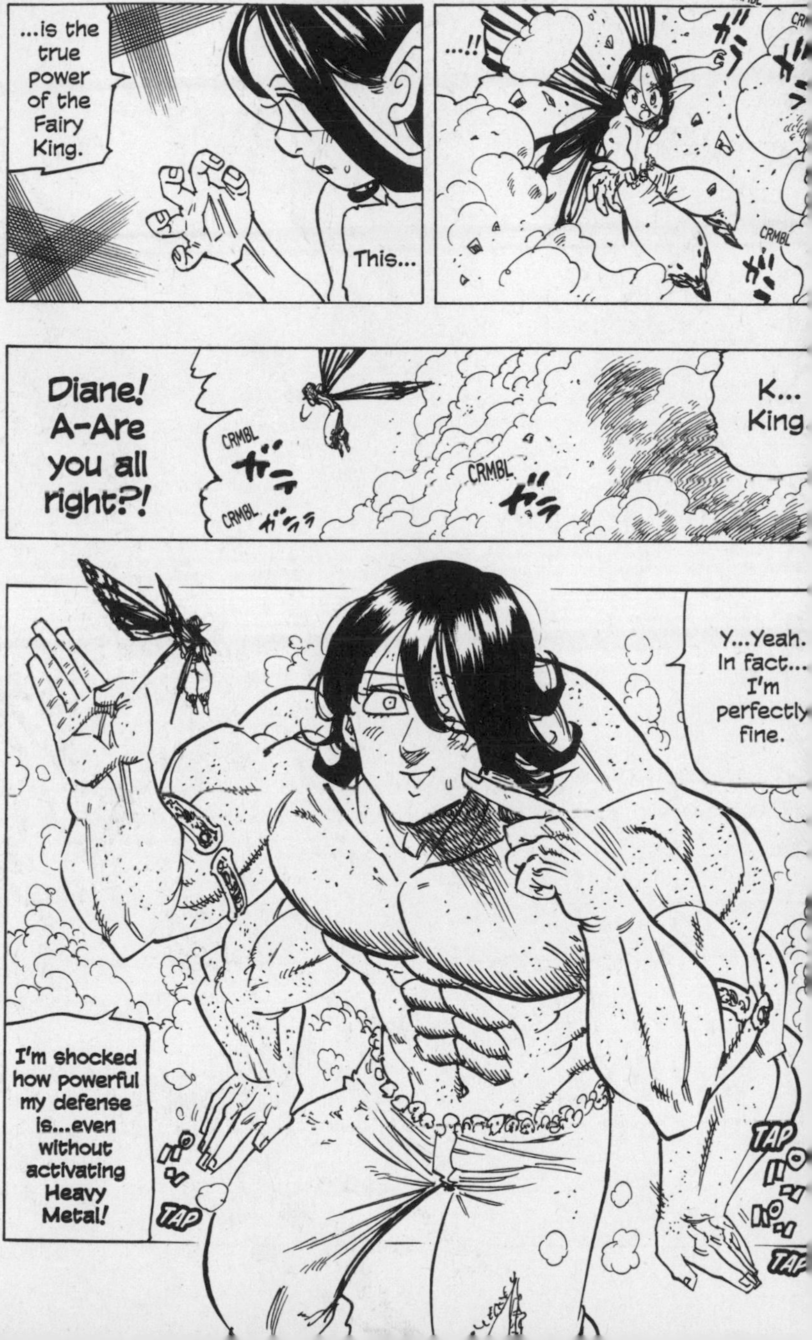
CRMBL
...!!
CRMBL
This...
...is the true power of the Fairy King.
K... King
CRMBL
CRMBL
CRMBL
Diane! A-Are you all right?!
Y...Yeah. In fact... I'm perfectly fine.
TAP
TAP
I'm shocked how powerful my defense is...even without activating Heavy Metal!

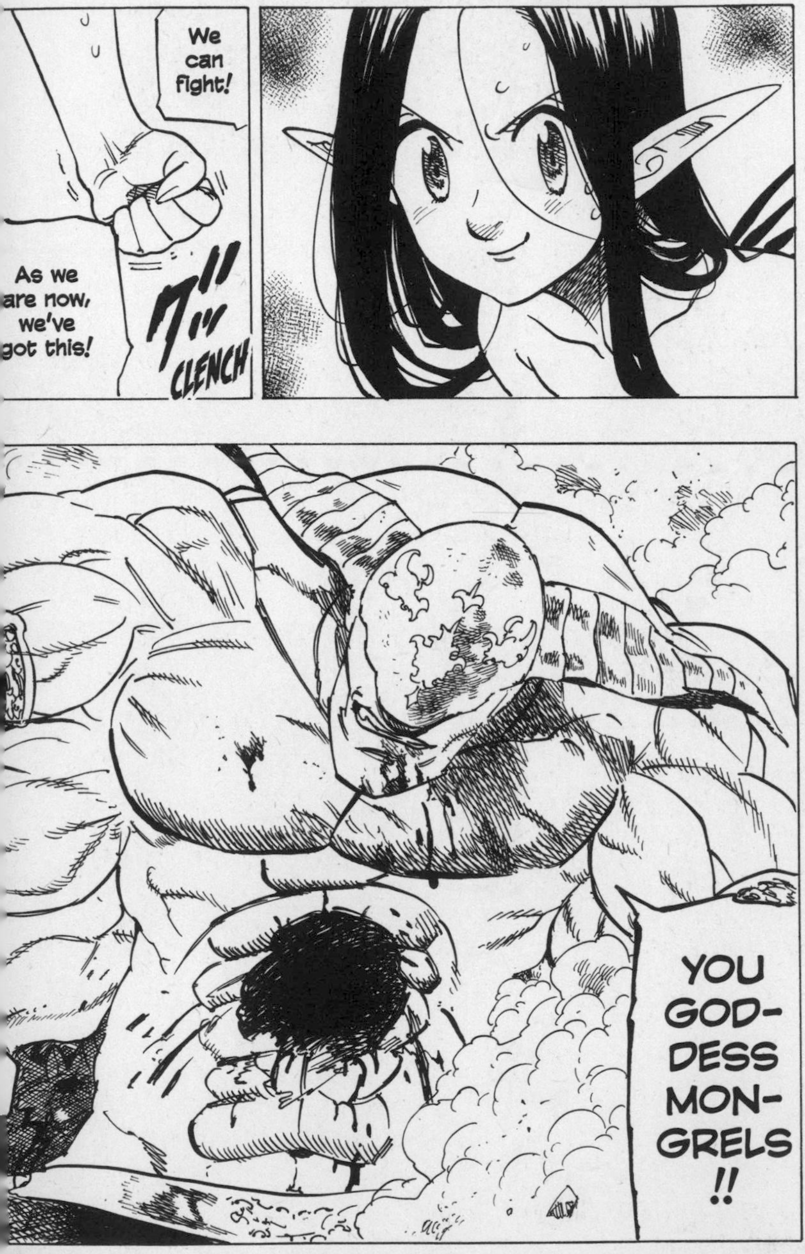
We can fight!
As we are now, we've got this!
CLENCH
YOU GOD-DESS MON-GRELS!!

THE SEVEN DEADLY SINS

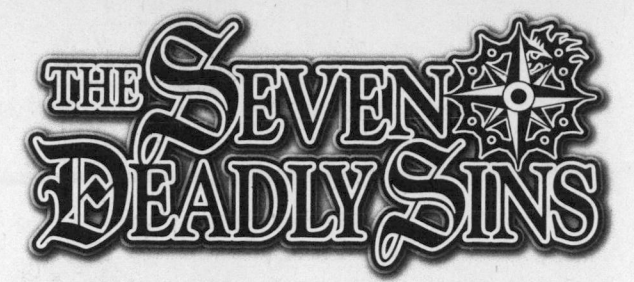

Chapter 202 - Players in the Holy War

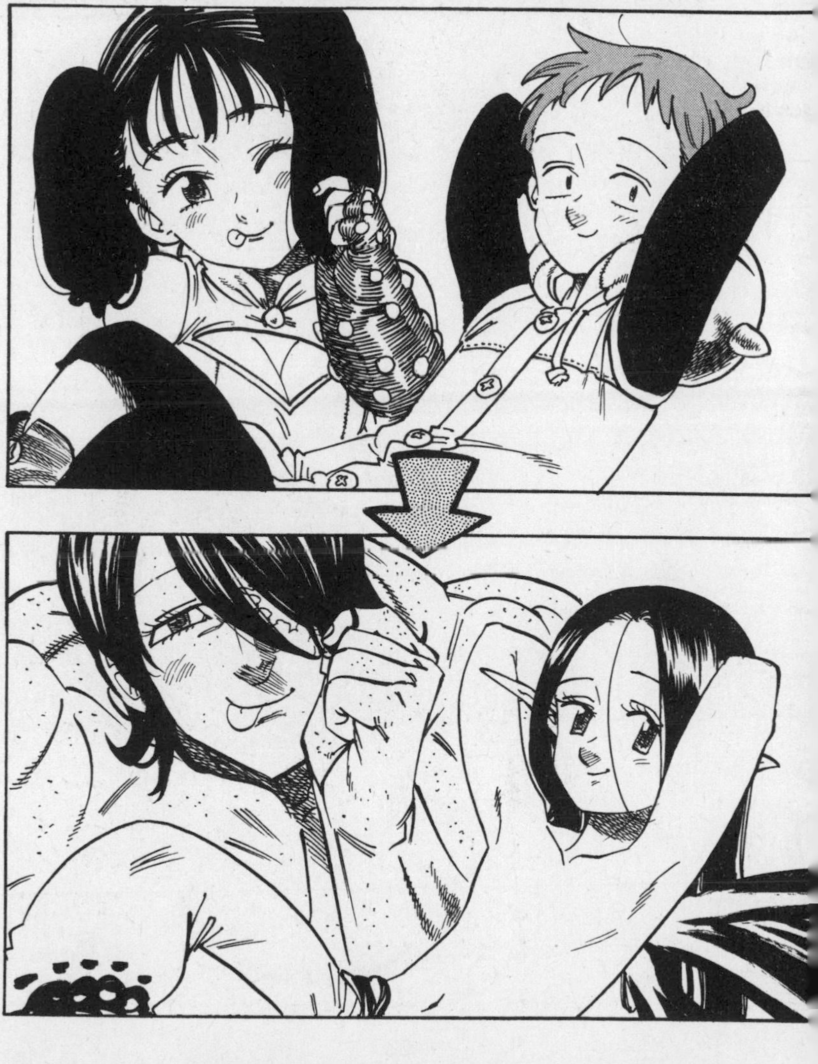

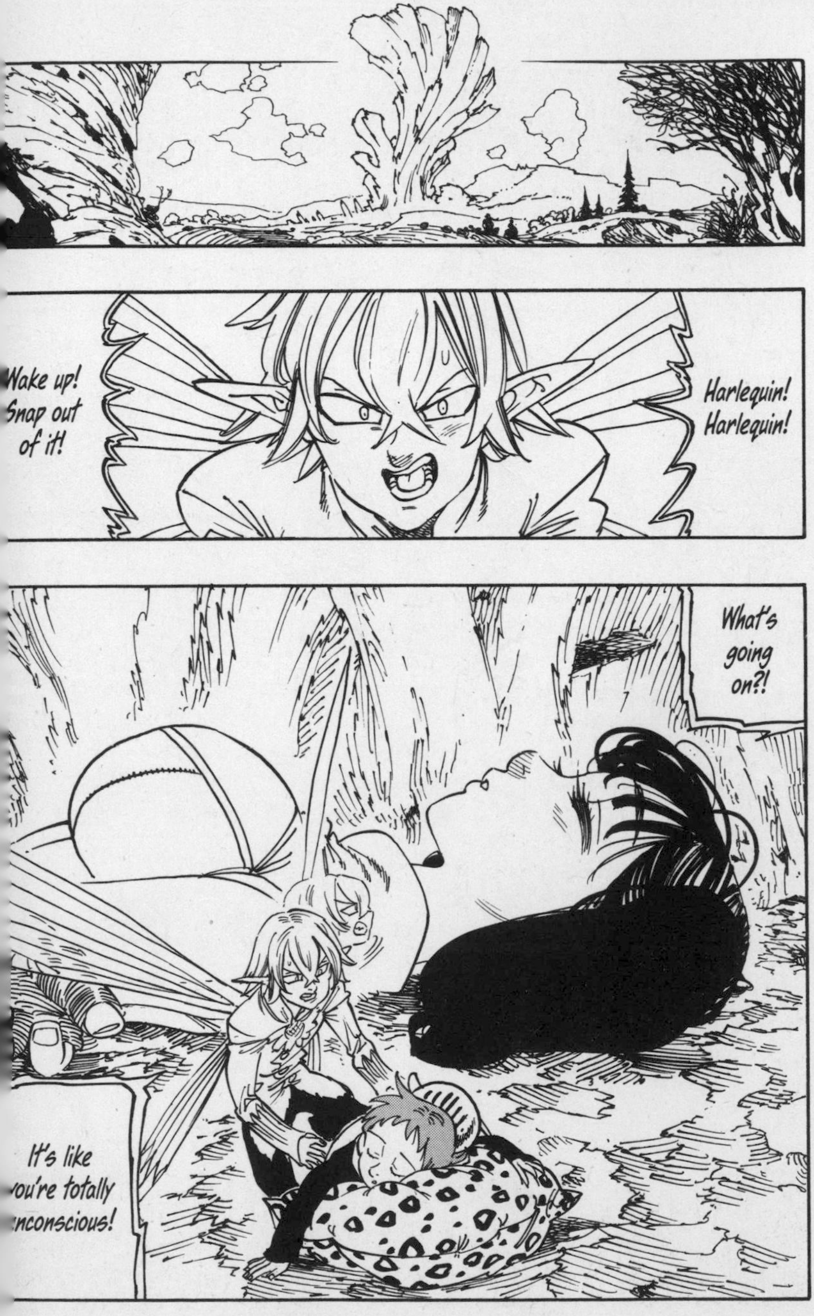

Harlequin! Harlequin!
Wake up! Snap out of it!
What's going on?!
It's like you're totally unconscious!

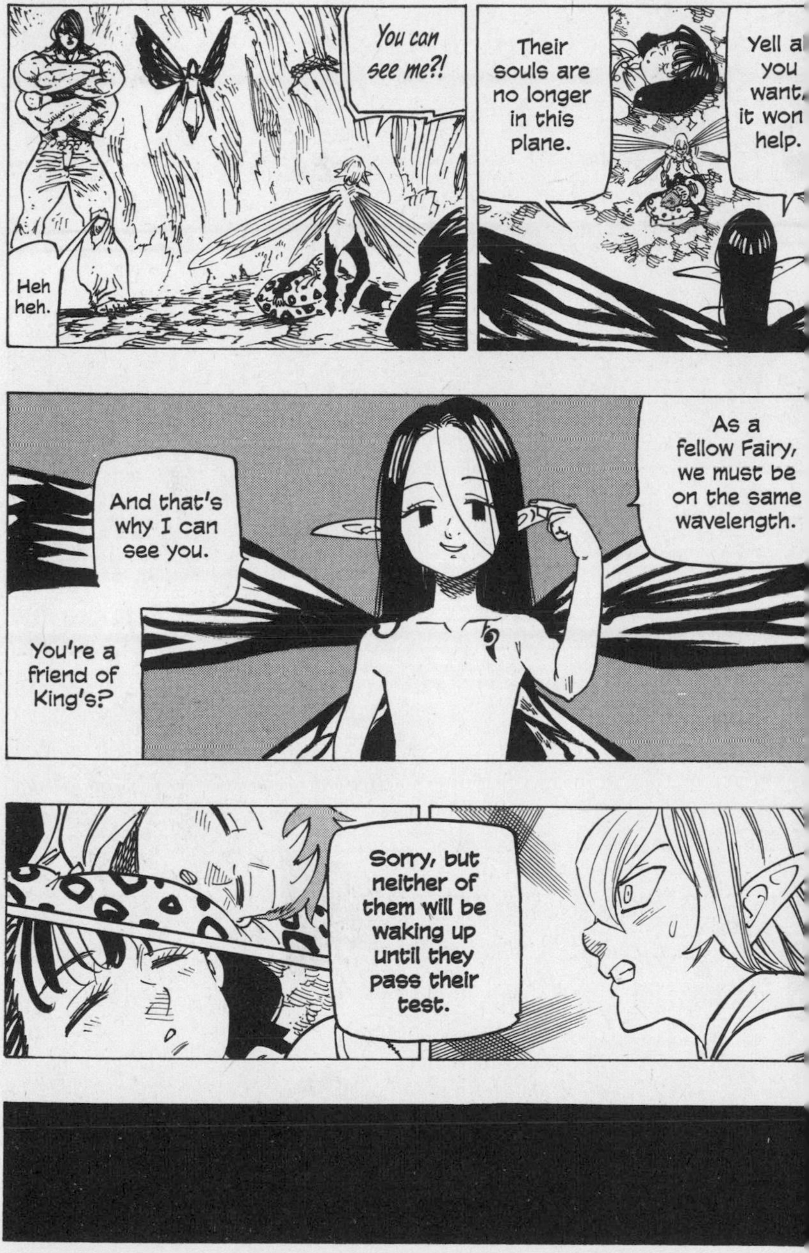
Yell a you want, it won help.
Their souls are no longer in this plane.
You can see me?!
Heh heh.
As a fellow Fairy, we must be on the same wavelength.
And that's why I can see you.
You're a friend of King's?
Sorry, but neither of them will be waking up until they pass their test.

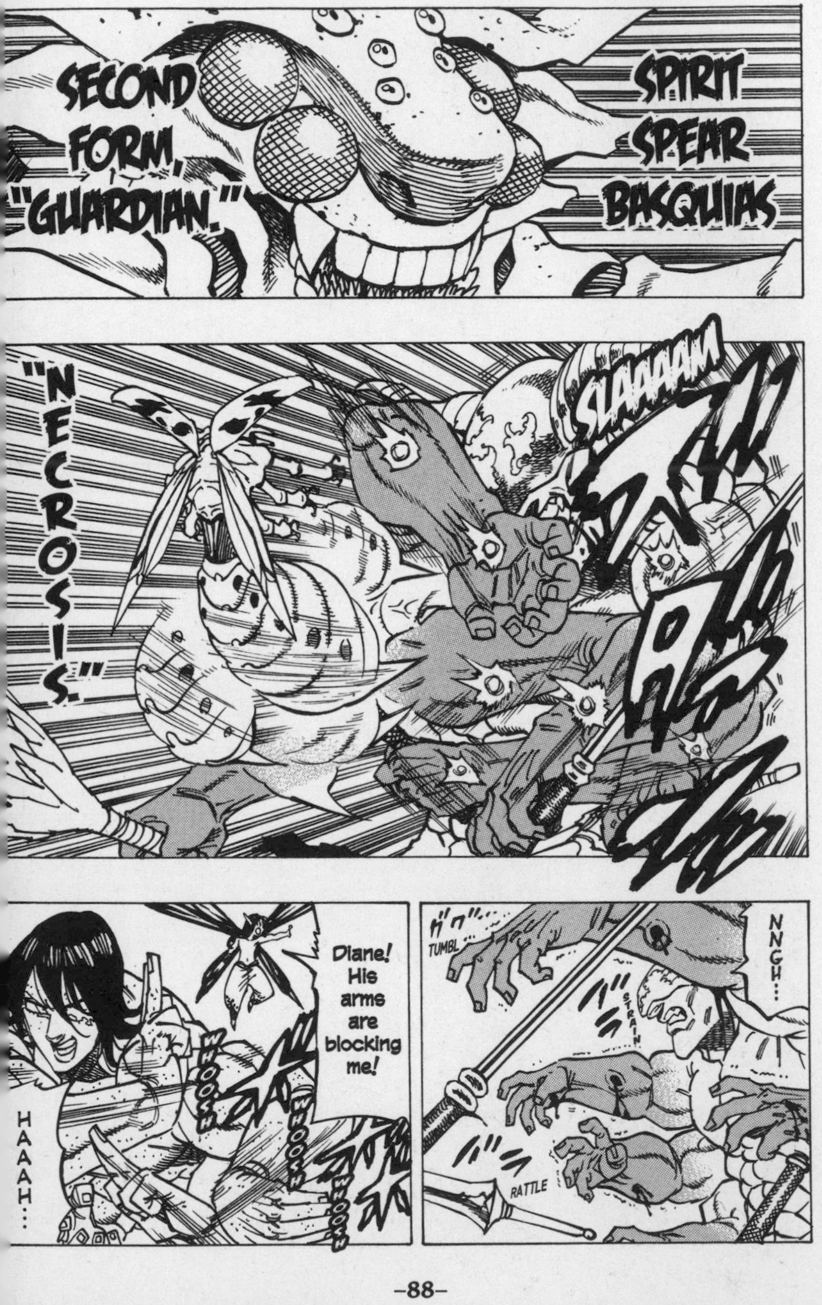
SPIRIT SPEAR BASQUIAS
SECOND FORM, "GUARDIAN."
SLAAAAM
"NECROSIS."
NNGH...
TUMBL
STRAIN
RATTLE
Diane! His arms are blocking me!
WHOOSH
WHOOSH
WHOOSH
HAAAH...

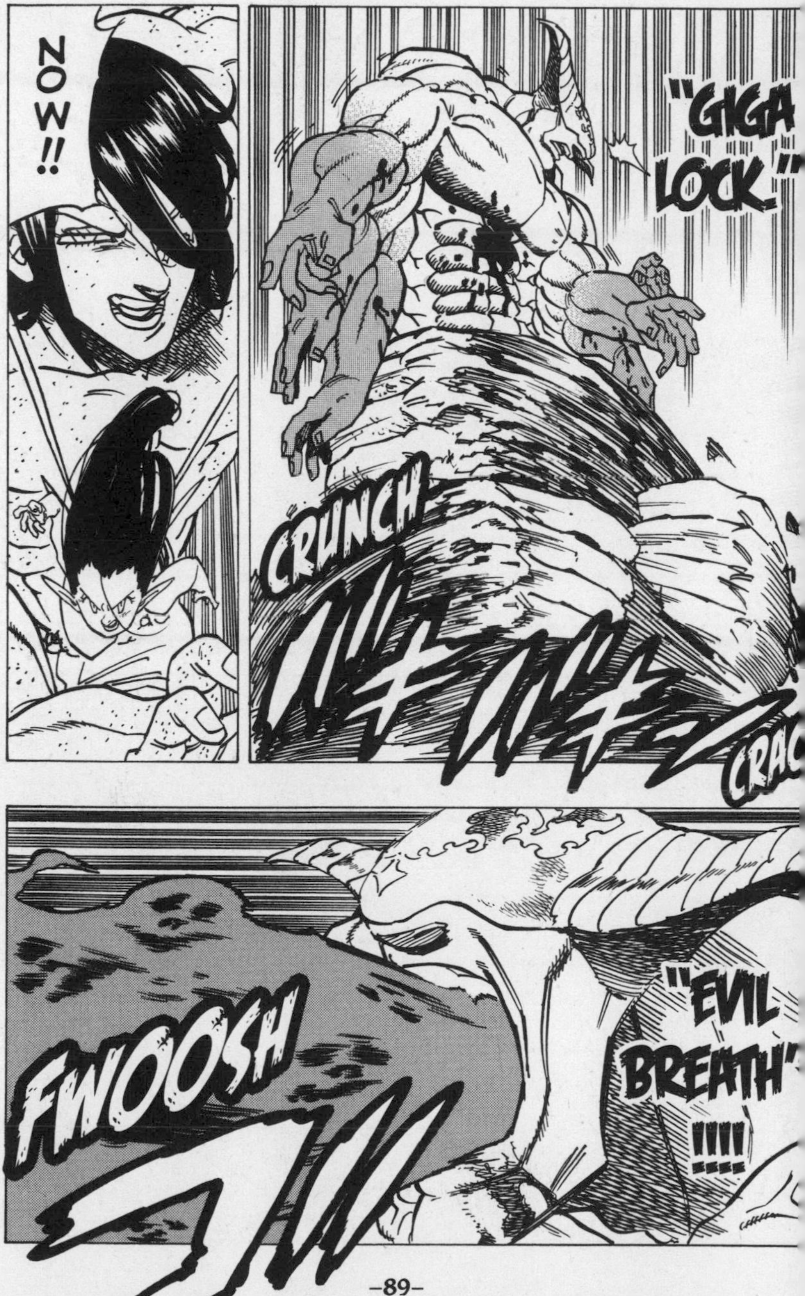
"GIGA LOCK"
CRUNCH
CRAC
NOW!!
"EVIL BREATH"!!!!
FWOOSH

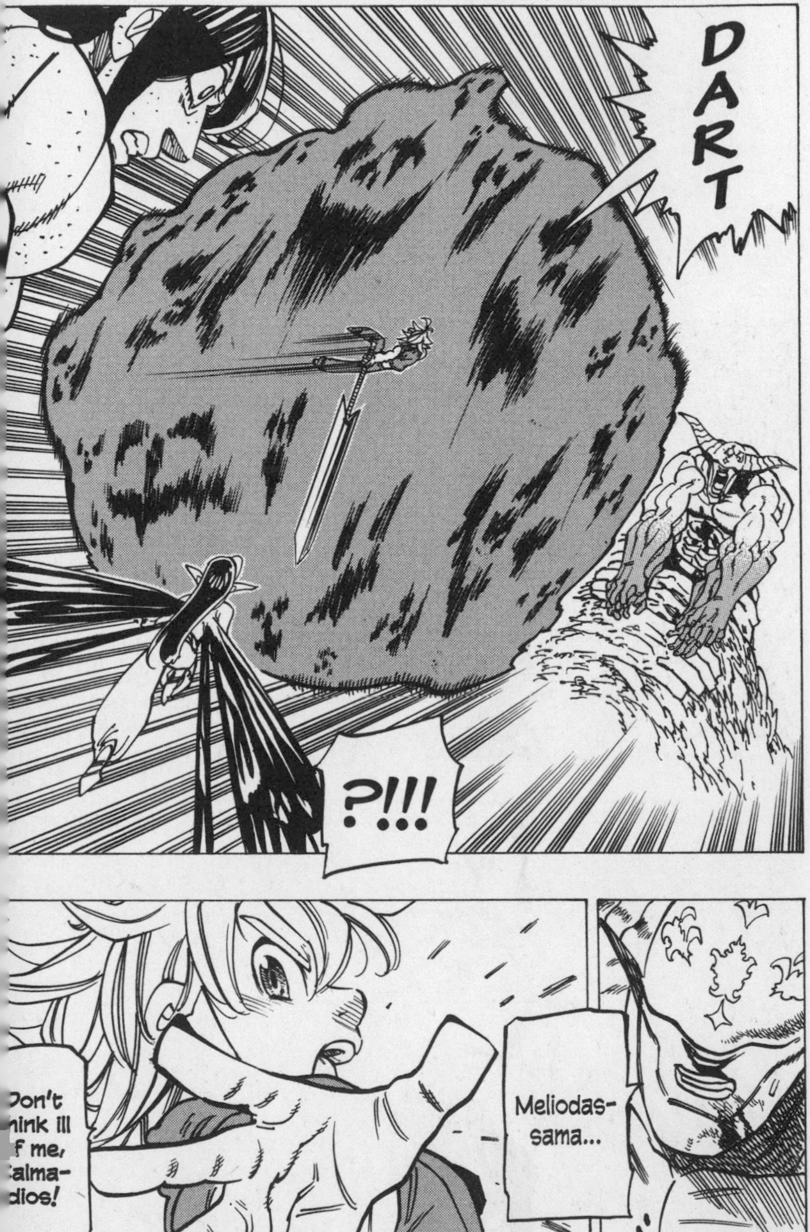
DART
?!!!
Meliodas-sama...
Don't hink ill f me, Calma-dios!

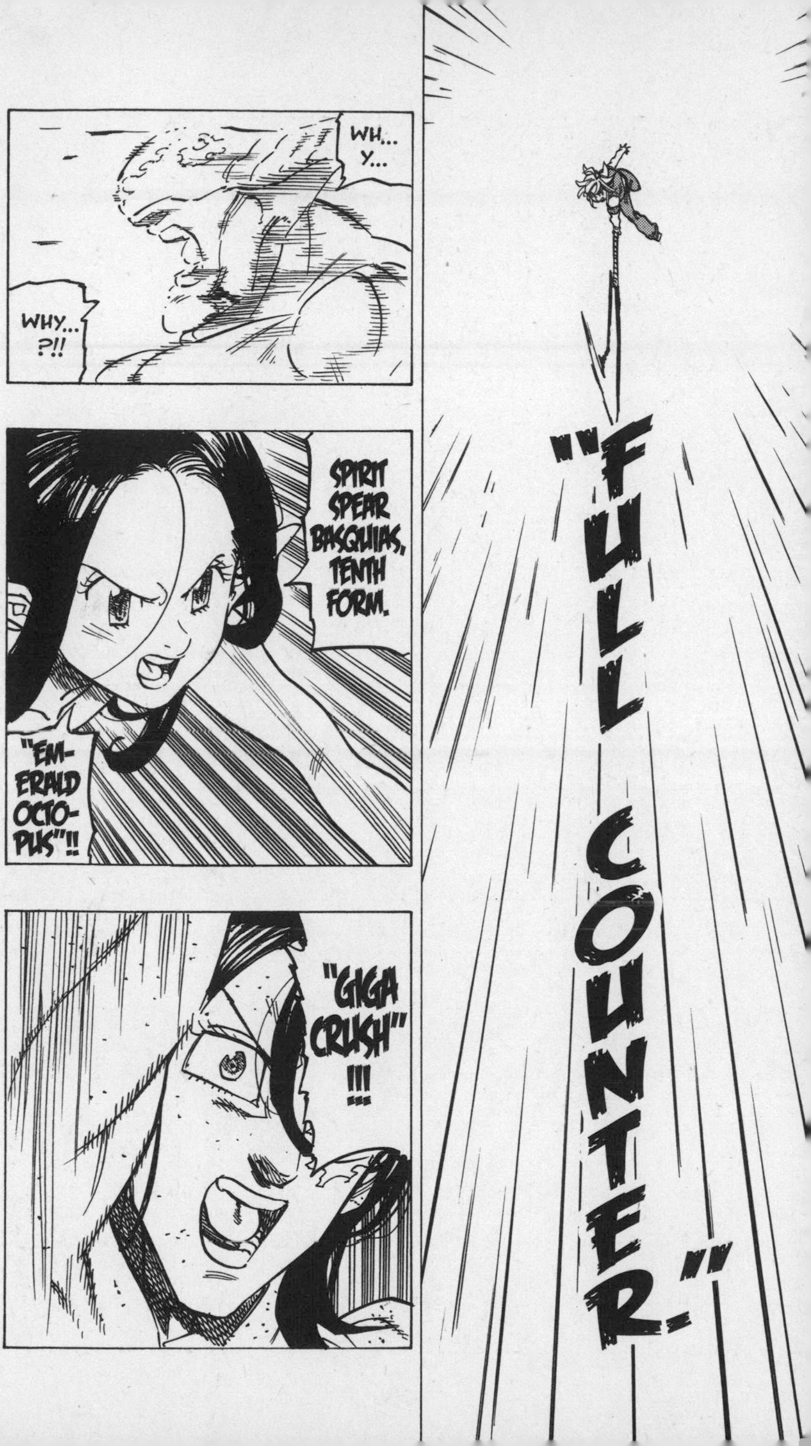
"FULL COUNTER"
WH... Y...
WHY... ?!!
SPIRIT SPEAR BASQUIAS, TENTH FORM.
"EMERALD OCTOPUS"!!
"GIGA CRUSH"!!!

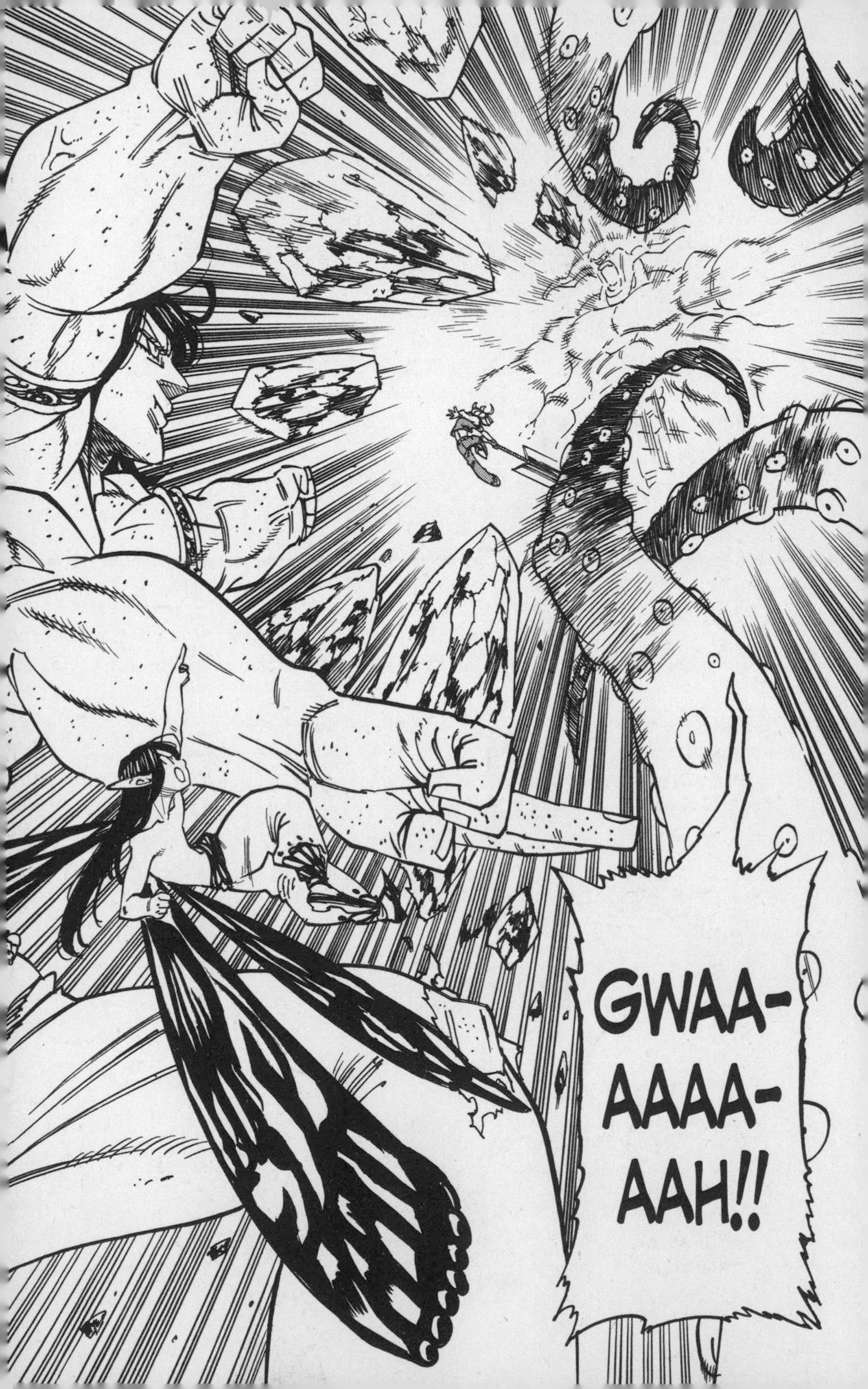
GWAA-AAAA-AAH!!

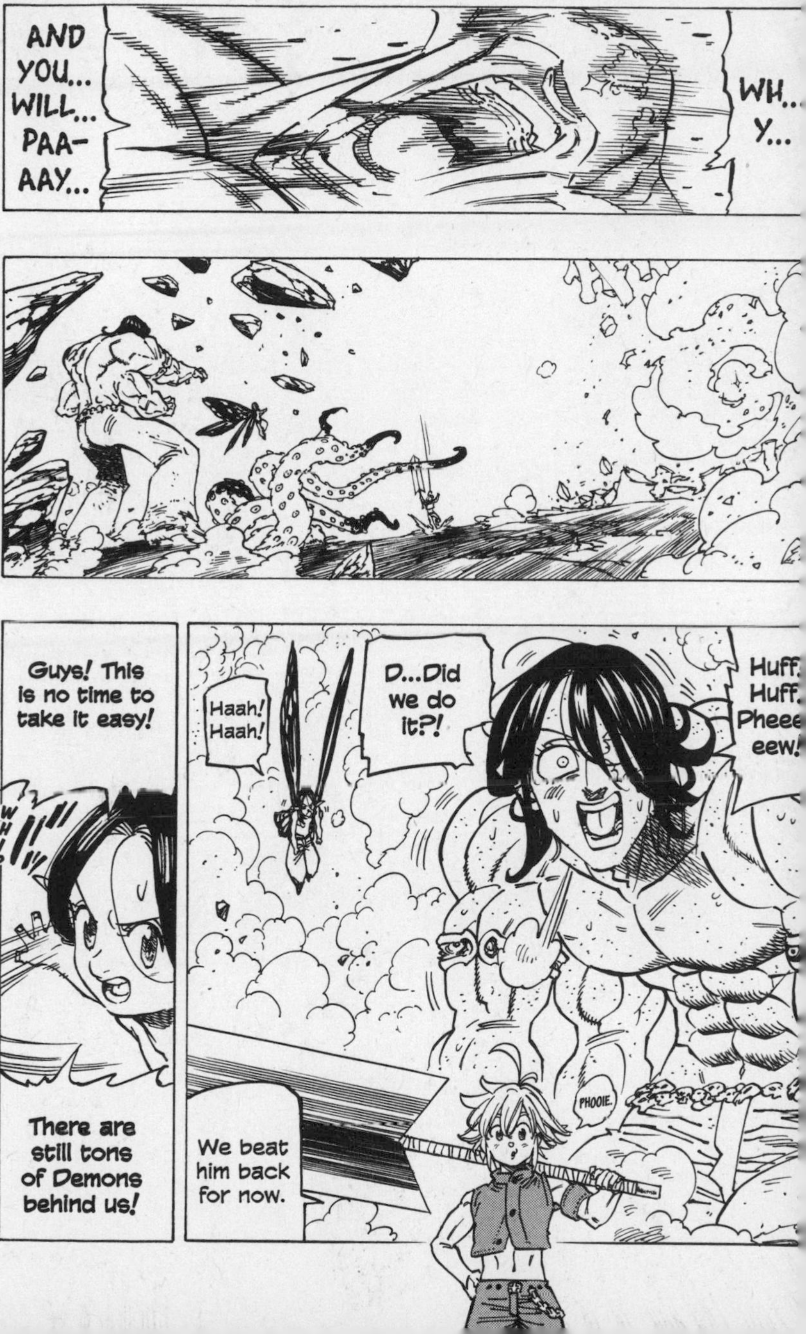
WH... Y...
AND YOU... WILL... PAA-AAY...
Huff. Huff. Pheee eew!
D...Did we do it?!
Haah! Haah!
PHOOIE.
We beat him back for now.
Guys! This is no time to take it easy!
WHIP
There are still tons of Demons behind us!

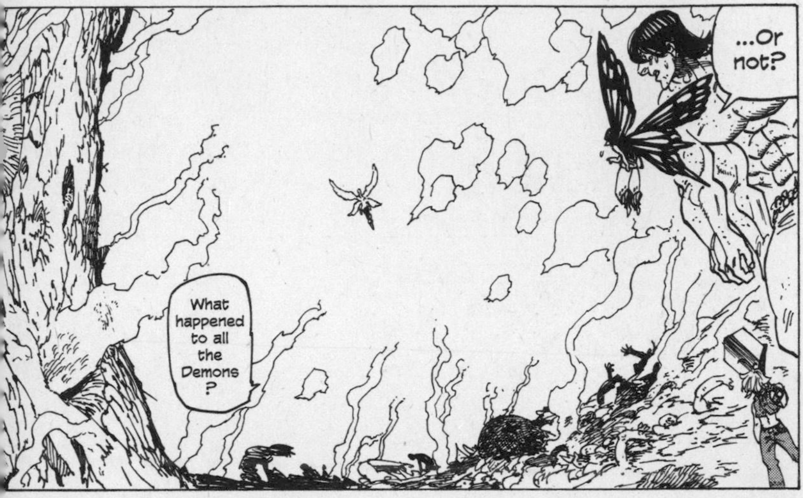
...Or not?
What happened to all the Demons?
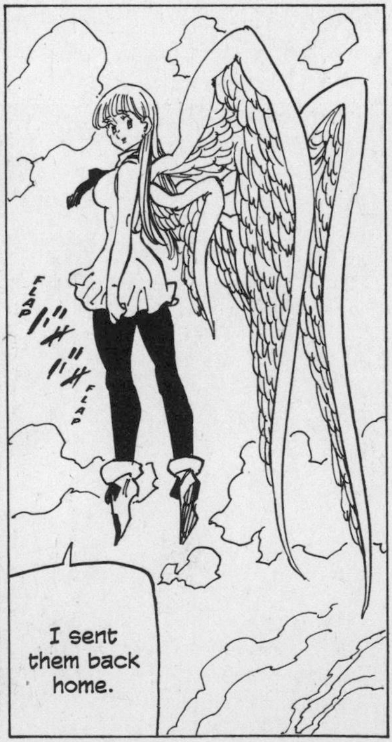
FLAP
FLAP
I sent them back home.
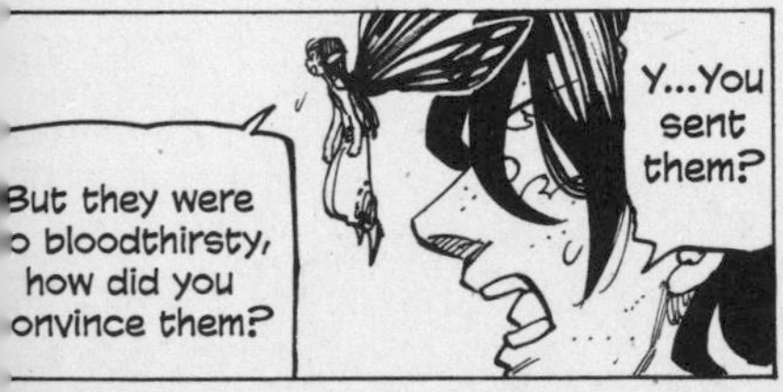
Y...You sent them?
But they were
o bloodthirsty,
how did you
onvince them?
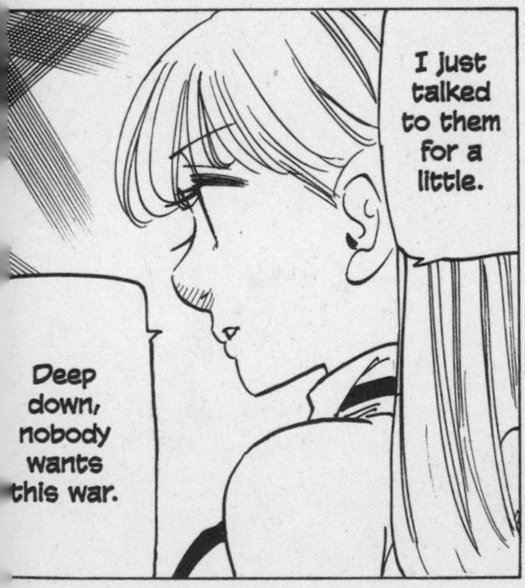
I just talked to them for a little.
Deep down, nobody wants this war.

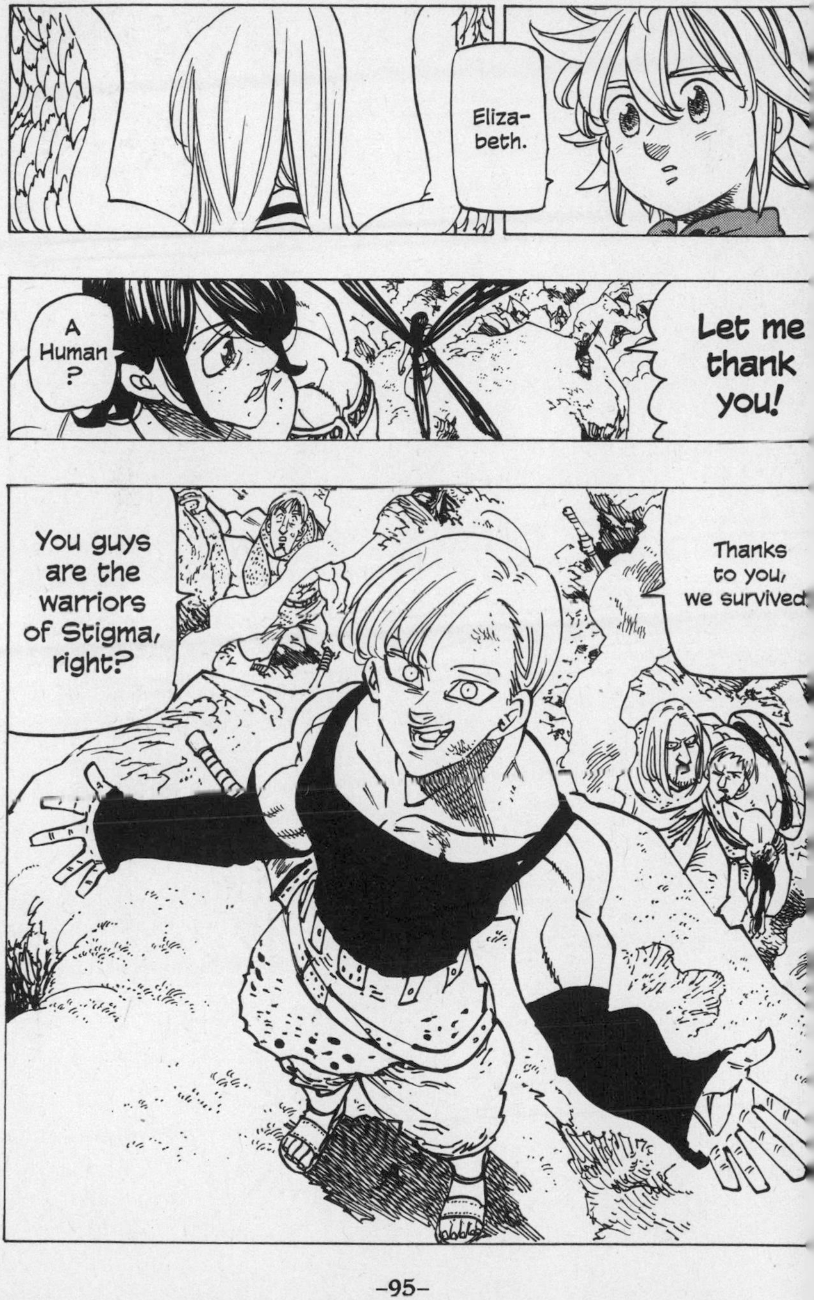
Eliza-beth.
Let me thank you!
A Human ?
Thanks to you, we survived.
You guys are the warriors of Stigma, right?

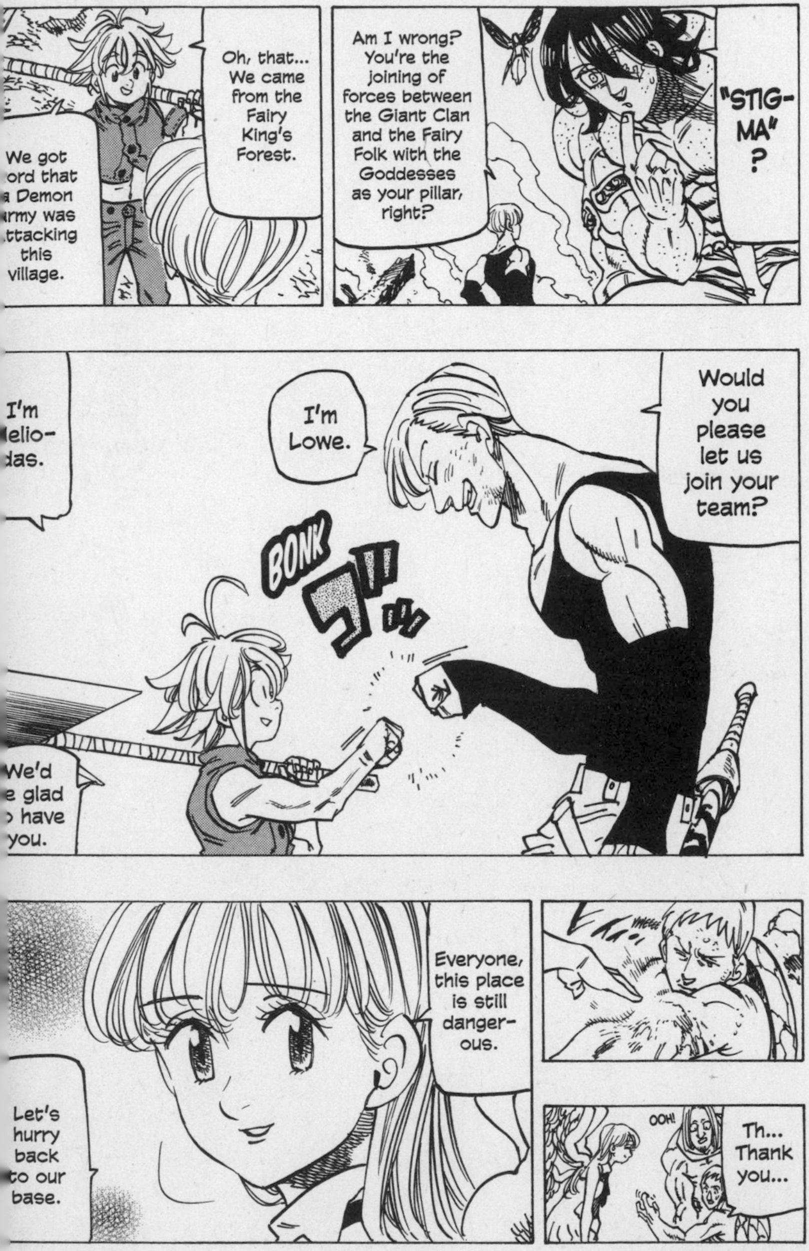
"STIG-MA"?
Am I wrong? You're the joining of forces between the Giant Clan and the Fairy Folk with the Goddesses as your pillar, right?
Oh, that... We came from the Fairy King's Forest.
We got ord that a Demon rmy was ttacking this village.
Would you please let us join your team?
I'm Lowe.
BONK
I'm lelio-das.
We'd e glad have you.
Th... Thank you...
OOH!
Everyone, this place is still danger-ous.
Let's hurry back to our base.

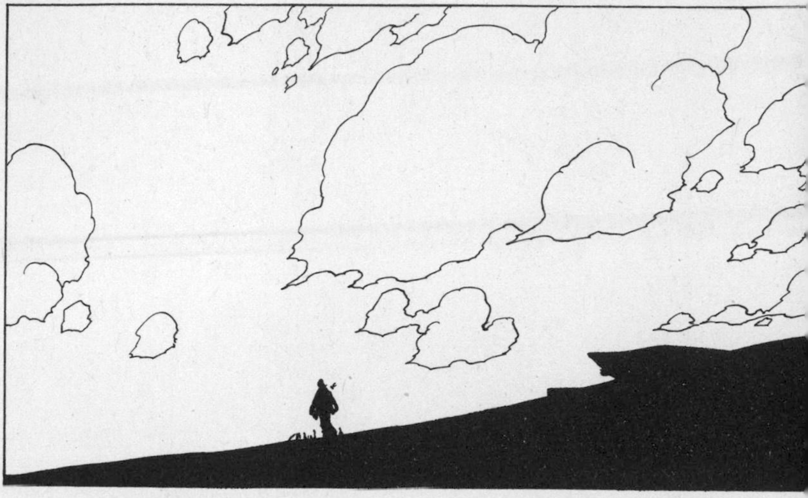

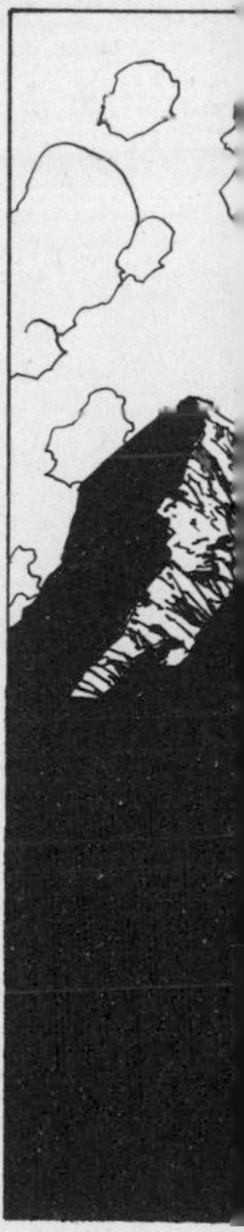

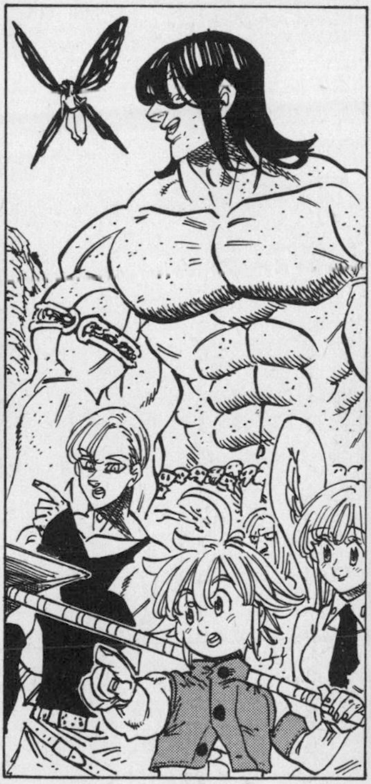

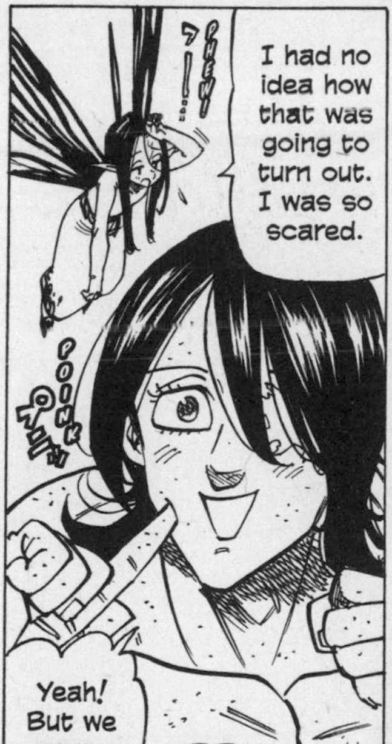
I had no idea how that was going to turn out. I was so scared.
PHEW!
POINK
Yeah! But we were pretty cool! ♥

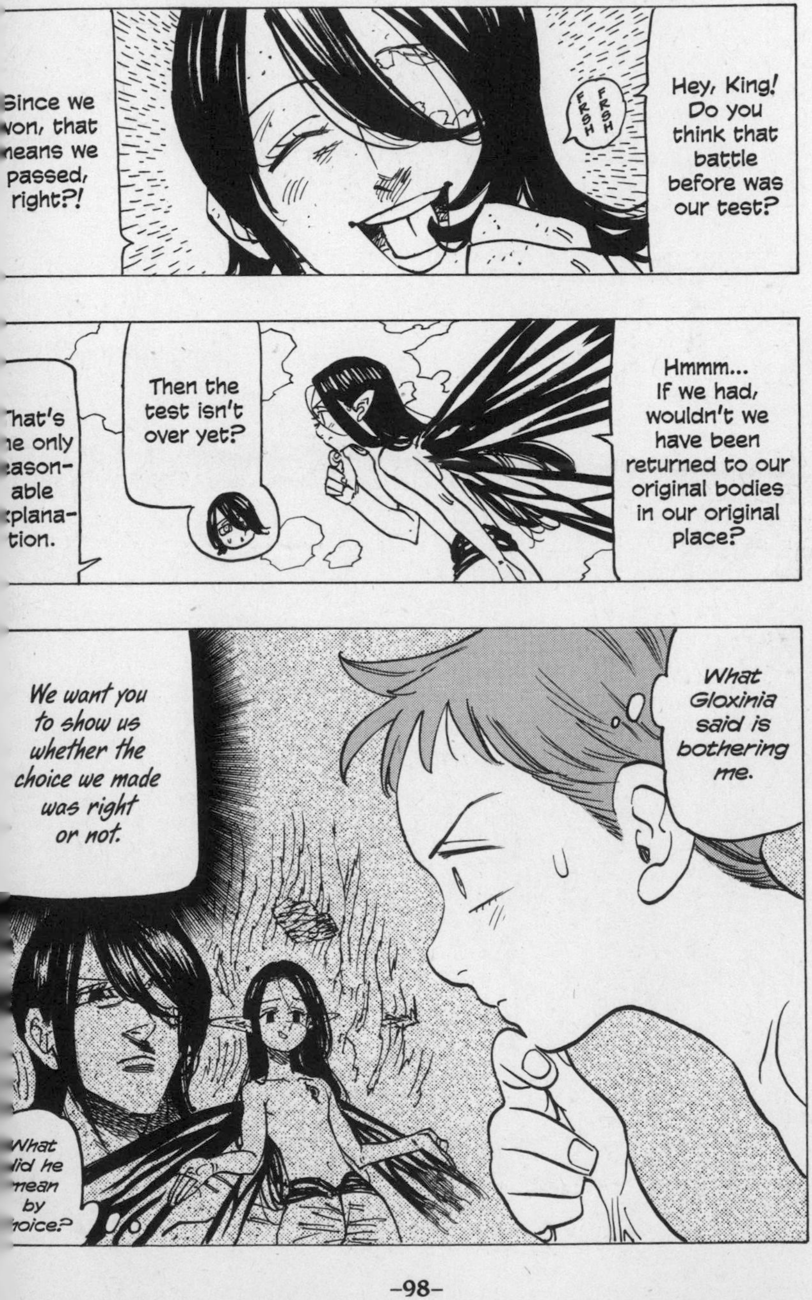
Hey, King! Do you think that battle before was our test?
FRSH FRSH
Since we von, that neans we passed, right?!
Hmmm... If we had, wouldn't we have been returned to our original bodies in our original place?
Then the test isn't over yet?
hat's ne only ason- able planation.
What Gloxinia said is bothering me.
We want you to show us whether the choice we made was right or not.
What lid he nean by oice?

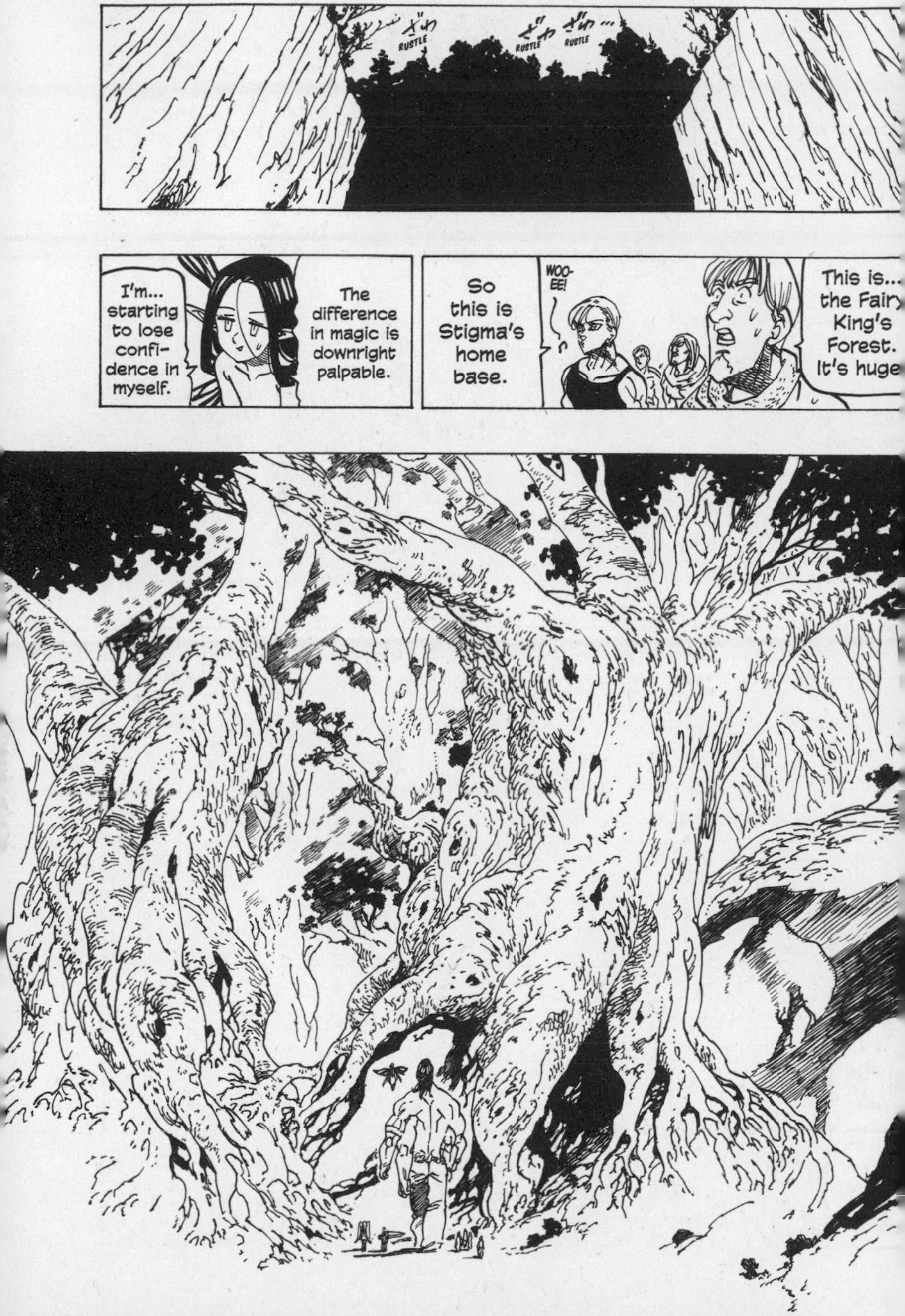
ざわ ざわ…
RUSTLE RUSTLE
ざわ
RUSTLE
This is... the Fair King's Forest. It's huge
WOO-EE!
So this is Stigma's home base.
The difference in magic is downright palpable.
I'm... starting to lose confi-dence in myself.

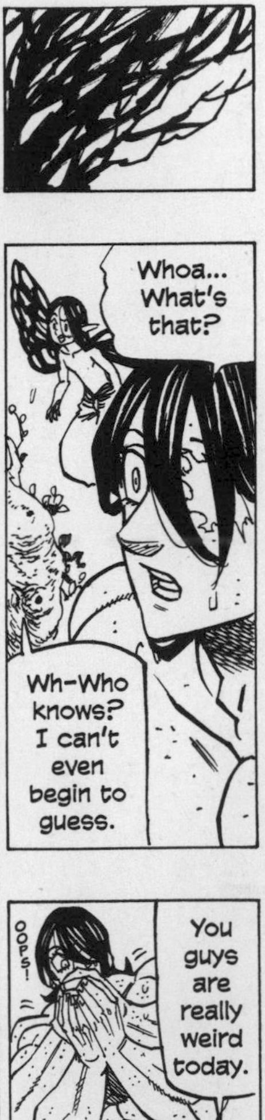
Whoa... What's that?
Wh-Who knows? I can't even begin to guess.
OOPS!
You guys are really weird today.
This is our home base, of course.

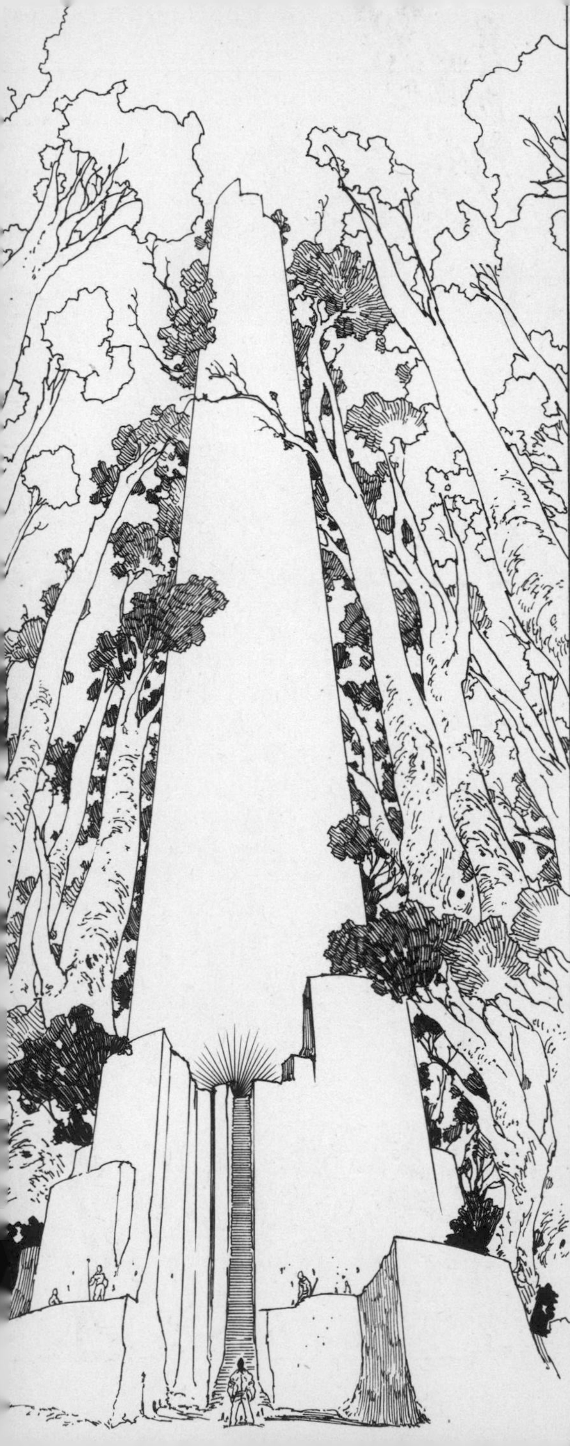

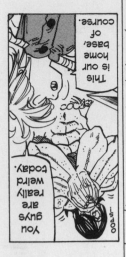

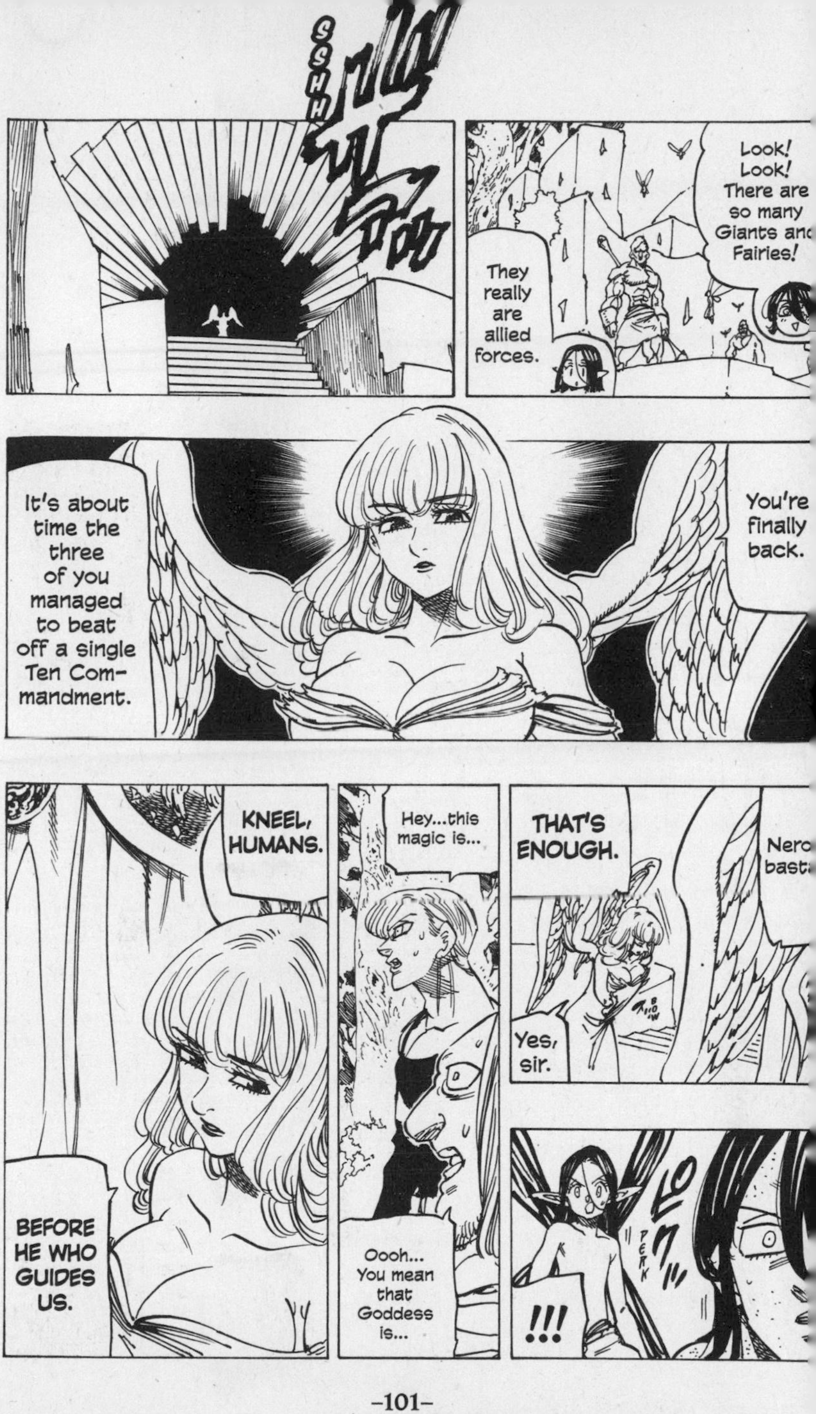
Look! Look! There are so many Giants an
Fairies!
They really are allied forces.
SSHH
You're finally back.
It's about time the three of you managed to beat off a single Ten Com-mandment.
Nero basta
THAT'S ENOUGH.
Yes, sir.
PERK
!!!
Hey...this magic is...
Oooh... You mean that Goddess is...
KNEEL, HUMANS.
BEFORE HE WHO GUIDES US.

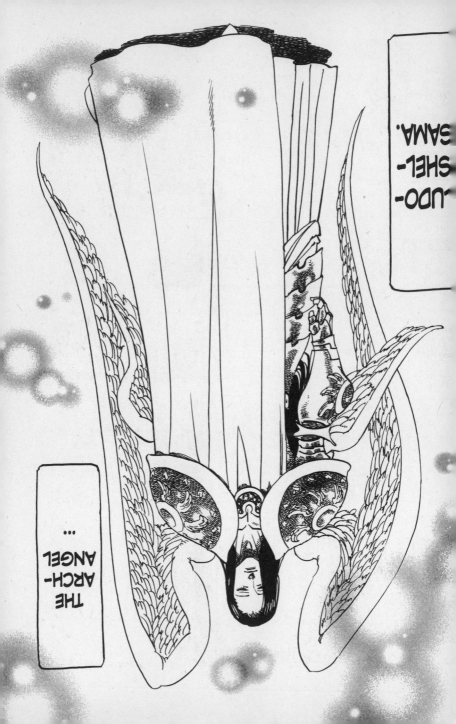

THE ARCH-ANGEL ...

...UDO-SHEL-SAMA.

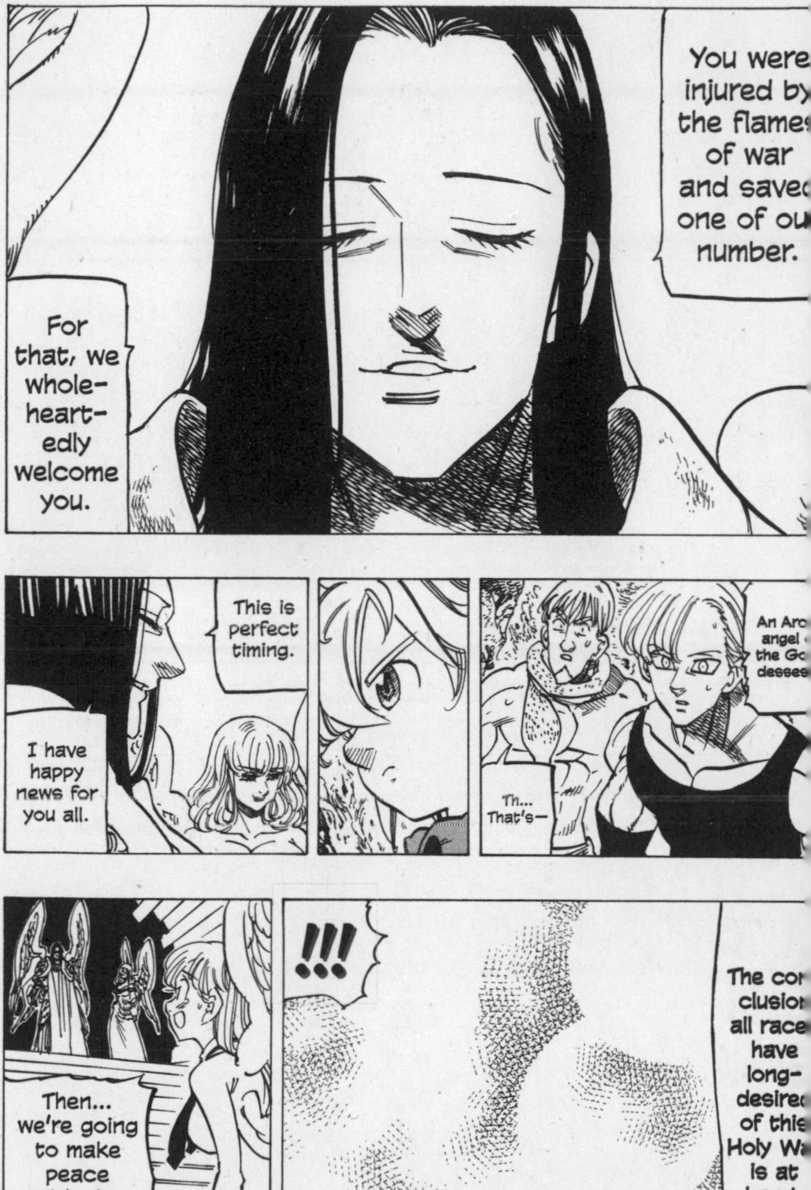
You were injured b the flame of war and save one of ou number.
For that, we whole-heart-edly welcome you.
An Arc angel the Go desse
Th... That's—
This is perfect timing.
I have happy news for you all.
The co clusio all race have long-desire of thi Holy W is at hand.
!!!
Then... we're going to make peace with the Demons?!

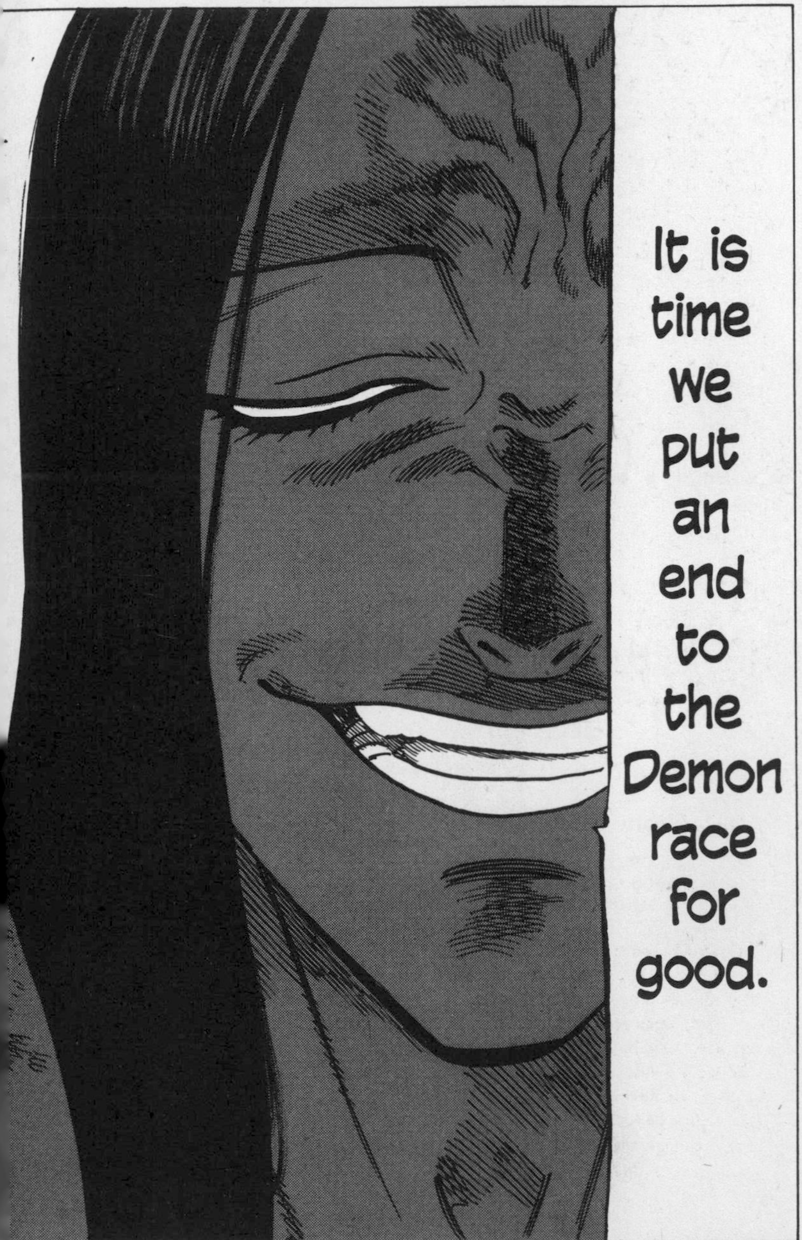
It is time we put an end to the Demon race for good.

THE SEVEN DEADLY SINS

Light of Divine Grace

**Total Height:
7,900 Feet
? Stories**

One of the bases for Stigma, built
by the Goddesses in the ancient
Fairy King's Forest. This massive
and windowless white castle has
been protected by the Archangel
Ludoshel's divine protection. It is
said that a gate that connects to
Heaven can be found within, but
details are obscure.

Chapter 203 - Ludoshel's Plan

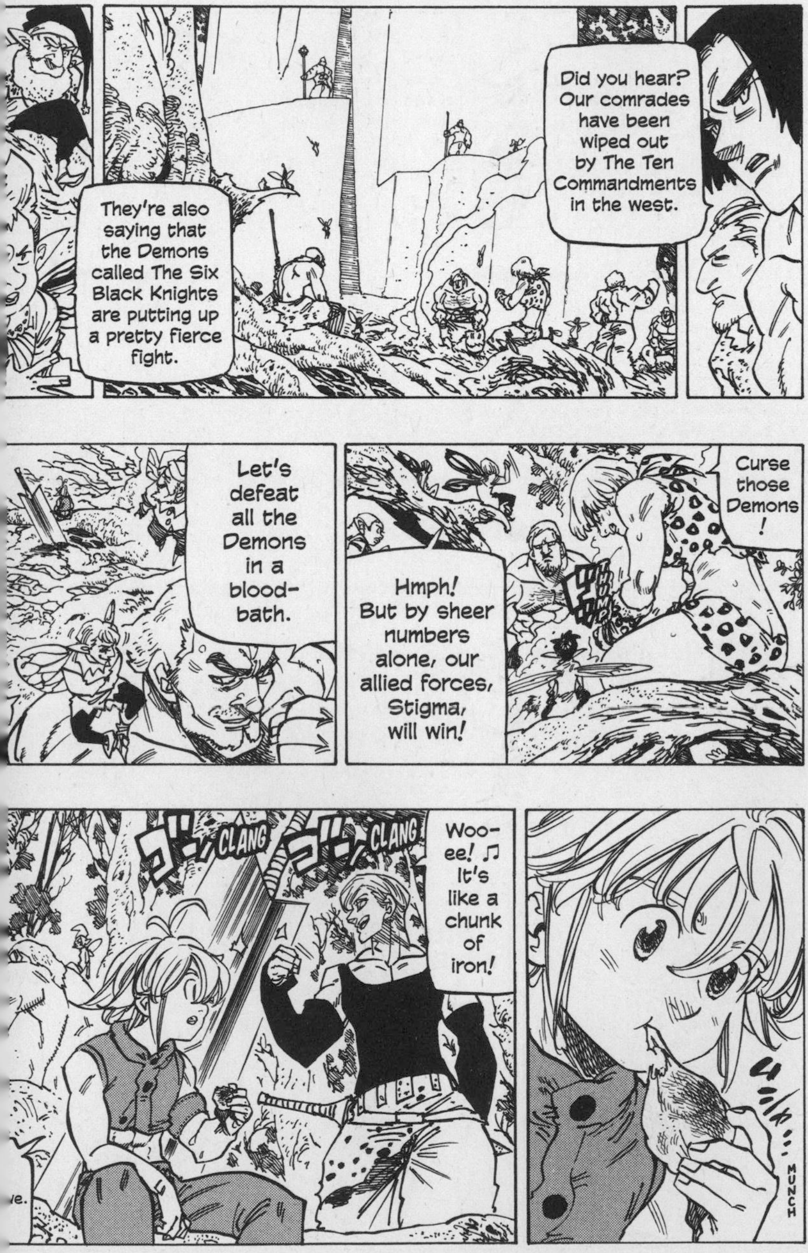
Did you hear? Our comrades have been wiped out by The Ten Commandments in the west.
They're also saying that the Demons called The Six Black Knights are putting up a pretty fierce fight.
Curse those Demons!
THUMP
Hmph! But by sheer numbers alone, our allied forces, Stigma, will win!
Let's defeat all the Demons in a blood-bath.
MUNCH
Woo-ee! ♫ It's like a chunk of iron!
CLANG
CLANG

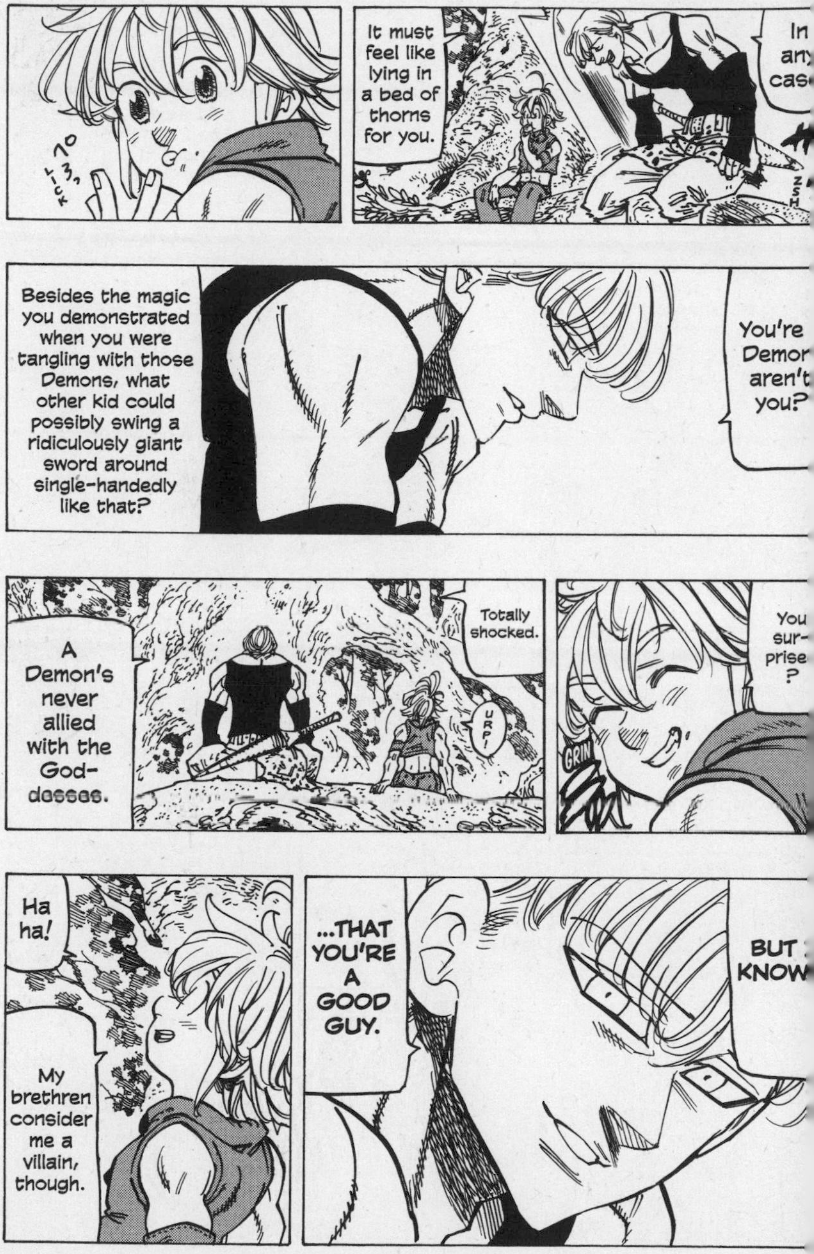
In any cas
It must feel like lying in a bed of thorns for you.
ZSH
LICK
You're Demor aren't you?
Besides the magic you demonstrated when you were tangling with those Demons, what other kid could possibly swing a ridiculously giant sword around single-handedly like that?
You sur-prise ?
GRIN
Totally shocked.
URP!
A Demon's never allied with the God-desses.
BUT KNOW
...THAT YOU'RE A GOOD GUY.
Ha ha!
My brethren consider me a villain, though.

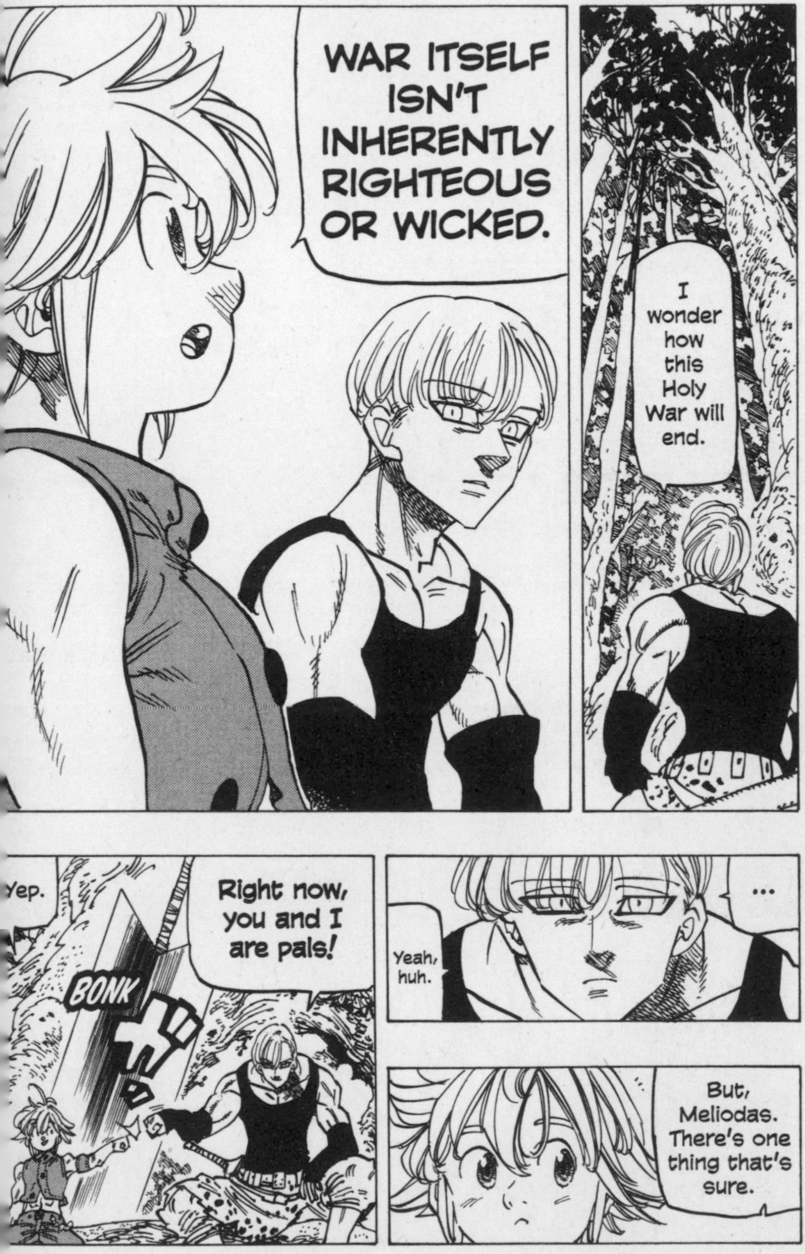
I wonder how this Holy War will end.
WAR ITSELF ISN'T INHERENTLY RIGHTEOUS OR WICKED.
...
Yeah, huh.
But, Meliodas. There's one thing that's sure.
Right now, you and I are pals!
Yep.
BONK

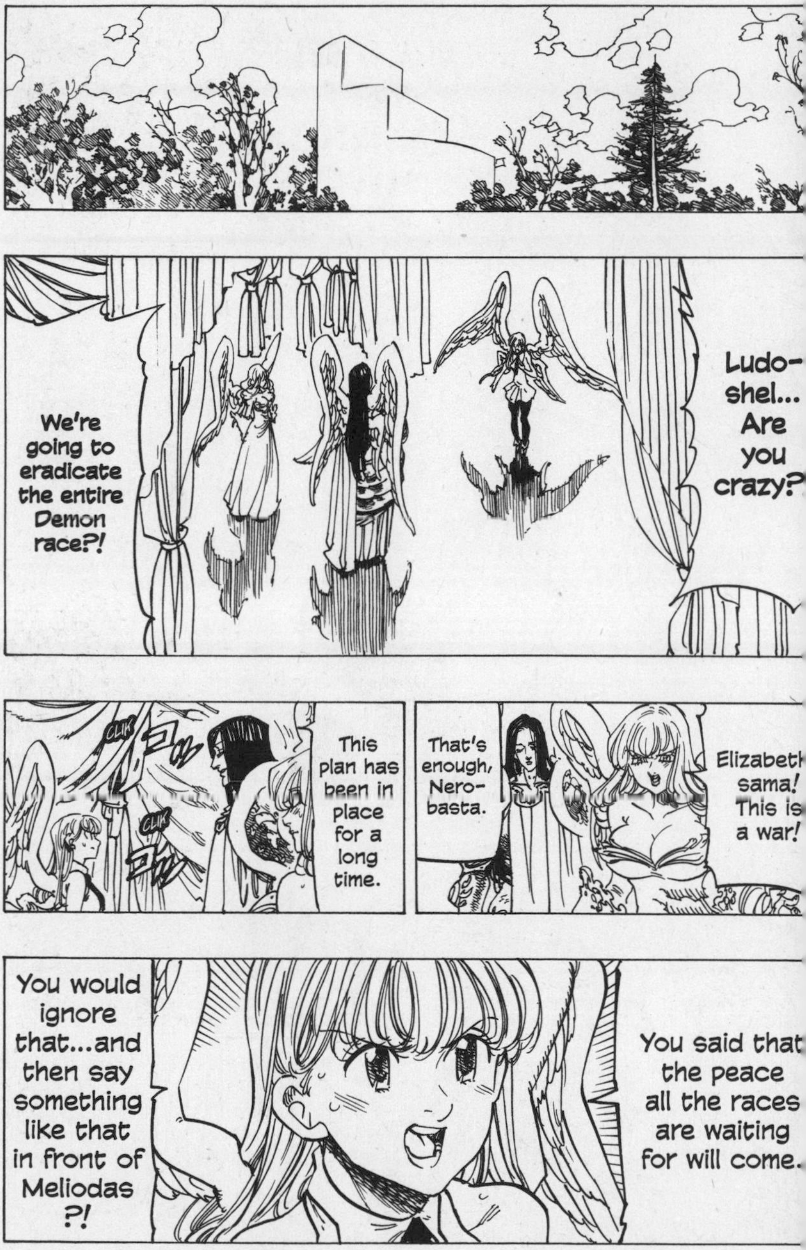
Ludo-shel... Are you crazy?
We're going to eradicate the entire Demon race?!
Elizabeth sama! This is a war!
That's enough, Nero-basta.
This plan has been in place for a long time.
CLIK
CLIK
You said that the peace all the races are waiting for will come.
You would ignore that...and then say something like that in front of Meliodas?!

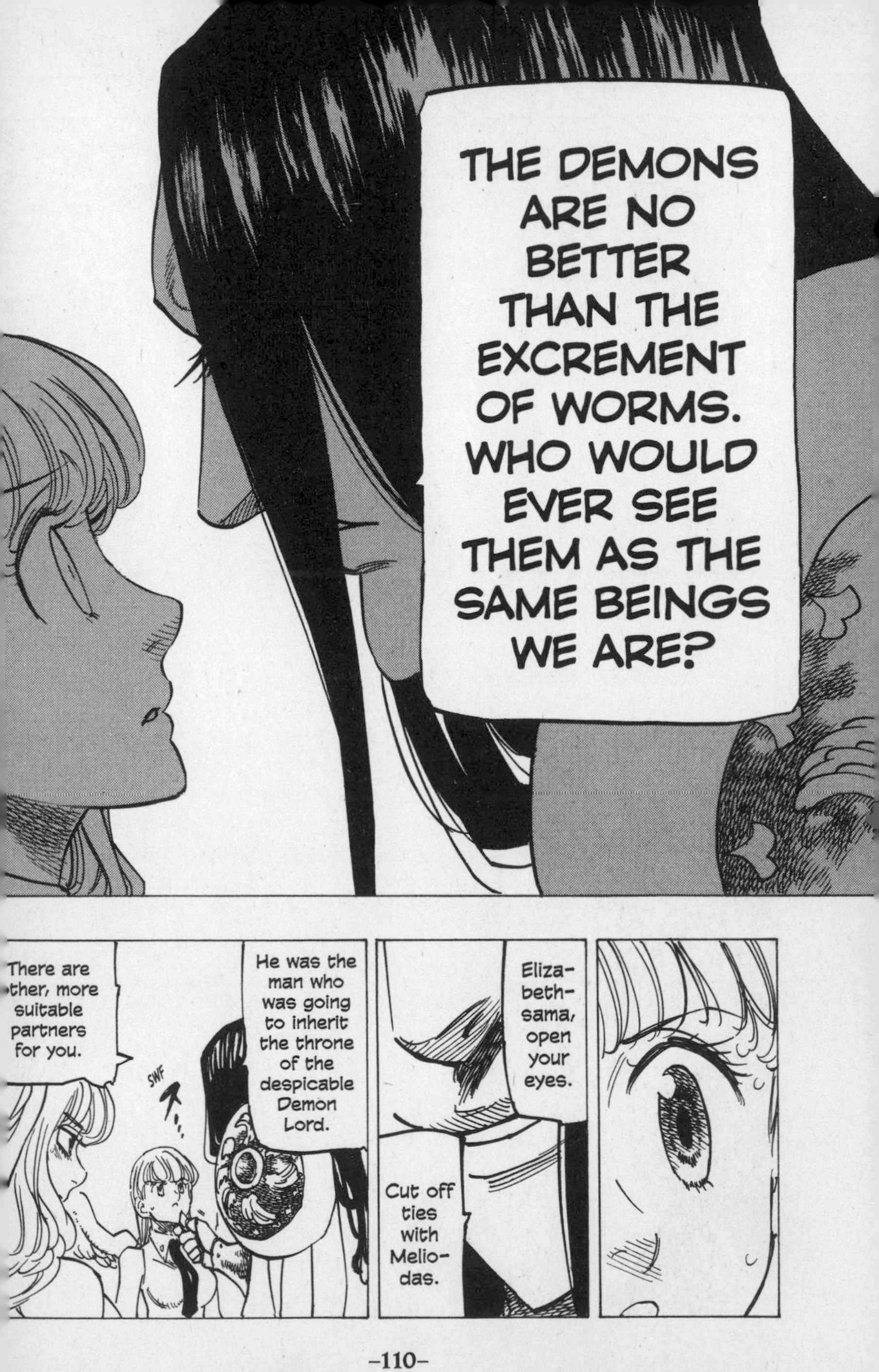
THE DEMONS ARE NO BETTER THAN THE EXCREMENT OF WORMS. WHO WOULD EVER SEE THEM AS THE SAME BEINGS WE ARE?
Eliza-beth-sama, open your eyes.
Cut off ties with Melio-das.
He was the man who was going to inherit the throne of the despicable Demon Lord.
SWF
There are ·ther, more suitable partners for you.

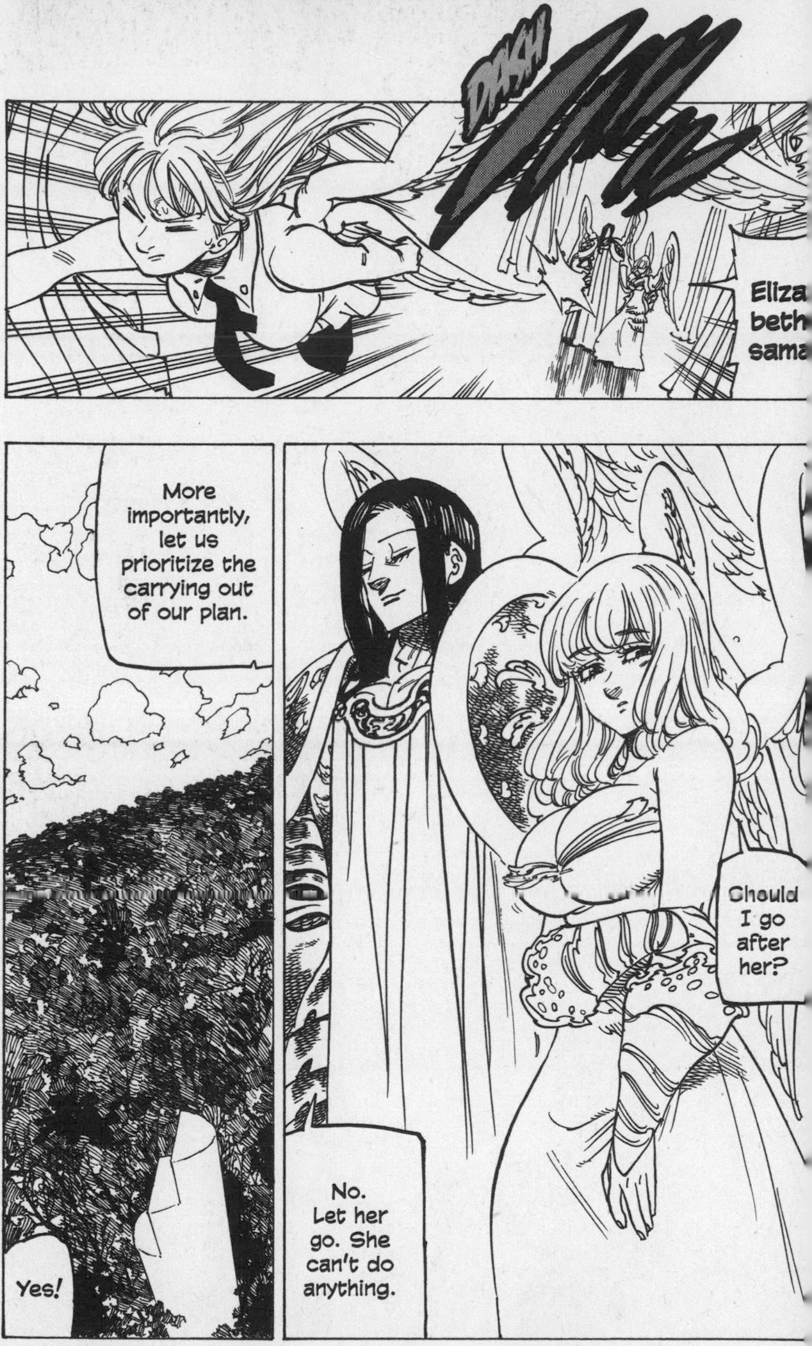
Eliza beth sama
DASH
Chould I go after her?
No. Let her go. She can't do anything.
More importantly, let us prioritize the carrying out of our plan.
Yes!

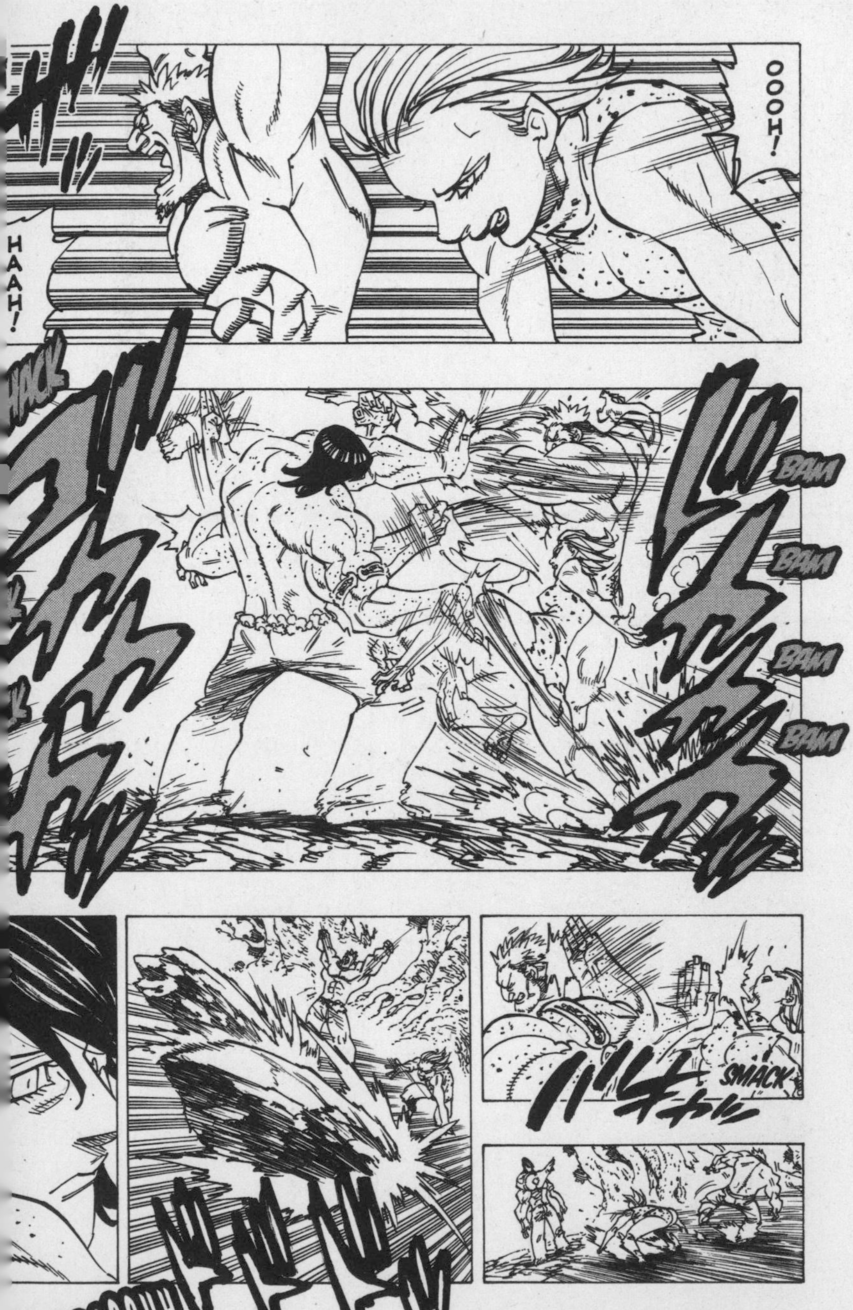
OOOH!
HAAAH!
BAM
BAM
BAM
BAM
SMACK
DOOSSSHH

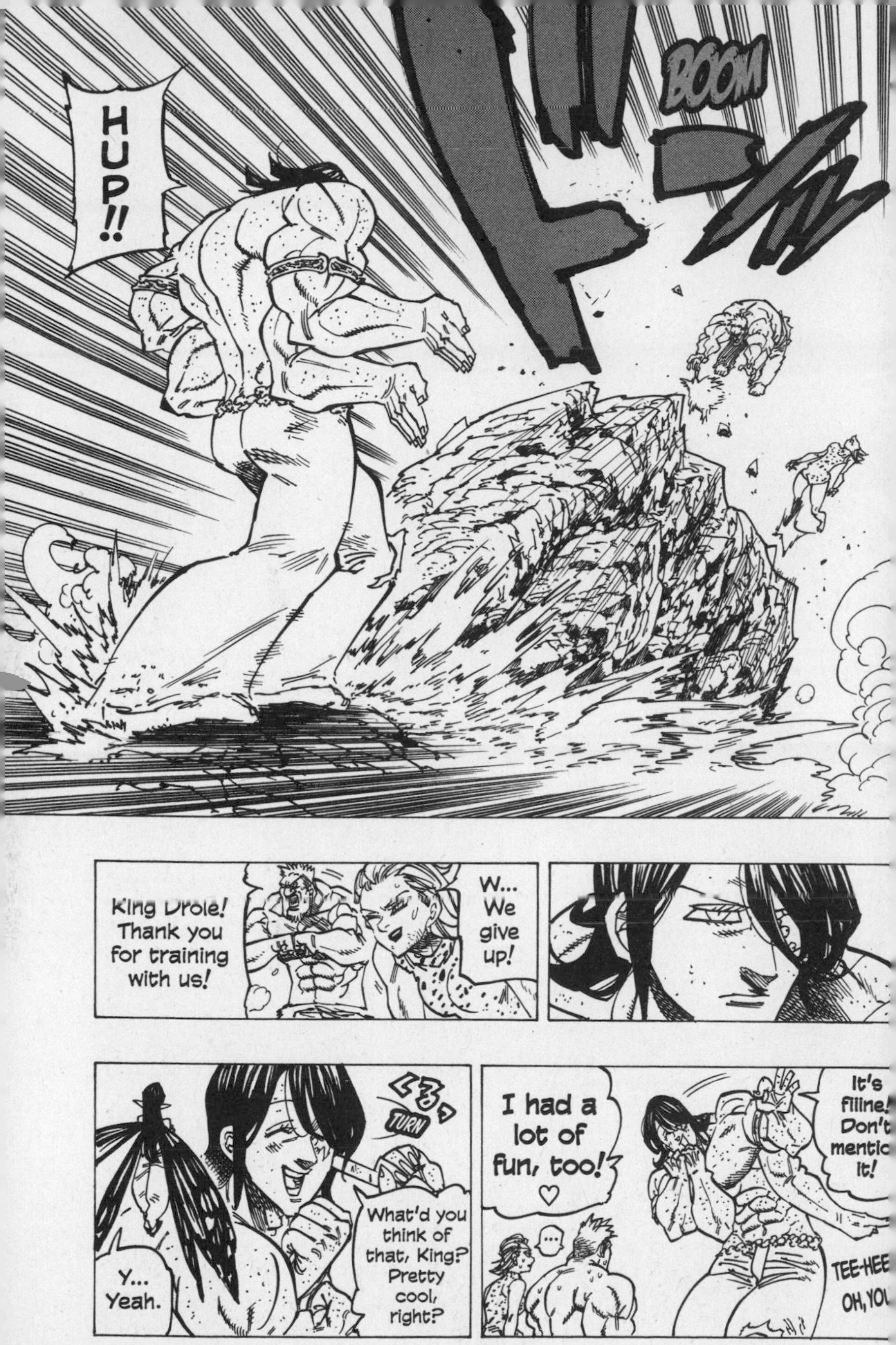
BOOM
HUP!!
W... We give up!
King Drole! Thank you for training with us!
It's fiiine! Don't mentic it!
TEE-HEE OH, YOU
I had a lot of fun, too! ♡
...
TURN
What'd you think of that, King? Pretty cool, right?
Y... Yeah.

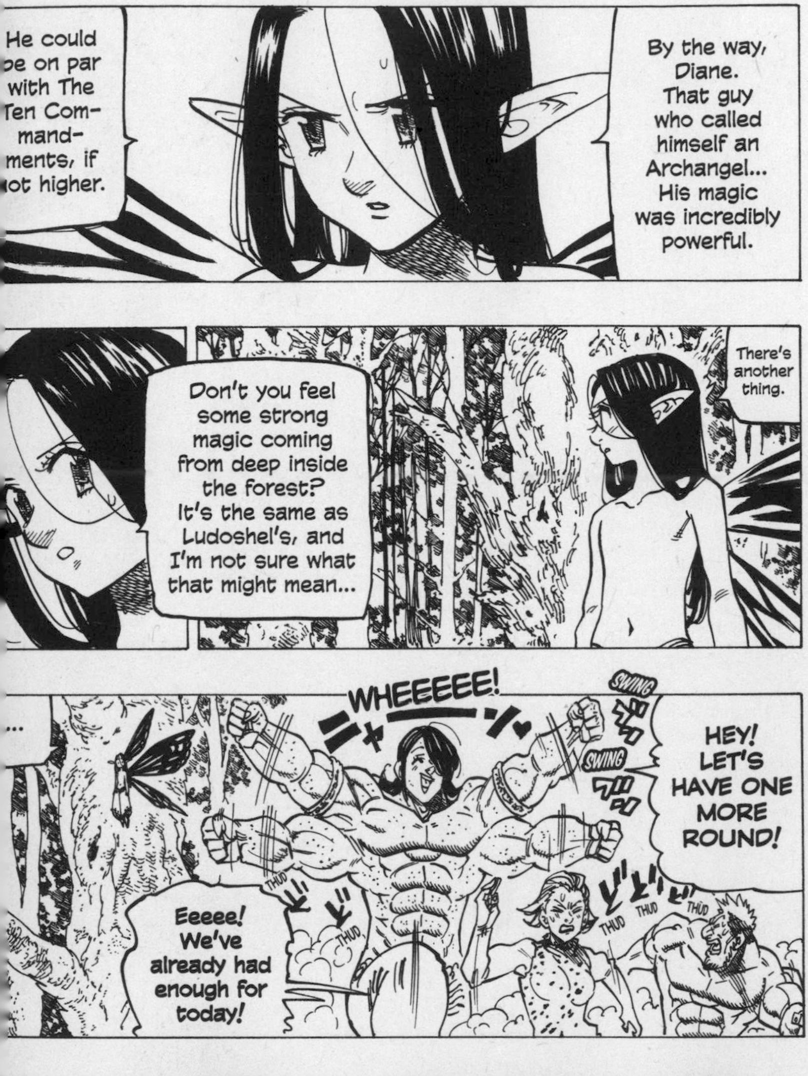
By the way, Diane. That guy who called himself an Archangel... His magic was incredibly powerful.
He could be on par with The Ten Commandments, if not higher.
There's another thing.
Don't you feel some strong magic coming from deep inside the forest? It's the same as Ludoshel's, and I'm not sure what that might mean...
HEY! LET'S HAVE ONE MORE ROUND!
SWING
SWING
WHEEEEEE!
THUD
THUD
THUD
THUD
THUD
Eeeee! We've already had enough for today!
...
Diane ...
Haah.
When will our test finally be over?

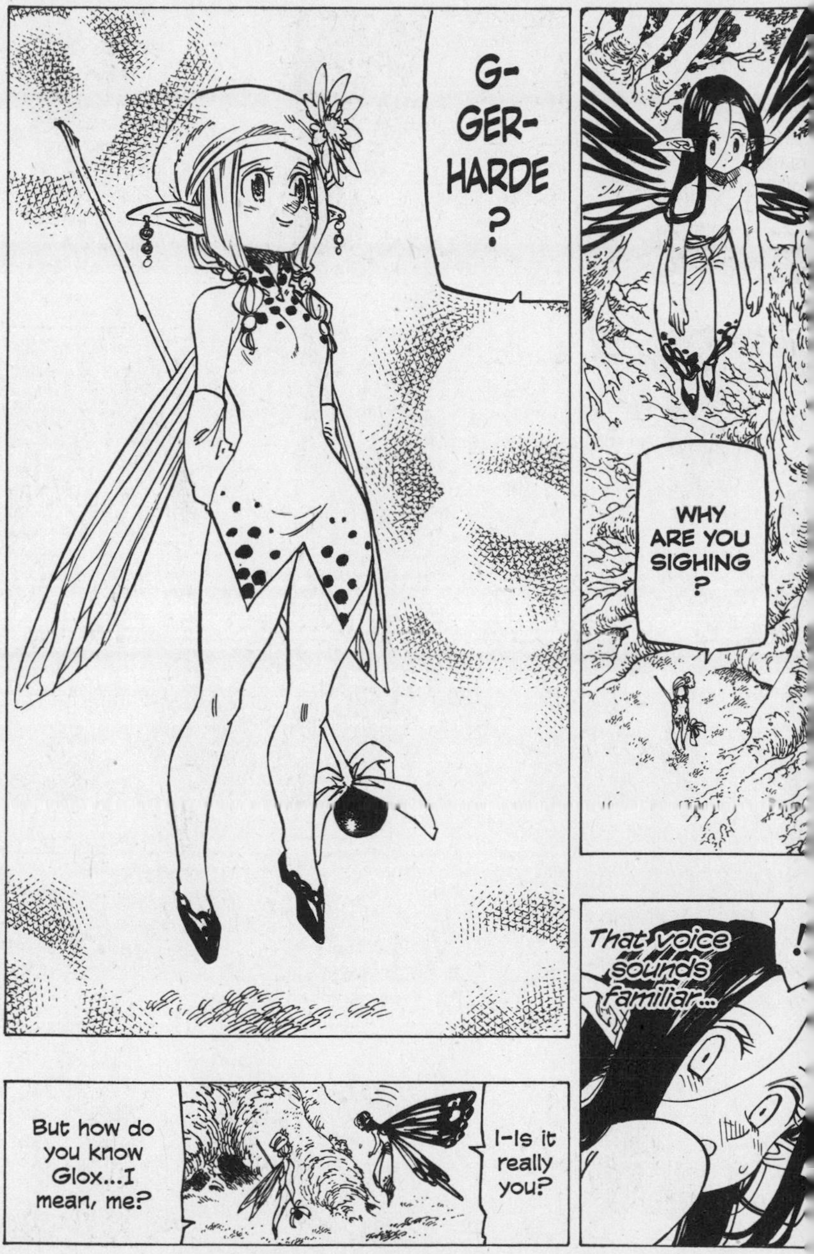
WHY ARE YOU SIGHING ?
!
That voice sounds familiar...
G- GER- HARDE ?
I-Is it really you?
But how do you know Glox...I mean, me?

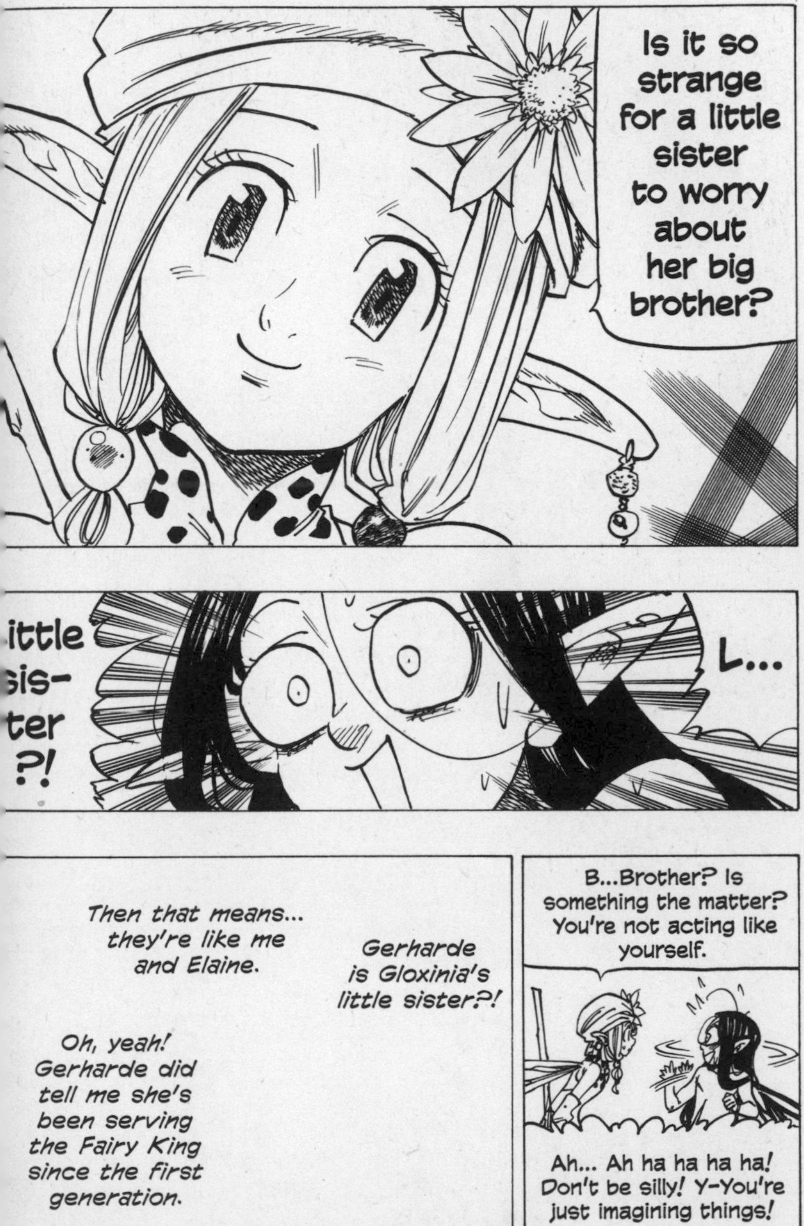
Is it so strange for a little sister to worry about her big brother?
L...
ittle sis-ter ?!
B...Brother? Is something the matter? You're not acting like yourself.
Ah... Ah ha ha ha ha! Don't be silly! Y-You're just imagining things!
Gerharde is Gloxinia's little sister?!
Then that means... they're like me and Elaine.
Oh, yeah! Gerharde did tell me she's been serving the Fairy King since the first generation.

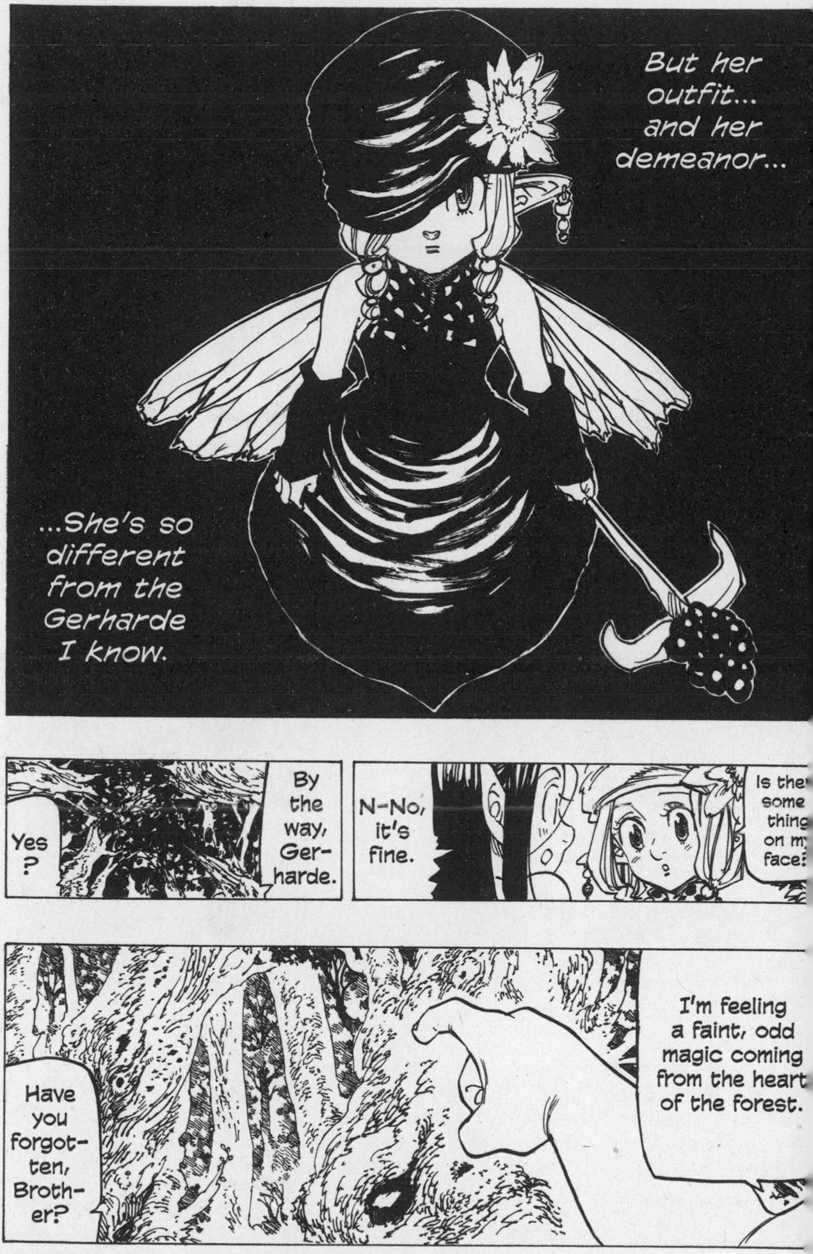
But her outfit... and her demeanor...
...She's so different from the Gerharde I know.
Is the some thing on m face
N-No, it's fine.
By the way, Ger-harde.
Yes ?
I'm feeling a faint, odd magic coming from the heart of the forest.
Have you forgot-ten, Broth-er?

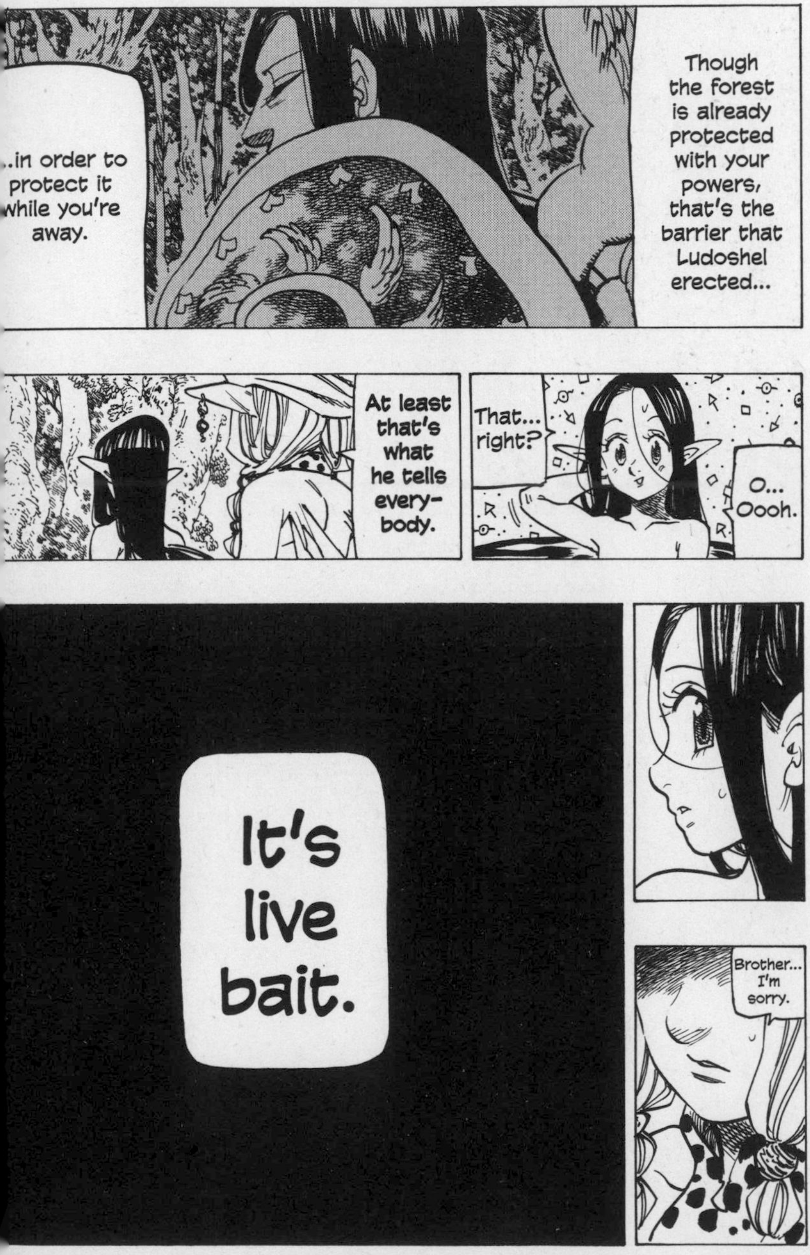
Though the forest is already protected with your powers, that's the barrier that Ludoshel erected...
..in order to protect it while you're away.
That... right?
O... Oooh.
At least that's what he tells every-body.
Brother... I'm sorry.
It's live bait.

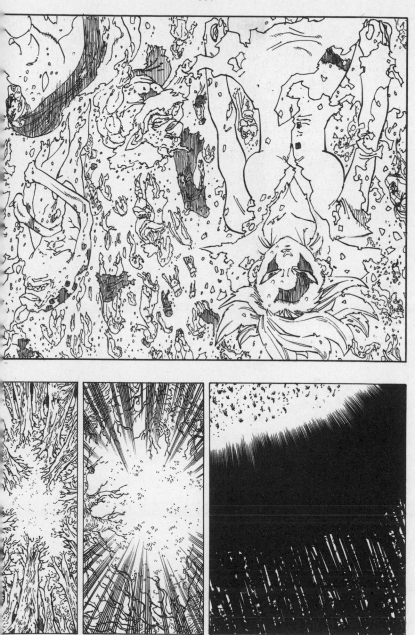

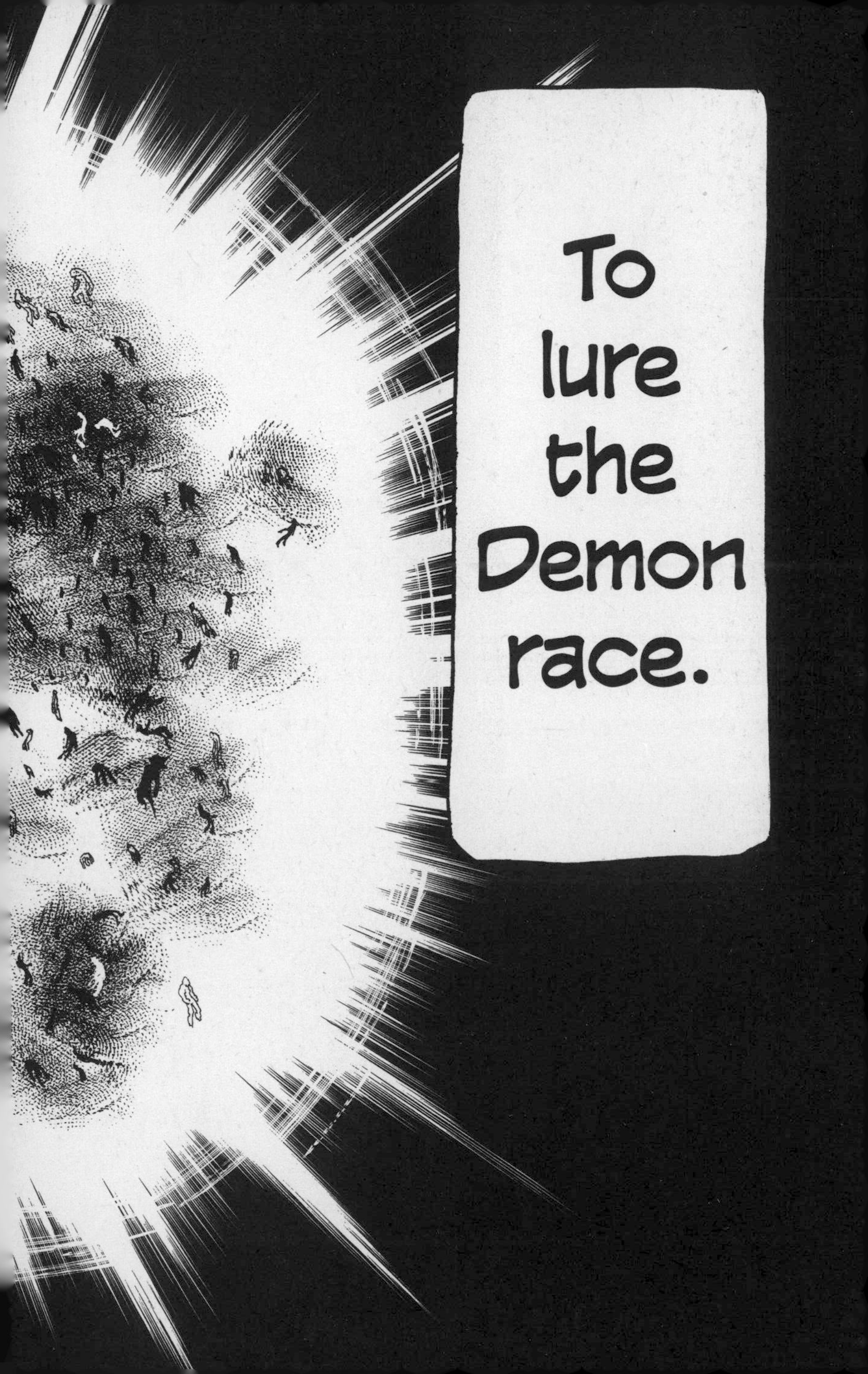
To lure the Demon race.

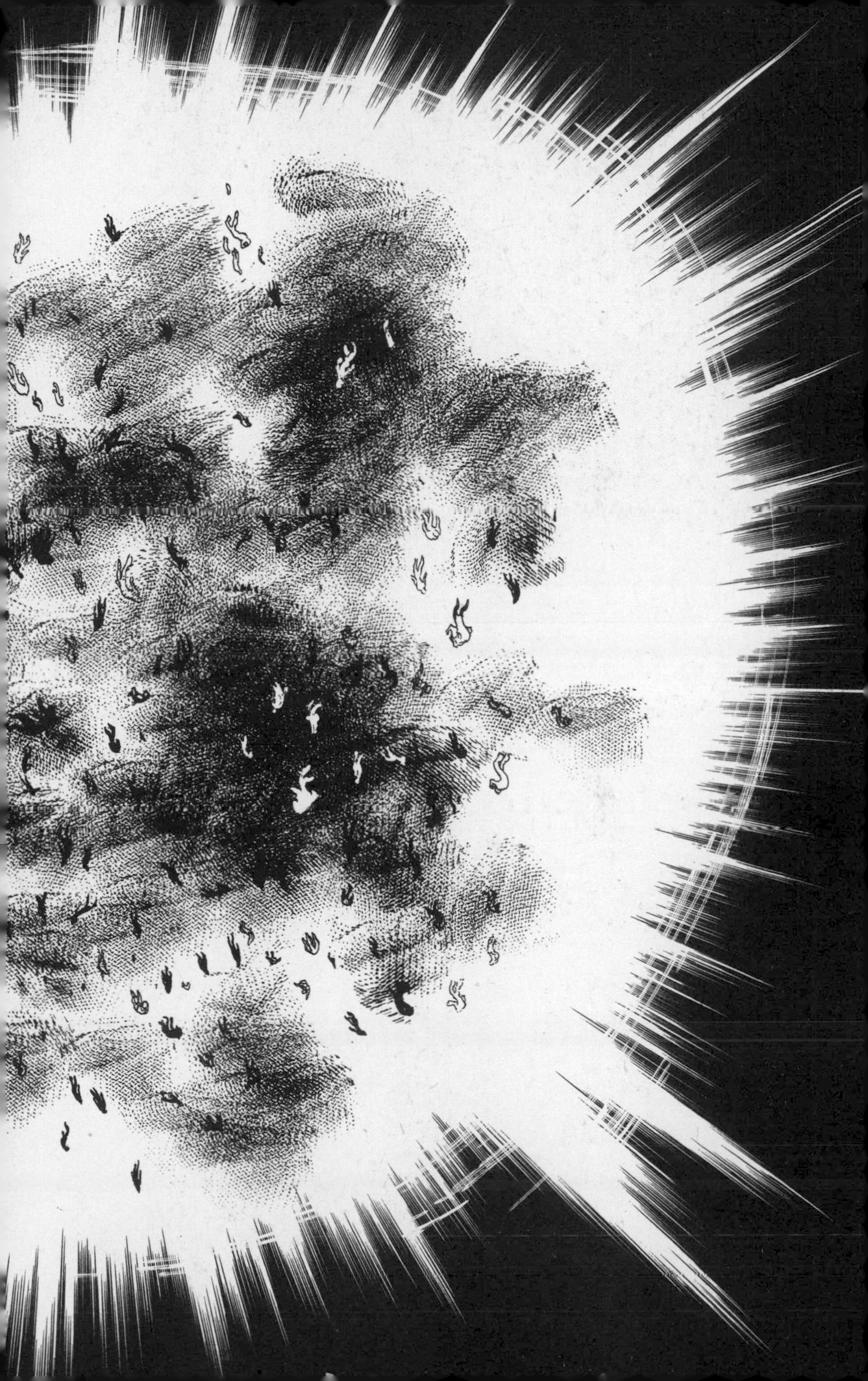

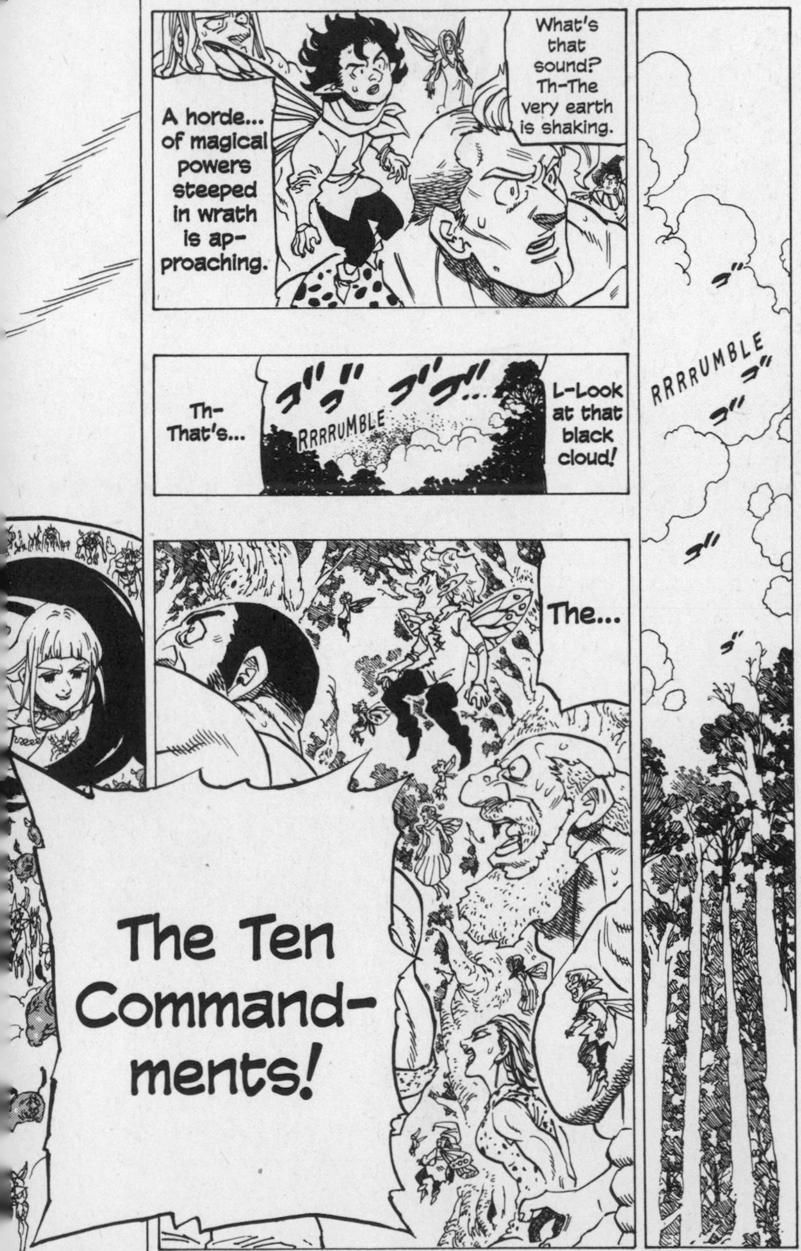

RRRRUMBLE
ゴゴ
What's that sound? Th-The very earth is shaking.
A horde... of magical powers steeped in wrath is approaching.
L-Look at that black cloud!
ゴゴ ゴゴ...
RRRRUMBLE
Th-That's...
The...
The Ten Commandments!

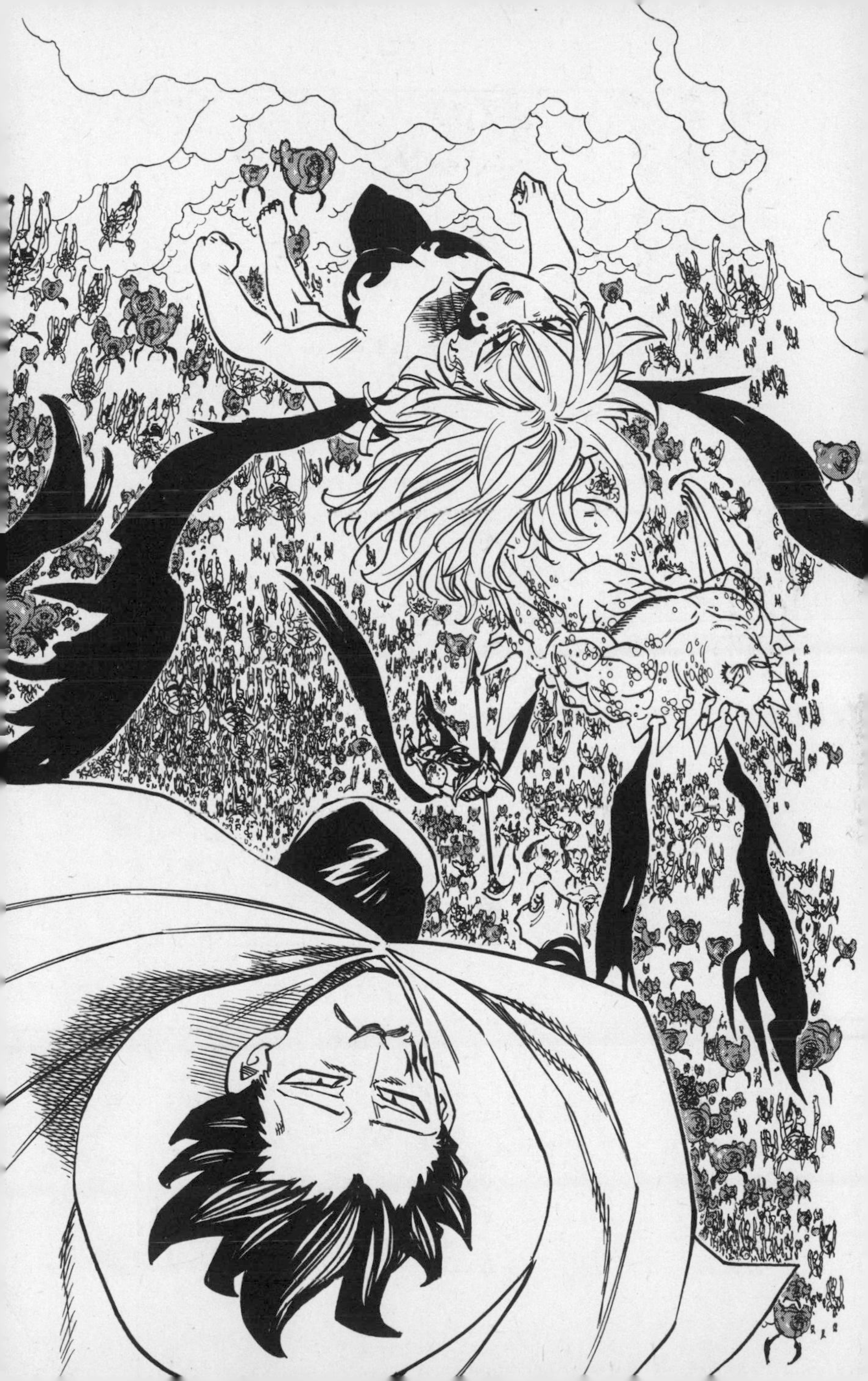

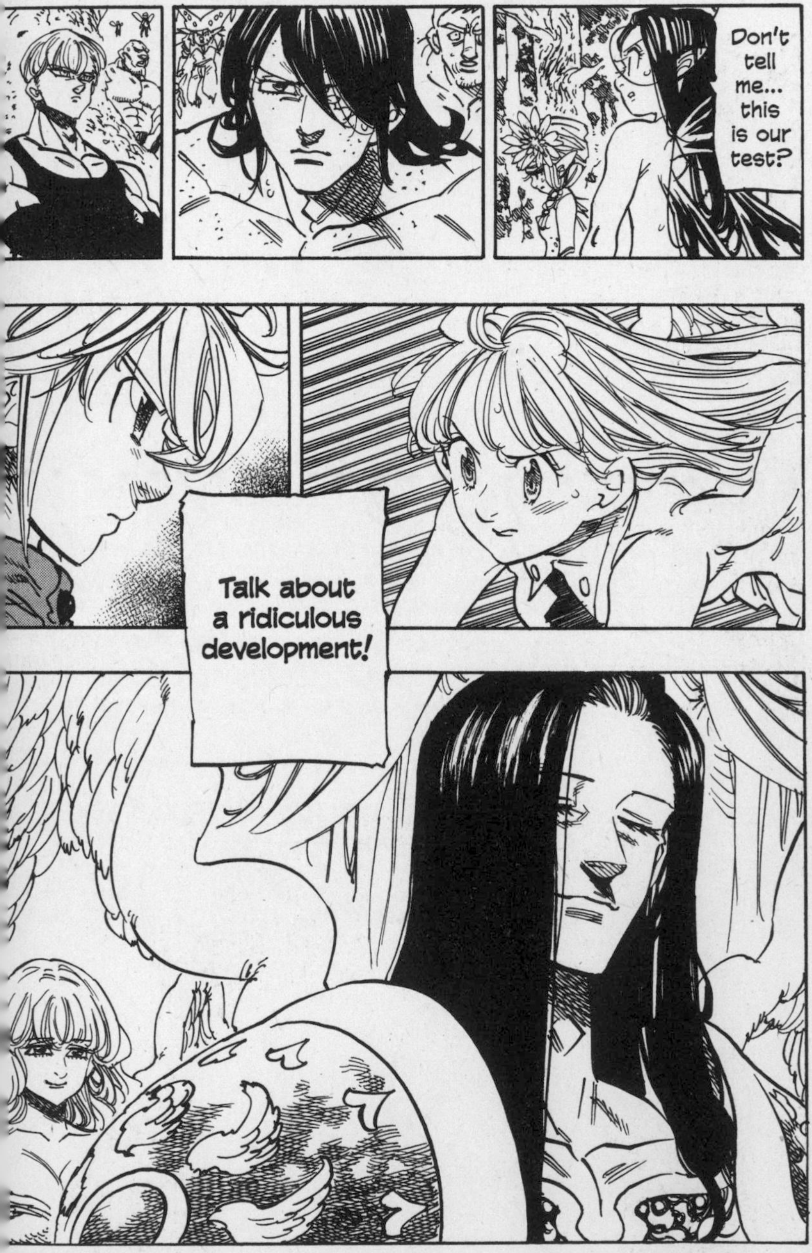
Don't tell me... this is our test?
Talk about a ridiculous development!

Chapter 204 - Let There Be Light

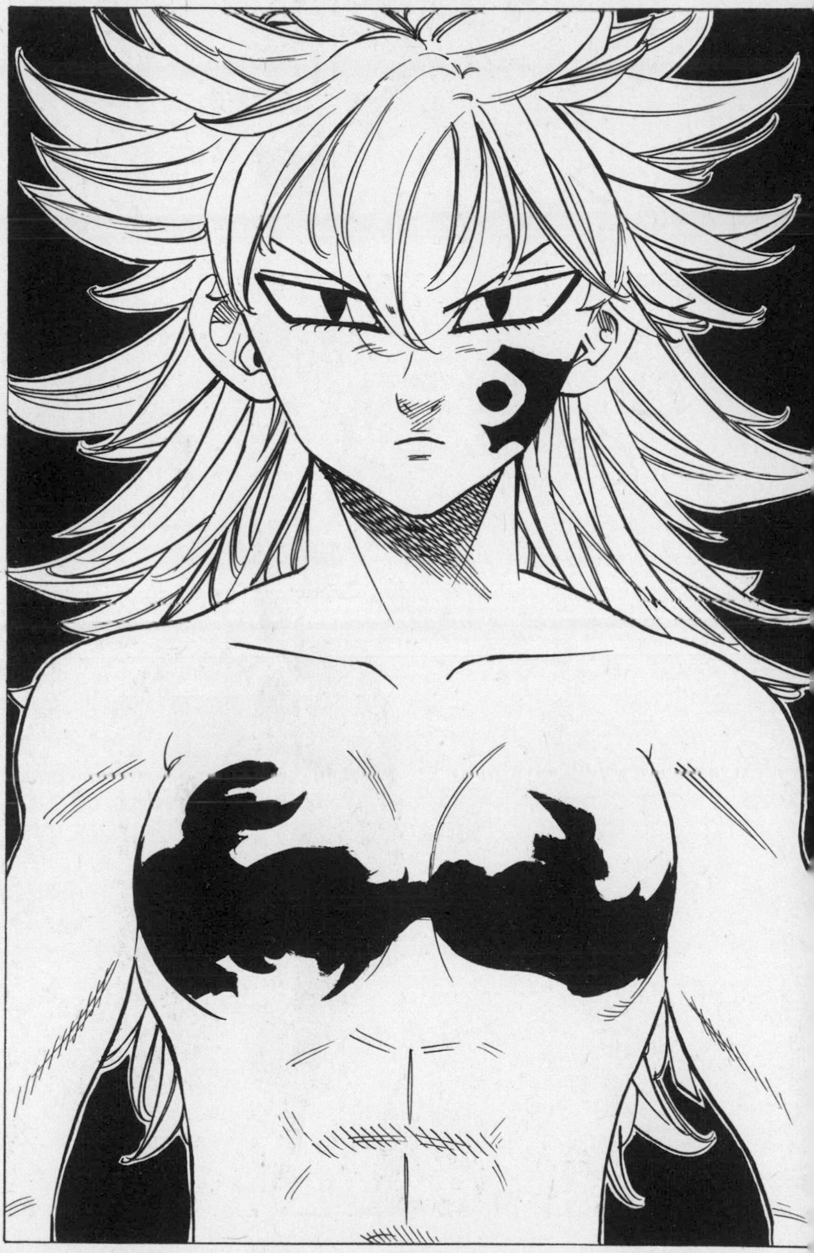

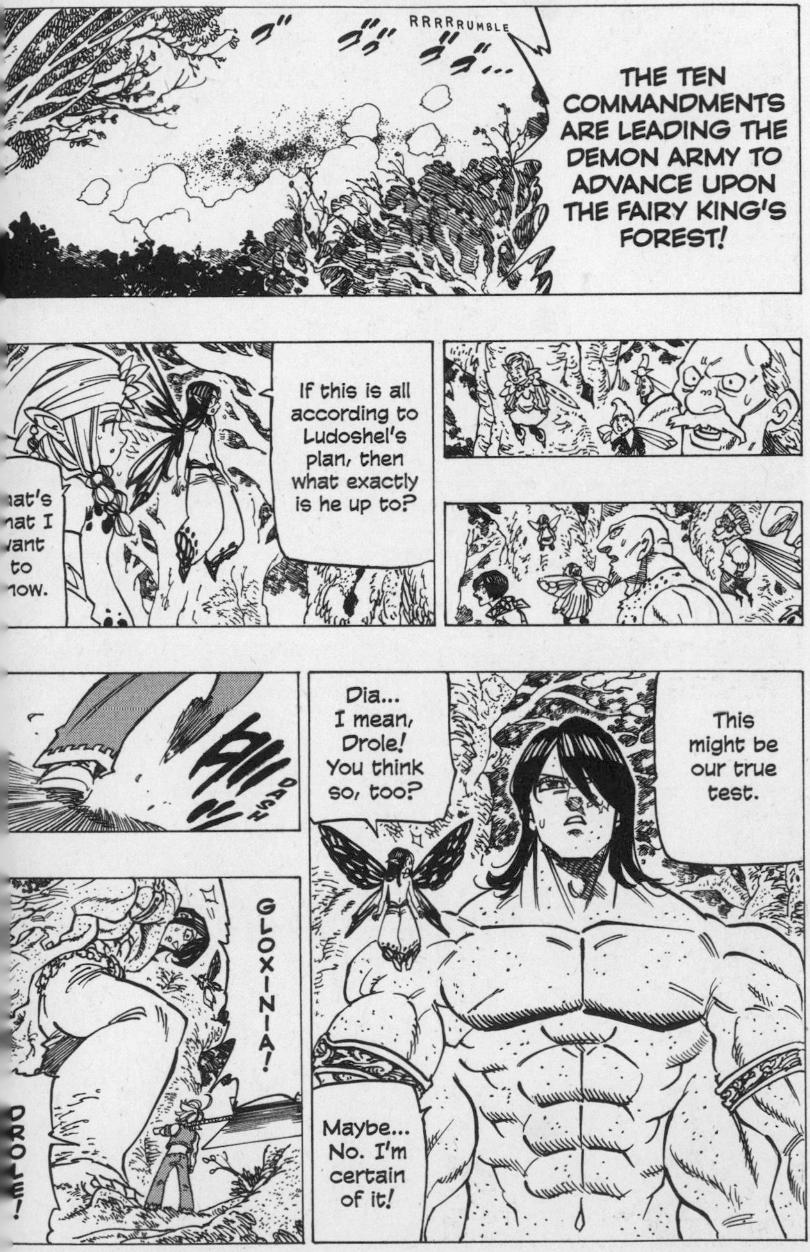
RRRRRUMBLE
THE TEN COMMANDMENTS ARE LEADING THE DEMON ARMY TO ADVANCE UPON THE FAIRY KING'S FOREST!
If this is all according to Ludoshel's plan, then what exactly is he up to?
This might be our true test.
Dia... I mean, Drole! You think so, too?
Maybe... No. I'm certain of it!
DASH
GLOXINIA!
DROLE!

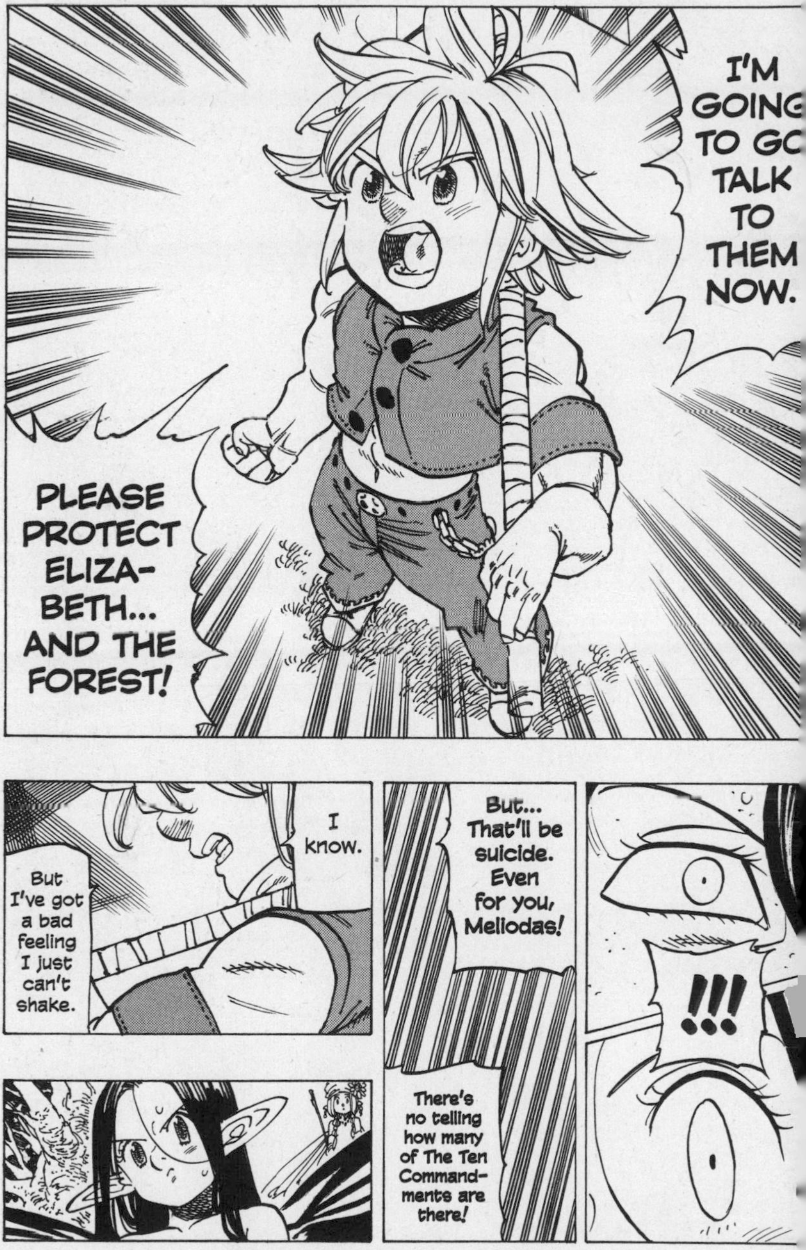
I'M GOING TO GO TALK TO THEM NOW.
PLEASE PROTECT ELIZA-BETH... AND THE FOREST!
!!!
But... That'll be suicide. Even for you, Meliodas!
There's no telling how many of The Ten Command-ments are there!
I know.
But I've got a bad feeling I just can't shake.

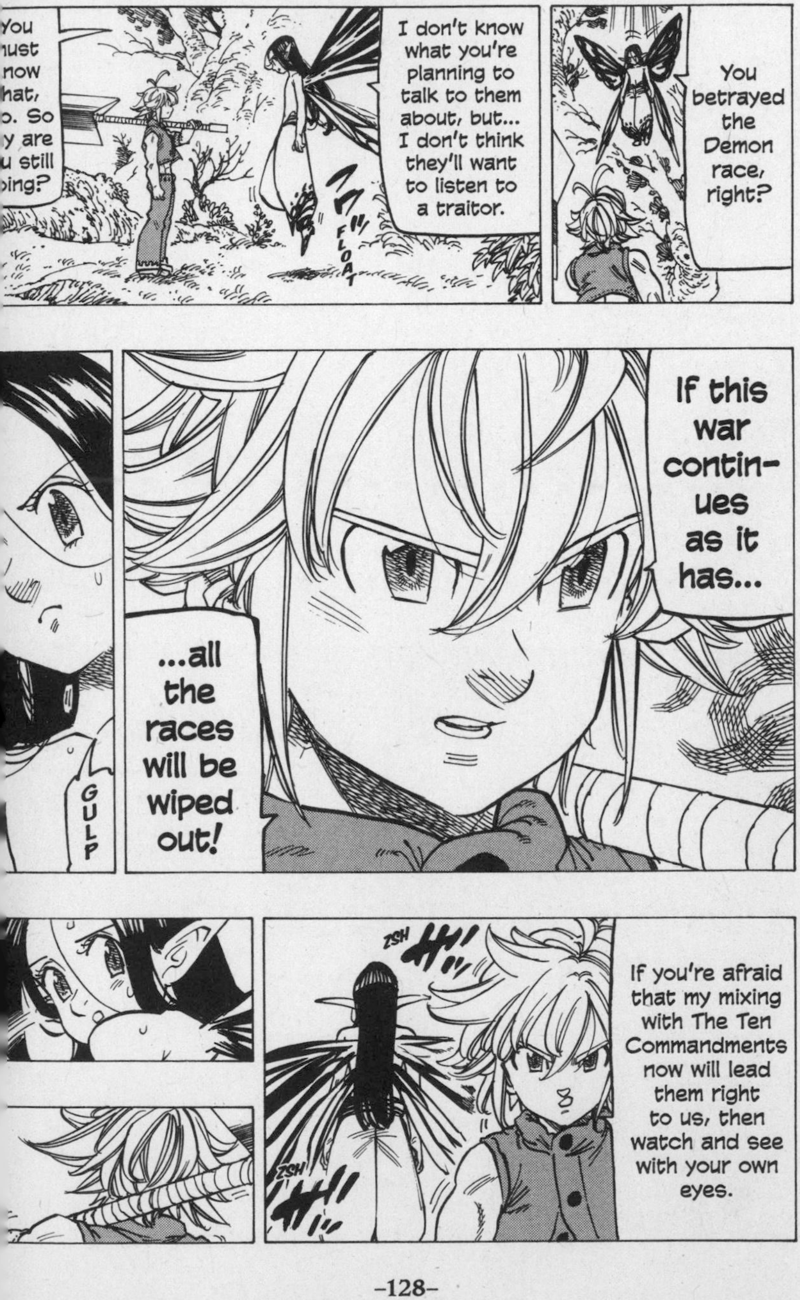
You betrayed the Demon race, right?
I don't know what you're planning to talk to them about, but... I don't think they'll want to listen to a traitor.
FLOAT
If this war contin-ues as it has...
...all the races will be wiped out!
GULP
If you're afraid that my mixing with The Ten Commandments now will lead them right to us, then watch and see with your own eyes.
ZSH
ZSH

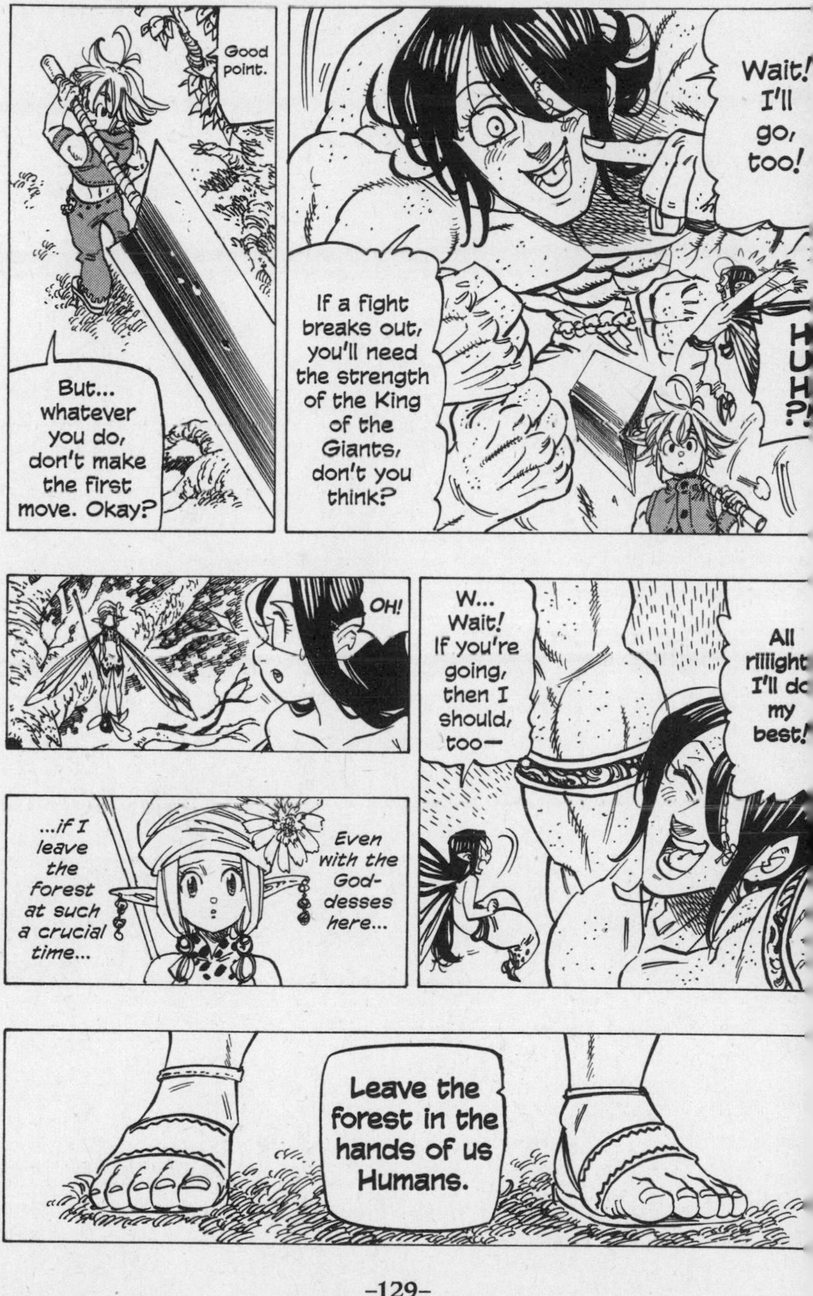
Wait! I'll go, too!
HUH?!
If a fight breaks out, you'll need the strength of the King of the Giants, don't you think?
Good point.
But... whatever you do, don't make the first move. Okay?
All riiight I'll do my best!
W... Wait! If you're going, then I should, too—
OH!
Even with the God-desses here...
...if I leave the forest at such a crucial time...
Leave the forest in the hands of us Humans.

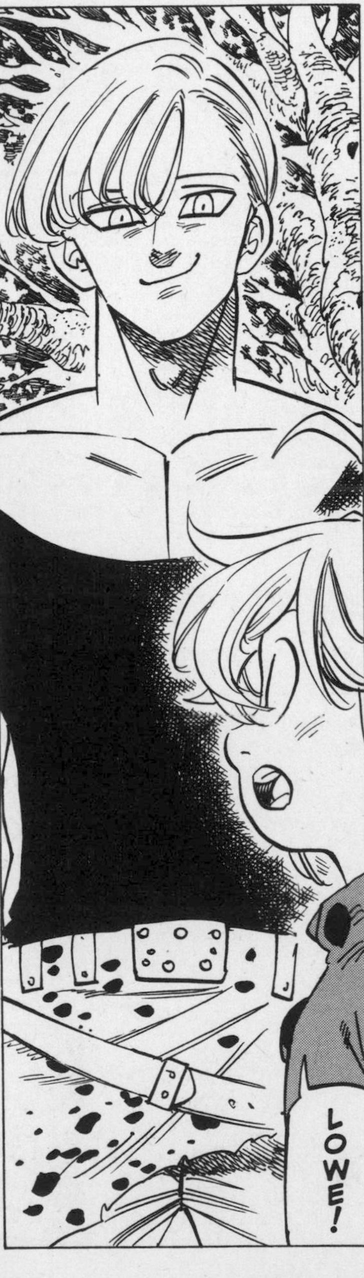
LOWE!

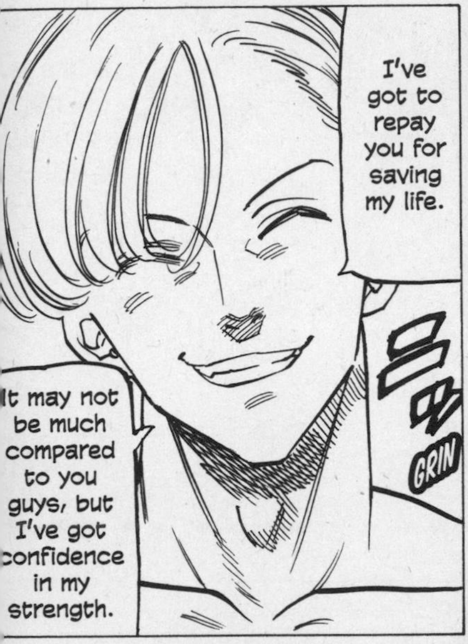
I've got to repay you for saving my life.
GRIN
It may not be much compared to you guys, but I've got confidence in my strength.

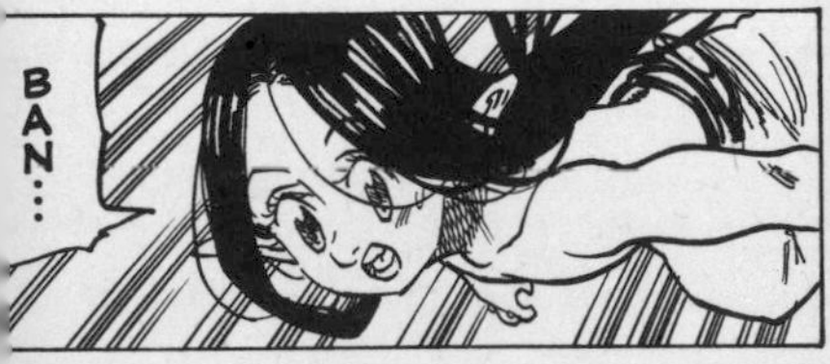
BAN...

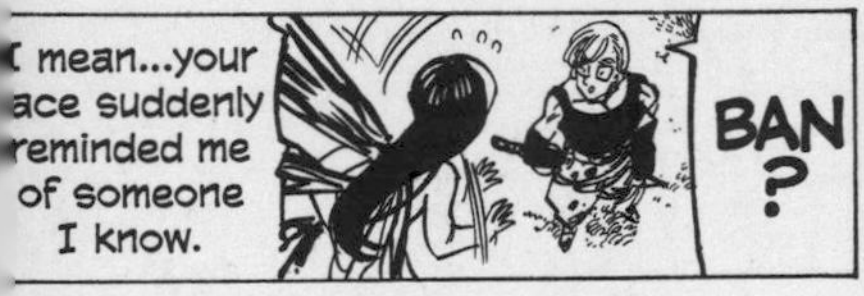
BAN?
I mean...your face suddenly reminded me of someone I know.

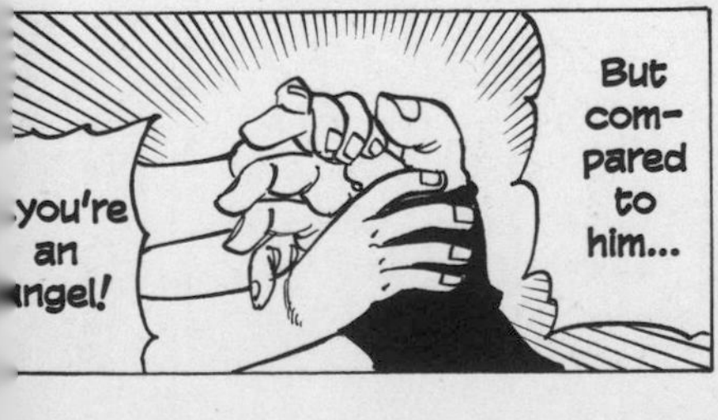
But compared to him...
you're an angel!

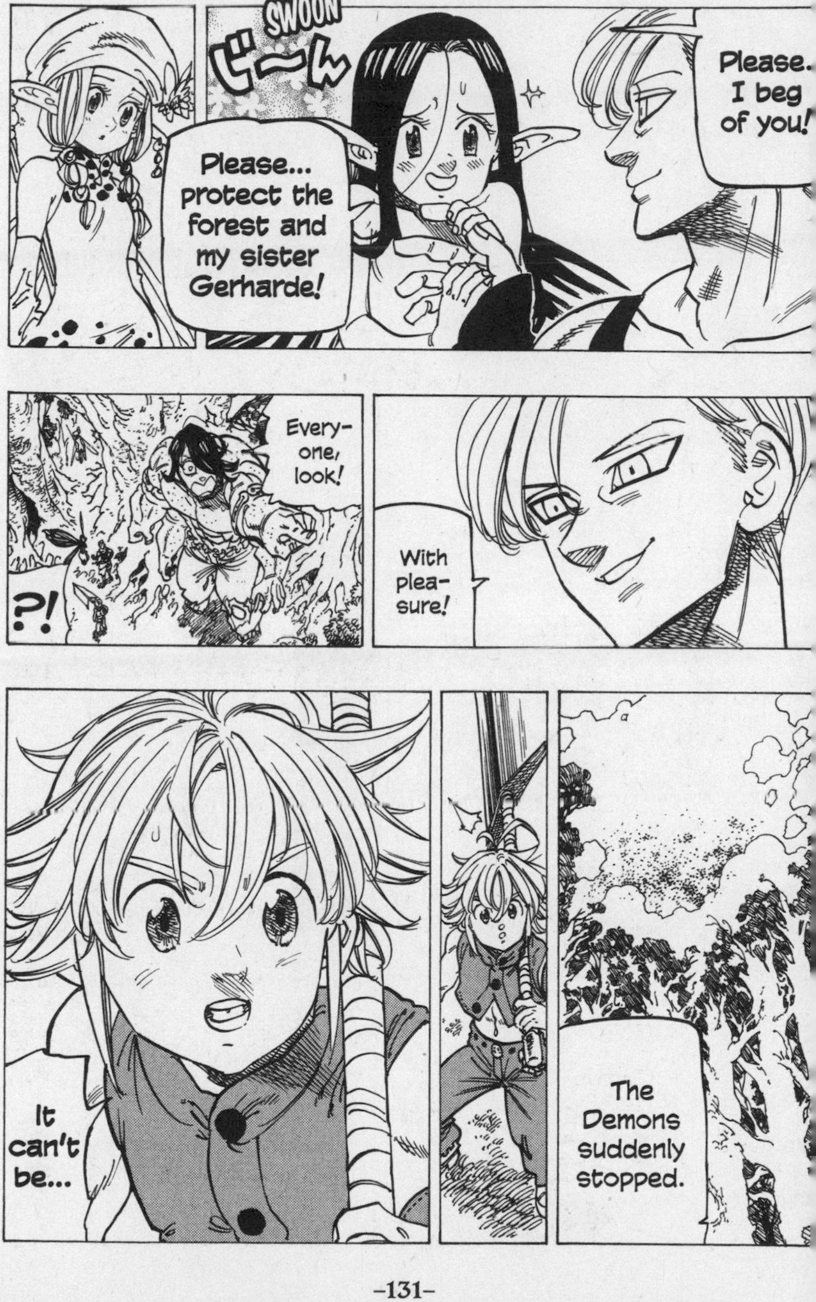
Please. I beg of you!
SWOON
Please... protect the forest and my sister Gerharde!
With plea-sure!
Every-one, look!
?!
The Demons suddenly stopped.
It can't be...

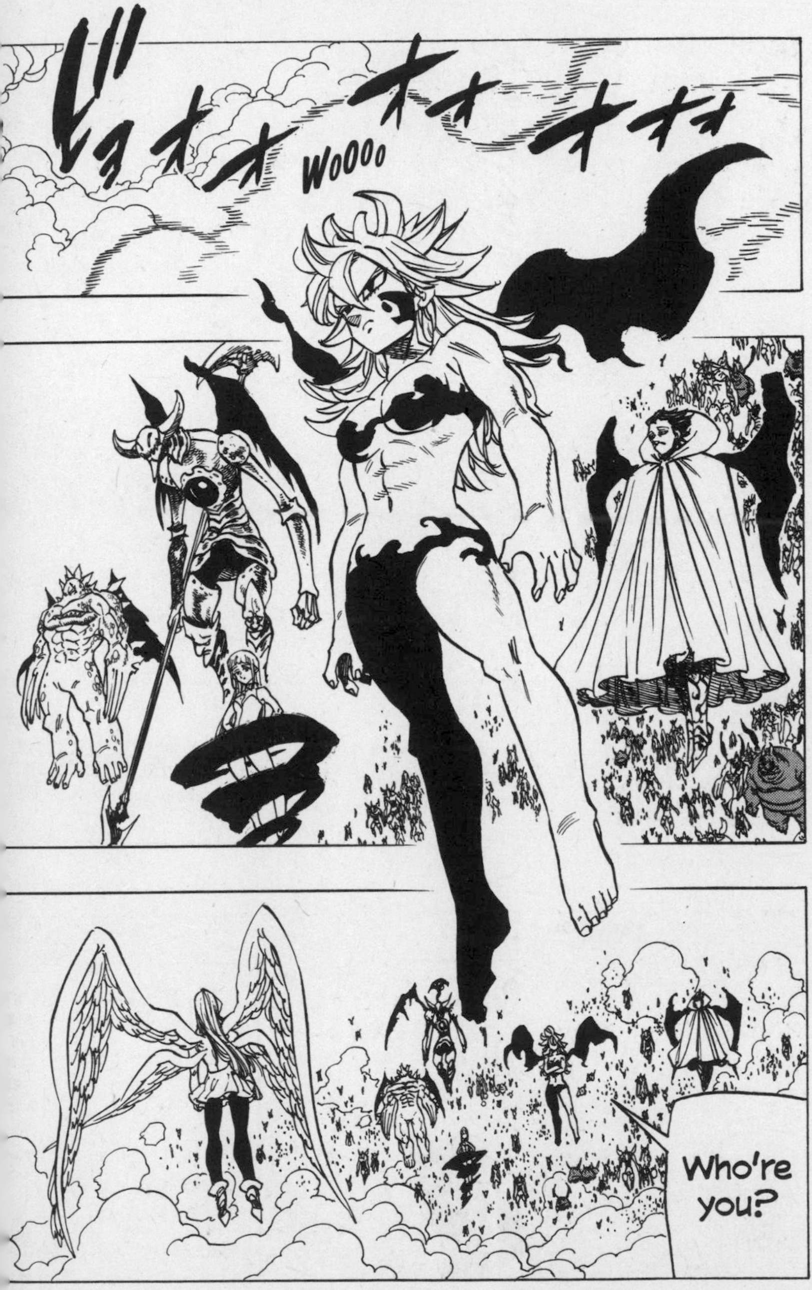
ジョオオオオオオオ
WOOOO
Who're you?

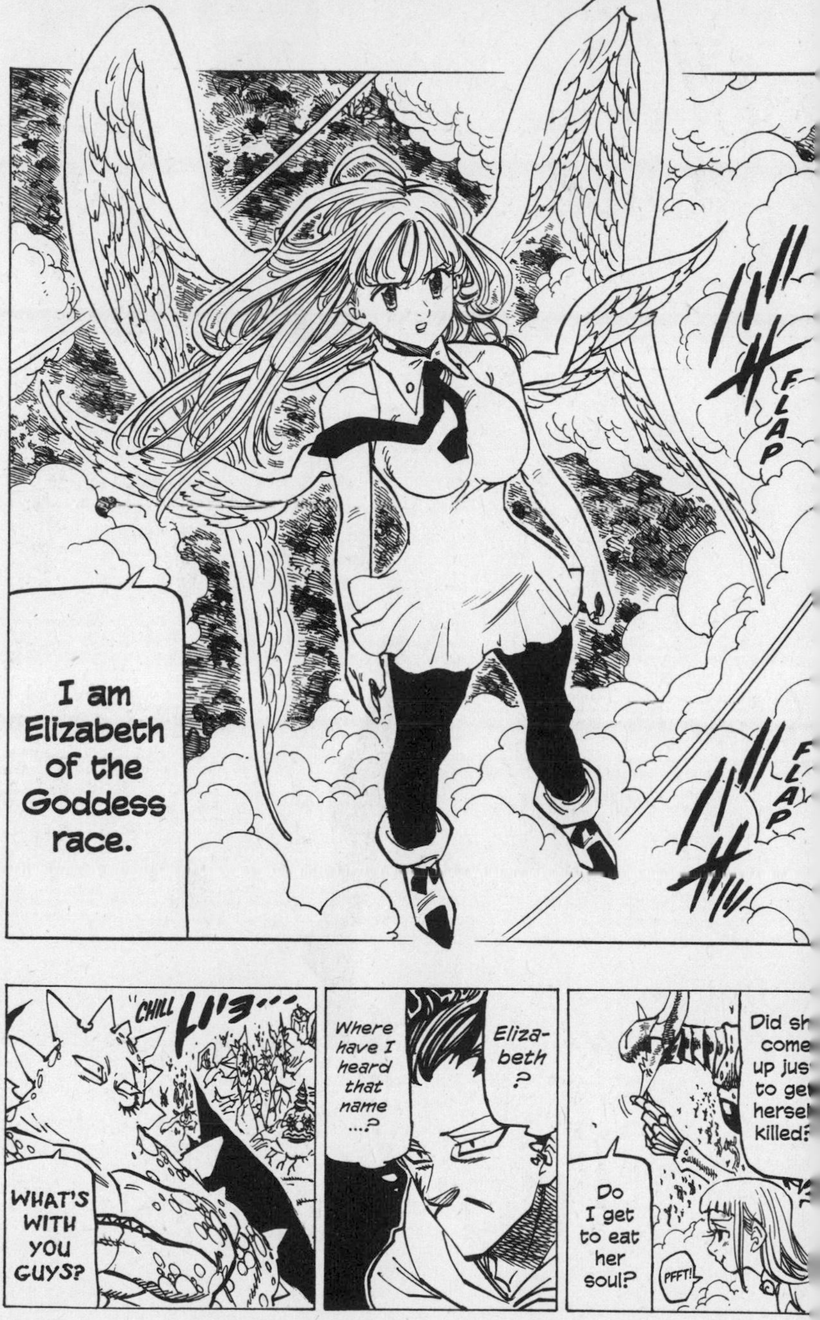
FLAP
FLAP
I am Elizabeth of the Goddess race.
Did sh come up jus to ge hersel killed?
Do I get to eat her soul?
PFFT!
Eliza-beth?
Where have I heard that name...?
CHILL
WHAT'S WITH YOU GUYS?

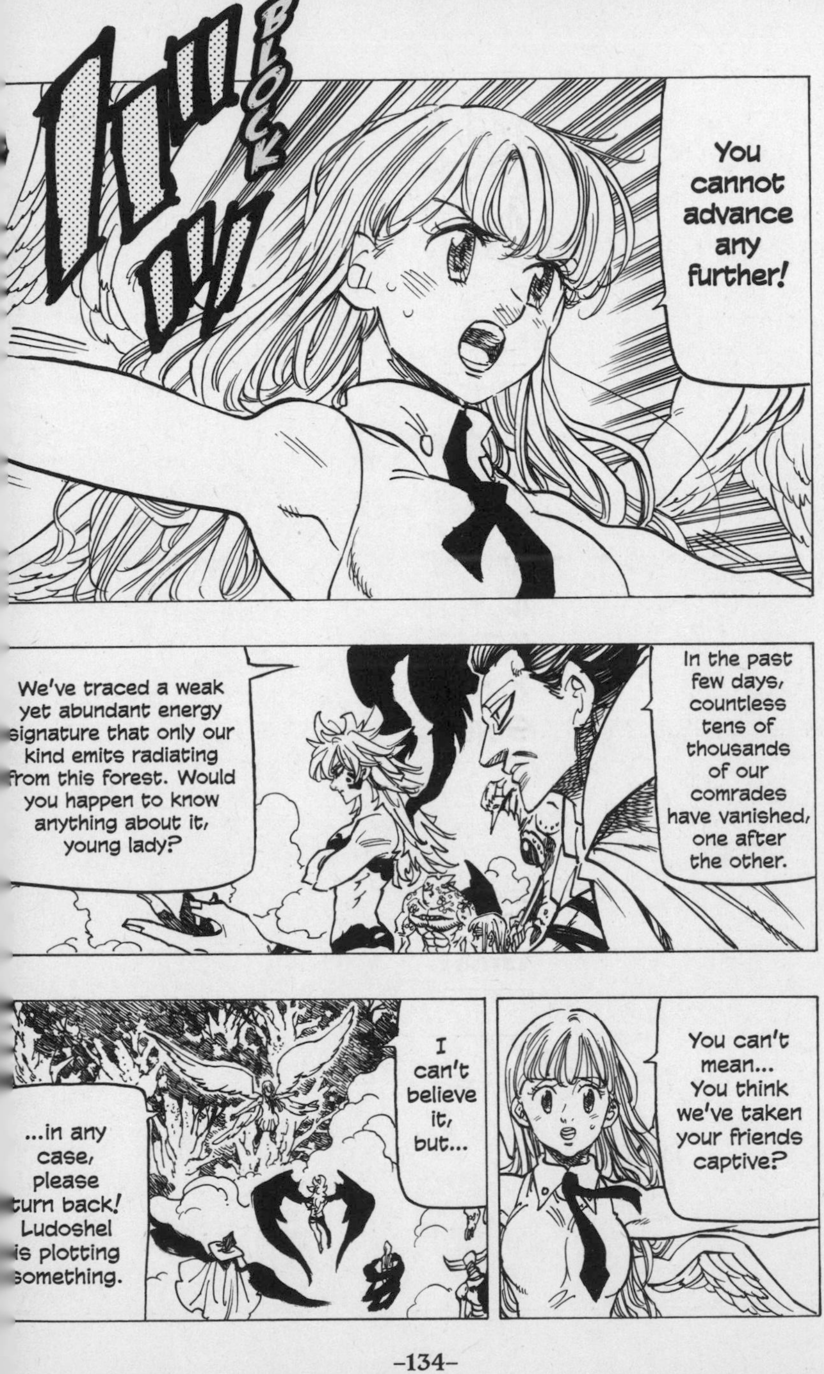
BLOCK
You cannot advance any further!
In the past few days, countless tens of thousands of our comrades have vanished, one after the other.
We've traced a weak yet abundant energy signature that only our kind emits radiating from this forest. Would you happen to know anything about it, young lady?
You can't mean... You think we've taken your friends captive?
I can't believe it, but...
...in any case, please turn back! Ludoshel is plotting something.

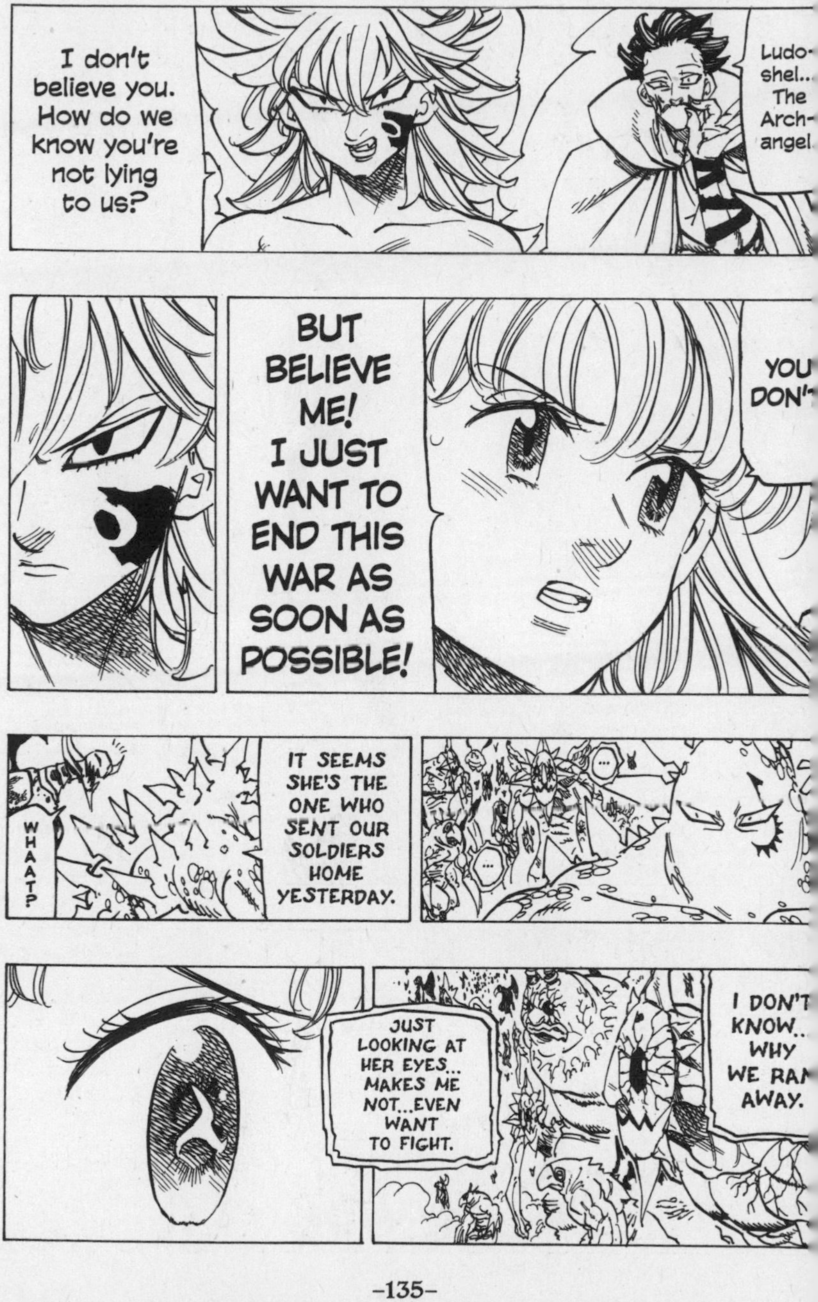
Ludo-shel... The Arch-angel...
I don't believe you. How do we know you're not lying to us?
YOU DON'
BUT BELIEVE ME! I JUST WANT TO END THIS WAR AS SOON AS POSSIBLE!
IT SEEMS SHE'S THE ONE WHO SENT OUR SOLDIERS HOME YESTERDAY.
WHAAT?
I DON'T KNOW... WHY WE RAN AWAY.
JUST LOOKING AT HER EYES... MAKES ME NOT...EVEN WANT TO FIGHT.

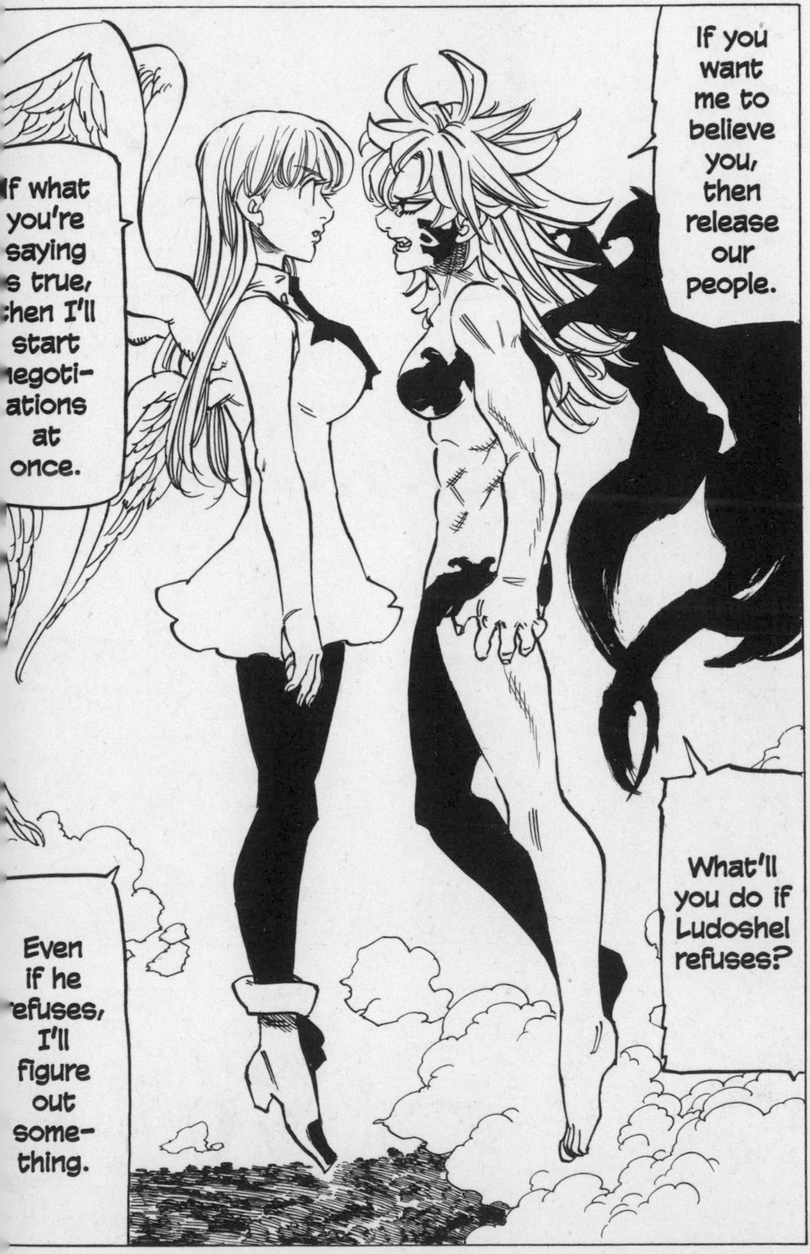
If you want me to believe you, then release our people.
If what you're saying s true, :hen I'll start negoti- ations at once.
What'll you do if Ludoshel refuses?
Even if he efuses, I'll figure out some- thing.

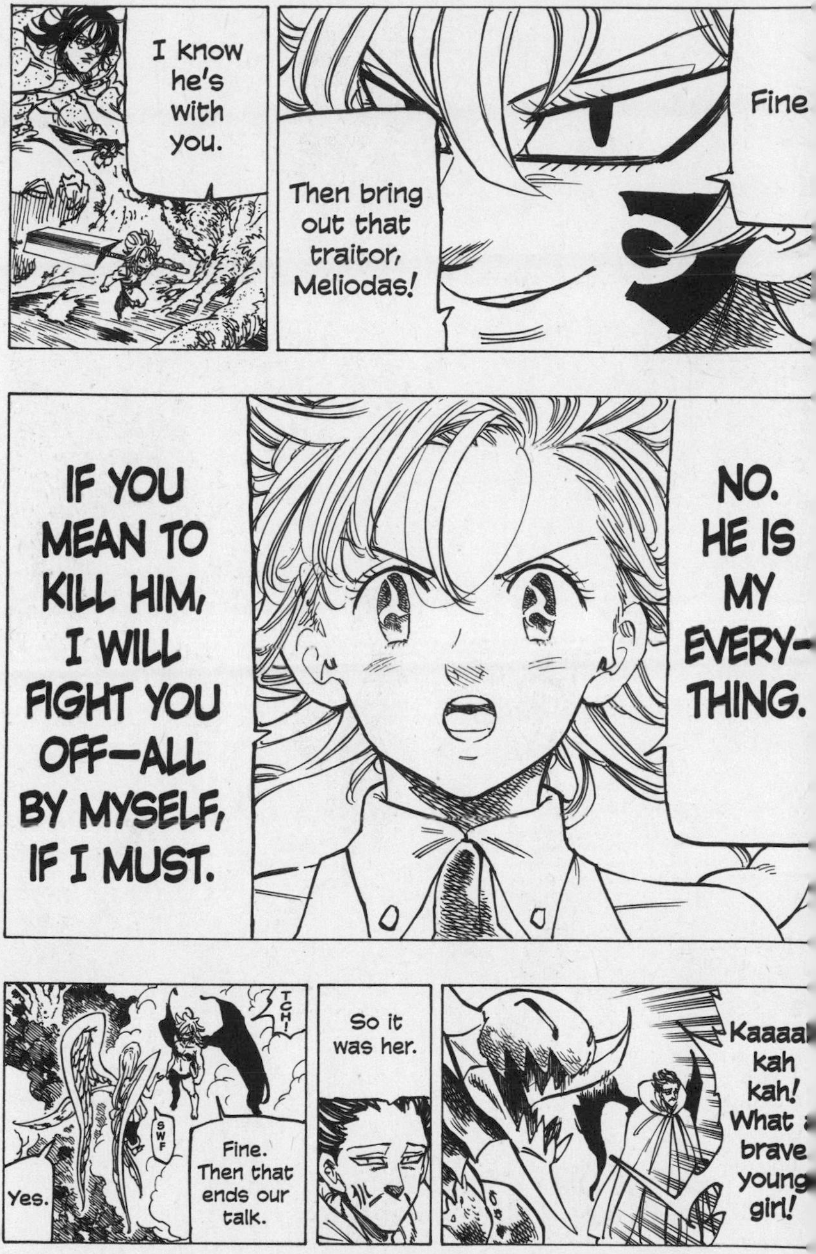
Fine
Then bring out that traitor, Meliodas!
I know he's with you.
NO. HE IS MY EVERY-THING.
IF YOU MEAN TO KILL HIM, I WILL FIGHT YOU OFF—ALL BY MYSELF, IF I MUST.
Kaaaa kah kah! What brave young girl!
So it was her.
TCH!
Fine. Then that ends our talk.
SWF
Yes.

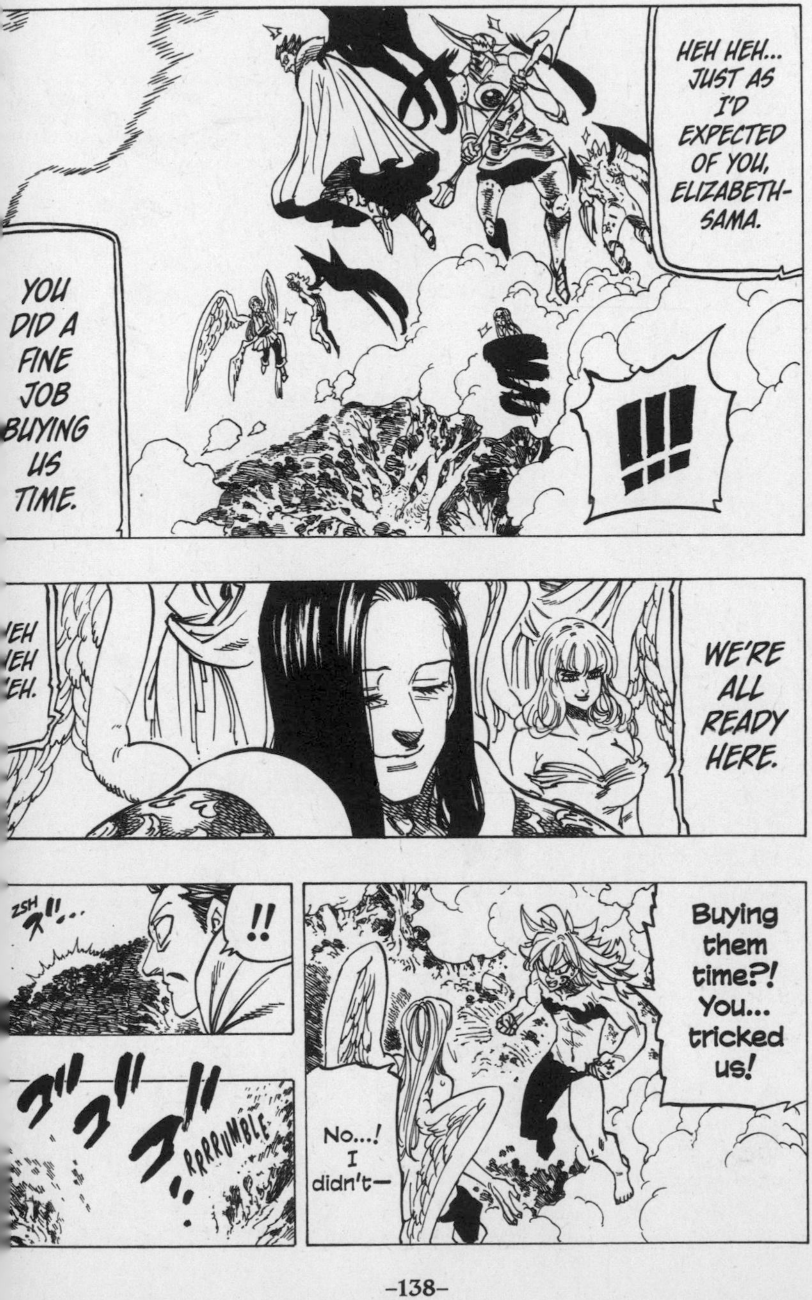
HEH HEH... JUST AS I'D EXPECTED OF YOU, ELIZABETH-SAMA.
!!!
YOU DID A FINE JOB BUYING US TIME.
WE'RE ALL READY HERE.
Buying them time?! You... tricked us!
No...! I didn't—
!!
ZSH
RRRUMBLE

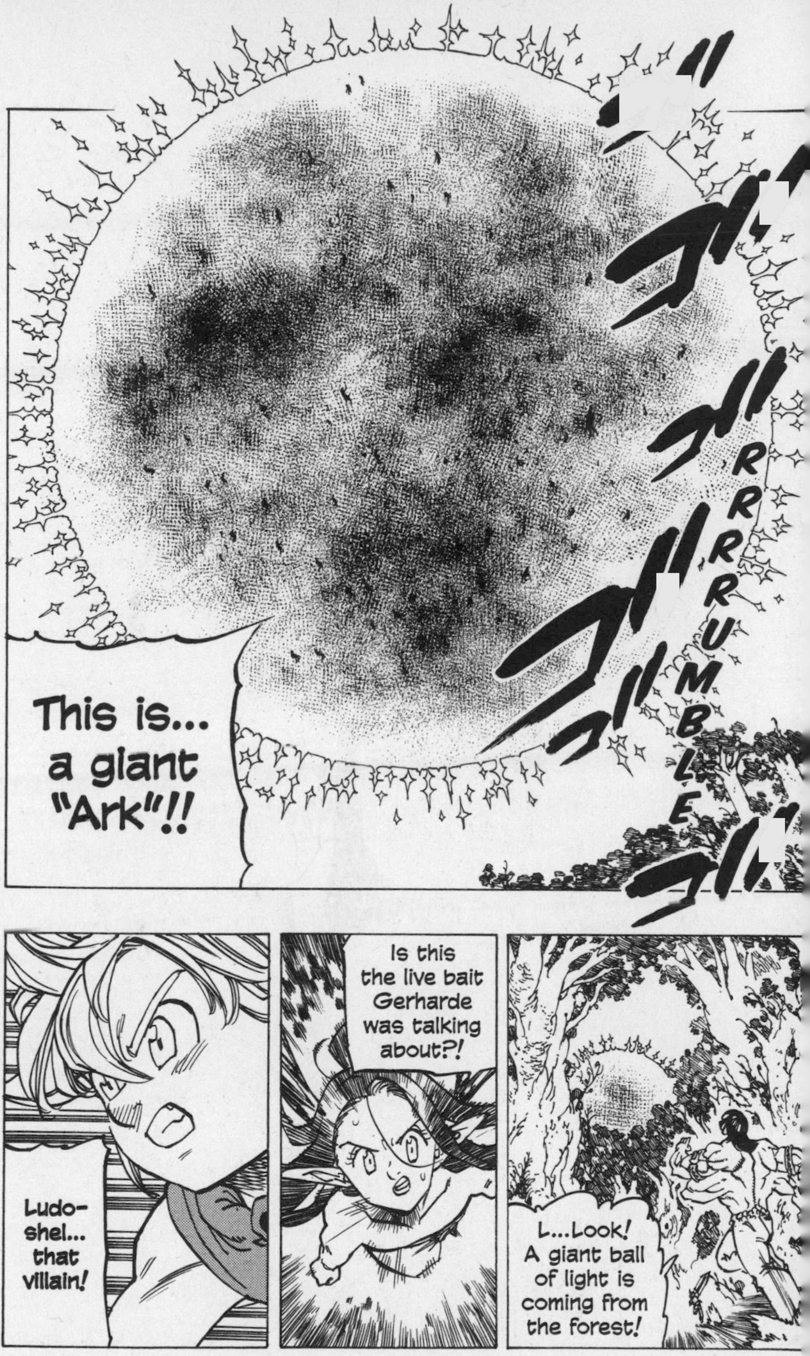
RRRRRUMBLE
This is... a giant "Ark"!!
L...Look! A giant ball of light is coming from the forest!
Is this the live bait Gerharde was talking about?!
Ludo-shel... that villain!

WOOOO
WOOOO
Within the "Ark," flesh and magic is eroding away... They're kept trapped in a state between life and death.
And none of them were even fighters in the war!
Sis-ter!
!!
DE...
...RI...
SWF
You've fulfilled your duty and earned your reward. Now rest.

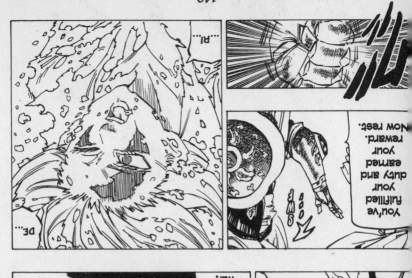

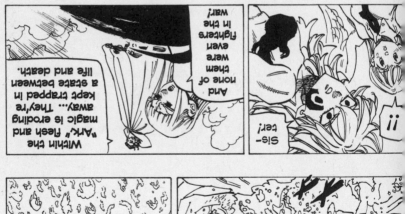

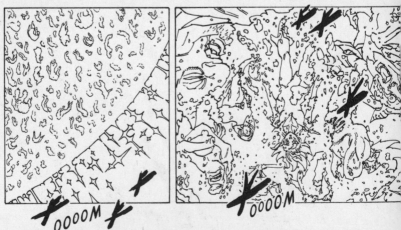

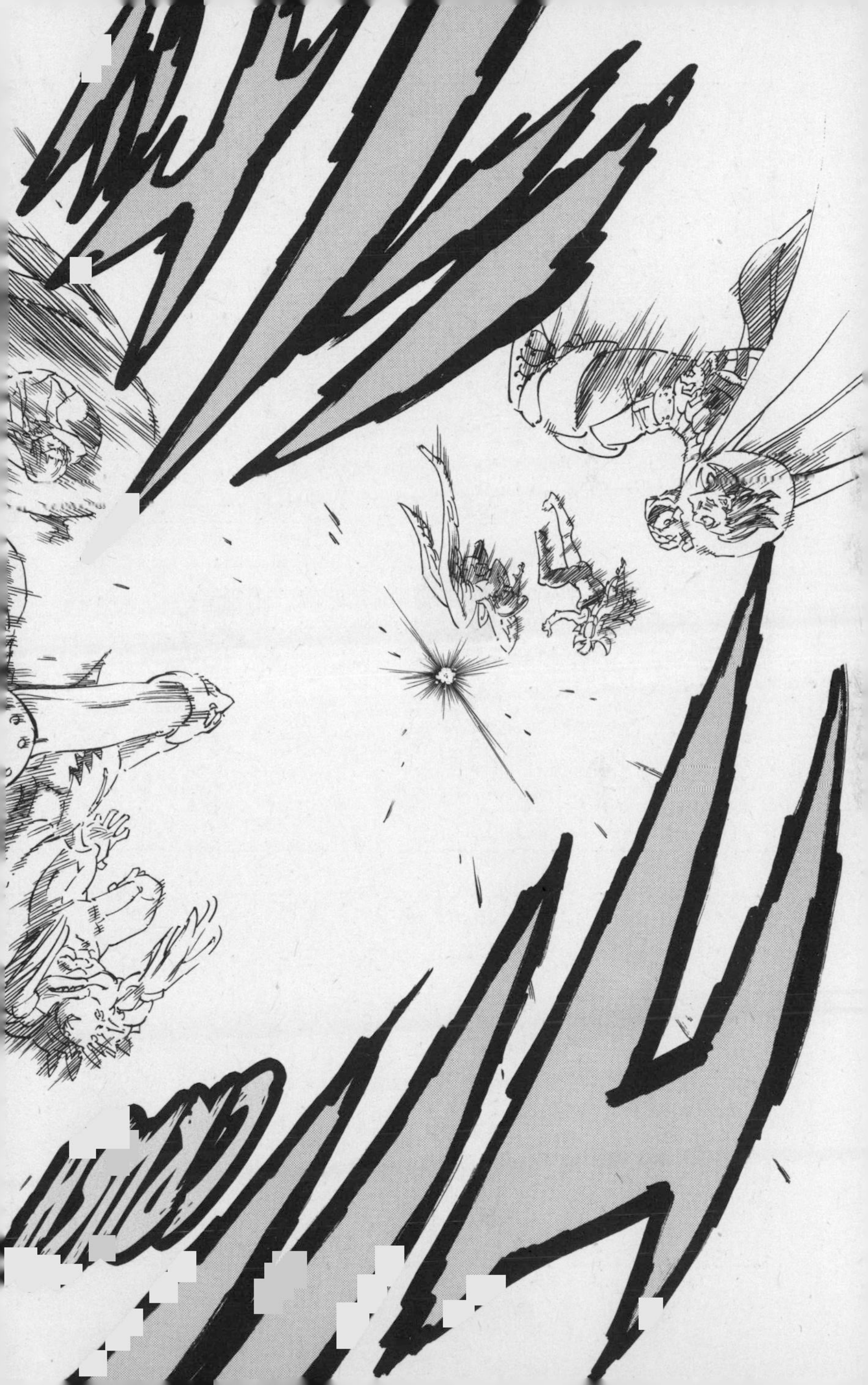

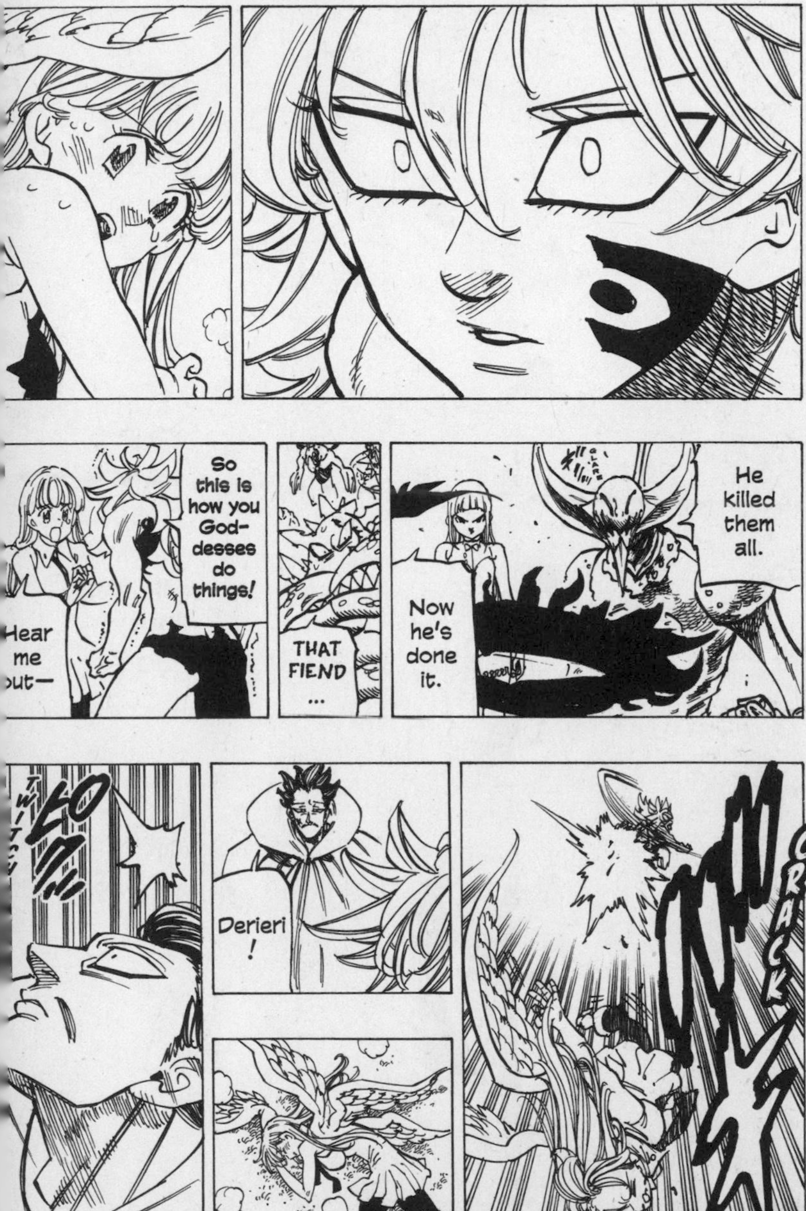
He killed them all.
Now he's done it.
THAT FIEND ...
So this is how you God-desses do things!
Hear me out—
Derieri!
CRACK

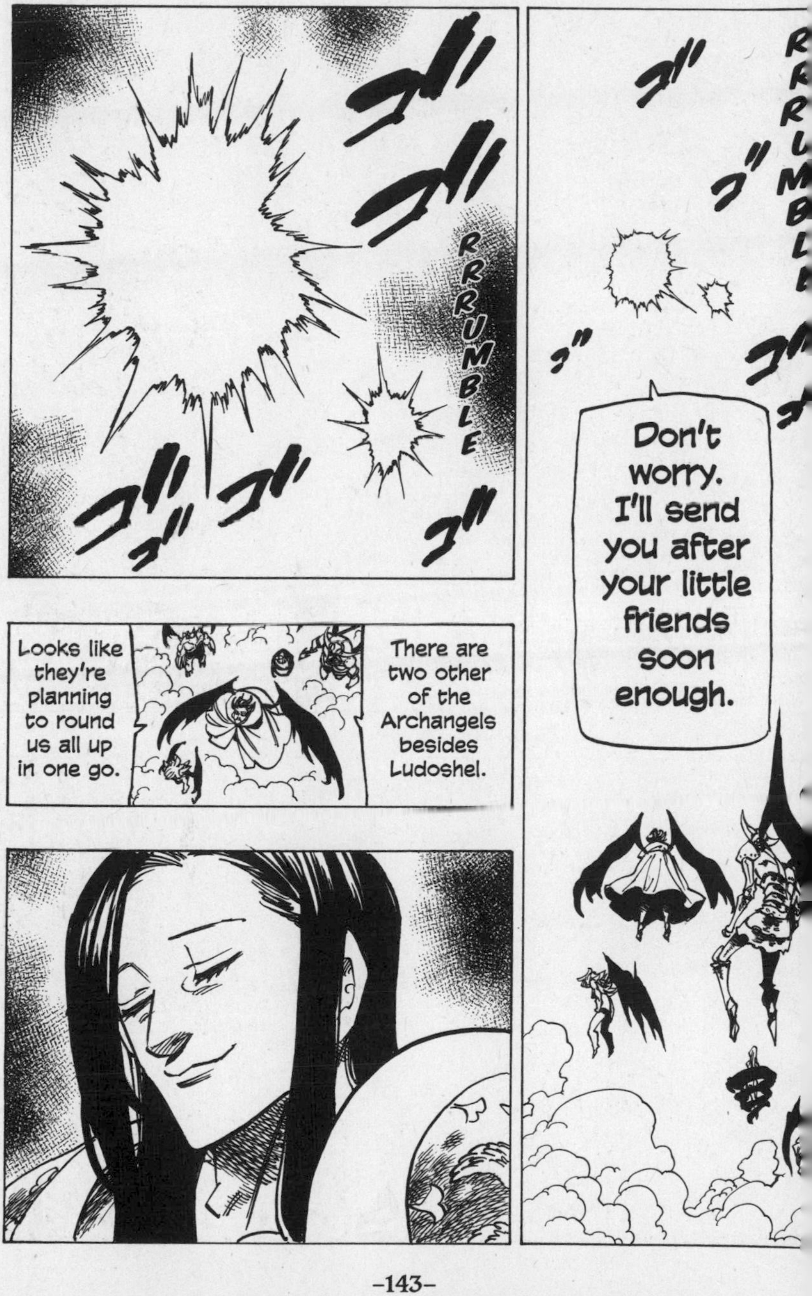
RRRUMBL
Don't worry. I'll send you after your little friends soon enough.
RRRUMBLE
There are two other of the Archangels besides Ludoshel.
Looks like they're planning to round us all up in one go.

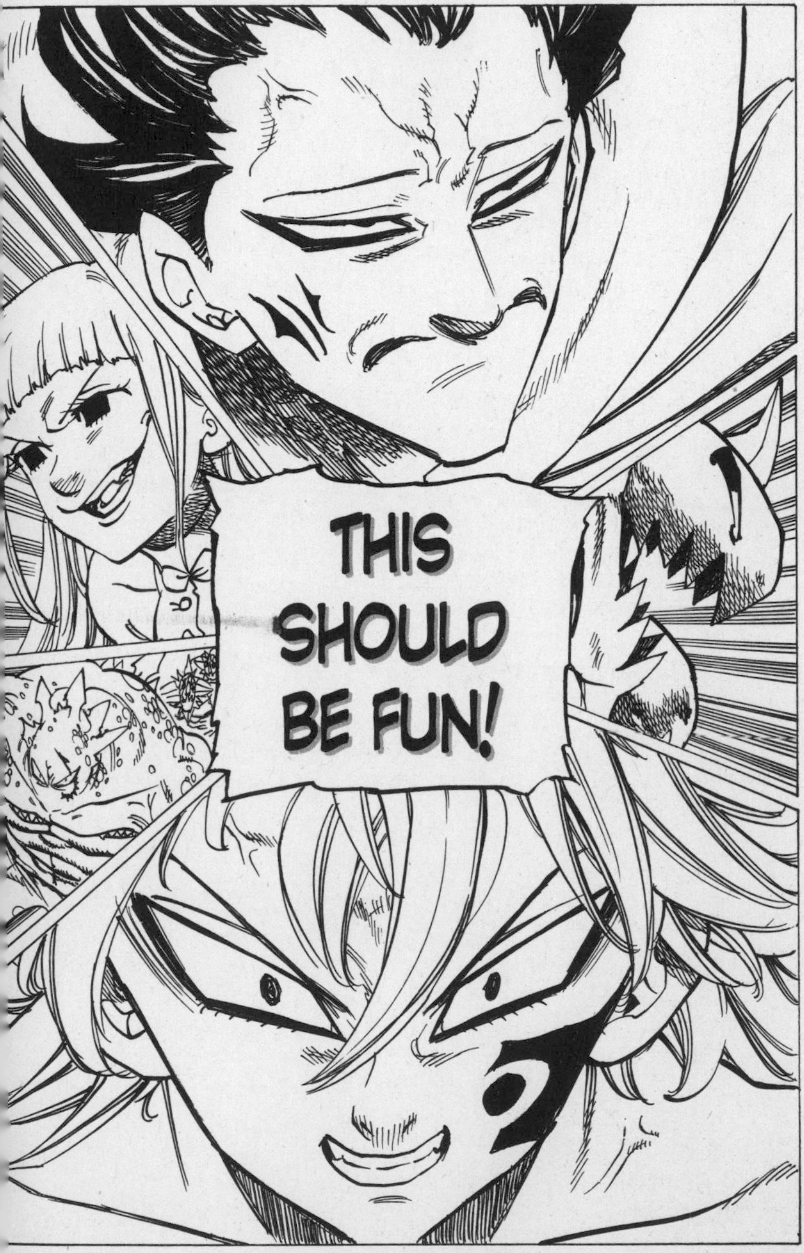
THIS SHOULD BE FUN!

Chapter 205 - The Ten Commandments vs. The Archangels

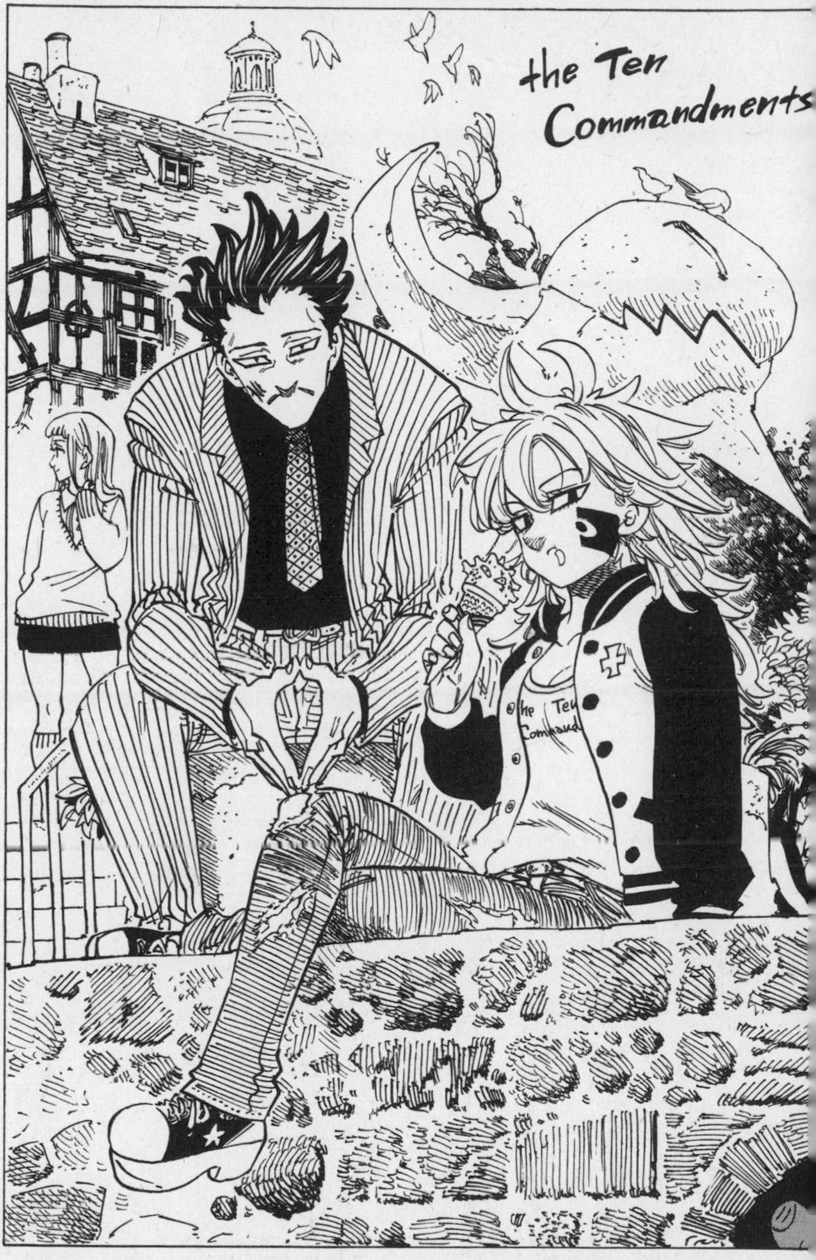
the Ten Commandments
the Ten Command

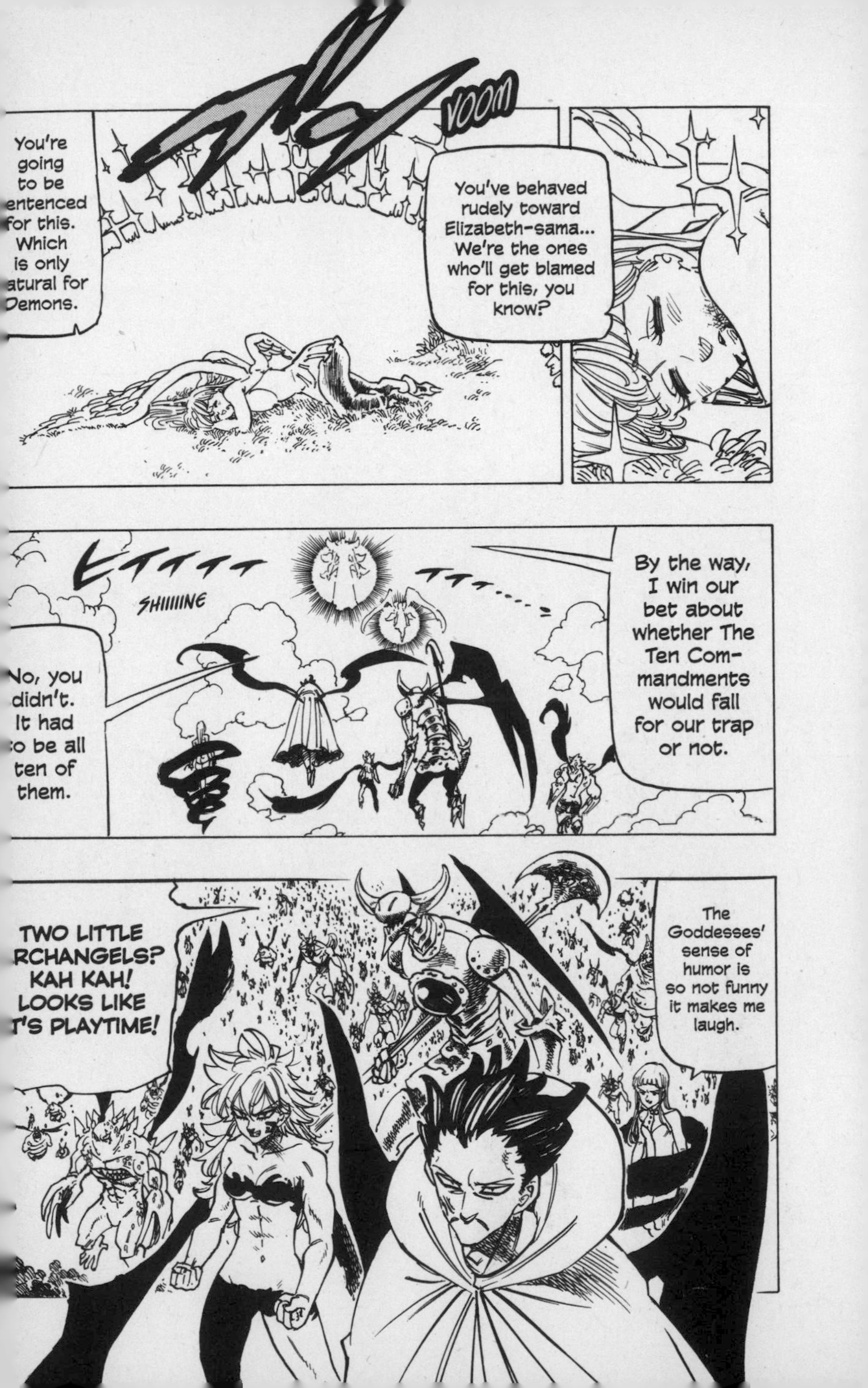
You've behaved rudely toward Elizabeth-sama... We're the ones who'll get blamed for this, you know?
VOOM
You're going to be entenced for this. Which is only atural for Demons.
By the way, I win our bet about whether The Ten Commandments would fall for our trap or not.
SHIIIIINE
No, you didn't. It had o be all ten of them.
The Goddesses' sense of humor is so not funny it makes me laugh.
TWO LITTLE RCHANGELS? KAH KAH! LOOKS LIKE T'S PLAYTIME!

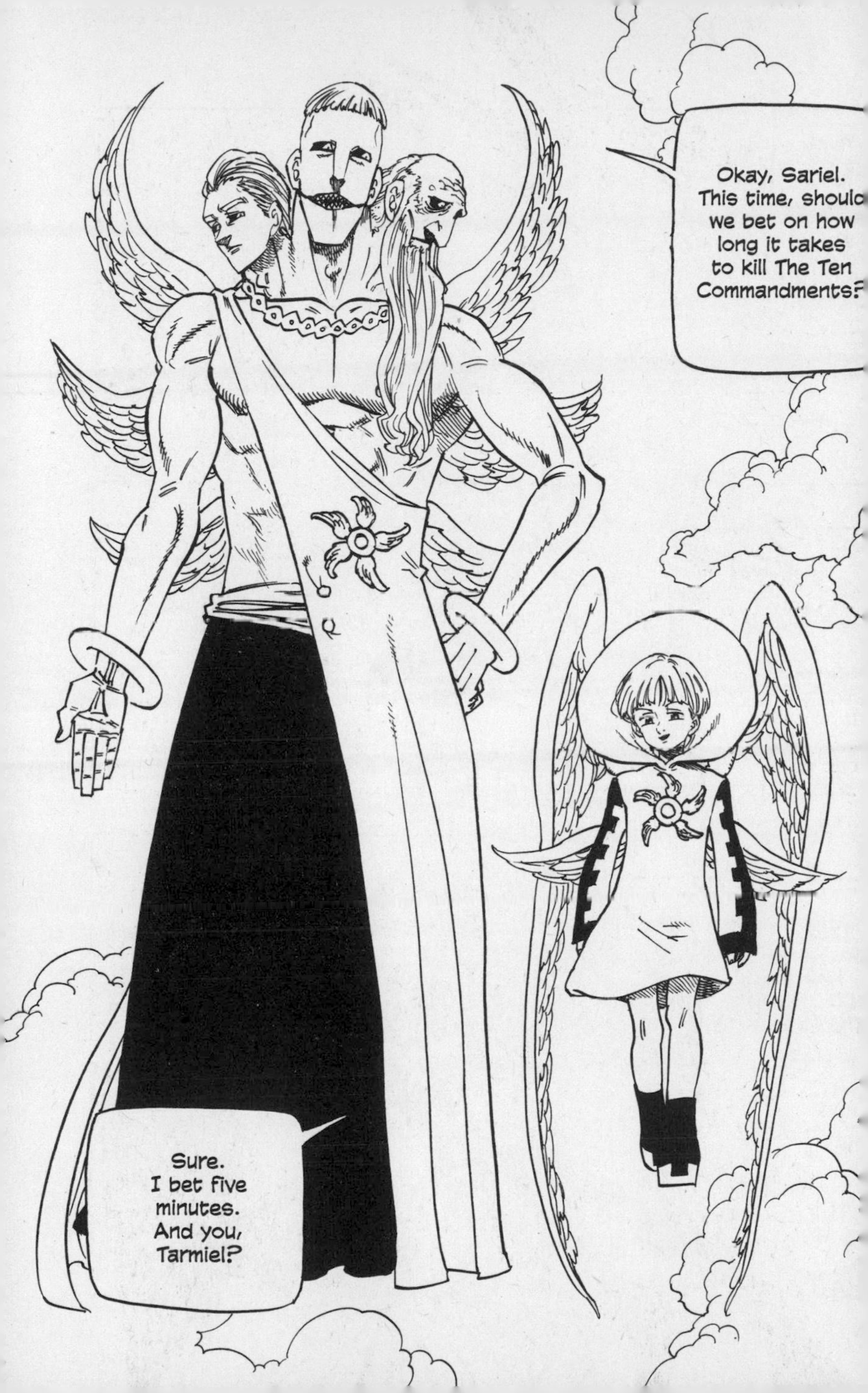
Okay, Sariel. This time, shoulc we bet on how long it takes to kill The Ten Commandments?
Sure. I bet five minutes. And you, Tarmiel?

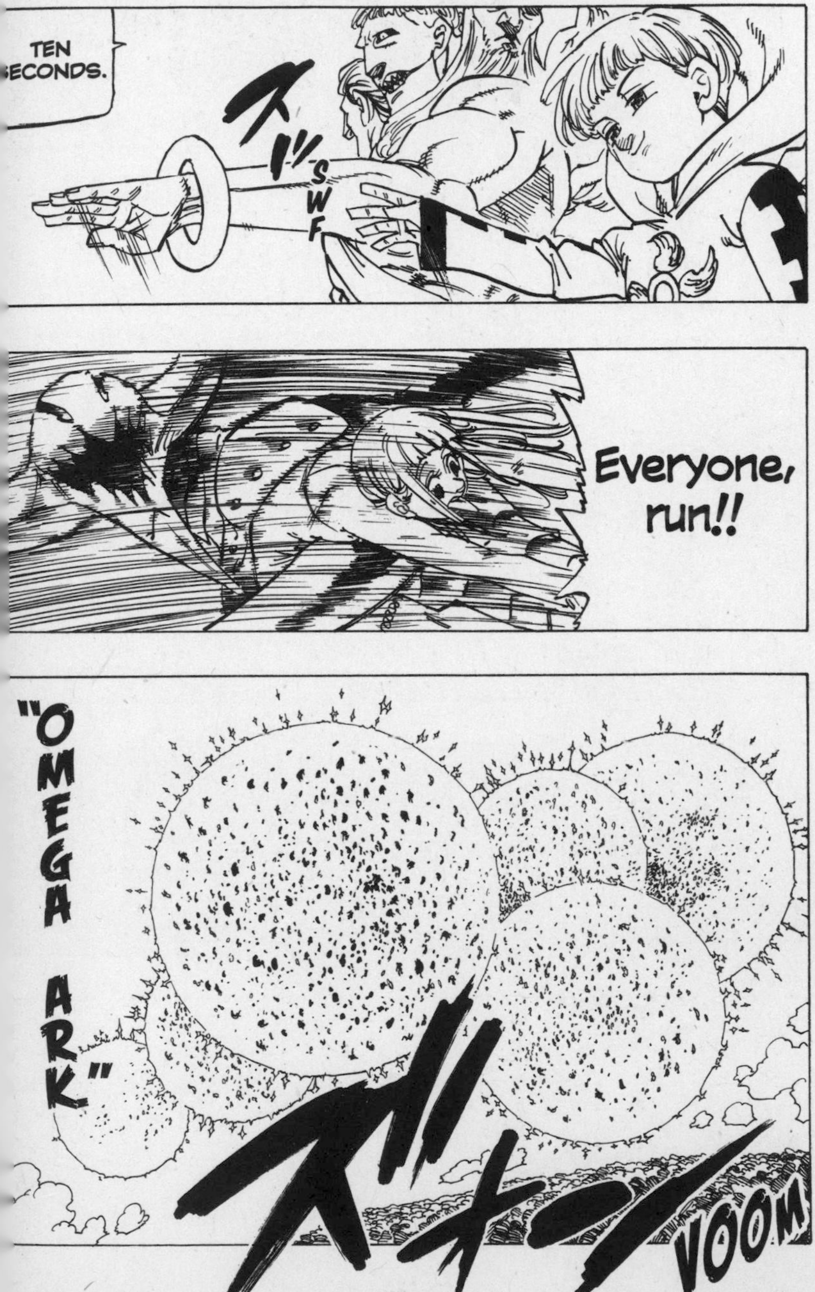
TEN SECONDS.
SWF
Everyone, run!!
"OMEGA ARK"
VOOM

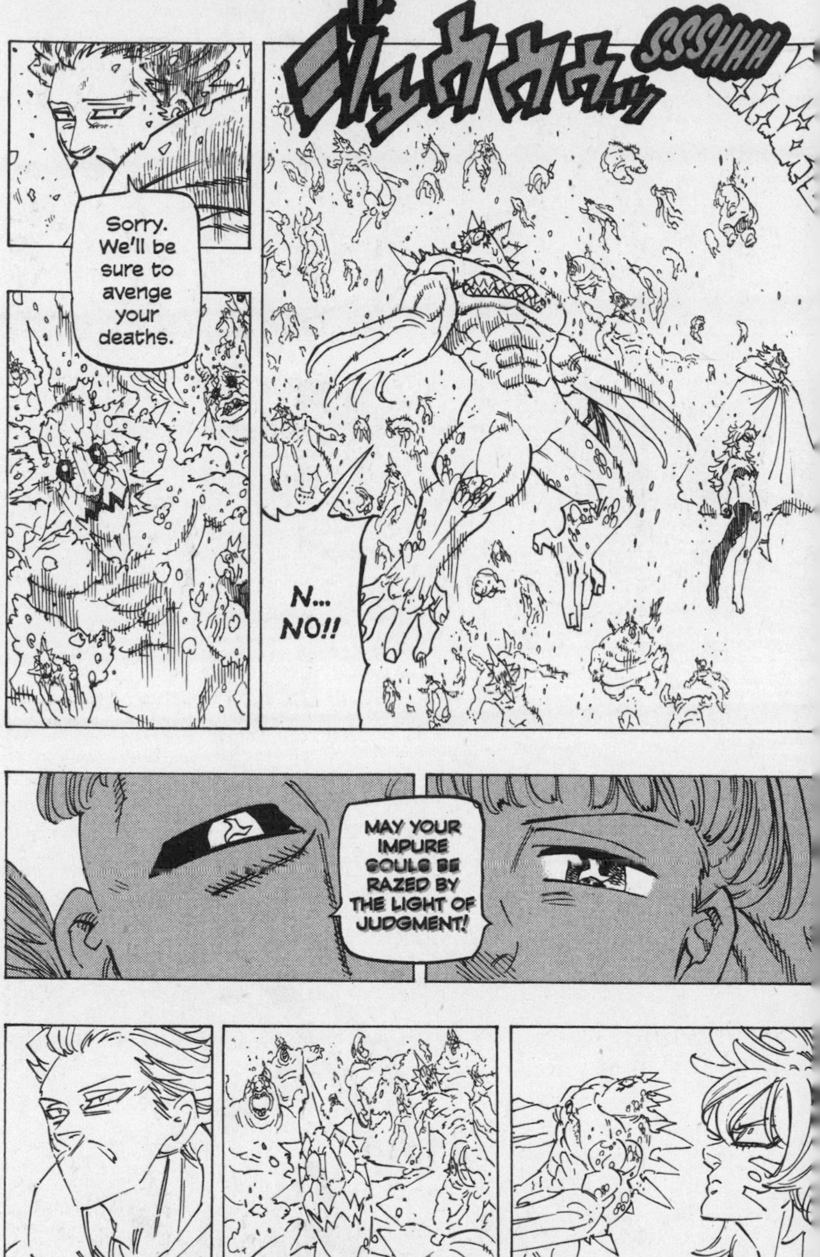
SSSHHH
N... NO!!
Sorry. We'll be sure to avenge your deaths.
MAY YOUR IMPURE SOULS BE RAZED BY THE LIGHT OF JUDGMENT!

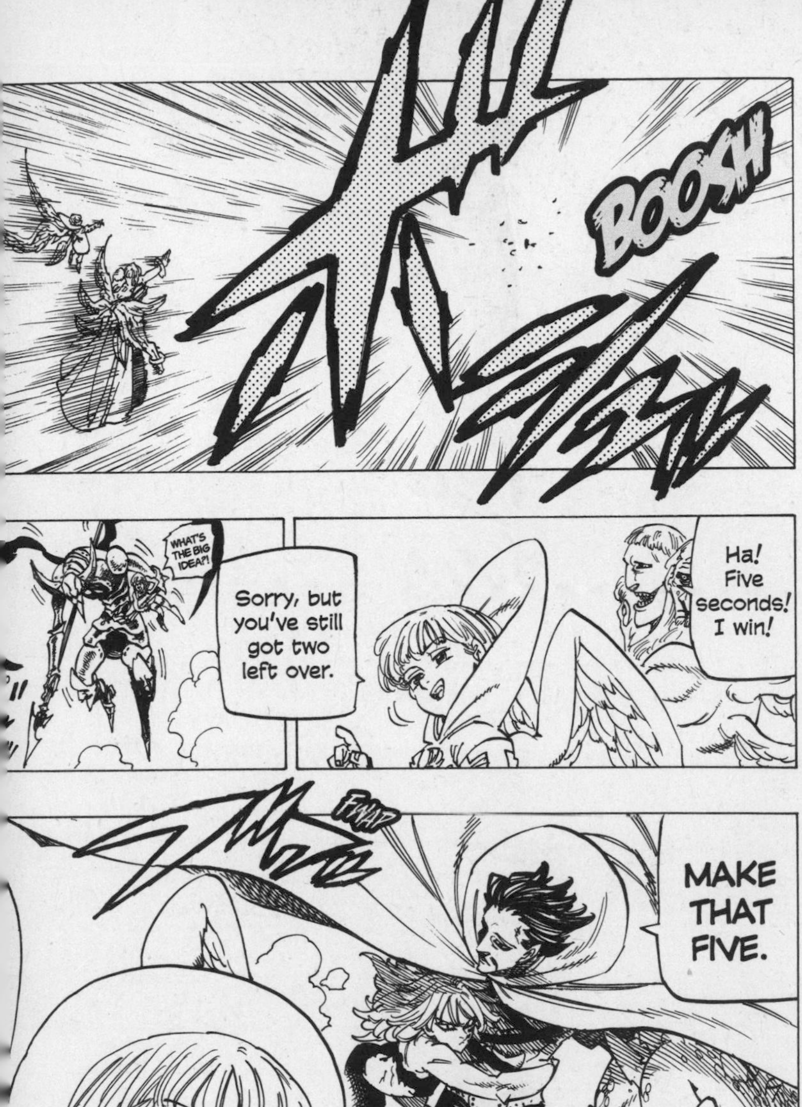
BOOSH
Ha! Five seconds! I win!
Sorry, but you've still got two left over.
WHAT'S THE BIG IDEA?!
FWAP
MAKE THAT FIVE.

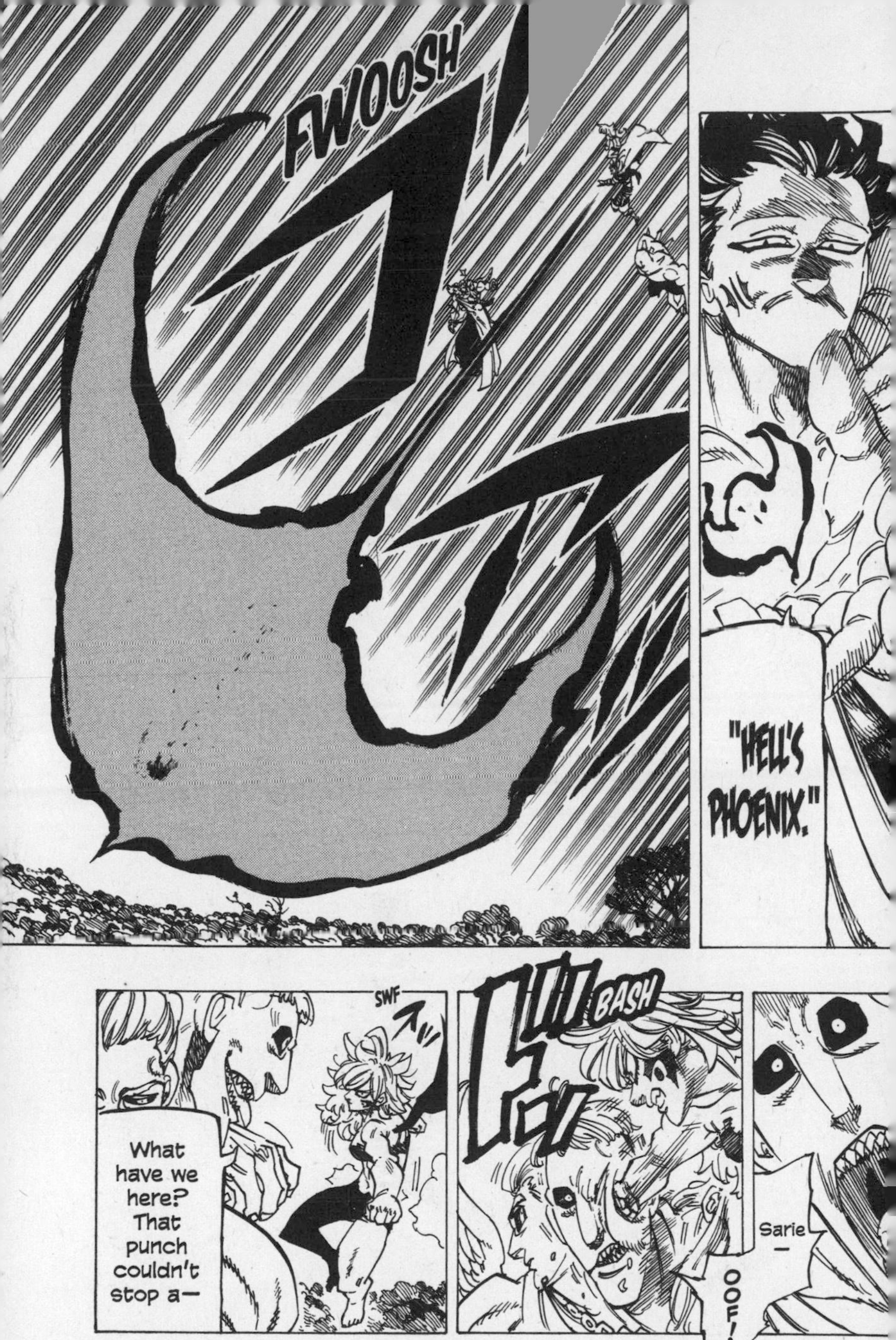
"HELL'S PHOENIX."
FWOOSH
Sarie—
OOF!
BASH
SWF
What have we here? That punch couldn't stop a—

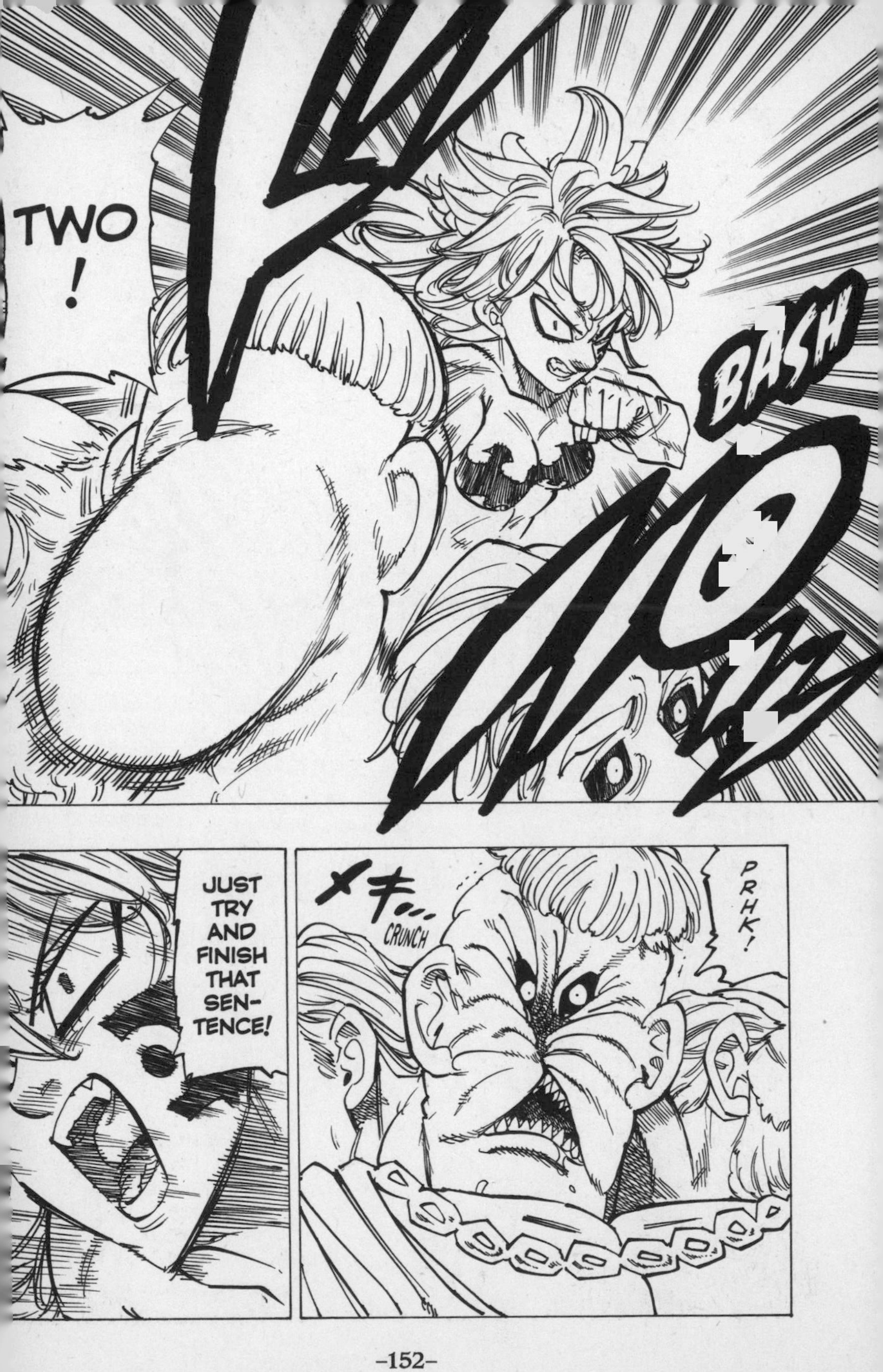
BASH
TWO!
メキ…
CRUNCH
PRHK!
JUST TRY AND FINISH THAT SEN-TENCE!

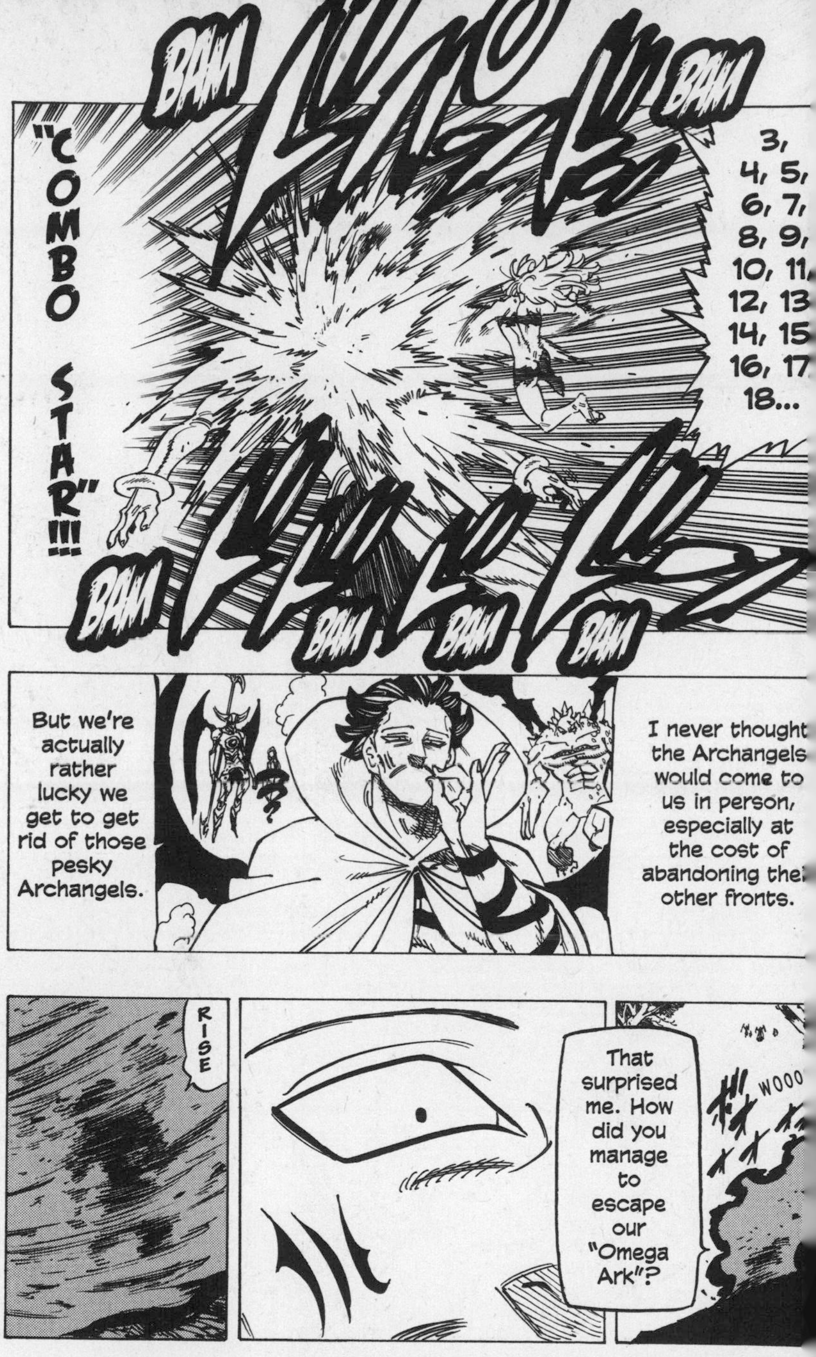
BAM
BAM
3, 4, 5, 6, 7, 8, 9, 10, 11, 12, 13 14, 15 16, 17 18...
"COMBO STAR"!!!
BAM
BAM
BAM
BAM
I never thought the Archangels would come to us in person, especially at the cost of abandoning the other fronts.
But we're actually rather lucky we get to get rid of those pesky Archangels.
WOOO
That surprised me. How did you manage to escape our "Omega Ark"?
RISE

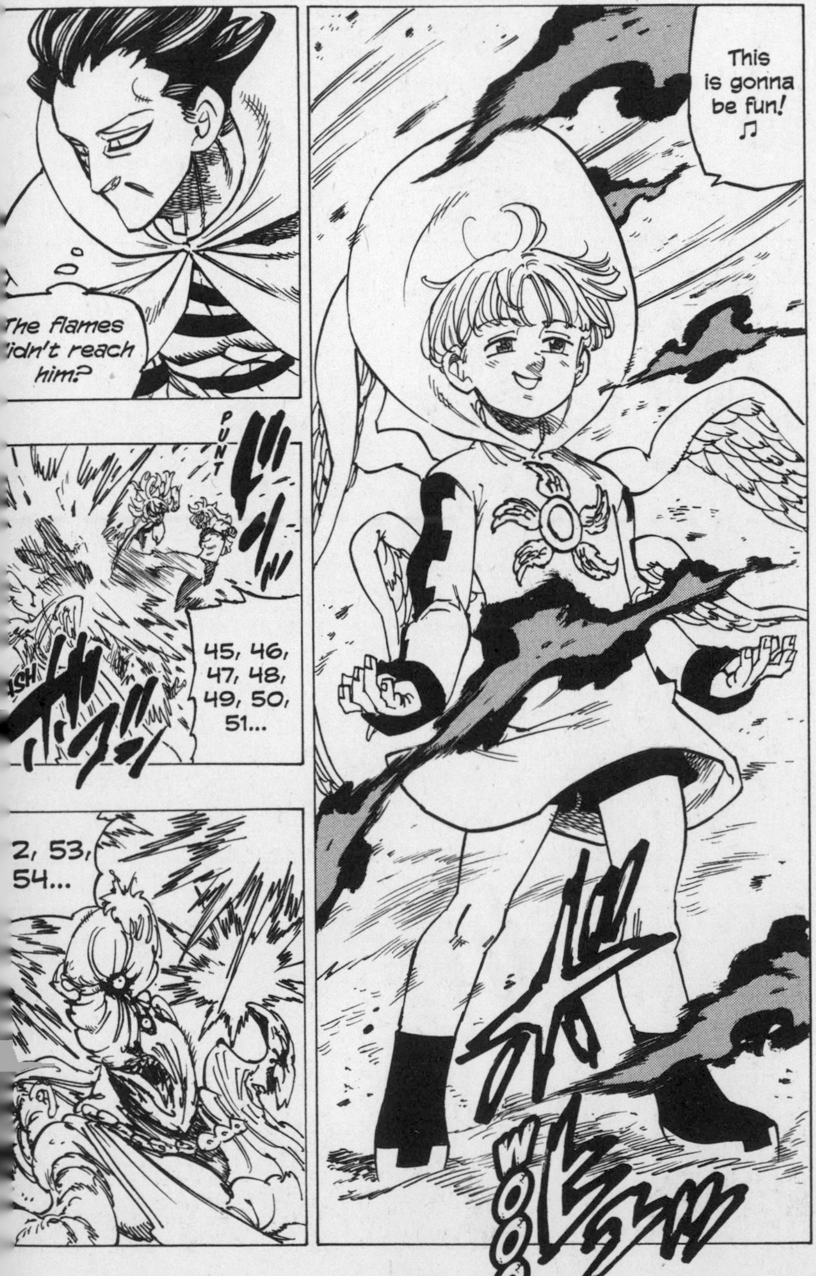
This is gonna be fun! ♫
WOOO
The flames didn't reach him?
PUNT
45, 46, 47, 48, 49, 50, 51...
2, 53, 54...

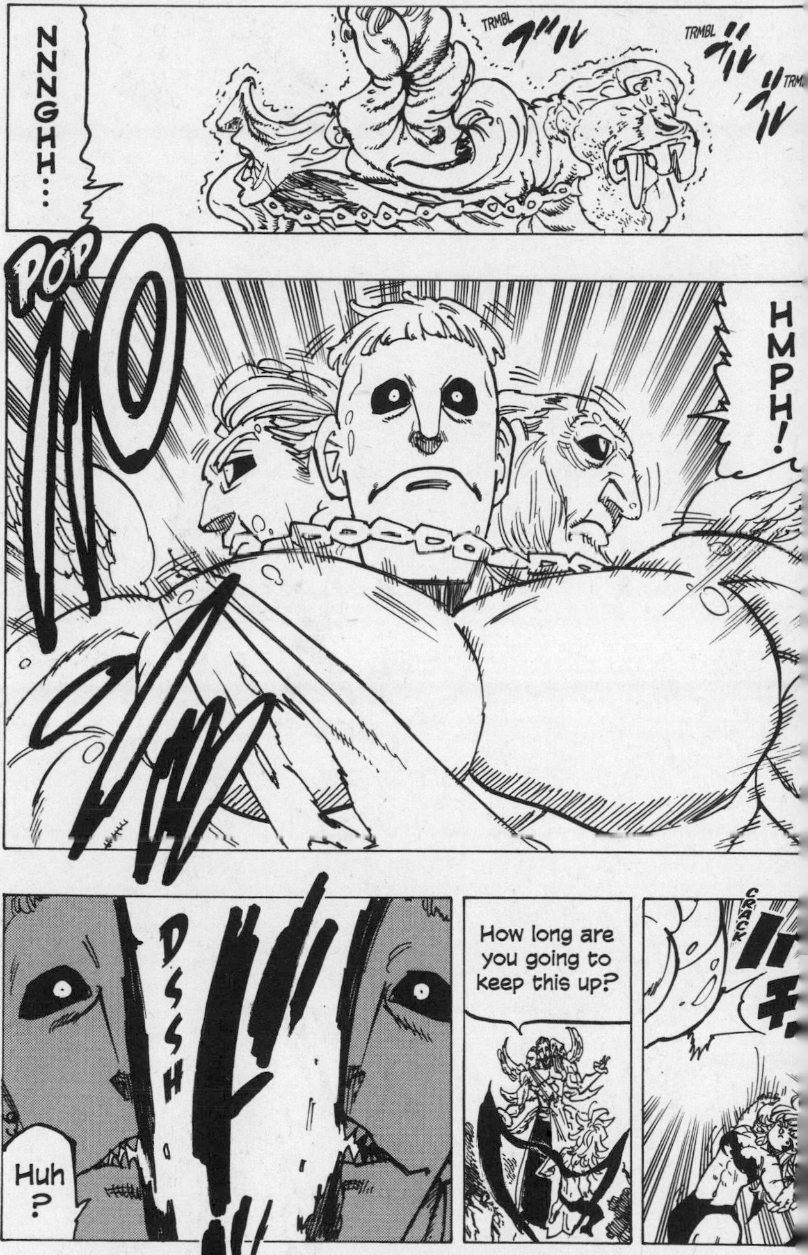
TRMBL
TRMBL
TRMBL
NNNGHH...
HMPH!
POP
CRACK
How long are you going to keep this up?
Huh?
DSSH

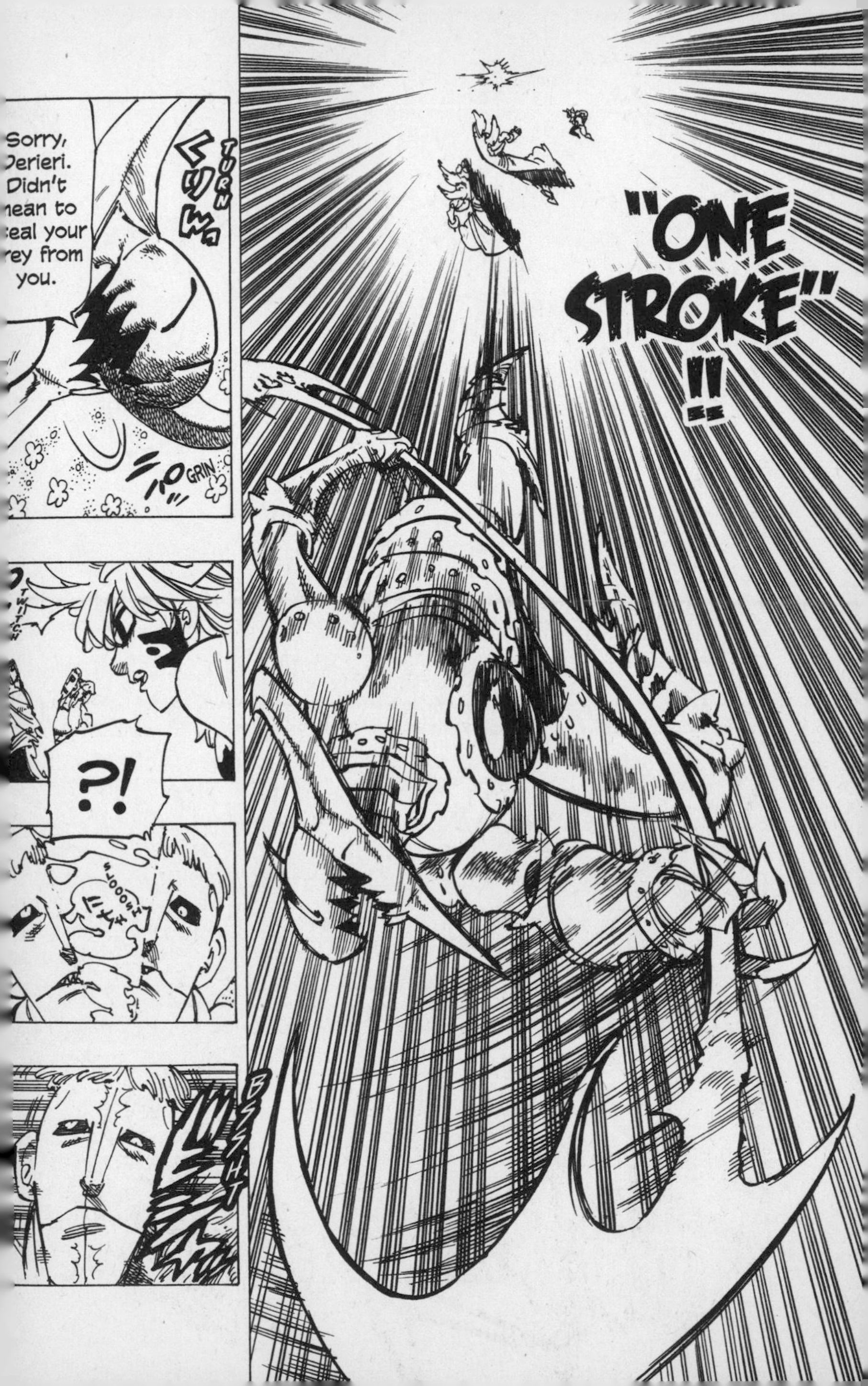
"ONE STROKE"!!
Sorry, Derieri. Didn't mean to steal your prey from you.
TURN
GRIN
TWITCH
?!
BSSHT

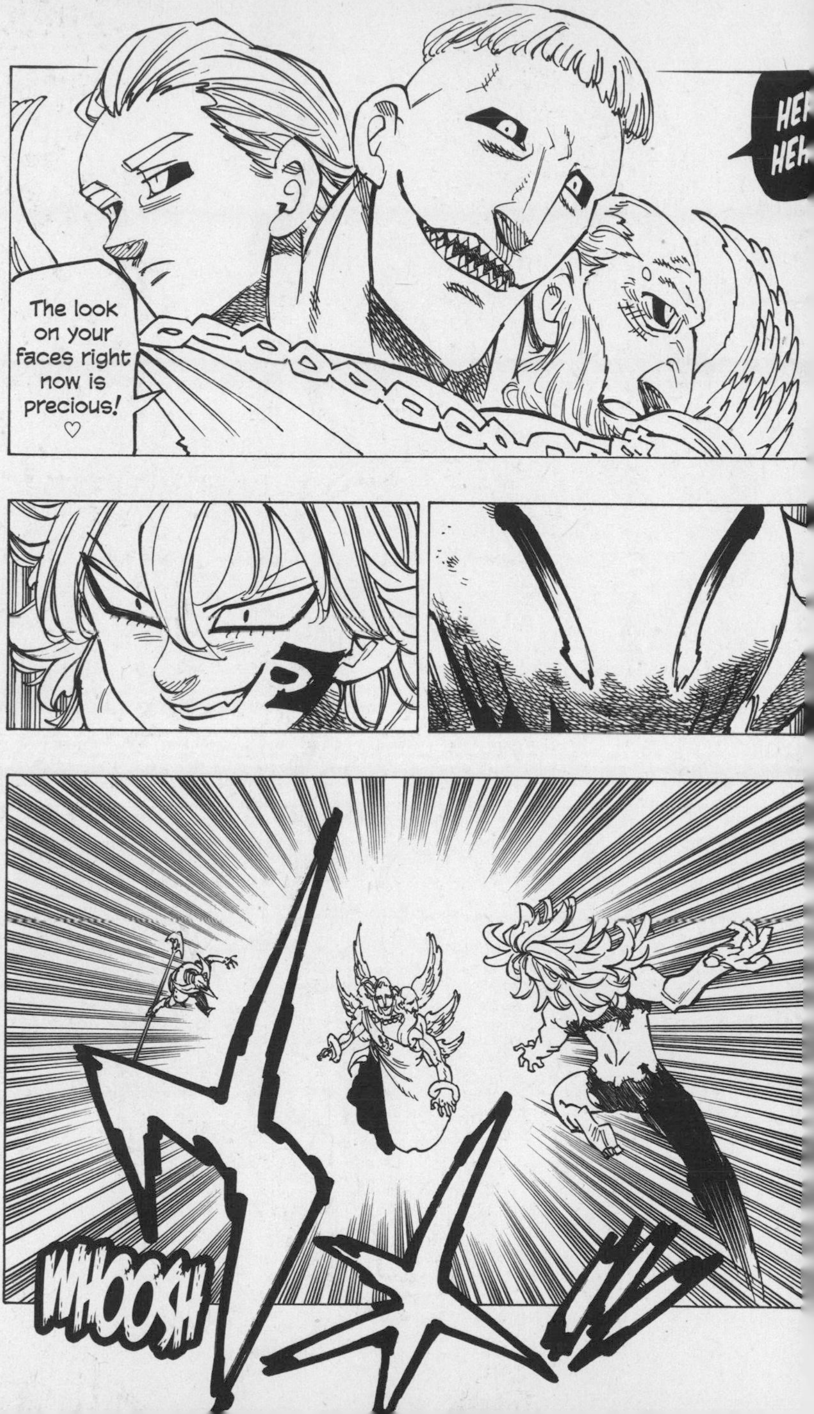
HEH HEH
The look on your faces right now is precious! ♡
WHOOSH

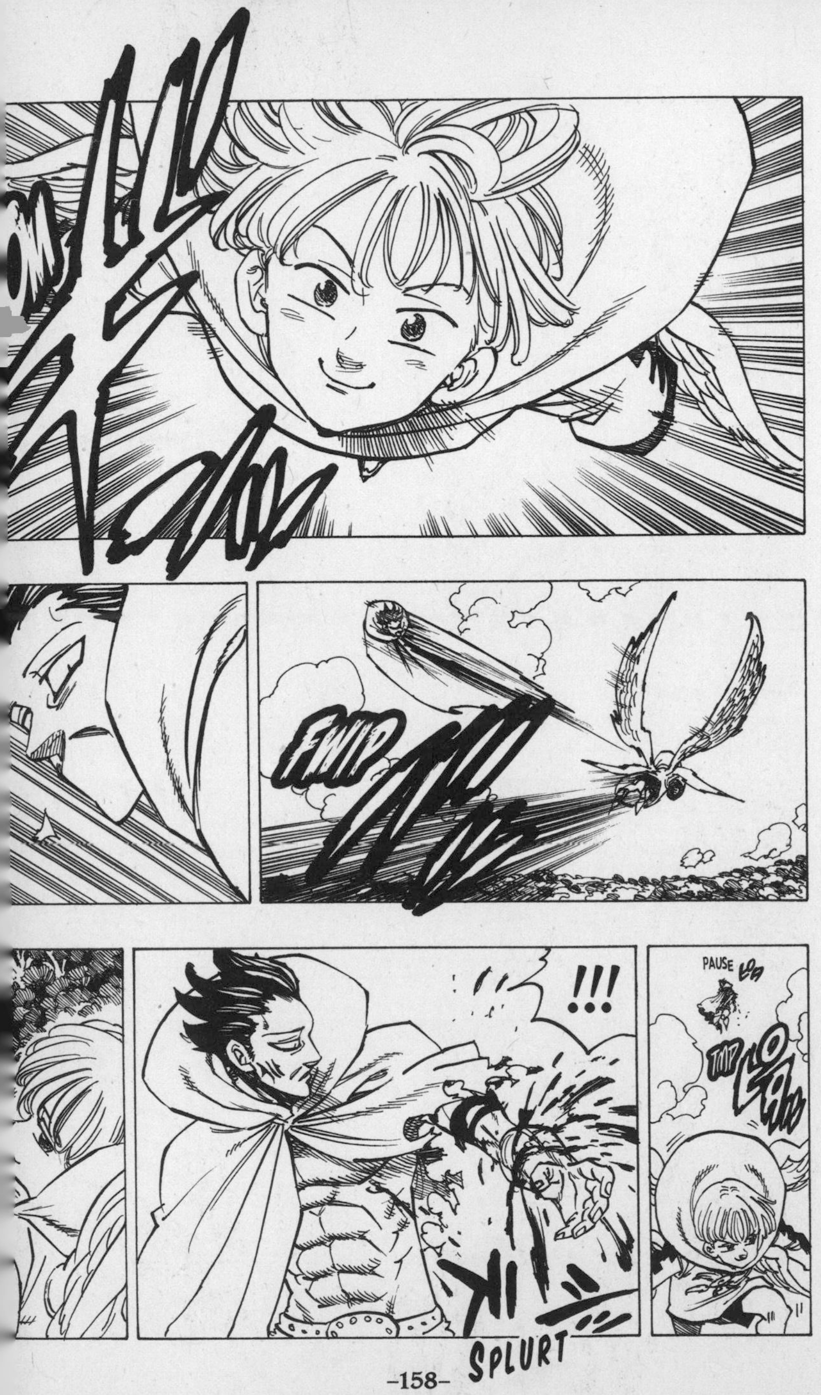
FWIP
PAUSE
TMP
!!!
SPLURT

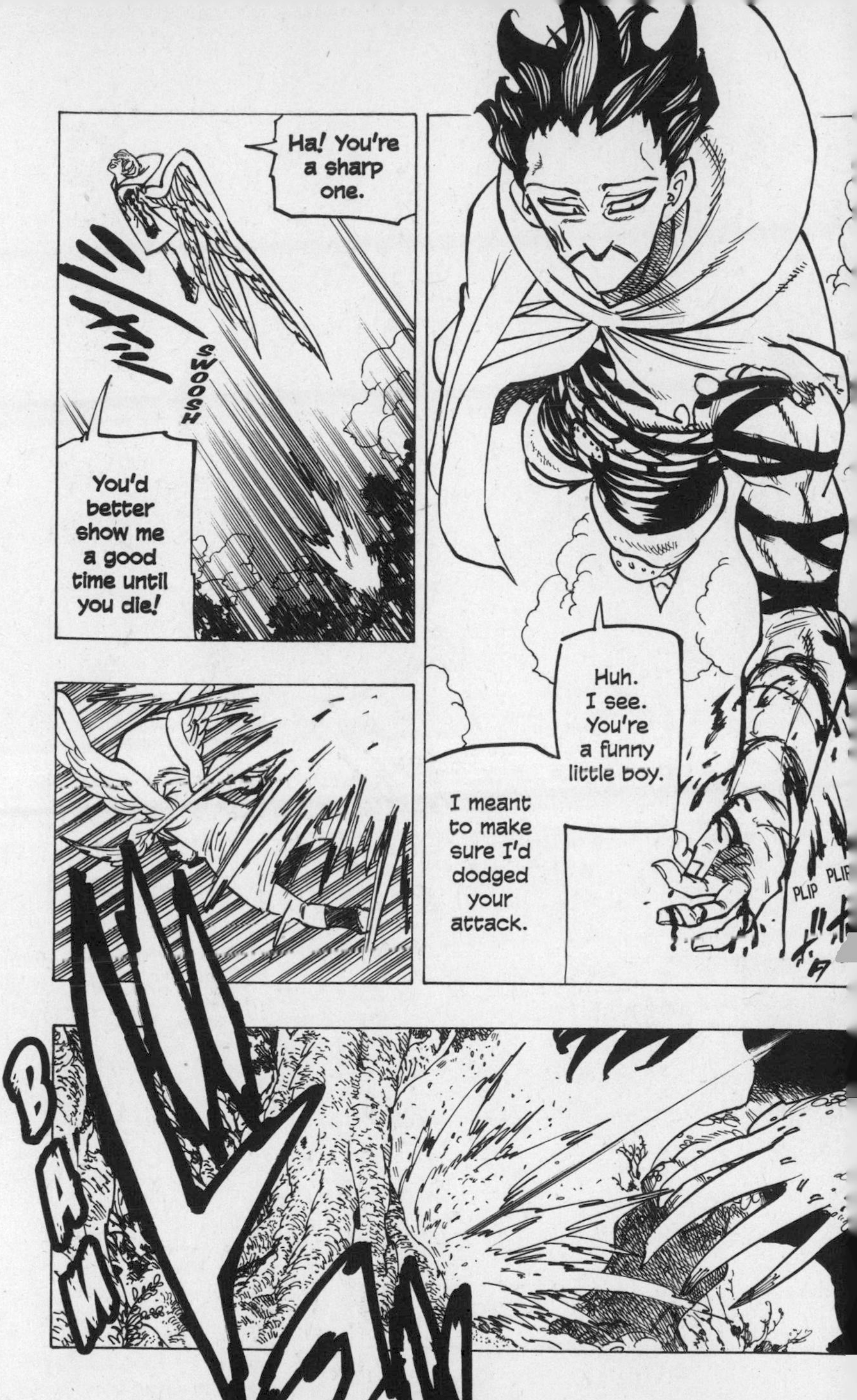
Huh. I see. You're a funny little boy.
I meant to make sure I'd dodged your attack.
PLIP PLIP
Ha! You're a sharp one.
SWOOSH
You'd better show me a good time until you die!
BAM

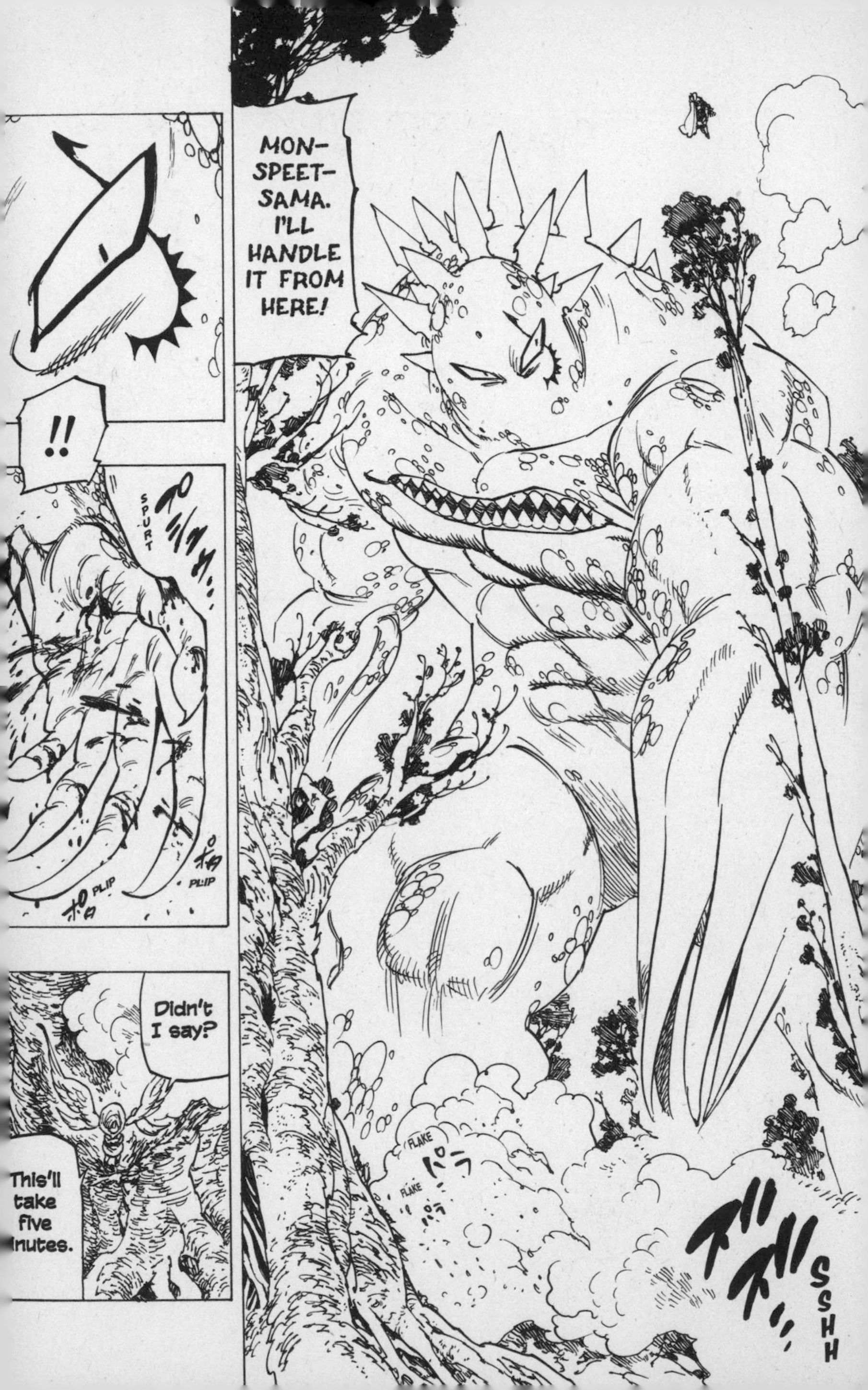
MON-SPEET-SAMA. I'LL HANDLE IT FROM HERE!
SSHH
FLAKE
FLAKE
!!
SPURT
PLIP
PLIP
Didn't I say?
This'll take five inutes.

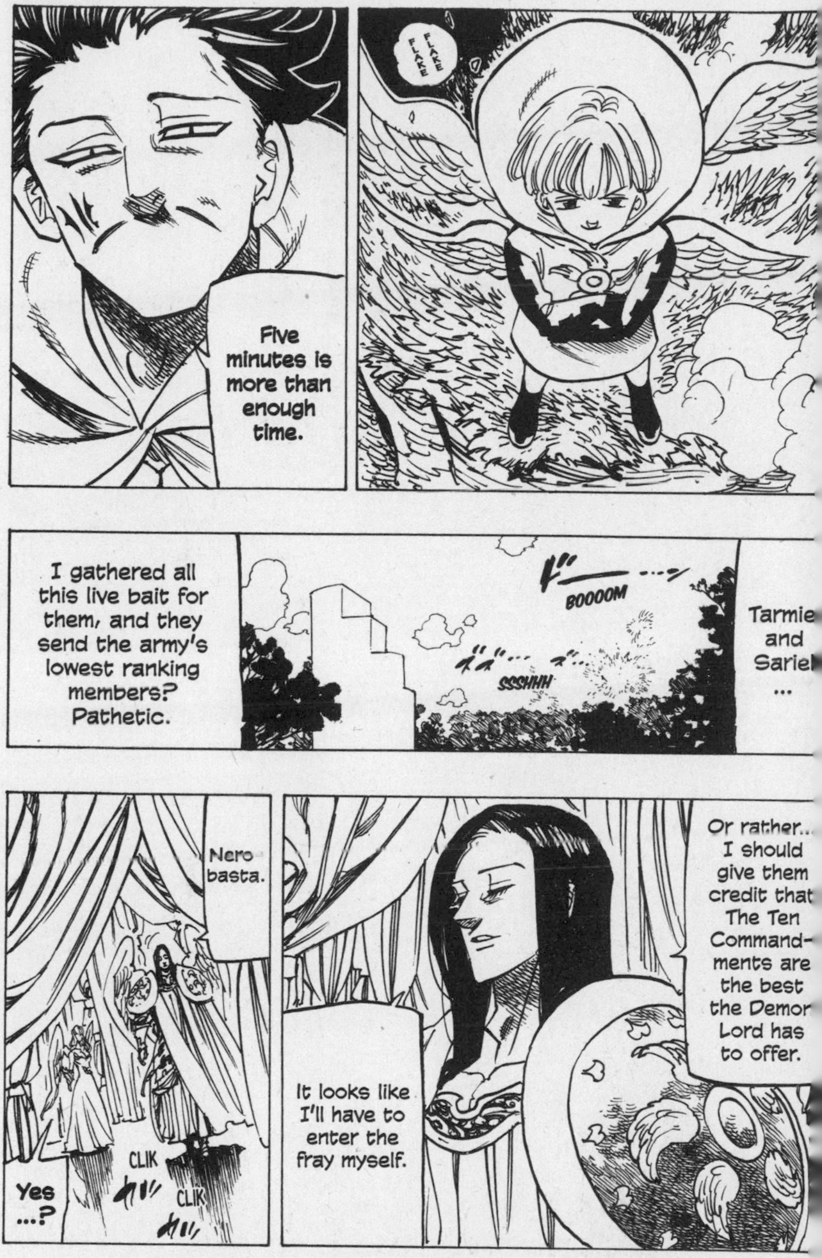
FLAKE FLAKE
Five minutes is more than enough time.
Tarmie and Sariel ...
BOOOOM
SSSHHH
I gathered all this live bait for them, and they send the army's lowest ranking members? Pathetic.
Or rather... I should give them credit that The Ten Commandments are the best the Demon Lord has to offer.
It looks like I'll have to enter the fray myself.
Nerobasta.
CLIK
CLIK
Yes ...?

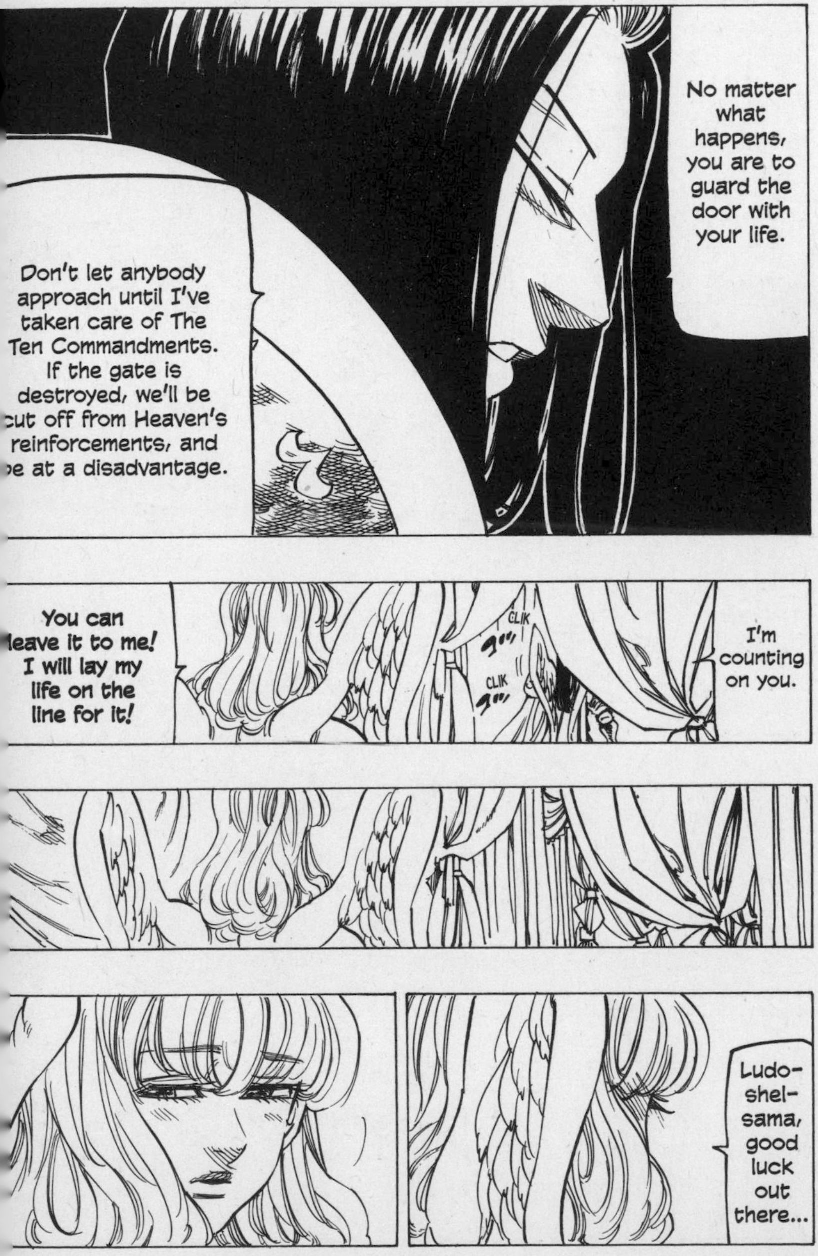
No matter what happens, you are to guard the door with your life.
Don't let anybody approach until I've taken care of The Ten Commandments. If the gate is destroyed, we'll be cut off from Heaven's reinforcements, and be at a disadvantage.
I'm counting on you.
CLIK
CLIK
You can leave it to me! I will lay my life on the line for it!
Ludo-shel-sama, good luck out there...

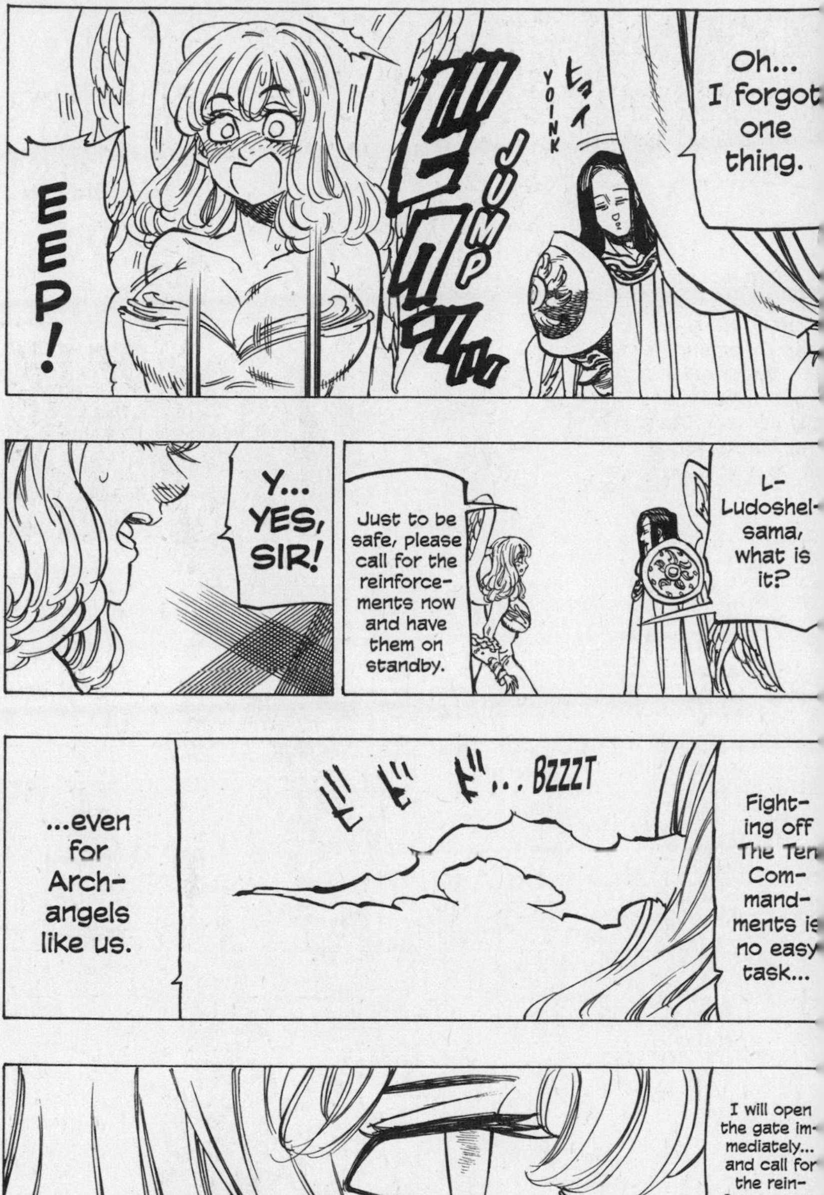
Oh... I forgot one thing.
YOINK
JUMP
EEP!
L-Ludoshel-sama, what is it?
Just to be safe, please call for the reinforcements now and have them on standby.
Y... YES, SIR!
Fighting off The Ten Commandments is no easy task...
BZZZT
...even for Archangels like us.
I will open the gate immediately... and call for the reinforcements.

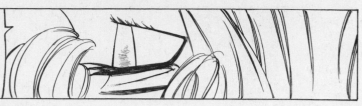

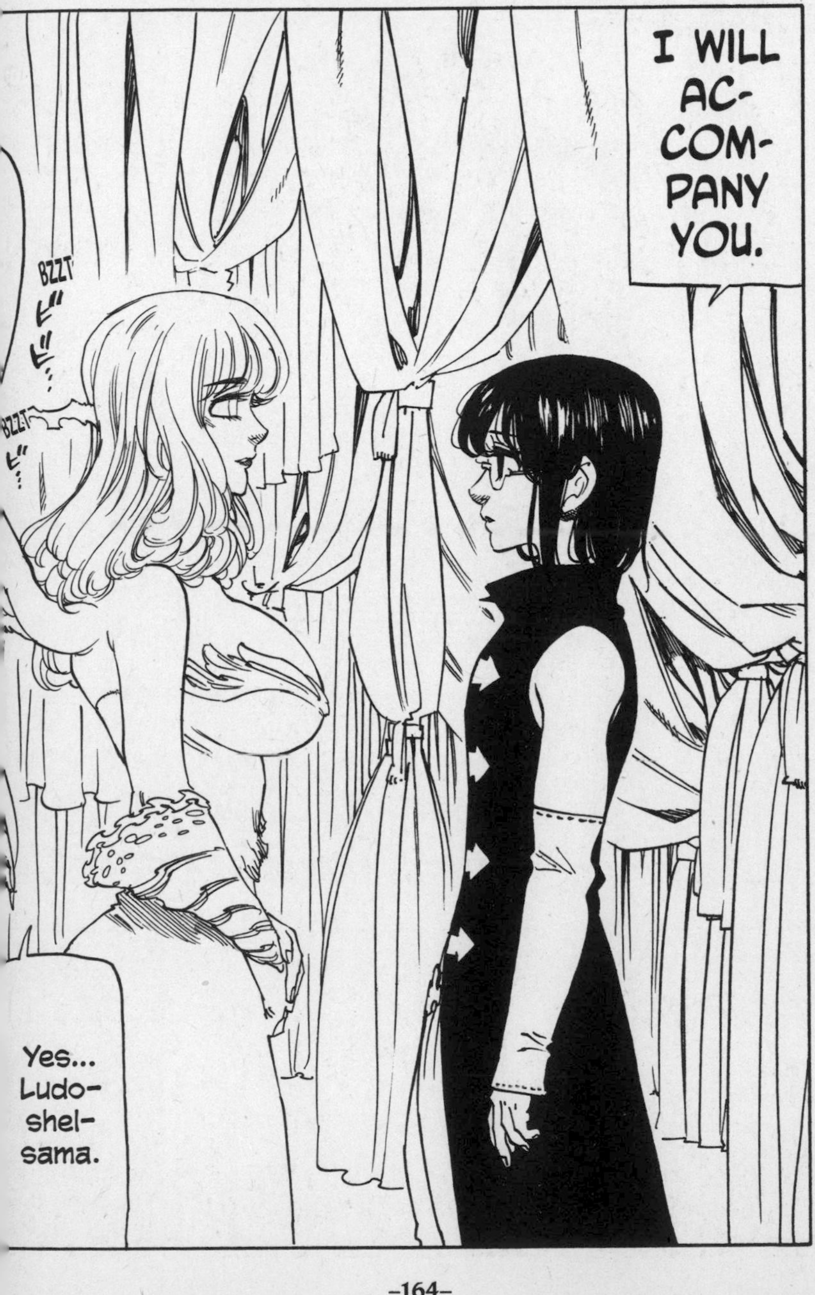
I WILL AC-COM-PANY YOU.
BZZT
BZZT
Yes... Ludo-shel-sama.

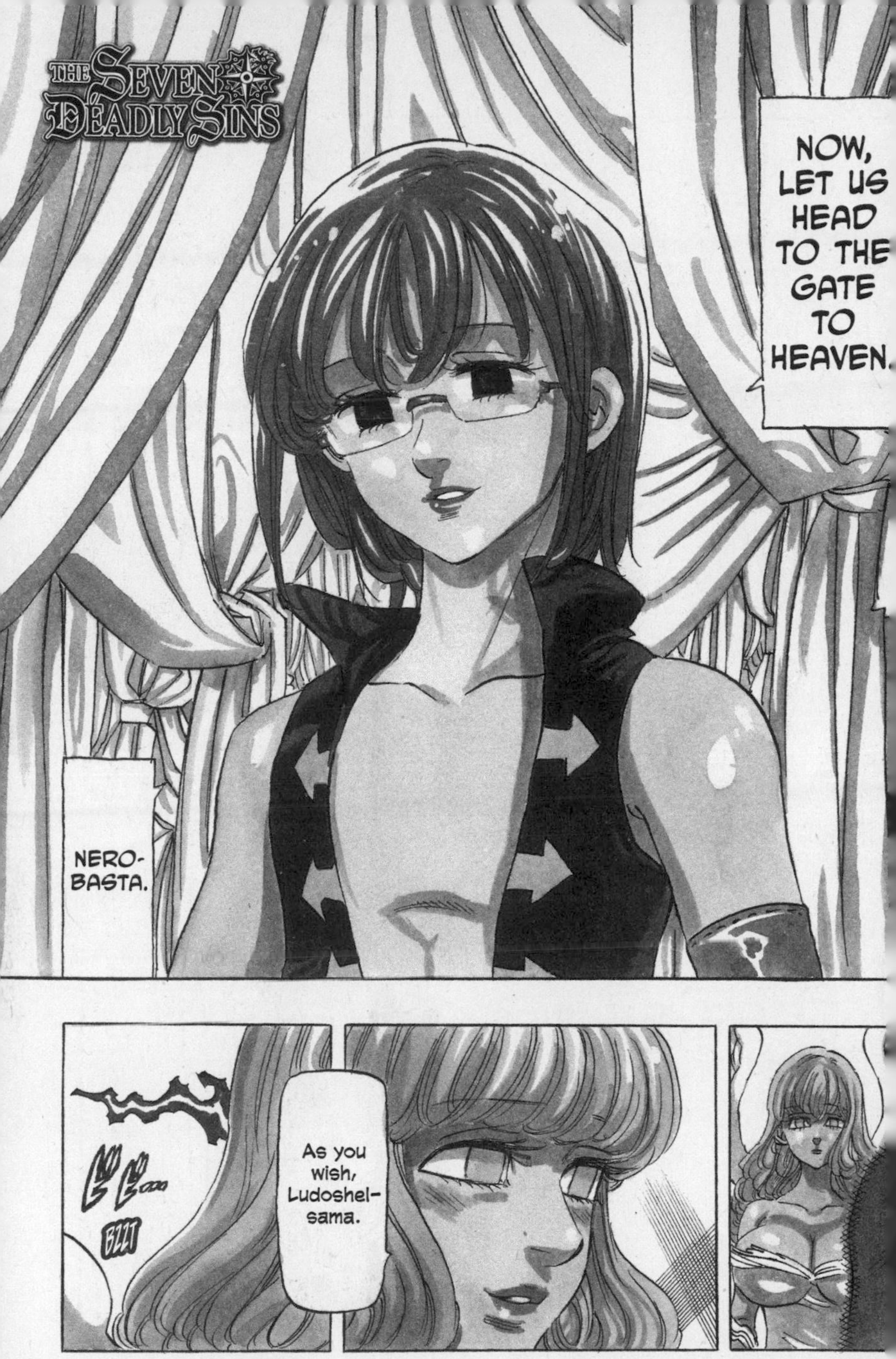
THE SEVEN DEADLY SINS
NOW, LET US HEAD TO THE GATE TO HEAVEN.
NERO-BASTA.
As you wish, Ludoshel-sama.
BZZT

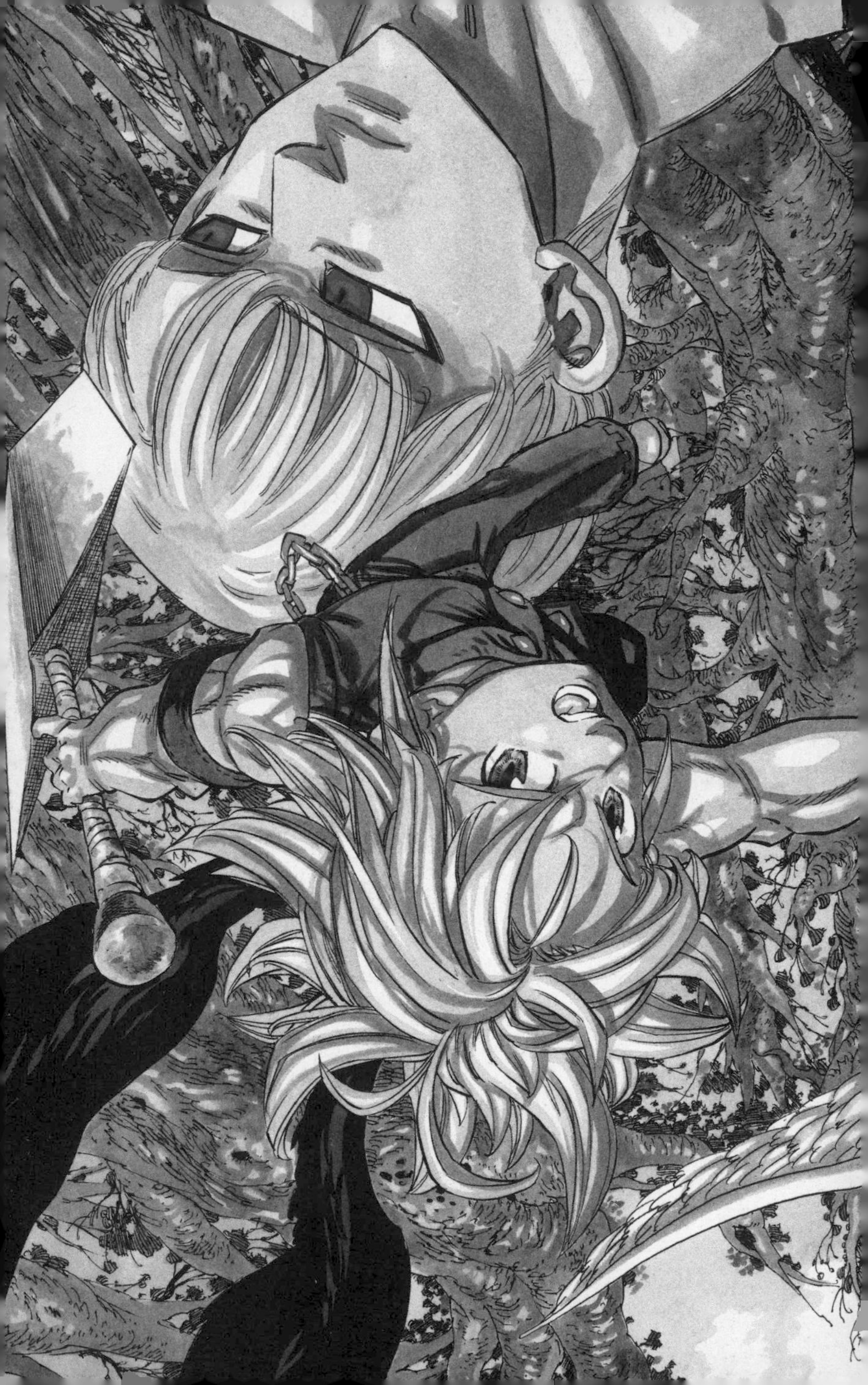

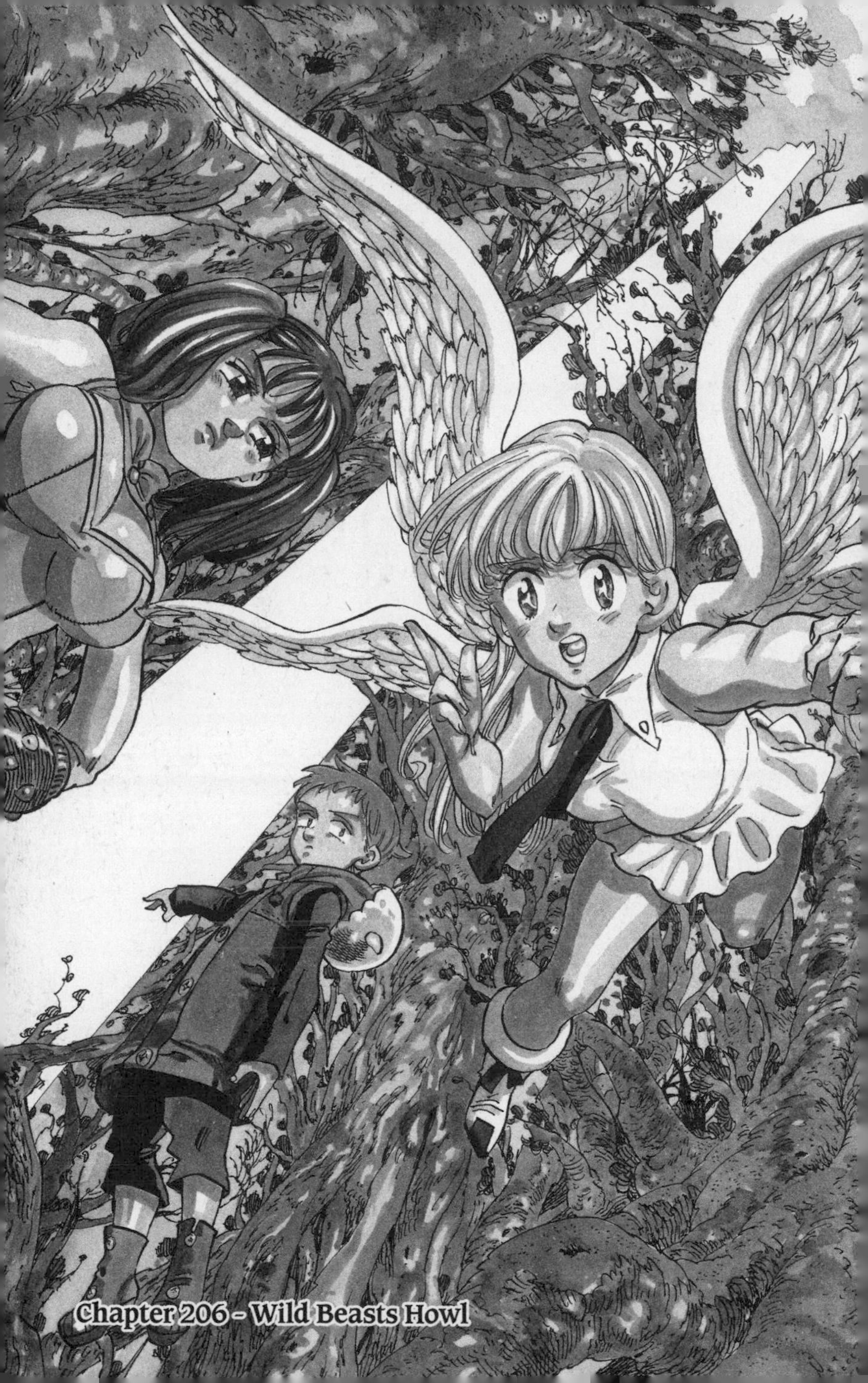
Chapter 206 - Wild Beasts Howl

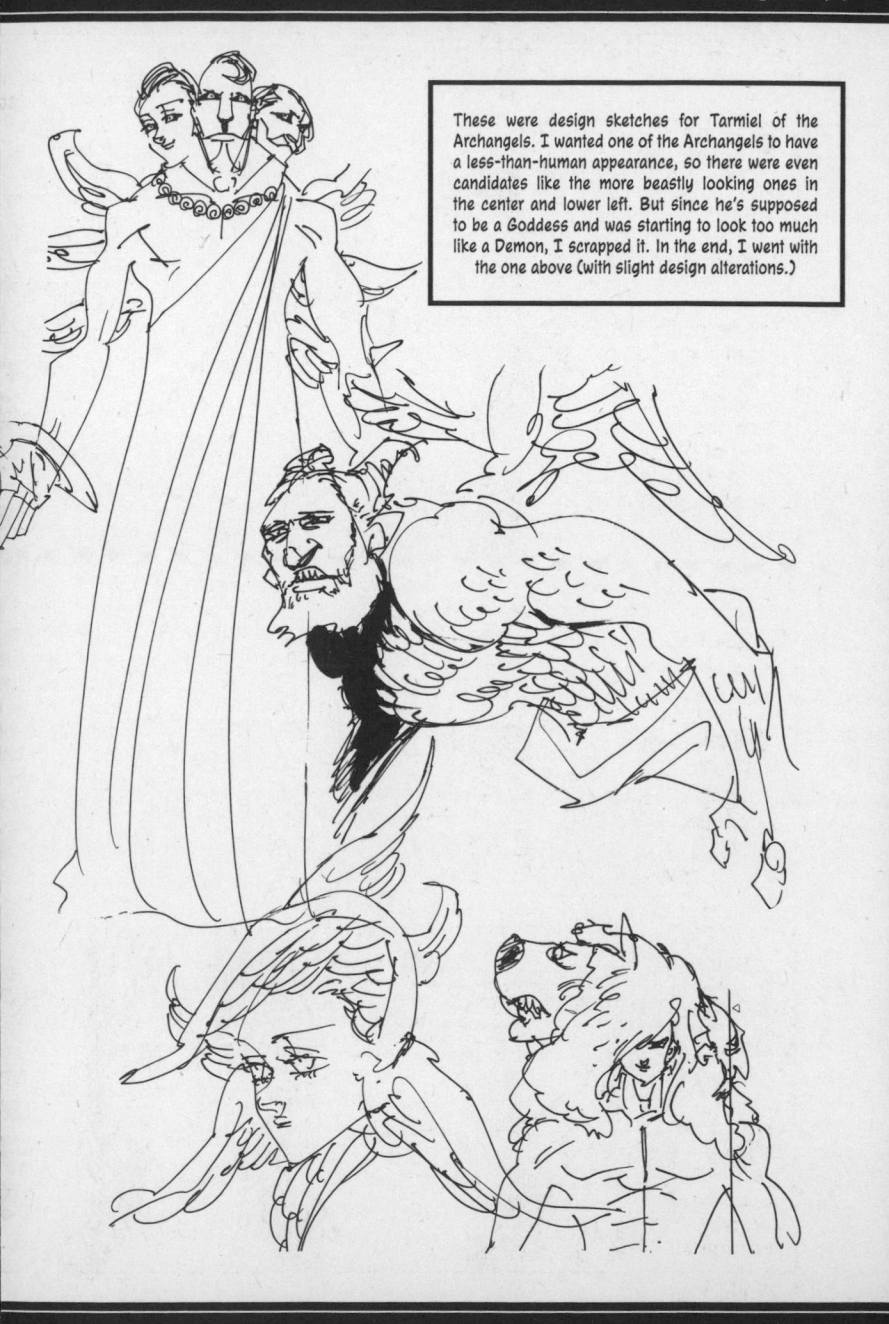

These were design sketches for Tarmiel of the Archangels. I wanted one of the Archangels to have a less-than-human appearance, so there were even candidates like the more beastly looking ones in the center and lower left. But since he's supposed to be a Goddess and was starting to look too much like a Demon, I scrapped it. In the end, I went with the one above (with slight design alterations.)

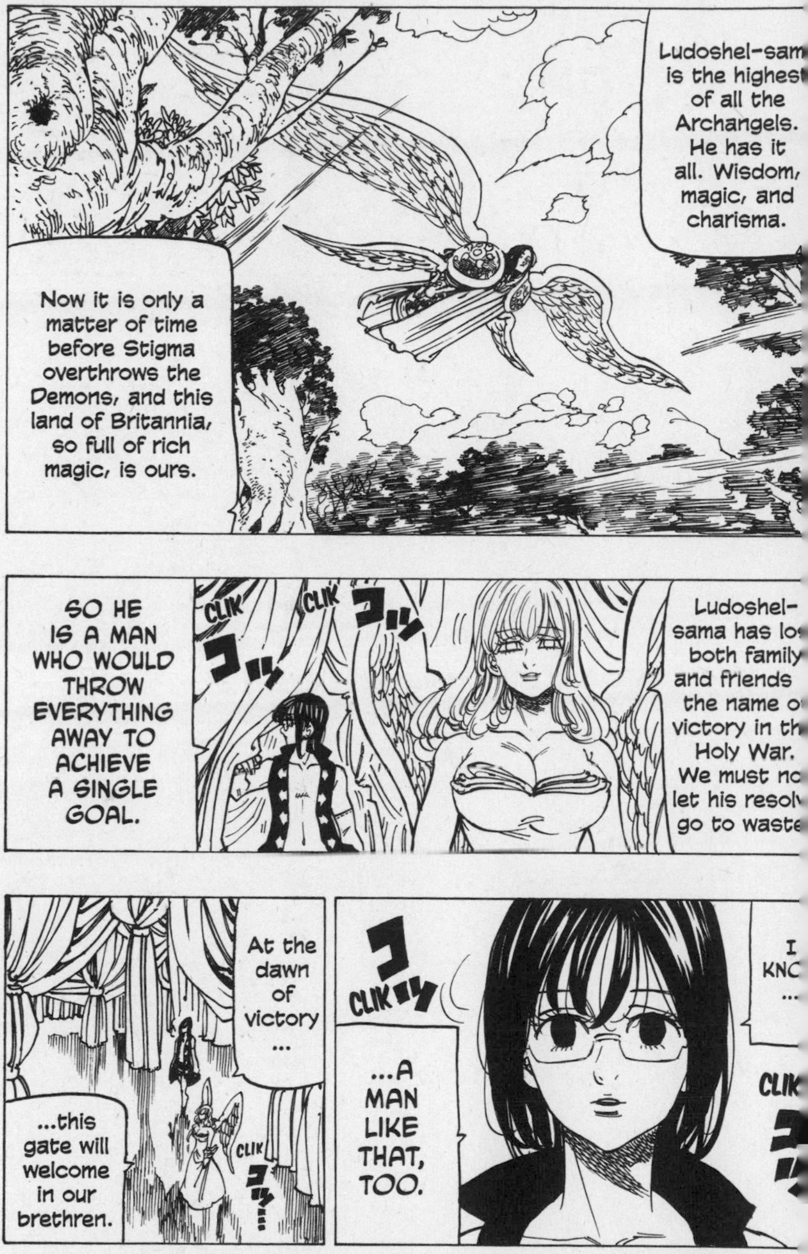
Ludoshel-sam is the highes of all the Archangels. He has it all. Wisdom, magic, and charisma.
Now it is only a matter of time before Stigma overthrows the Demons, and this land of Britannia, so full of rich magic, is ours.
Ludoshel-sama has lo both family and friends the name o victory in th Holy War. We must no let his resolv go to waste
CLIK
CLIK
SO HE IS A MAN WHO WOULD THROW EVERYTHING AWAY TO ACHIEVE A SINGLE GOAL.
I KNO ...
CLIK
CLIK
...A MAN LIKE THAT, TOO.
At the dawn of victory ...
CLIK
...this gate will welcome in our brethren.

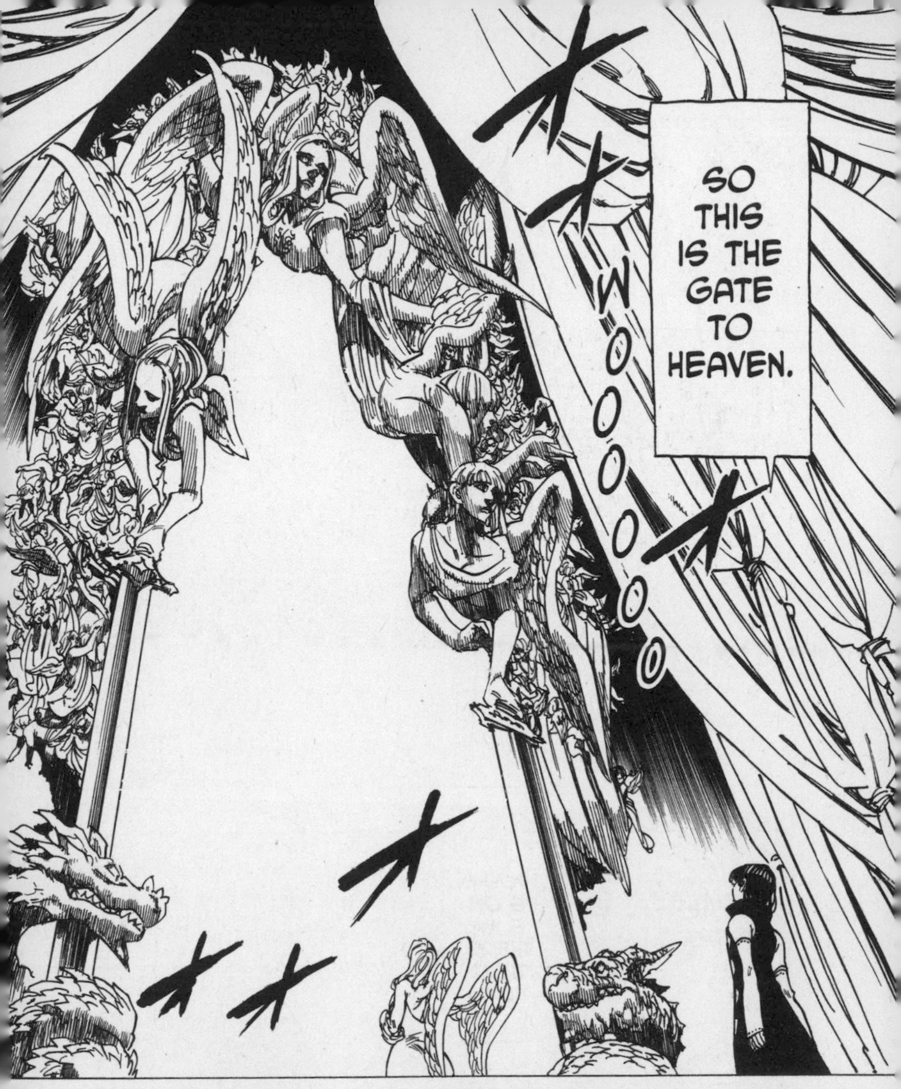
SO THIS IS THE GATE TO HEAVEN.
WOOOOOOOO
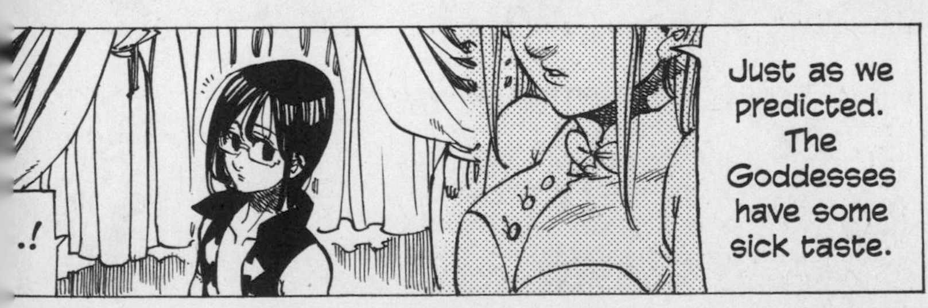
Just as we predicted. The Goddesses have some sick taste.
..!

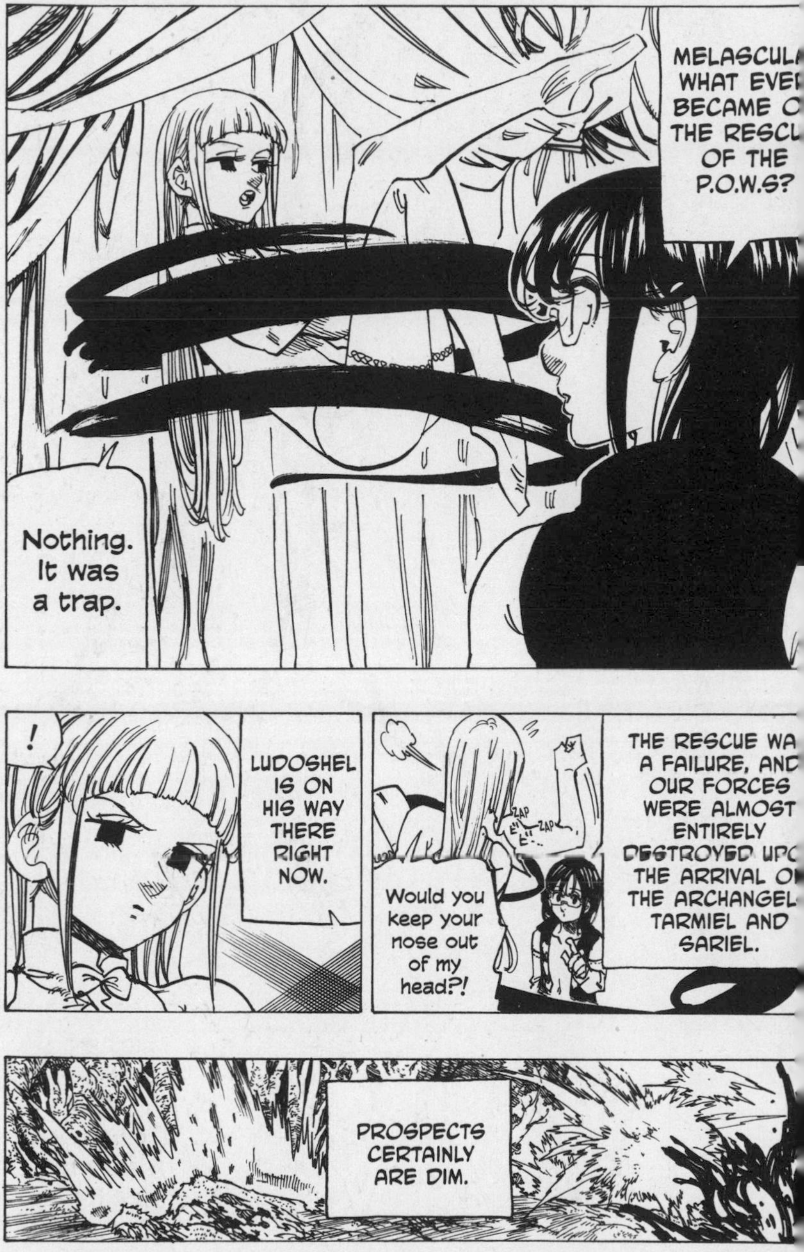
MELASCULA WHAT EVEI BECAME O THE RESCU OF THE P.O.W.S?
Nothing. It was a trap.
THE RESCUE WA A FAILURE, AND OUR FORCES WERE ALMOST ENTIRELY DESTROYED UPO THE ARRIVAL OI THE ARCHANGEL TARMIEL AND SARIEL.
ZAP
ZAP
Would you keep your nose out of my head?!
LUDOSHEL IS ON HIS WAY THERE RIGHT NOW.
!
PROSPECTS CERTAINLY ARE DIM.

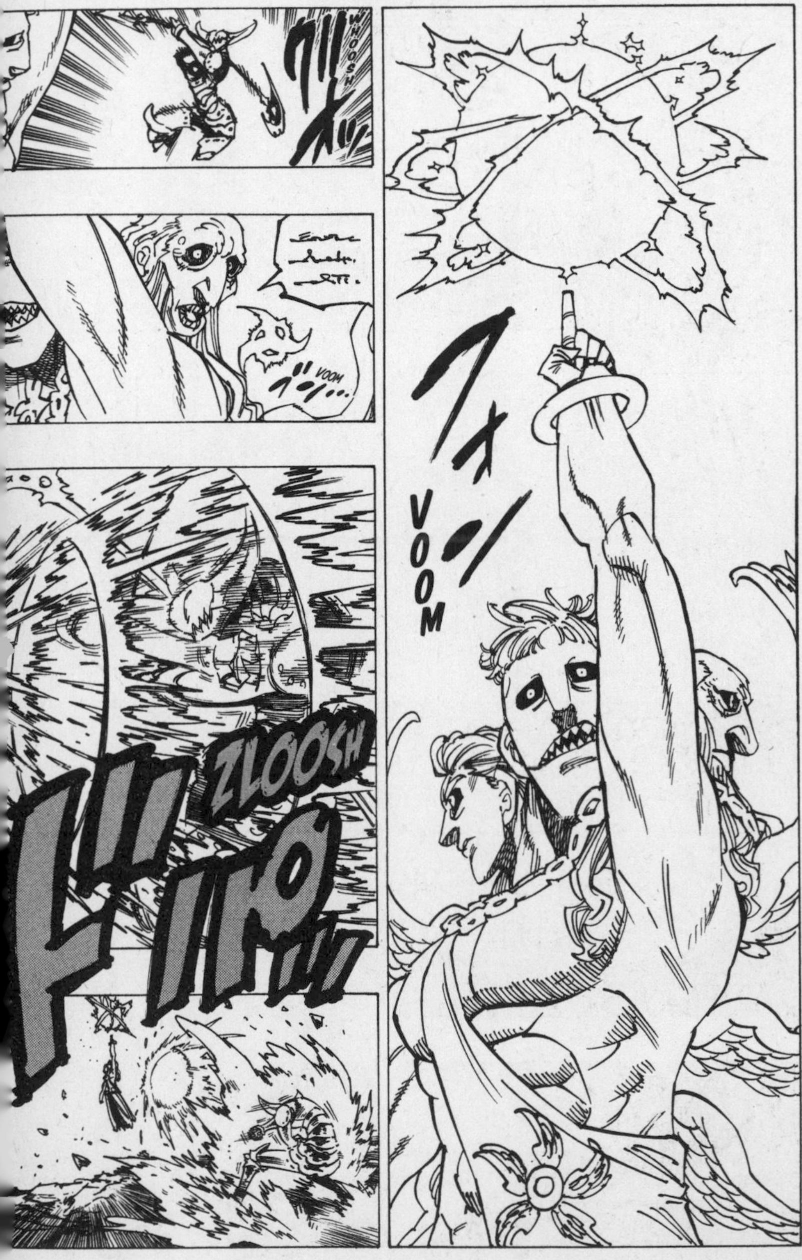
VOOM
WHOOSH
VOOM
ZLOOSH

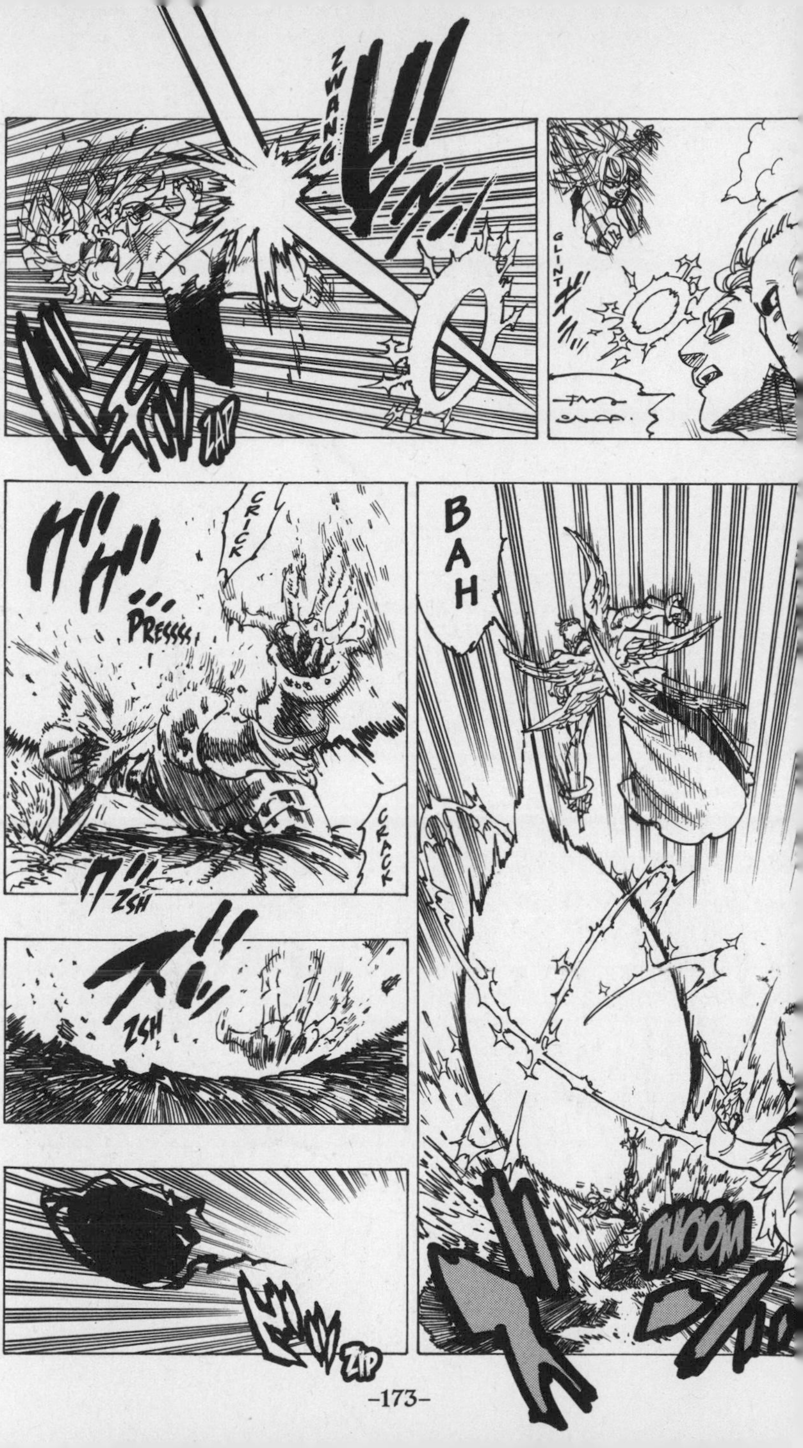
GLINT
ZWANG
ZAP
BAH
THOOM
CRICK
PRESSSS
CRACK
ZSH
ZSH
ZIP

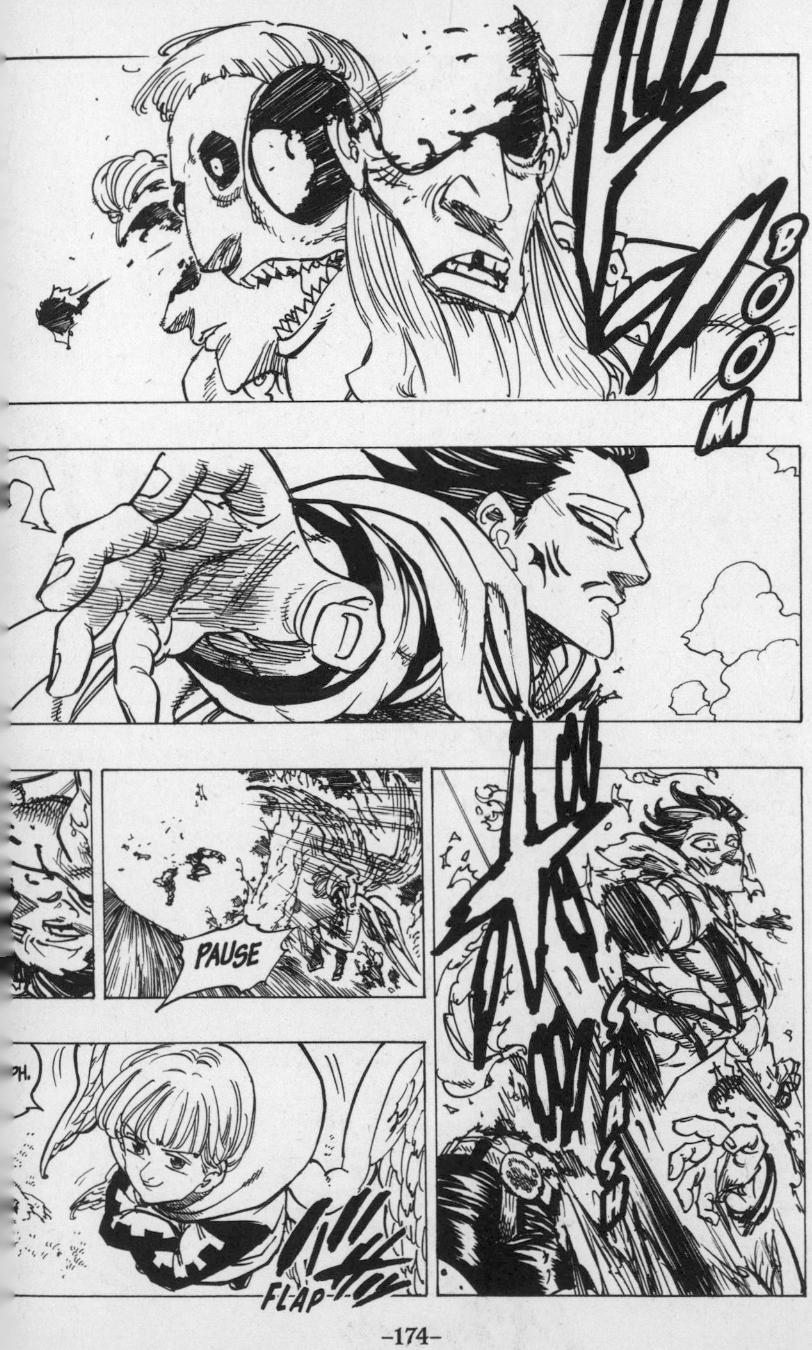
BOOOM
SLASH
PAUSE
FLAP-P-P

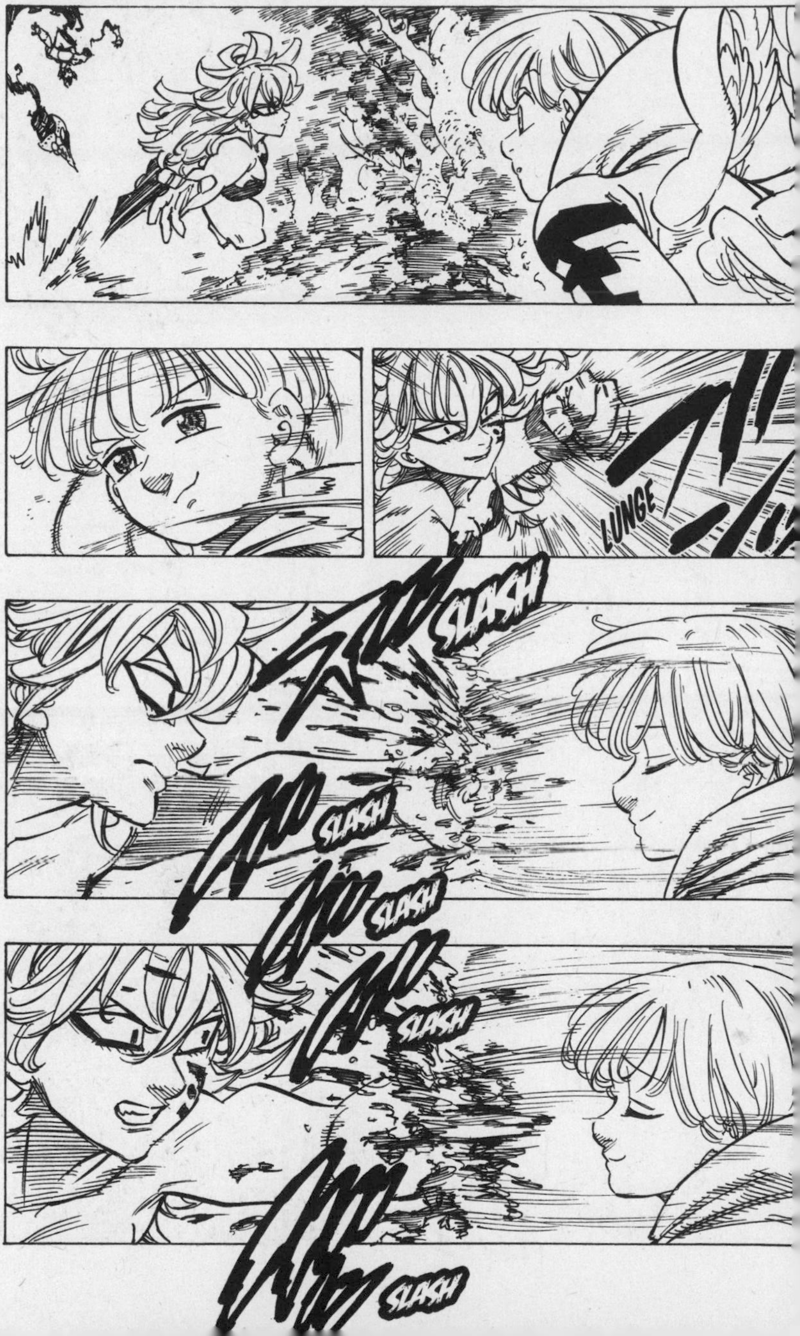
LUNGE
SLASH
SLASH
SLASH
SLASH
SLASH

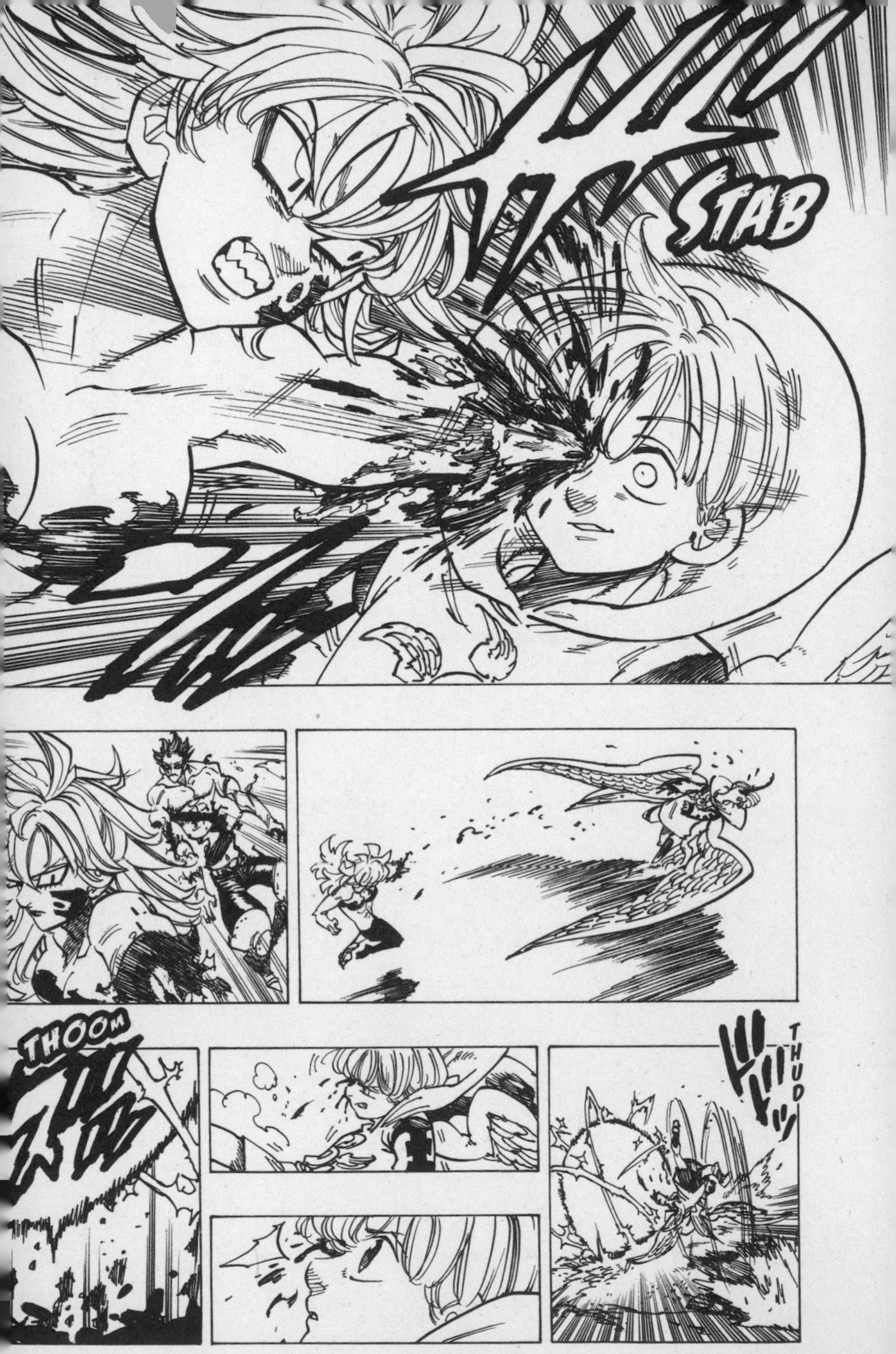
STAB
THUD
THOOM

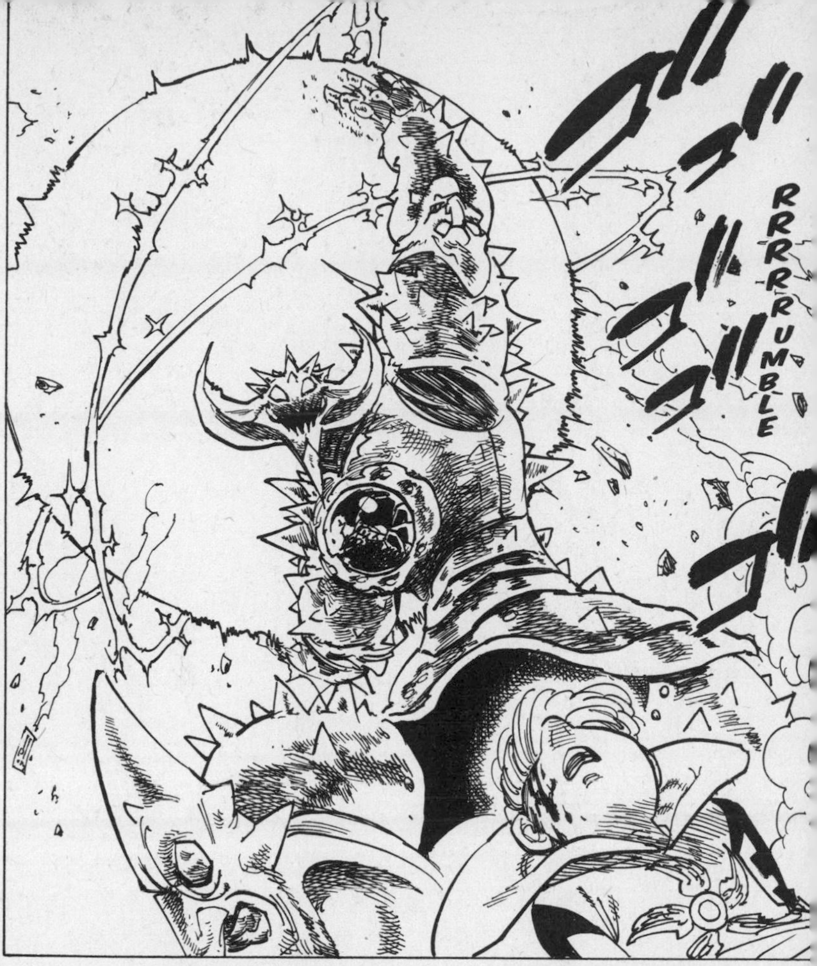
RRRRRUMBLE

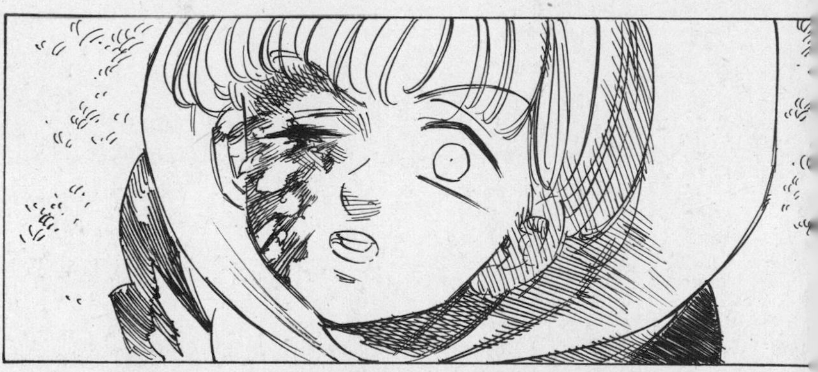

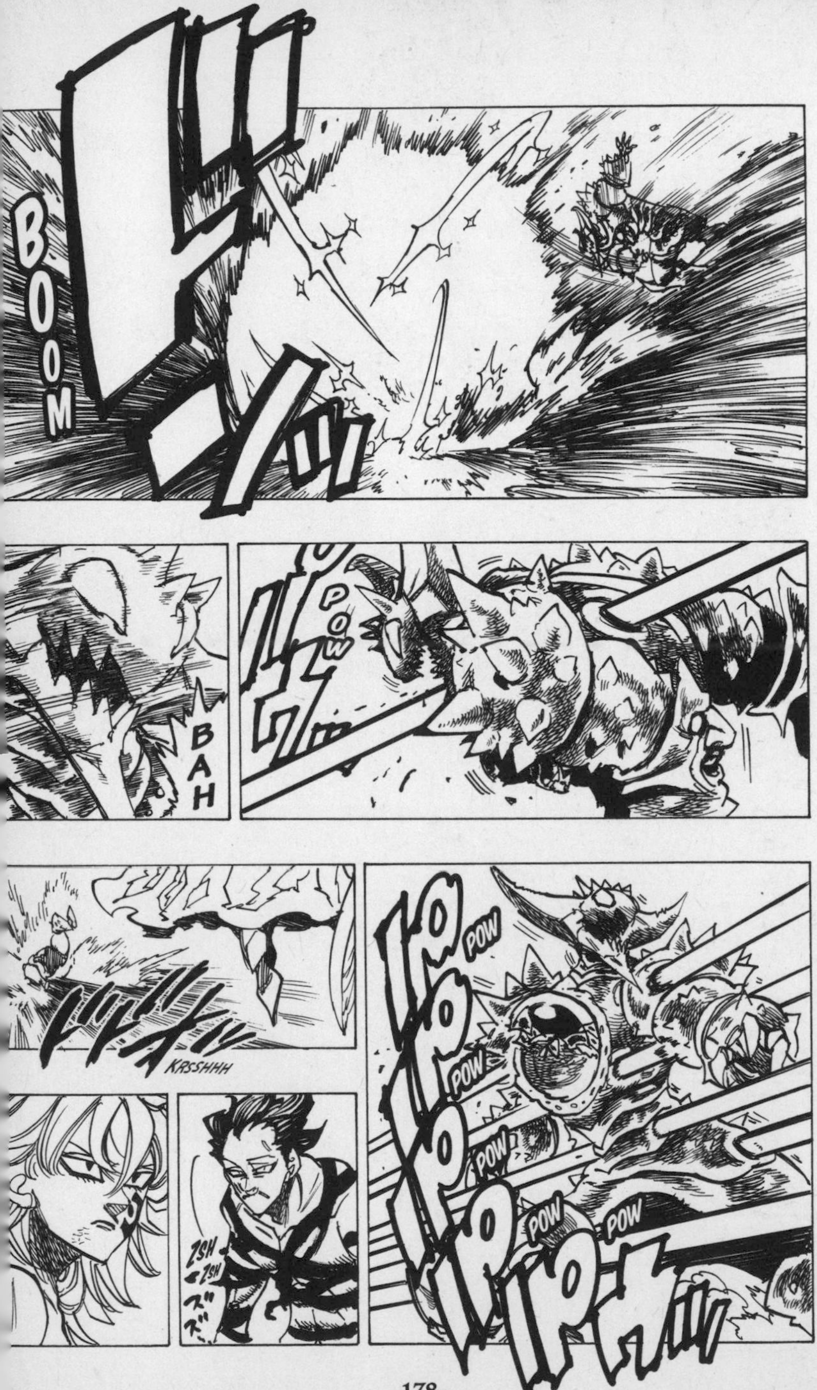
BOOM
POW
BAH
POW
POW
POW
POW
POW
POW
KRSSHHH
ZSH ZSH

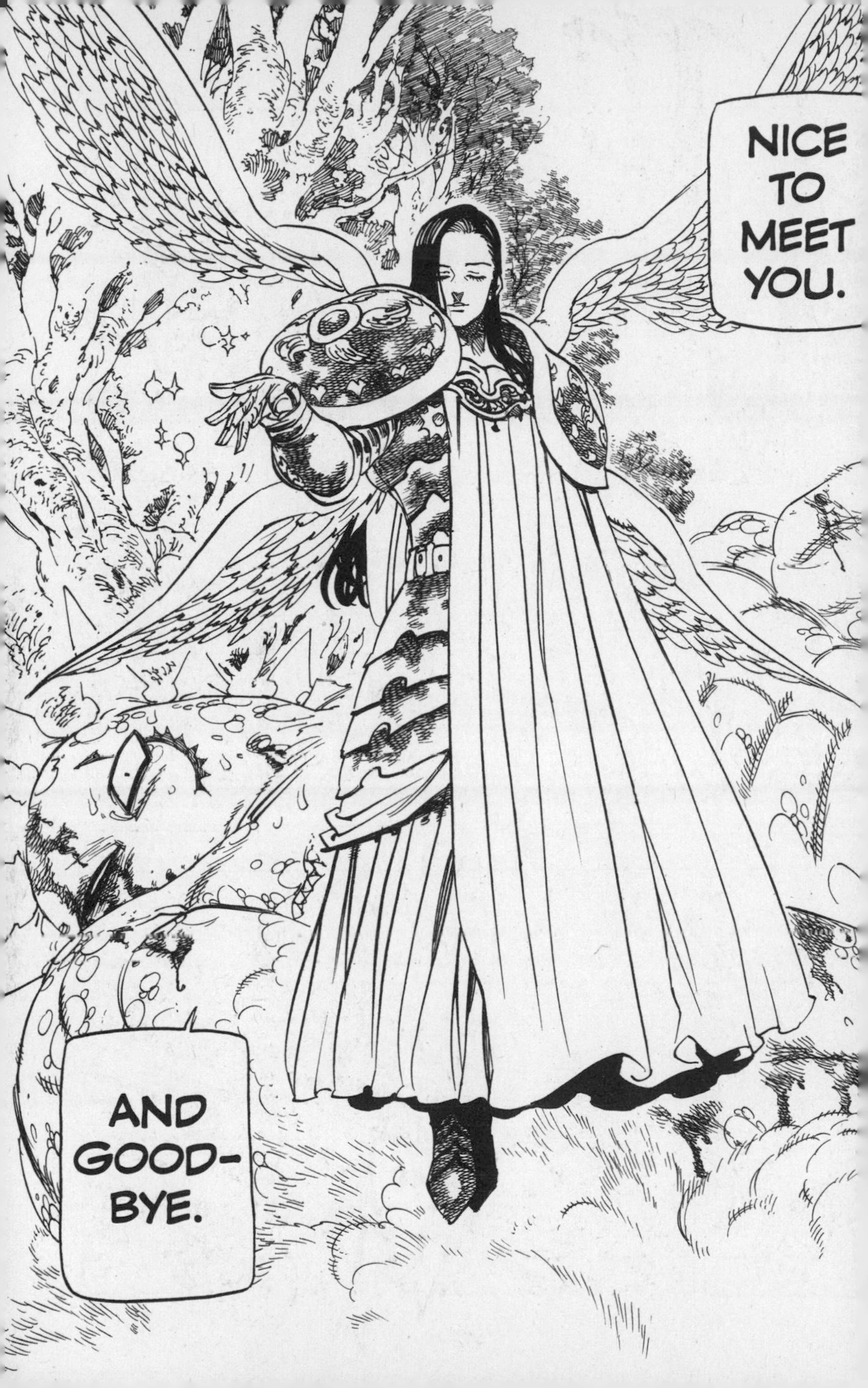
NICE TO MEET YOU.
AND GOOD-BYE.

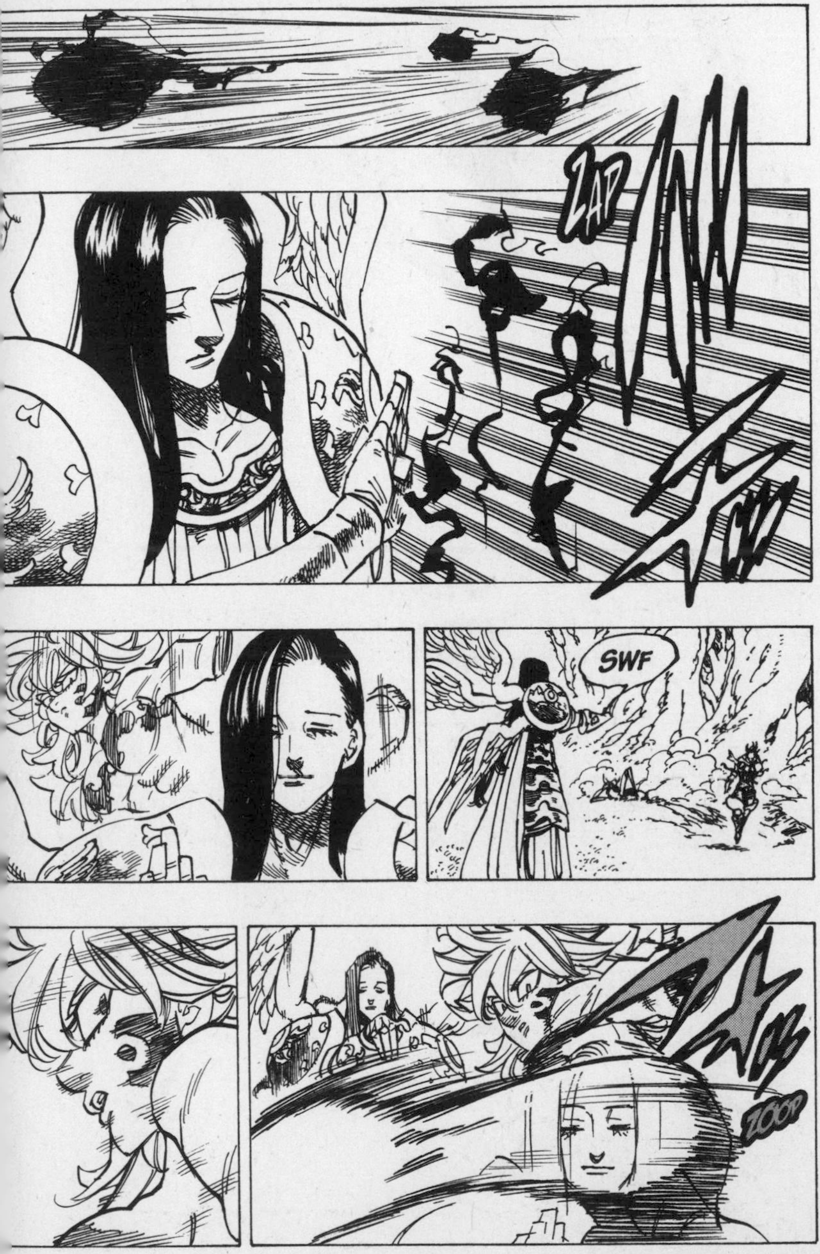
ZAP
SWF
ZOOP

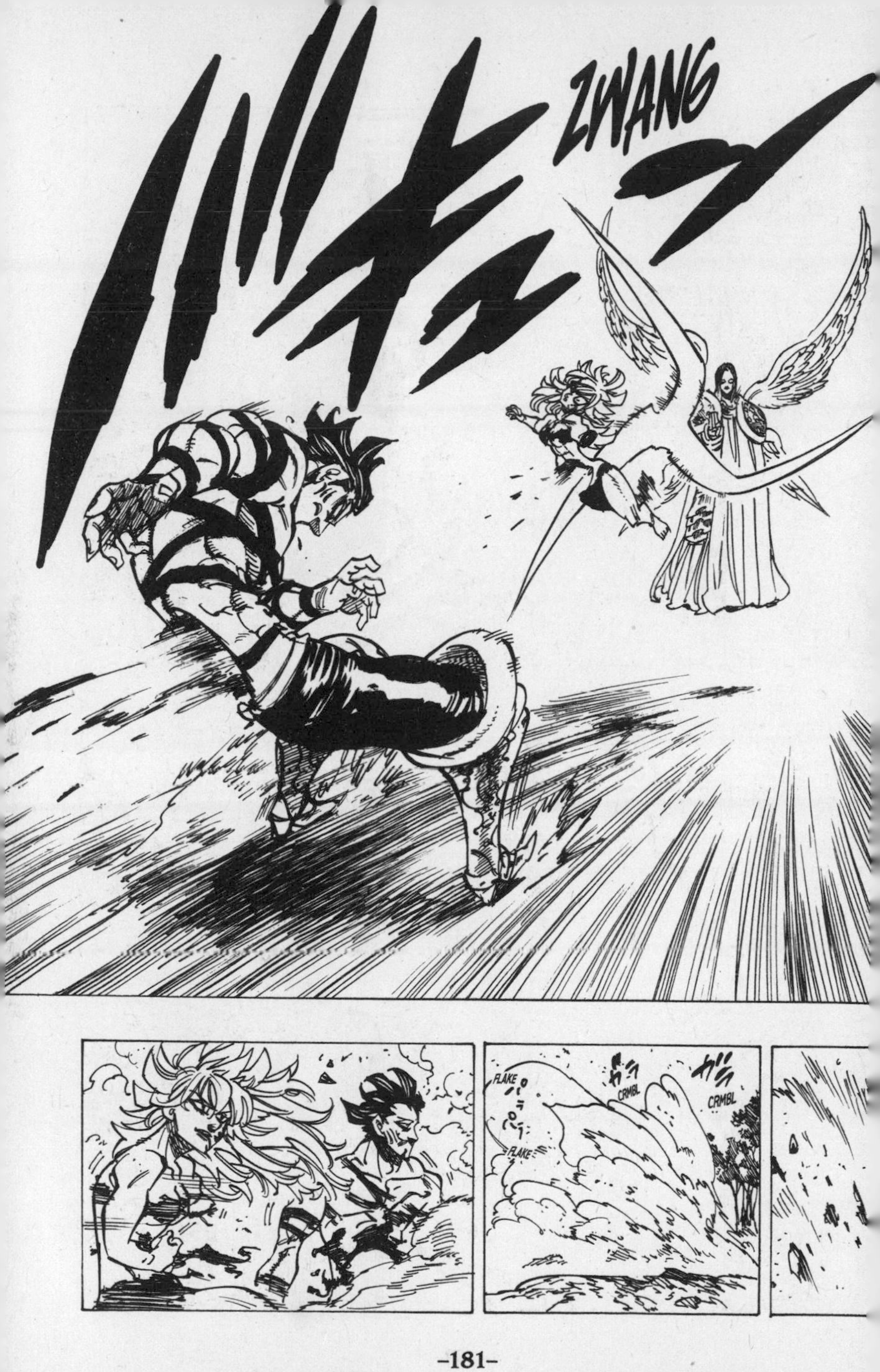
ZWANG
CRMBL
CRMBL
FLAKE
FLAKE

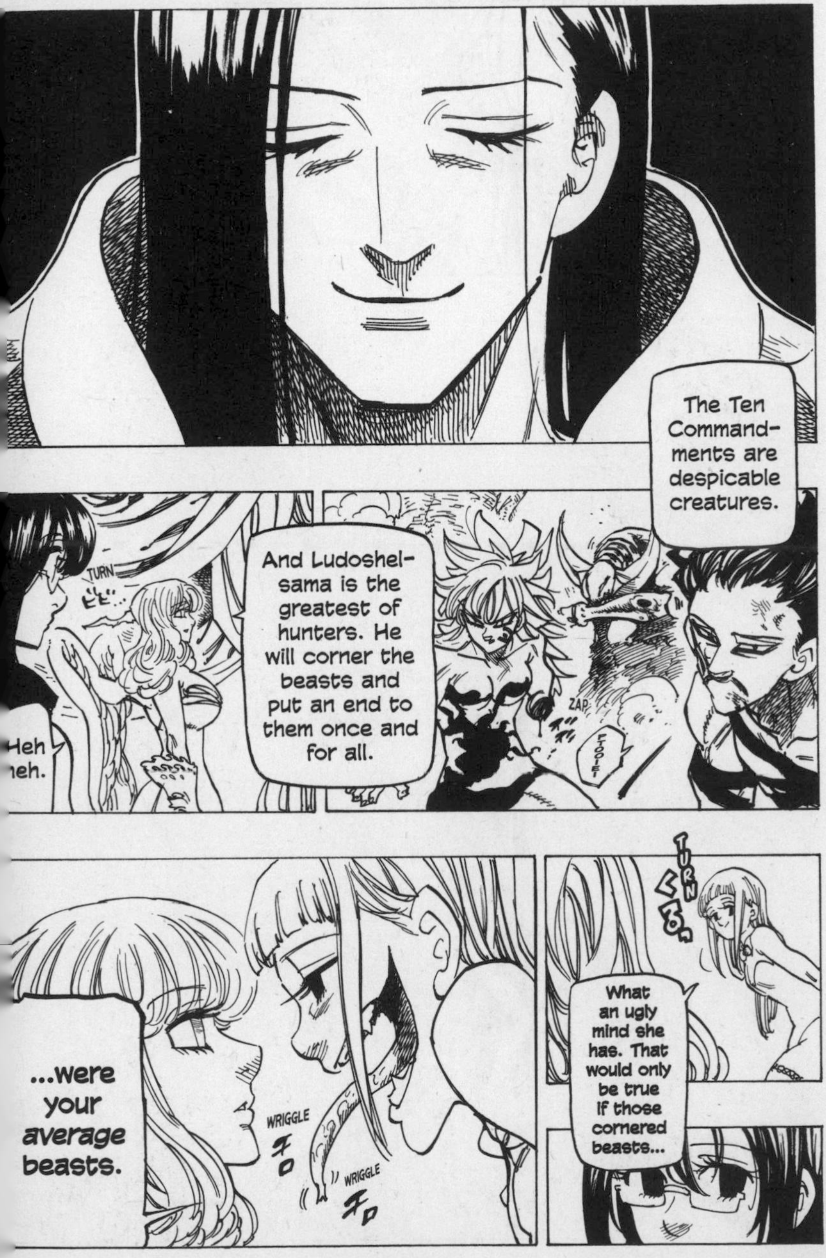
The Ten Commandments are despicable creatures.
ZAP
FTOOIE!
And Ludoshel-sama is the greatest of hunters. He will corner the beasts and put an end to them once and for all.
TURN
Heh heh.
TURN
What an ugly mind she has. That would only be true if those cornered beasts...
WRIGGLE
WRIGGLE
...were your average beasts.

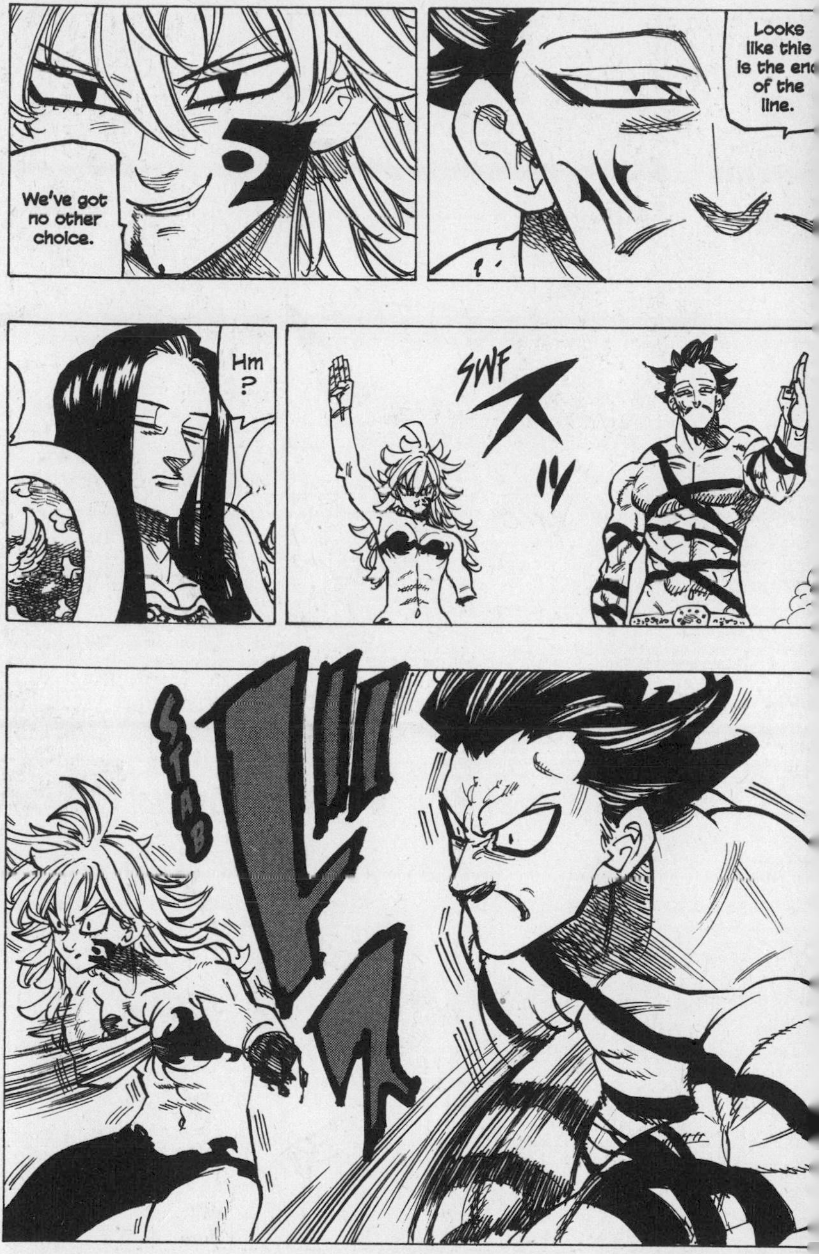
Looks like this is the en of the line.
We've got no other choice.
Hm?
SWF
STAB

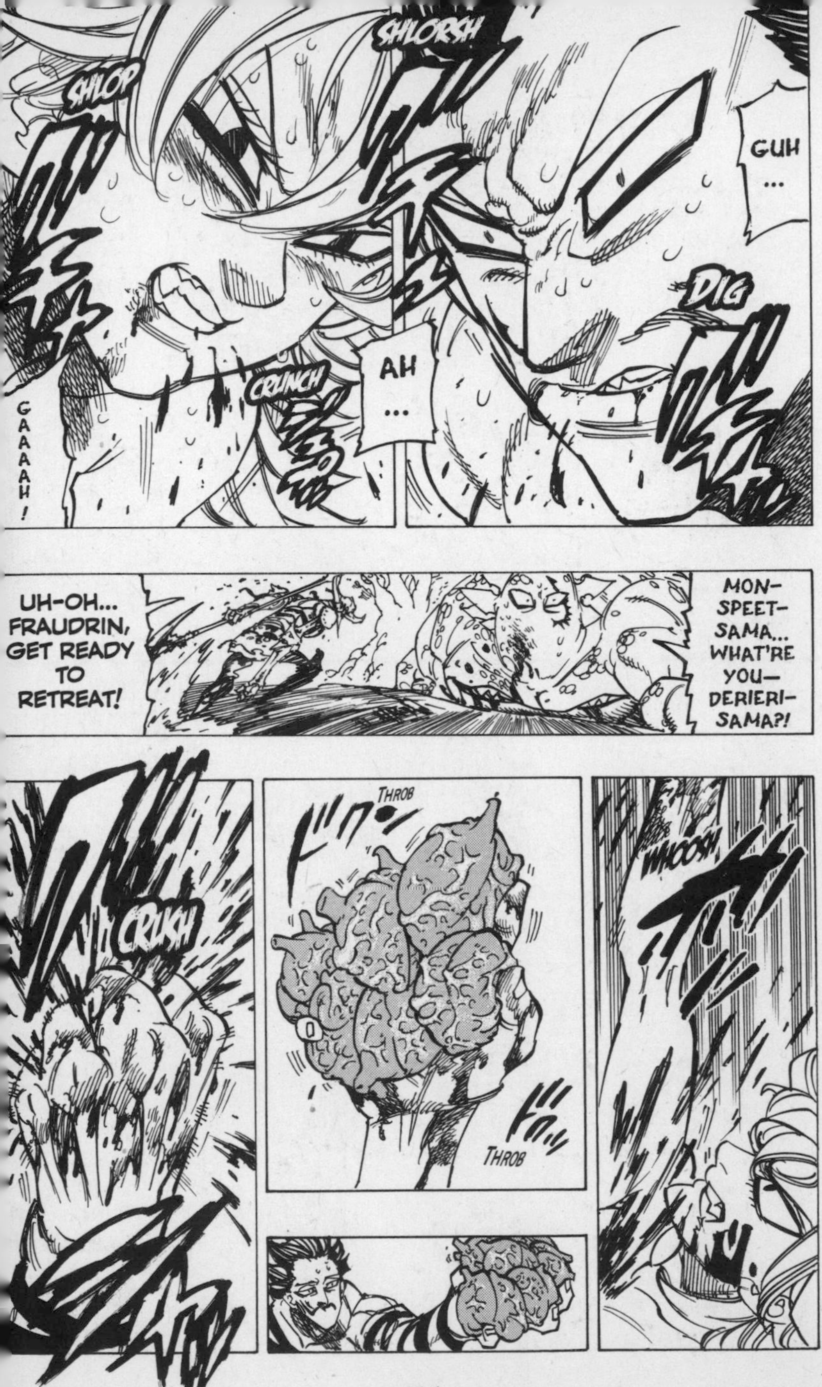
GUH ...
DIG
SHLORSH
AH ...
SHLOP
CRUNCH
GAAAAAH!
MON-SPEET-SAMA... WHAT'RE YOU—DERIERI-SAMA?!
UH-OH... FRAUDRIN, GET READY TO RETREAT!
WHOOSH
THROB
THROB
CRUSH

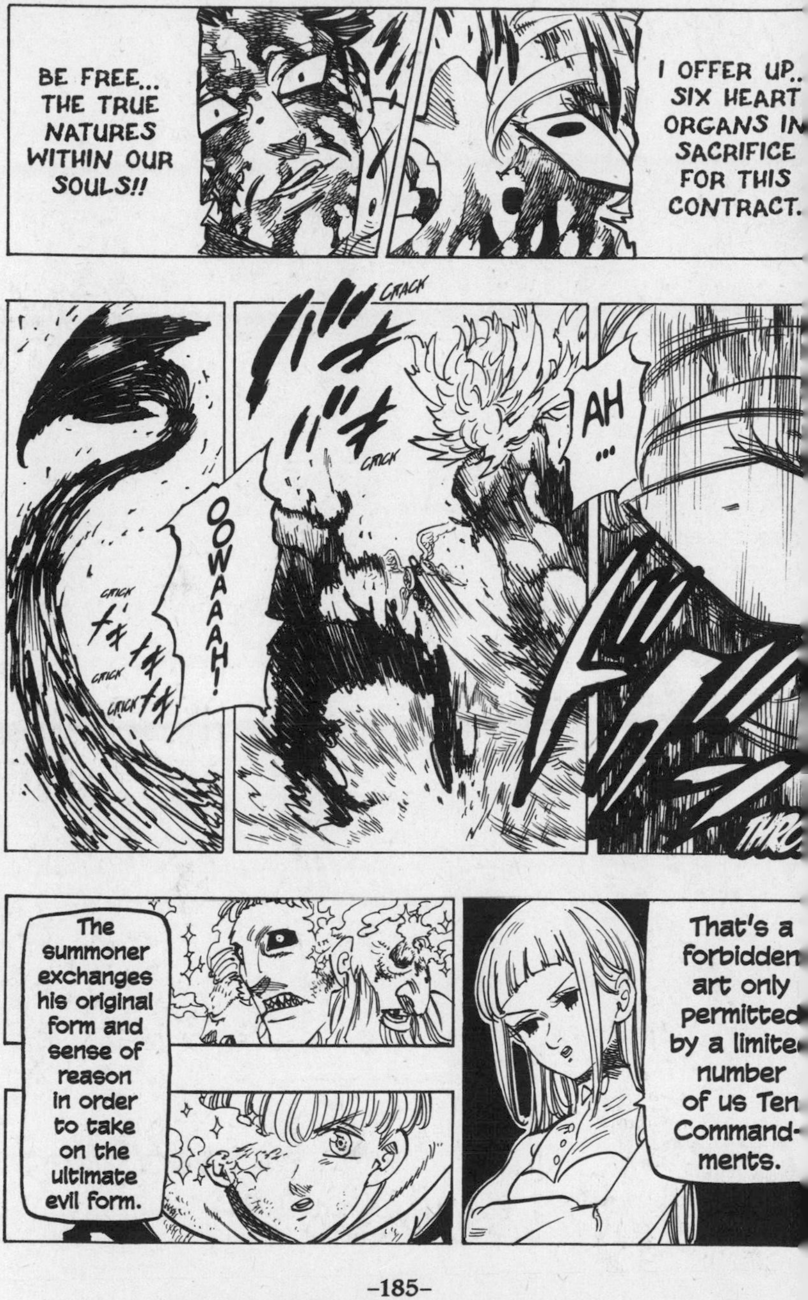
I OFFER UP... SIX HEART ORGANS IN SACRIFICE FOR THIS CONTRACT.
BE FREE... THE TRUE NATURES WITHIN OUR SOULS!!
AH...
CRACK
CRACK
OOWAAAAH!
CRACK
CRACK
CRACK
That's a forbidden art only permitted by a limited number of us Ten Command-ments.
The summoner exchanges his original form and sense of reason in order to take on the ultimate evil form.

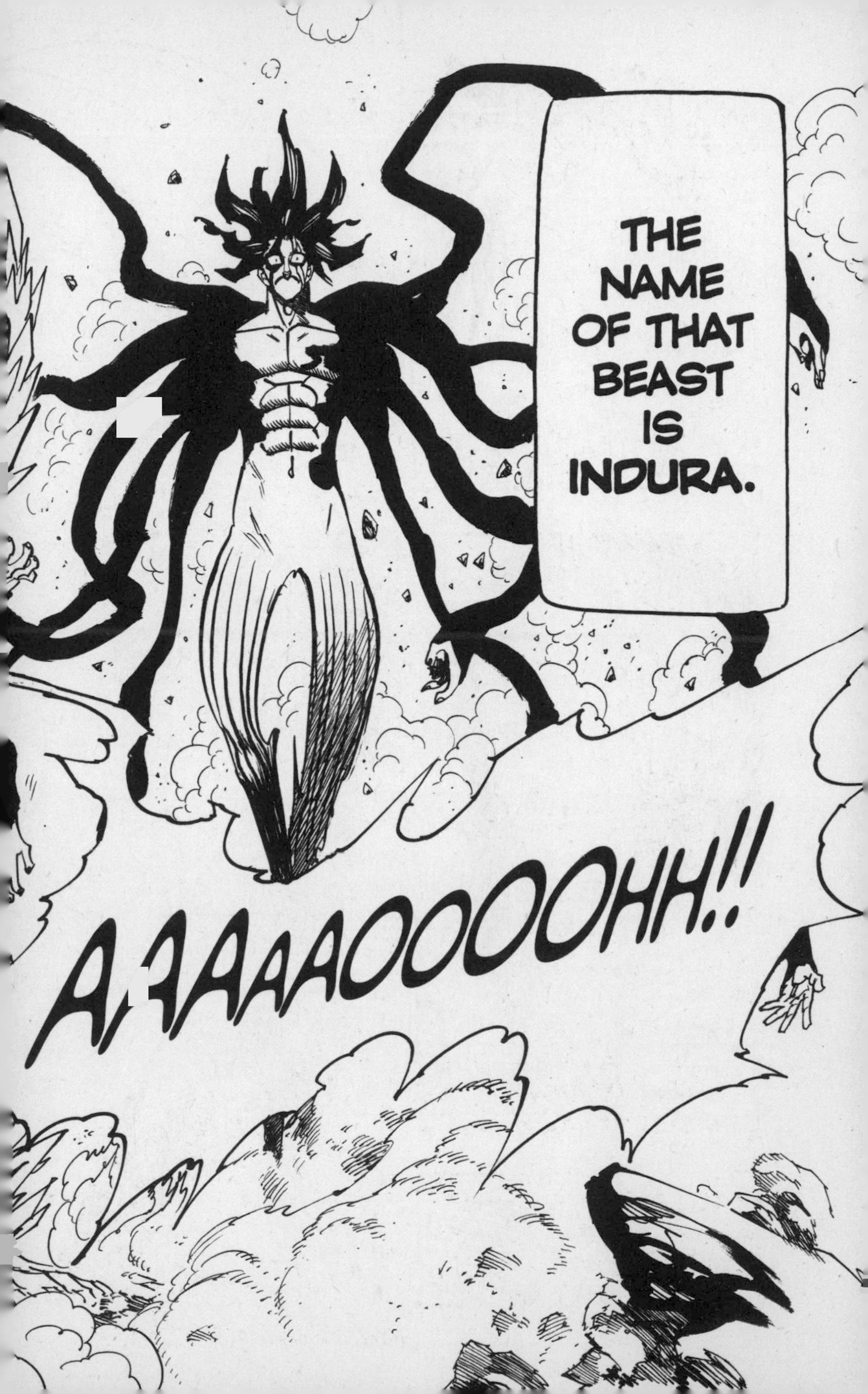
THE NAME OF THAT BEAST IS INDURA.
AAAAAOOOOOHH!!

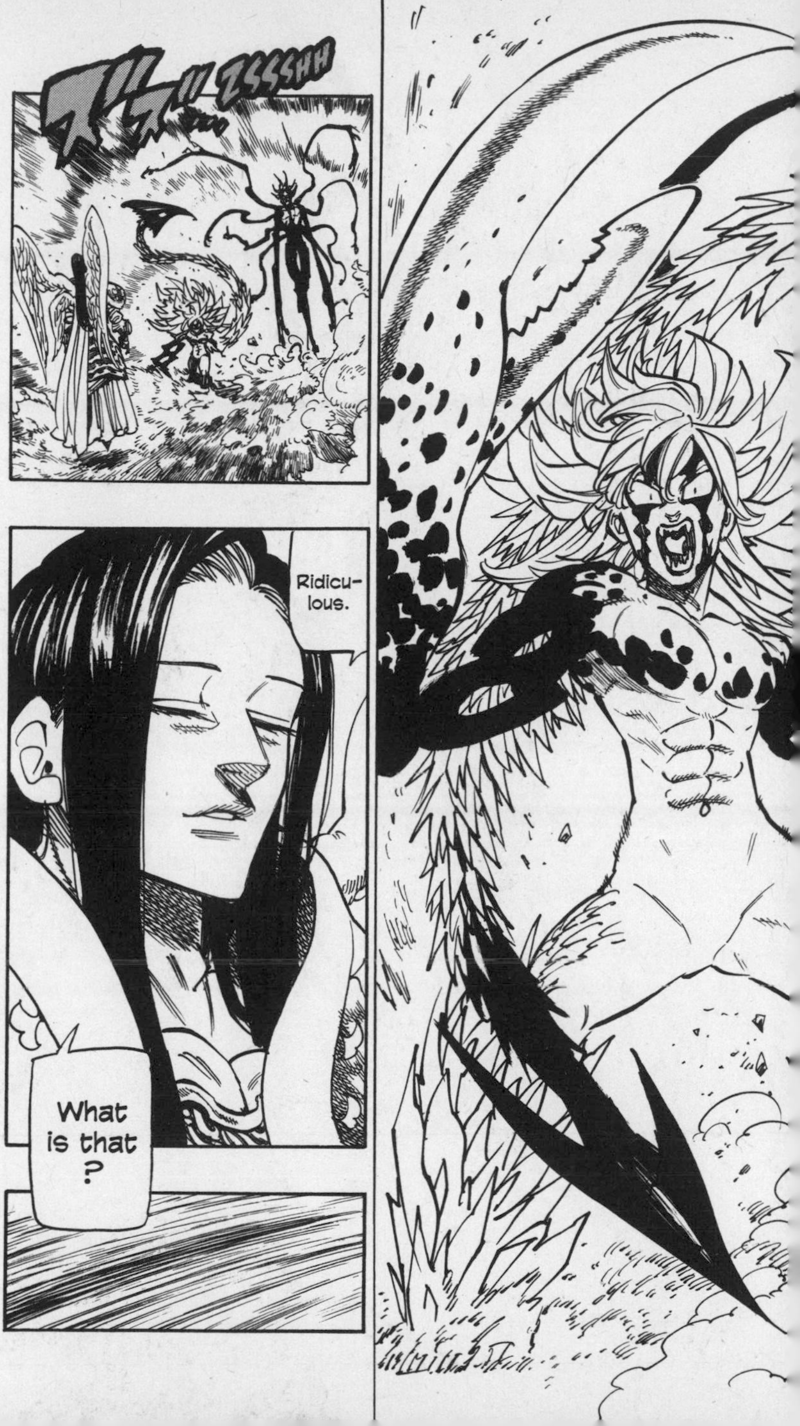
ZSSSHH
Ridiculous.
What is that ?

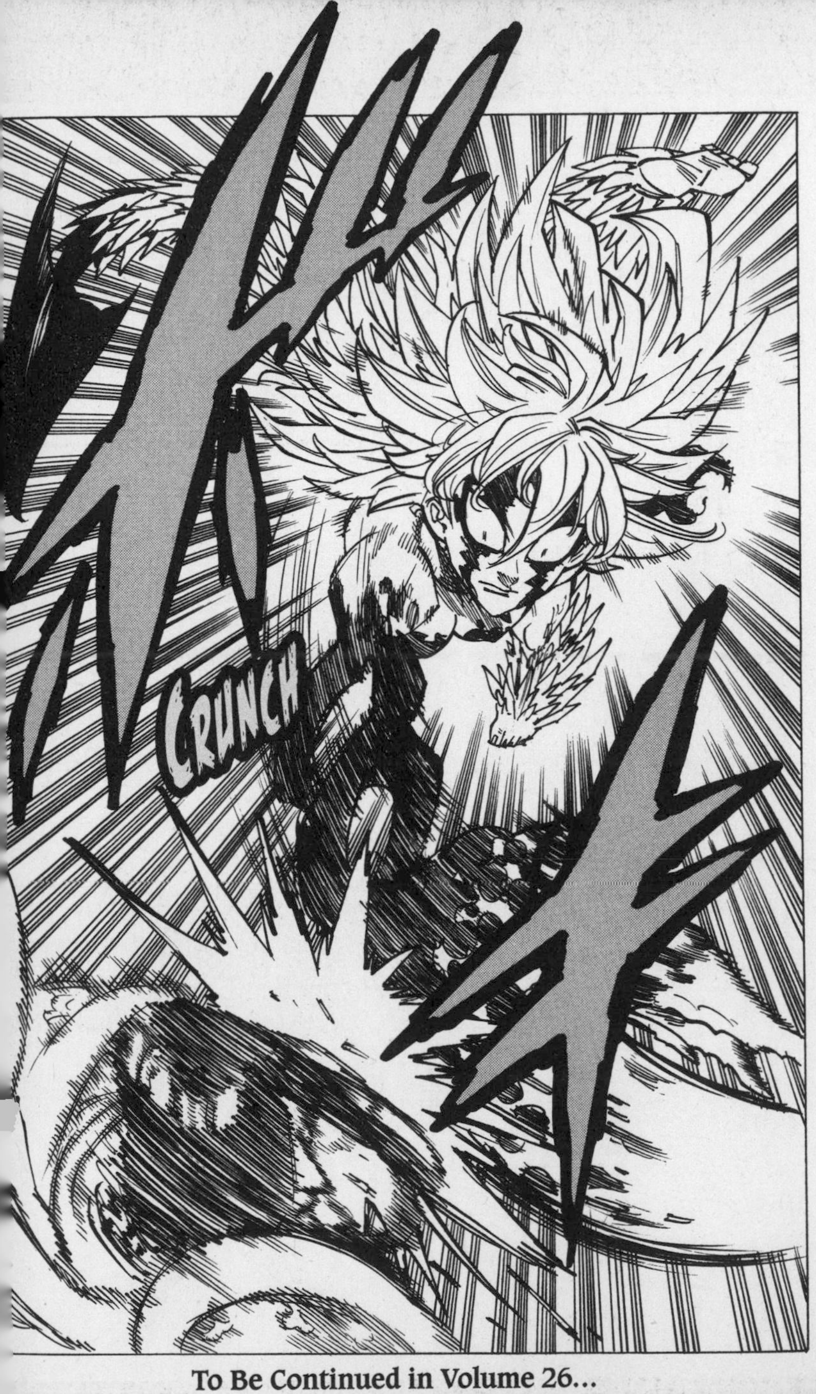
CRUNCH

To Be Continued in Volume 26...

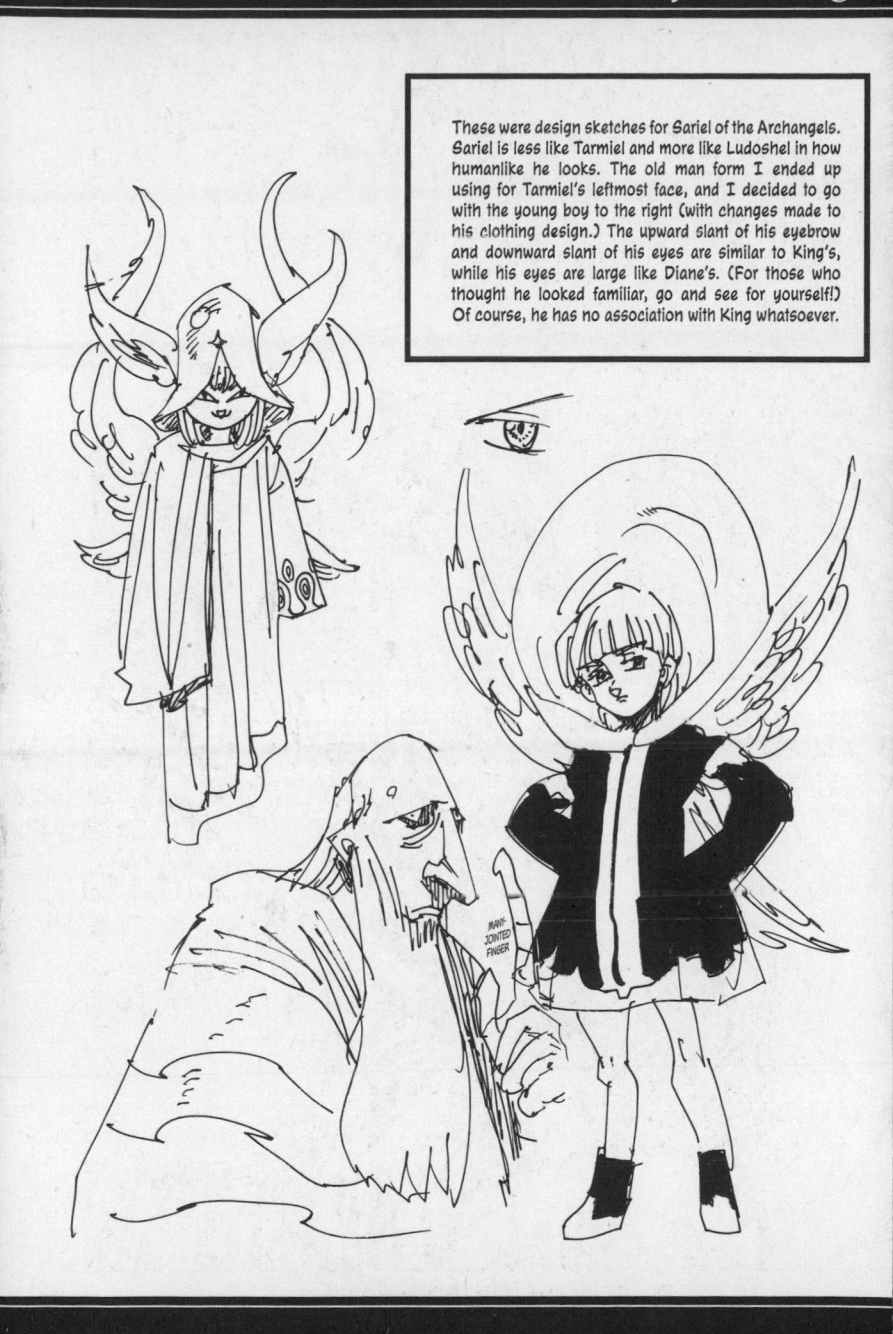

These were design sketches for Sariel of the Archangels. Sariel is less like Tarmiel and more like Ludoshel in how humanlike he looks. The old man form I ended up using for Tarmiel's leftmost face, and I decided to go with the young boy to the right (with changes made to his clothing design.) The upward slant of his eyebrow and downward slant of his eyes are similar to King's, while his eyes are large like Diane's. (For those who thought he looked familiar, go and see for yourself!) Of course, he has no association with King whatsoever.

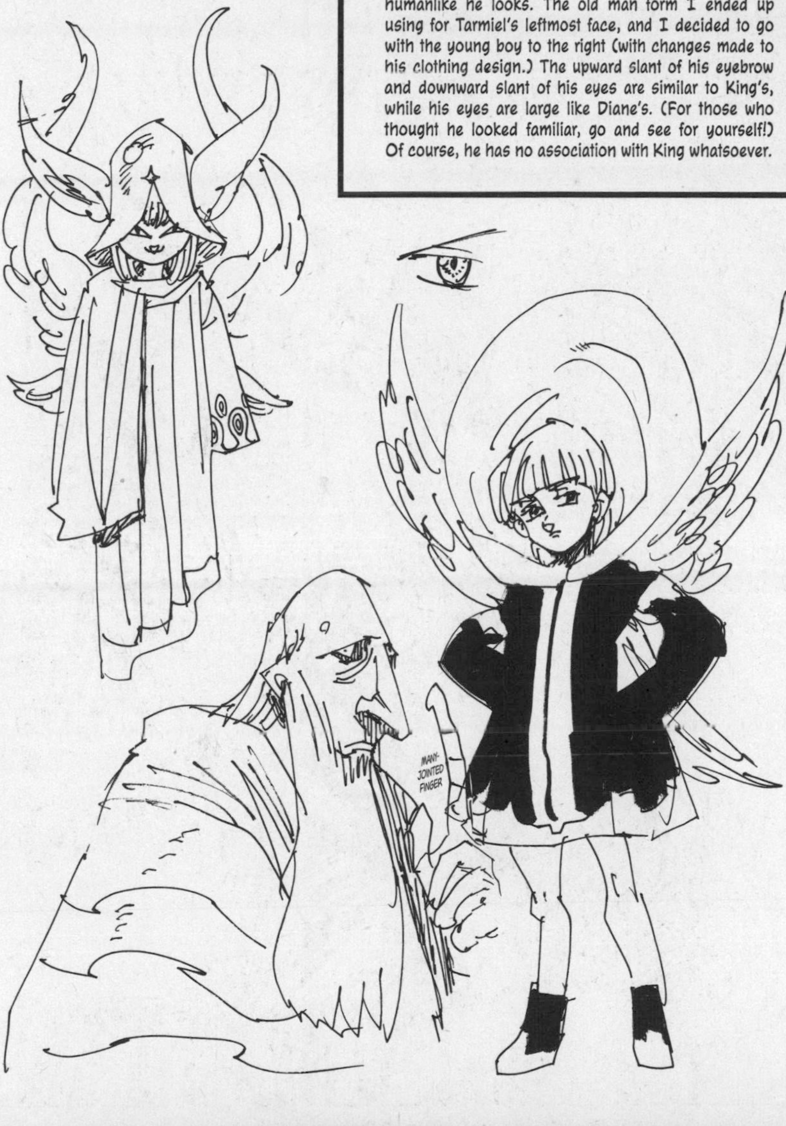
MANY-
JOINTED
FINGER

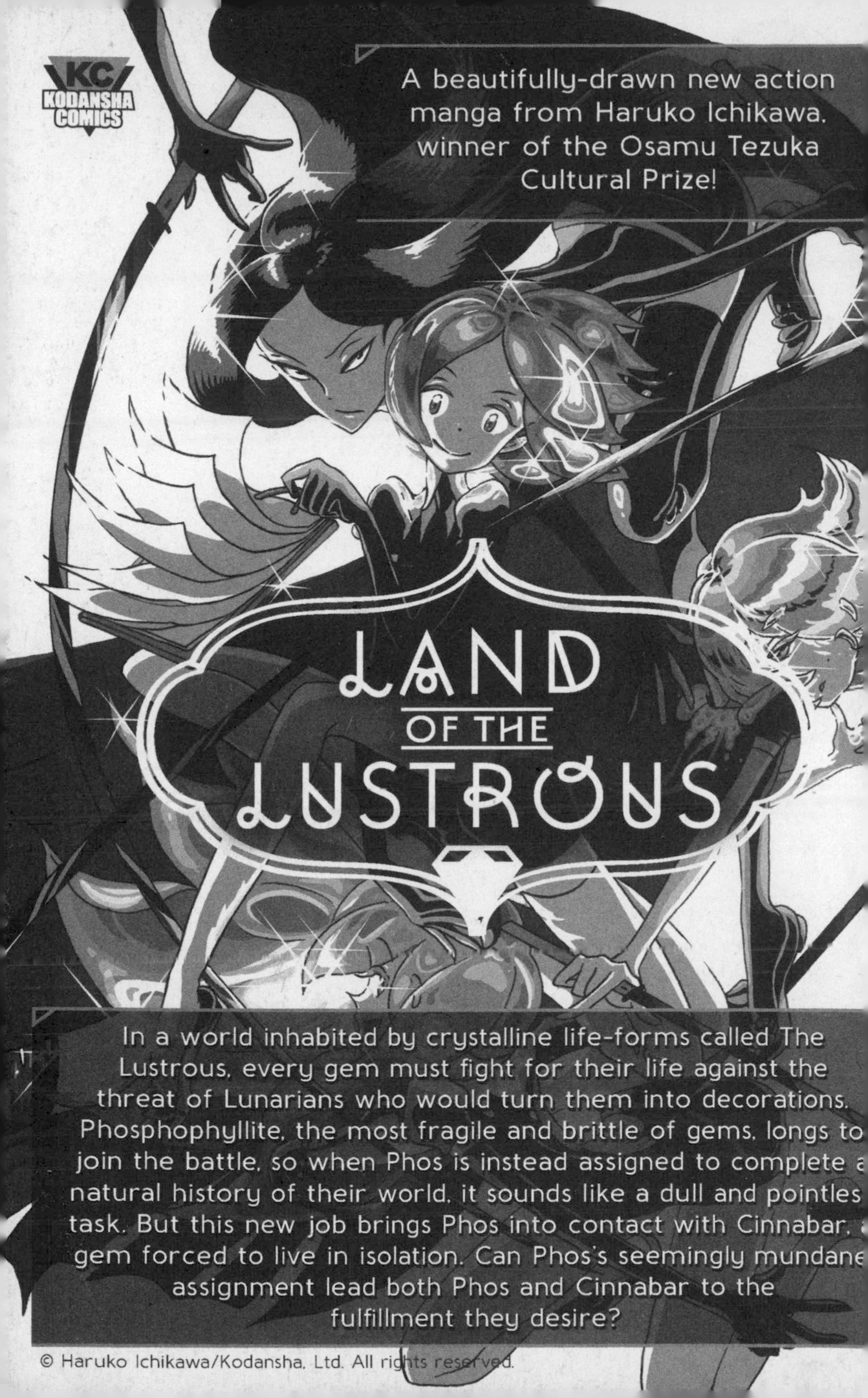
KC KODANSHA COMICS
A beautifully-drawn new action manga from Haruko Ichikawa, winner of the Osamu Tezuka Cultural Prize!
LAND OF THE LUSTROUS
In a world inhabited by crystalline life-forms called The Lustrous, every gem must fight for their life against the threat of Lunarians who would turn them into decorations. Phosphophyllite, the most fragile and brittle of gems, longs to join the battle, so when Phos is instead assigned to complete natural history of their world, it sounds like a dull and pointles task. But this new job brings Phos into contact with Cinnabar, gem forced to live in isolation. Can Phos's seemingly mundane assignment lead both Phos and Cinnabar to the fulfillment they desire?
© Haruko Ichikawa/Kodansha, Ltd. All rights reserved.

A Kodan

The Seve ba Suzuki
English

All right

Publishe nprint of
Kodansha USA Publishing, LLC, New York.

Publication rights for this English edition arranged through
Kodansha Ltd., Tokyo.

First published in Japan in 2017 by Kodansha Ltd., Tokyo.

ISBN 978-1-63236-567-5

Printed in the United States of America.

www.kodanshacomics.com

9 8 7 6 5 4 3 2 1

Translation: Christine Dashiell
Lettering: James Dashiell
Editing: Lauren Scanlan
Kodansha Comics edition cover design: Phil Balsman